CLARENDON LIBRARY OF LO

General Editor: L. Jo

THE CEMENT OF THE
UNIVERSE

THE
CEMENT OF THE
UNIVERSE

A Study of Causation

—

J. L. MACKIE

OXFORD
AT THE CLARENDON PRESS
1980

Oxford University Press, Walton Street, Oxford OX2 6DP

OXFORD LONDON GLASGOW
NEW YORK TORONTO MELBOURNE WELLINGTON
KUALA LUMPUR SINGAPORE HONG KONG TOKYO
DELHI BOMBAY CALCUTTA MADRAS KARACHI
NAIROBI DAR ES SALAAM CAPE TOWN

ISBN 0 19 824642 0

First published 1974
Reprinted in paperback 1980

Published in the United States by
Oxford University Press, New York

Printed in Great Britain
at the University Press, Oxford
by Eric Buckley
Printer to the University

...and as these [*Resemblance, Contiguity, and Causation*] are the only ties of our thoughts, they are really *to us* the cement of the universe, and all the operations of the mind must, in a great measure, depend on them.

HUME, Abstract

Preface

THIS work, like my previous *Truth, Probability, and Paradox*, was completed during the tenure of a Radcliffe Fellowship for the years 1971–2 and 1972–3, and I have to thank the Radcliffe Trustees for this award, the Master and Fellows of University College for allowing me to accept it, and Mr. Peter Singer for taking over, as Radcliffe Lecturer, nearly all my undergraduate teaching.

Several parts of the book are based on previously published work, and I have to thank the editors and publishers in question for permission to use this. Chapter 3 includes material from an article, 'Causes and Conditions', published in the *American Philosophical Quarterly*, ii (1965), 245–64, which is used by permission of the publishers, Basil Blackwell and Mott Ltd. Chapter 7 is a considerably revised version of an article, 'The Direction of Causation', published in the *Philosophical Review*, lxxv (1966), 441–66, which is incorporated by permission of the editors. The Appendix is similarly a revised version of an encyclopedia article for which I have been asked to use the following form of acknowledgement: ' "Mill's Methods of Induction" by J. L. Mackie. Reprinted with permission of the Publisher from the ENCYCLOPEDIA OF PHILOSOPHY edited by Paul Edwards. Volume 5, pages 324–332. Copyright © 1967 by Crowell Collier and Macmillan, Inc.'

Several other parts are based on unpublished papers which I have read and discussed at various times and places. My views about causation have developed in a haphazard way over many years, and I have profited from many arguments and suggestions which I cannot now trace to their original source. I can only express my gratitude and offer my apologies generally to those whose ideas I have unconsciously plagiarized.

I would also like to thank Mrs. E. Hinkes for typing the book.

J. L. M.

February 1973

Preface to the
Paperback Edition

IN this edition a serious misprint has been corrected on page 164, where sixteen words were omitted after line 24; in order to accommodate these words small changes, which do not alter the sense, have been made on this page, minor misprints have been corrected on pages 51 (line 11), 52 (line 10), 99 (line 8 up), 224 (note 28), 255 (line 12), 263 (line 15 up), 303 (line 12), and 328 (under 'Inus condition' and 'Laws'). Additional notes have been inserted referring to pages 80, 143, 190, 214, and 238, being marked by asterisks and printed on p. 322. There is a short Additional Bibliography on page 326. Otherwise the text is unchanged.

Some reviewers and other readers have found my argument hard to follow, mainly because, instead of first stating my theory of causation and then defending it, I work towards it from several different starting points and by way of attempts to solve a number of problems, partly criticizing and partly taking over the views of a good many writers. My position is in some respects intermediate between those of the best known rival schools of thought about causation—it has, understandably, been attacked both for being too Humean and for not being Humean enough —and I could hardly define it intelligibly or explain why I hold it except by tracing the struggles through which I have reached it. Nevertheless, it might have been helpful if I had begun with a rough outline and conspectus of my final view, and I shall now try to make good that deficiency. This may be of some use as an introduction, but it will itself be more fully understood if readers also come back to it after having read the book; it may then guard against misinterpretations by indicating how the different parts of my theory fit together.

My treatment is based on distinctions between three kinds of analysis, factual, conceptual, and epistemic. It is one thing to ask what causation is 'in the objects', as a feature of a world that is wholly objective and independent of our thoughts, another to ask what concept (or concepts) of causation we have, and yet another to ask what causation is in the objects so far as we know it and how we know what we do about it. Verificationism, which has been (openly or covertly) influential in much recent philosophy, has tended to blur these distinctions, suggesting that our concepts and what our statements mean, and also what we can intelligibly claim to be the case, or even speculate about, are tied to what is somehow verified or at least verifiable. My contrary insistence on these distinctions reflects a fundamentally realist view.

In the objects, causation can be seen as a relation between concrete events. But more precisely it is a relation between instantiated features: there will be some conjunction of features in the cause-event (including the 'circumstances' of what we initially identify as the cause) which are all and only those causally relevant to the set of features that we take as the effect. (Once a specific effect has been chosen, it is a wholly objective matter what features are causally relevant to it.) But what constitutes this causal relevance which connects the cause-features with the effect-features? There are regularities of succession, typically complex (what is regularly related to some effect-feature will be a disjunction of conjunctions of positive and negative causal factors), and these regularities may be quantitative, involving functional dependences as well as simple presences and absences of items on either the cause or the effect side, and again may be statistical or probabilistic rather than deterministic. But regularities, of any sort, do not exhaust the matter. There is also a direction of causation, an asymmetry between cause and effect which is not simply temporal order, though it is related to this. I say something below about our knowledge of this asymmetry and our concept of it; but the objective asymmetry is, I admit, obscure and elusive. Again, in an individual cause–effect sequence, over and above the fact that it instantiates some regularity, there is more than one sort of continuity of process, in particular, as well as spatio-temporal continuity, there is what I call qualitative continuity: something carries over from cause to effect, causal relations are forms of partial persistence as well as of change. Thus, contrary to the Humean view, there is more in objective causation than regularity, but contrary to the traditional rationalist view, this extra element is nothing like logical necessity. Since this objective causation significantly resembles both the continuation of self-maintaining processes and the survival of things without change (or without easily observable change), these two kinds of persistence might well be included in an extended concept of causation in the objects.

Causation as we know it commonly falls far short of this. The above-mentioned regularities are usually very incompletely known. Yet I stress that such 'gappy' regularities can be empirically discovered or confirmed (particularly by methods of eliminative induction) and can also be *used*. Causal relations are not knowable *a priori*, and I also reject all transcendental arguments. But I suggest that there is some ground for a presumption of some element of persistence. I also hold that the traditional problem of induction can be solved (though the solution is not given in this book), and hence that there is empirical support for the assumption that there are some regularities to be found, an assumption which is used in applications of the eliminative methods. The continuity or persistence which, in my view, replaces the rationalists' necessity is a thoroughly empirical feature, in no way mysterious, but observable or discoverable in principle, though in many cases it is not immediately perceivable. Our knowledge of causal asymmetry is based partly on our experience of bringing about one thing by way of another. But causal asymmetry in itself is not constituted by this experience, and even our knowledge of it does not rest wholly on this experience: there is also an observable asymmetry with respect to what I call the dispersal of order, which yields a non-reversible direction of explanation.

Whereas regularities of one sort or another play a large part in causation both in the objects and as we know it, our concept of causation is not primarily a concept of the instantiation of regularities: we locate causation in singular cause–effect sequences, and assume that there is some distinctively causal relation, some influence or operation, in each such sequence taken on its own. But neither is it a concept of anything like logical necessity or even *a priori* knowability or intelligibility of sequences. The basic notion is best captured by various contrary-to-fact conditionals. What we call a cause typically is, and is recognized as being, only a partial cause; it is what makes the difference in relation to some assumed background or causal field. And where we take A to be thus a partial cause of B, we can say that if A had not occurred, B would not; a cause is taken to be in this counterfactual sense necessary in the circumstances for B, though sometimes also sufficient in the circumstances as well, or perhaps only sufficient in the circumstances and not necessary: we have alternative counterfactual concepts of causation. But these counterfactual conditional relationships do not exhaust our concept of causation, for this concept includes also the notion of the asymmetry between cause and effect; conceptually, that asymmetry seems to be based on a contrast between what is fixed and what is (at any time) not fixed: effects become fixed only by way of their causes. Our concept of causation also includes some presumption of a 'causal mechanism', and hence of the continuities, both spatio-temporal and qualitative, that I have ascribed to causation in the objects.

Since I distinguish the analysis of the concept of causation from the factual analysis of causation in the objects, I am not committed to giving a fully determinate or tidy conceptual analysis; rather I insist that our concept is in several ways a bit indeterminate: 'cause' can mean slightly different things on different occasions, and about some problematic cases, for example of over-determination, we may be unsure what to say. But it is still a fairly unitary concept: we do not have one concept for physical causation and another for human actions and interactions (as someone might be forced to say who took our concept of physical causation to be that of regular succession); we can and do assert similar counterfactual necessity (and at times sufficiency) about fields of all different sorts.

Having thus distinguished our concept of causation from causation as it is and even as it is known, I must also explain how these different items are related to one another. The counterfactual conditionals which are central in our concept are not, I hold, capable of being simply true, of describing literally a fully objective reality. But they are suggested by the resemblances and differences that we find when we compare observed sequences with one another. They are also sustained by statements about regularities of sequence, even incompletely known regularities; while these regularities are themselves confirmed (by way of the eliminative methods of induction) by those same combinations of resemblance and difference. A world in which events take place in accordance with such laws of working as I ascribe to causation in the objects, even though these laws are very incompletely known, will be one in which the ways of thinking that constitute our causal concepts are both reasonable and useful. Also, both our experience of action and manipulation and the observable asymmetry with respect to the dispersal of order, which are central in our discovery of the direction of causation, suggest the contrast between fixity and non-fixity which is at the heart of our concept of this asymmetry, and which may also belong to the objective world.

I should also explain how the various chapters contribute to this rather complex account.

Chapter 1 is a critical study of Hume's account of causation, arguing that while his negative theses are largely correct, Hume radically misinterprets the ordinary notion of causal efficacy or necessity which he then proceeds to explain away. Chapter 2 is devoted to the analysis of this ordinary concept in terms of counterfactual conditionals along with a preliminary treatment of the asymmetry which this concept involves; it offers a psychological explanation of our counterfactual thinking, much as Hume offered a psychological explanation of the different sort of necessity—*a priori* knowability—which he wrongly took to be what, in our concepts, distinguishes causal from non-causal sequences. Chapter 3 studies the complex form of causal regularities and relates this to our uses of them and to our methods of discovering them; these methods are studied in further detail and defended against some stock objections in the Appendix on Eliminative Methods of Induction. Chapter 4 contains mainly negative criticism both of Kant and of more recent writers, Strawson and Bennett, who have developed some of his ideas. Its conclusion is that no sort of transcendentalism is needed as a supplement to Hume or as a replacement of some of his doctrines, though it is conceded that causation is a very pervasive and structurally important feature of the world as we know it, and one on which much of our knowledge of the world depends—for example, it plays a vital part in the determination of the metric of the time dimension. Chapter 5 defends the conceptual analysis already given by comparing it with the account given by Hart and Honoré (and by applying it to some of their legal examples), and also with the accounts of Ducasse and of some thinkers who appeal to a commonsense knowledge of particular kinds of causing. It shows that we do not need to recognize a radical plurality of causal concepts, but also that there is more in causing than can be *simply* perceived; though causing can indeed be observed, the observation includes an important element of interpretation and relies greatly on knowledge drawn from the observation of other cases.

Chapter 6 rebuts Russell's thesis that the concepts of causation and causal law are obsolete, and shows that the relation of functional dependence, which he would substitute for it, is better understood as an addition to and extension of the 'neolithic' concept. It adds that once this extension has been made, we might well extend the concept in two further ways, to include the continuation of a uniform process and the persistence of an unchanging thing as further varieties of causation.

Chapter 7 deals with the direction of causation, mainly as a problem in conceptual analysis. More criticism has been directed against this chapter, I believe, than against all the others together, and I admit that the topic is highly controversial and that the positive account suggested at the end of the chapter is not altogether satisfactory. But most of the chapter is given to the establishing of a number of negative theses: the soundness of these has been acknowledged, at least implicitly, for they have hardly been challenged. Thus it is shown that the concept of causal asymmetry is not simply that of temporal succession, but equally that the direction of time cannot be reduced to the direction of causation (pages 161–6), that it is not that of one-way determination, as Russell suggested (pages 166–7), and that though causal direction is related to 'effectiveness', to the possibility of using a cause to bring about an effect, and our knowledge of the asymmetry depends partly on this sort of experience, our concept is of an objective asymmetry on which effectiveness somehow depends, and is not the anthropocentric concept of effectiveness itself (pages 168–73). My discussion (pages 173–83) of backward (time-reversed) causation has often been misunderstood. I do not suggest, and I do not believe, that backward causation occurs, but only that it is conceptually possible, and I use this conceptual possibility and an examination of what might be evidence for backward causation merely to throw light on the concept of causal direction. This examination strongly suggests that this concept is connected with a contrast between fixity and non-fixity. It is also shown that entropy increase does not itself constitute the asymmetry of either time or causation. But a notion of the dispersal of order, based on examples introduced particularly by Popper, is shown to be related to a direction of explanation which must also connect with the contrast between fixity and non-fixity, and this dispersal of order is shown to be involved in the stock examples of the increase of entropy (pages 183–9). These criticisms and preliminary discussions point clearly towards a conceptual analysis based on the notion of fixity; but I concede that the analysis actually offered on pages 190 will not do. I have returned to this problem in a later article on 'Mind, Brain, and Causation' (see the Additional Bibliography). Whether the conceptual analysis based on fixity can be read also as factual analysis is briefly discussed on pages 191–2, where it is also considered what objective asymmetries will be left if it cannot.

The theme of Chapter 8 is the supposed necessity in causal connections and the distinction (in concept, knowledge, and reality) between causal laws and accidental universal propositions. After distinguishing many different jobs that 'necessity' has been expected to do, I argue that whereas it is often thought that the ability of causal laws to entail or sustain counterfactual conditionals is what marks them off from accidental universals and shows them to have some meaning stronger than that of merely factual universality, this is a mistake: merely factual universals, if supported directly or indirectly by inductive evidence, will sustain counterfactuals (pages 193–204). So far, then, I am supporting the Humean rejection of any necessity stronger than factual universality. But after this problem has been completely resolved, there is still some distinction between causal laws and merely accidental universals, and this is not adequately accounted for in the standard Humean way by noting that causal laws fit together into a body of scientific theory (pages 204–8). My positive solution of this problem contains two elements. I show how we can distinguish the basic laws of working of some system both from pure collocation statements and from derived laws which are mixed products of the basic laws and the pure collocations; but this distinction is not made by the application of any simple criteria, but requires a thorough understanding of the system in question. I then suggest that the basic laws of working are forms of persistence, that qualitative continuity is to be found (though it is often not obvious) in causal processes. This notion underlies the demand for 'causal mechanisms', and is an empirical counterpart of the necessity postulated by Kneale and other rationalists. I also claim (against, e.g., Nagel) that there is some *a priori* expectability about such continuity or persistence (pages 208–30). In these respects I go beyond Humean views.

Chapter 9 discusses the form of statistical or probabilistic laws, and shows that these may be of three different kinds, only one of which introduces a basic indeterminism. Chapter 10 discusses the ontology of causation. After criticizing the use often made of a Fregean argument to show that causal statements cannot be extensional (pages 250–6), I note that both concrete events and facts are, and can coherently be, recognized as causes and effects, and so distinguish 'producing causes' from 'explanatory causes' (pages 257–60). The latter name has, unfortunately, proved to be misleading: since explanation is relative to interests and previous beliefs and expectations, it has been thought by some readers that explanatory causation is similarly relative or subjective. But this is not what I intend. I develop the notion of fact causes or explanatory causes by distinguishing causally relevant features and formulating the ideal of a minimally complete causal account which would mention all and only the relevant features. This relevance of cause-features to effect-features is a thoroughly objective matter, owing nothing to interests or previous beliefs or expectations; explanatory causation, thus developed, is the form which causation in the objects is most accurately seen as taking, while our ordinary recognition of concrete event causes is seen as a legitimate concession to the incompleteness of our knowledge (pages 260–9).

Chapter 11 begins with a summary of the previous ten chapters and an outline of the view of efficient causation developed in them, as an introduction to the question whether teleology, final causation, and purposive behaviour can be fully explained in terms of efficient causation, or whether some kind of irreducible teleology should be recognized in addition to efficient causes. The 'logical connection argument' which has been thought to show that the relation between will or desire and action cannot be causal (in anything like a Humean sense) is rebutted. While several uses of distinctively teleological descriptions of processes and behaviour are admitted and explained, it is argued that no objective processes are in themselves irreducibly teleological. We have teleological concepts, and teleology belongs to some processes as we know them, but not to the processes in the objects. In reality, efficient causation only is the cement of the universe.

This account of causation does not, of course, stand entirely on its own, but is connected with things that I have said elsewhere. It rests partly on logical and epistemological views which are not defended here; for the logical ones I have argued particularly in *Truth, Probability, and Paradox*, for the epistemo-logical ones particularly in *Problems from Locke* but also in 'A Defence of Induction'. The project of defending an essentially empiricist view of causation which, however, explains elements in our thinking which are initially at variance with such a view is also connected with my main meta-ethical thesis in *Ethics: Inventing Right and Wrong*. The most radical challenge to my denial of the objectivity of values is the argument that it presupposes an empiricism which is unable to cope with many other features of the world, including causation, that it would nevertheless be intolerable to deny. This challenge is (in part) rebutted by showing that the empiricism in question can, after all, give an adequate account of causation and our know-ledge of it.

August 1979   J. L. M.

Contents

Introduction

THIS book has as its theme an attempt to discover or elucidate the nature of causation. It is, of course, part of the business of the various sciences to discover particular causal relationships and causal laws; but it is part of the business of philosophy to determine what causal relationships in general are, what it is for one thing to cause another, or what it is for nature to obey causal laws. As I understand it, this is an ontological question, a question about how the world goes on. In Hume's phrase, the central problem is that of causation 'in the objects'. In approaching this ontological question it will indeed be necessary to examine the meaning, and the logic, of several kinds of causal statements, the uses of what we can classify as causal language; to engage, in other words, in conceptual analysis. But questions about the analysis of concepts or meanings are distinct from questions about what is there, about what goes on. Of course, we may, or rather must, accept the use of causal language as a rough guide to what we are to take as causal relationships, as indicating— though not as authoritatively marking out—our field of study. But it is always possible that our causal statements should, in their standard, regular, and central uses, carry meanings and implications which the facts do not bear out, that our ways of speaking and reasoning about the situations or sequences which we recognize as causal should (explicitly or implicitly) assert of them something which is not true. It is equally possible that some or even all of the situations and sequences that we recognize as causal should have features which we have not fully recognized, or perhaps which we have not discovered at all, and which therefore are not built into the meaning of our causal language. Conceptual and linguistic analysis in the causal area, then, is a guide to our main topic and an introduction to it; but it is not itself our main topic, and with regard to that topic its authority is far from absolute.

Also subsidiary to our main topic, but even more important

as an introduction to it, is the epistemological question how we can and do acquire causal knowledge, how we learn about causal relationships, test, refute, establish, or confirm causal claims and hypotheses. I would reject the verificationist theory that the meanings of causal statements, among others, are directly determined by the ways in which they are, or even can be, verified or tested, though of course it must be conceded that there are indirect connections between what a statement means and the ways in which it can be checked. Equally I would reject any phenomenalist or subjective idealist theory that what is there is constituted or determined by how things appear to us (or to me). But the possibilities of finding things out may set limits, perhaps quite narrow limits, to what we have any right to assert to be there. An ontological claim which lacked epistemological support would be nothing but an airy speculation, and, while an outright denial of it would not be in order, to spend any great time on it would be as much out of place in philosophy as in science.

When I say that the theme is the nature of causation, I am taking the word 'causation' in a very broad sense. What goes on may be governed by laws of functional dependence rather than, or as well as, by connections between distinguishable cause-events and result-events. There may be continuing processes which it would be not at all natural to describe in the ordinary terminology of cause and effect. There may be statistical laws, probabilistic laws of working in contrast with strict causal, that is, deterministic laws. There may be human actions and reactions which do not fit into some preferred framework of mechanical or Humean causation. There may be some room or even some need for teleological description of some or all of what goes on. None of these topics is excluded *a priori* by a narrow interpretation of the causation whose nature is the subject of this inquiry, and in fact some attention will be paid to each of them. The causation that I want to know more about is a very general feature or cluster of features of the way the world works: it is not merely, as Hume says, *to us*, but also *in fact*, the cement of the universe.[1]

---

[1] *An Abstract of a Treatise of Human Nature*, p. 32.

I

Hume's Account of Causation

THE most significant and influential single contribution to the
theory of causation is that which Hume developed in Book I,
Part III, of the *Treatise*, summarized in the *Abstract*, and re-
stated in the first *Enquiry*. It seems appropriate to begin by
examining and criticizing it, so that we can take over from it
whatever seems to be defensible but develop an improved
account by correcting its errors and deficiencies.

Hume's conclusion seems to be summed up in the two definitions of a cause as 'an object precedent and contiguous to another, and where all the objects resembling the former are
placed in a like relation of priority and contiguity to those
objects that resemble the latter', and again as 'an object precedent and contiguous to another, and so united with it in the
imagination, that the idea of the one determines the mind to
form the idea of the other, and the impression of the one to
form a more lively idea of the other'.

These definitions, repeated with minor changes in the
Enquiry, identify causation first with regular succession and then
with succession together with a psychological association. They
at once give rise to well-known and obvious difficulties and
objections. How are the two definitions even to be reconciled
with one another? They are clearly not equivalent, nor even
coextensive.[1] There may well be regular successions such that
ideas of the successive items provoke no associations, and again
successions which are not regular but are such that the ideas of
the successive items are suitably associated. Even if we confine
ourselves to the first definition there are still many problems.
How close or how remote are the resemblances to be? Is

---

[1] Cf. J. A. Robinson, 'Hume's Two Definitions of "Cause"', *Philosophical
Quarterly*, xii (1962), reprinted in *Hume*, ed. V. C. Chappell.

contiguity required or not (it is not included in the first definition in the *Enquiry*, and reasons for not insisting on it are mentioned later in the *Treatise*)?[2] If there is a unique, never repeated, sequence of events, does it count as causal or not by this definition? Would we not want to say that such a unique sequence might either be, or not be, causal, but that this question would not be settled either way merely by its uniqueness? And in general, would we not want to say that there can be sequences which are regular, but in which the earlier item does not cause the later, either where the two items are collateral effects of a common cause, or where the regularity of their succession is just accidental? More dubiously, are there not causal sequences which nevertheless are not regular: e.g. if tossing a coin were an indeterministic process, so that my tossing this coin just as I did this time might equally well have led to its falling heads or tails, still, since it in fact fell heads, did not my tossing it cause its falling heads? In any case, there are complications about necessary causes, sufficient causes, necessary and sufficient causes, combinations of causal factors, counteracting causes, a plurality of alternative causes, causal over-determination, and so on which are entirely neglected if we speak just of regular succession, about 'all the objects resembling the former . . .'. Can even precedence in time be insisted on? Are there not causes which are simultaneous with their effects, and might there not conceivably be causes which succeed their effects?

Even the first definition, then, does not seem to agree at all well with what we ordinarily require for causation. It might be clarified and made precise and perhaps qualified or extended, and so turned into something more satisfactory. This would be a fairly lengthy task. I shall undertake this task later,[3] but to pursue it now would lead us away from Hume's distinctive contribution to the subject. In fact, we may suspect that while the two definitions in some way represent the conclusion of Hume's discussion, the way we have just been looking at them somehow misses the point, that what Hume took himself to have established was something to which the difficulties I have been hastily surveying have little relevance. Perhaps a *definition* of 'cause', in the sense in which a definition is shown to be defective by such points as those mentioned, is not what Hume was primarily concerned to give. This suspicion is strengthened by the reflection that in the *Abstract*, where Hume selects for special attention this 'one simple argument' and claims to have 'carefully traced [it] from the beginning to the end'[4]—thereby indicating that he regarded the discussion of causation as his greatest achievement in the first two Books of the *Treatise*—he does not give the two definitions: the conclusion is stated (on pages 22 and 23) without them.

Indeed, the main topic of all the passages to which I have referred is 'the nature of our reasonings concerning matter of fact'.[5] This is made explicit in the *Enquiry* and in the *Abstract* (p. 11). In the *Treatise*, Part III of Book I is entitled 'Of Knowledge and Probability'; knowledge is dispatched in Section 1, leaving the other fifteen sections for probability. In Section 11 he explains that he is using the word 'probability' in an unnaturally broad sense[6] to cover all 'arguments from causes or effects'; in view, therefore, of his repeated claim that all inferences concerning matter of fact, that is, all non-demonstrative inferences, are founded on the relation of cause and effect, 'probability' equally covers all inferences concerning matter of fact. Hume's broad purpose, then, is 'to enquire what is the nature of that evidence which assures us of any real existence and matter of fact, beyond the present testimony of our senses, or the records of our memory',[7] in other words to establish the character and the justification, if any, of all non-demonstrative inferences about empirical matters; causation comes into view because Hume thinks that it is the foundation and immediate subject of all such inferences. Very soon, of course, he focuses on necessity or necessary connection both as what distinguishes causal sequences from non-causal ones and as somehow intimately linked with causal inference, so that his specific task is to give an account of the idea of necessary connection and of whence and how it is derived, but this is still only part of the wider study of empirical inferences. And of course his serious conclusion is the largely negative one that these inferences are to be ascribed to imagination and custom rather than to reason, that we do not discover any necessity in 'the objects' that could

---

[4] *Abstract*, p. 5. [5] *Enquiry*, Sect. IV, Pt. II, Selby-Bigge, p. 32.
[6] Borrowed, as he says in *Enquiry* (Selby-Bigge, p. 56 n.), from Locke.
[7] *Enquiry*, Selby-Bigge, p. 26.

serve as a basis and justification for these inferences, but that
instead our very idea of necessity arises from those inferences:
the supposed necessity is based on the inference, not the inference upon any perceived necessity.[8] This negative thesis, this
reversal of what seems to be the true or natural order[9] of things,
is what appears to Hume himself to be his great new discovery.

Since this is his main theme and purpose, it is not very surprising if his first definition, his account of causation as we know
it in the objects, is imprecise and carelessly formulated. Precision about this was not required for the job in hand. He
might, indeed, have explained himself somewhat as follows:

Causation as we observe it in 'objects' of any kind—physical processes, mental processes, the transition from willing to bodily movement, or anywhere else—is something that we might roughly
describe as regular succession. Exactly what it is or may be, within
the bounds of this rough description, does not matter for the present
purpose. All that matters is (i) that it should be something that
could, in those cases in which we form our idea of causation, give
rise to a suitable association of ideas and hence, in accordance with
my psychological theory of belief, to belief in the effect when the
cause is observed or in the cause when the effect is, and (ii) that it
should not be anything in which there is an observable necessity (or
efficacy or agency or power or force or energy or productive quality)
or anything at all that could supply a rival explanation of our idea
of necessity, competing with the explanation given in terms of
association, belief, and projection.

With this understanding of Hume's purpose, we can now
study the arguments by which he reached and supported what
he acknowledged to be a paradoxical conclusion. But these
arguments are complicated, and it will be helpful, in dis-
entangling them, to use the device of a *structure diagram*.[10] Hume's
thesis (*a*) that causation in the objects, so far as we know, is only
regular succession, is a corollary or further conclusion based
(partly) on his main conclusion (*b*) that necessity is in the mind,
not in objects, though we tend to project it onto the objects.

[8] *Treatise*, I, III, 6, Selby-Bigge, p. 88.
[9] *Treatise*, I, III, 14, Selby-Bigge, pp. 167–8.
[10] Such a diagram is, I hope, self-explanatory. Propositions are represented by
letters, and arrows between letters, as in *b* → *a*, indicate that the author whose
argument is being analysed is saying that *b* gives some support to *a*. In constructing
the diagram I am not myself asserting that there are such logical or evidential
relationships.

This main conclusion is supported by the confluence of three lines of thought. The first of these says that (c) no knowledge of one 'object' on its own would tell us that it would cause a certain effect or that it was the effect of a certain cause, and hence that (d) what might be variously described as causal knowledge or causal beliefs or the making of inferences from observed events to their causes or to their effects—'the inference from the impression to the idea'—arises purely from the experience of constant conjunction. The second line of thought culminates in the claim (e) that this experience does not reveal any necessity in the objects, in particular, what in view of Hume's use of the term 'necessity' is closely related to this, that the experience of constant conjunction does not provide materials for any *rational* inference from cause to effect (or vice versa) in a new instance. The third line of thought is the psychological theory of belief, summed up in the thesis (f) that belief consists in the liveliness given to an idea by an associative link with a present impression.

That is, the main structure of the argument is as shown in Diagram (i). (In this, d is shown twice because it is both used along with e and f to support b and also used along with b to support a.)

Diagram (i)

That the main structure of Hume's argument consists in the bringing together of these three lines of thought to support what I have called his main conclusion is confirmed by his own summary of his argument in the *Treatise*, which I quote, merely inserting the letters of reference:

Before we are reconciled to this doctrine, how often must we repeat to ourselves, *that* (c) the simple view of any two objects or actions, however related, can never give us any idea of power, or of a connexion betwixt them: *that* (d) this idea arises from the repetition of their union: *that* (e) the repetition neither discovers nor causes anything in the objects, but (f) has an influence only on the mind by that customary transition it produces: *that* (b) this customary transition is therefore the same with the power and necessity; which are consequently qualities of perceptions, not of objects, and are internally felt by the soul, and not perceived externally in bodies?[11]

This account is equally confirmed by Hume's lengthier summary of his argument in the *Abstract*; there the first line of thought is found on pages 13 and 14, the second is foreshadowed on page 12 and developed on pages 14 and 15, and the third is given on pages 16 to 21, while the conclusion is stated several times in slightly different forms in those pages.

In the *Treatise* (Book I, Part III) the first line of thought is presented partly at the beginning of Section 6 and partly at the beginning of Section 14 (though associated points are made in Section 3); the second line of thought occupies the central part of Section 6; the third begins at the end of that Section, and, with a wealth of illustration, fills Sections 7 to 10, while Sections 11 to 13 further illustrate it by attempting to explain reasoning about probabilities (in the narrow, ordinary, sense, not in the broad one in which 'probability' covers all inferences concerning matters of fact) in terms of this same psychological theory of belief. Section 14 puts the whole argument together and draws the conclusions.

In the first *Enquiry*, Section IV, Part I develops the first line of thought, stressing point *c*; Section IV, Part II gives the second line of thought; Section V gives the third; Section VII, Part I contributes further points to the first line of thought, and Section VII, Part II again puts the whole argument together.

What I have given so far is only the broad structure of Hume's argument. We may now fill in some details.

Leading up to *c*, in the first line of thought, is the argument that (*g*) cause and effect are distinct existences and the ideas of a cause and its effect are also distinct, so that (*h*) a particular cause is always conceivable without its effect, and a particular effect without its cause. From *g* it also follows—in a branch argument—that (*i*) there can be no demonstrative proof of the principle that every event has a cause, and this is further supported by detailed criticisms (*j*) of specific attempts to prove this.[12] But *c* needs, and is given, further support in addition to *h*. We *might* be able to observe something about *C* that would

[11] *Treatise*, I, III, 14, Selby Bigge, p. 166.   [12] *Treatise*, I, III, 3.

tell us *a priori* that it would produce *E* (or something about *E* that would tell us *a priori* that it had been produced by *C*), even if *C* were conceivable without *E* and vice versa: the *C–E* sequence might be necessary *a priori* without being analytic. This possibility is excluded partly by a challenge to anyone to produce an example of such detection of power or necessity, and partly by a search through different areas of experience for an impression that might give rise to the idea of power or necessity.[13] The negative result is that (*k*) no impression of power or necessity is supplied by any observed relation or sequence. Also, to support *d*, *c* needs the help of the claim that (*l*) causal knowledge is actually acquired in cases where we experience constant conjunction. Inserting these details, we can give in Diagram (ii) a fuller picture of the first line of thought.

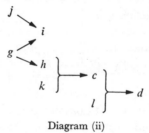

Diagram (ii)

The second line of thought could be similarly expanded. It turns upon the problem-of-induction dilemma. The conclusion (*e*) that the experience of constant conjunction does not provide materials for any *rational* inference from cause to effect (or vice versa) in a new instance is supported by the claim that any such rational inference would have to rest on the principle that unobserved instances must resemble observed ones, or that nature is uniform, while this principle can be established neither by demonstration (since its falsity is conceivable) nor by 'probable reasoning' (since that would be circular). This argument clearly has a further detailed structure, but I need not analyse it because it has been very thoroughly analysed by D. C. Stove[14] whose conclusions I shall simply take over and apply. I shall refer to the whole problem-of-induction dilemma as *m*.

---

[13] *Treatise*, early part of Section 14; *Enquiry*, Sect. VII, Pt. I.

[14] 'Hume, Probability, and Induction' in *Philosophical Review*, lxxiv (1965), reprinted in *Hume*, ed. V. C. Chappell. Stove develops his analysis more fully in *Probability and Hume's Inductive Scepticism* (1973).

The third line of thought is developed at great length in the *Treatise*, and again there would be scope for a detailed analysis of the subsidiary arguments. But it may be sufficient to note one important premiss, that (*n*) belief is not a separate idea but a peculiar feeling or manner of conceiving any idea; it is on this, together with the whole body of examples (*o*) where belief seems to be produced by association, that thesis *f* rests.

The structure of the whole argument, in as much detail as we require, can then be shown by Diagram (iii) with the following 'dictionary':

(*a*) Causation in the objects, so far as we know, is only regular succession.
(*b*) Necessity is in the mind, not in objects.
(*c*) The simple view of objects gives us no idea of power or necessary connection, i.e. no knowledge of one 'object' on its own allows causal inference to another 'object'.
(*d*) Causal knowledge and inference, and the idea of necessary connection, arise purely from the experience of constant conjunction.
(*e*) This experience neither reveals nor produces any necessity in the objects; that is, it does not provide materials for any rational inference from cause to effect (or vice versa) in a new instance.
(*f*) Belief consists in the liveliness given to an idea by association with a present impression.
(*g*) Cause and effect are distinct existences, and the ideas of a cause and of its effect are distinct.
(*h*) A cause is conceivable without its effect and vice versa.
(*i*) There can be no demonstrative proof that every event has a cause.
(*j*) Specific attempts to prove that every event has a cause fail.
(*k*) No impression of power or necessity is supplied by any observed relation or sequence.
(*l*) Causal knowledge is acquired in cases where we experience constant conjunction.
(*m*) The problem-of-induction dilemma.
(*n*) Belief is not a separate idea but a feeling.
(*o*) Belief is produced by association.

We have already noted a curious duality in this argument,

which comes out in the double formulation that we need to give for such propositions as *c*, *d*, and *e*. The main topic is the character and justification of inferences about matters of fact, but bound up with this is the secondary topic of the nature of causal connection. These are further linked by a very important assumption which is implicit in a double treatment of necessity or necessary connection. On the one hand this is taken to be

Diagram (iii)

the distinguishing feature of causal as opposed to non-causal sequences. On the other hand, it is taken to be something that would allow rational *a priori* inference, e.g. something such that if we detected it holding between *C* and *E*, we should (if we knew enough about *C* itself) be able to infer rationally that *E* would follow *C*. This is clearest when necessity is equated with power: 'if the original power were felt, it must be known: were it known, its effect must also be known; since all power is relative to its effect.' And again 'We must distinctly and particularly conceive the connexion betwixt the cause and effect, and be able to pronounce, from a simple view of one, that it must be followed or preceded by the other. This is the true manner of conceiving a particular power . . .'.[15]

This second interpretation of necessity is used, with important results, in the survey that establishes *k*. It is, for example, partly because we do not know *a priori* which movements are under the control of the will that we cannot be detecting necessity in

[15] *Enquiry*, Sect. VII, Pt. I, Selby-Bigge, p. 66; *Treatise*, I, III, 14, Selby-Bigge, p. 161.

the will–movement sequence. And again if we could detect
necessity in this sequence, the whole transition from will to
movement would have to be transparent to our understanding,
whereas in fact the intermediate links are utterly obscure.

Now it is a sheer assumption that these two interpretations
belong together, that the distinguishing feature of causal
sequences must be something that would justify *a priori* inference. Hume gives no argument to support it. Moreover, it has
no basis in the ordinary concept of causation. This ordinary
concept may include suggestions that there is some intimate tie
between an individual cause and its effect, that the one produces the other, that it somehow pushes or pulls it into existence, and the like. But none of these suggestions would carry
with it a justification of *a priori* inference. The notion of a necessity that would justify *a priori* inference is indeed to be found
in rationalistic philosophy, for example in Locke as well as
Descartes.[16] It has repeatedly cropped up in the thinking
of some scientists and philosophers of science, particularly in
the form of the view that no explanation is satisfactory unless
it is *intelligible*, unless it gets beyond brute fact and shows that
what does happen has to happen, and therefore, if only we
knew enough, could be firmly expected to happen. But it is a
rationalist scientists' and philosophers' notion, not part of the
ordinary concept of a cause.

We should, therefore, distinguish the two things which this
assumption has unwarrantably identified. We might call *necessity*$_1$ whatever is the distinguishing feature of causal as opposed
to non-causal sequences, and *necessity*$_2$ the supposed warrant for
an *a priori* inference, for example, the power which if we found

---

[16] Locke (*An Essay concerning Human Understanding*, Book IV, Chapter III, § 13)
says that we can see 'some connexion' in mechanical processes, and he clearly
thinks (Book III, Chapter VI) that things have real essences which are the 'foundation' of all their properties, from which their qualities flow, and from which, if
only we knew those essences, we should be able to infer those qualities. The trouble
is merely that these real essences 'are so far from our discovery or comprehension',
that 'we know them not'. Similarly Descartes (*Principles of Philosophy*, II, §§ 37 ff.)
states such laws as 'Every reality, in so far as it is simple and undivided, always
remains in the same condition so far as it can . . .' and 'A moving body, so far as
it can, goes on moving'. The behaviour of things will be intelligible in so far as it
can be shown to be a consequence of such laws as these, which are themselves
based on 'God's immutability'. Again 'if I move one end of a staff . . . I easily
conceive the power by which that part of the staff is moved as necessarily moving
at one and the same instant all its other parts' (*Regula* IX).

it in C would tell us at once that C would bring about E, or some corresponding feature which if we found it in E would tell us at once that E had been produced by C, or some relation between one kind of thing and another which told us that things of those kinds could occur only in sequences, with a thing of the second kind following a thing of the first. But once we have drawn this distinction, we must concede that while Hume has a strong case for asserting k about necessity$_2$, he has no case at all for asserting it about necessity$_1$.

This point can be put in another way. I have interpreted the passages we are discussing as presenting an *argument* in which it is assumed that necessity is something that, if found, would justify *a priori* inference, and in which it is concluded that this necessity is not found but is felt and then improperly objectified. But Hume also pretends to be engaged in a very different pursuit, a *search* rather than an argument. Necessary connection is introduced as that of which the idea is the as yet unidentified third element (along with contiguity and succession) in our idea of causation, which will be identified only when we have found the impression from which it is derived.[17] But if this second pursuit were to be conducted fairly, it would have to be carried on in an innocent, open-minded way; Hume would have to be prepared to accept as the sought-for impression whatever seemed in practice to differentiate the sequences we accept as causal from those we do not. As we have seen, this is not how he proceeds: he starts with a firm conviction that nothing can count as necessary connection unless it will somehow support *a priori* inference. His search for necessity$_1$ is sacrificed to his argument about necessity$_2$. His ostensible procedure is to look for the impression from which the idea of power or necessity is derived in order to decide what this idea is, since, on Hume's principles, the idea must be just a fainter copy of the impression. But his real procedure is to examine various sorts of observation which might be supposed to include the required impression, and to reject these in turn on the ground that they include nothing which could yield, as a copy, such an idea of power as he has already postulated. And when he finally reaches his thesis that necessity is in the mind, explained in terms of the psychological theory of belief,

17 *Treatise* I, III, 2, Selby-Bigge, p. 77.

associative links, and the 'determination of the thought', he finds it convincing just because this, and perhaps this alone, *could* supply a source, in the form of an impression, for what he has from the start assumed the idea of power or necessity to be, a licence to infer effect from cause or vice versa.

After this analysis and clarification of Hume's arguments we can turn to evaluation. How good are they? What, if anything, do they establish?

If we accepted Hume's conceptual framework, and assumed that all kinds of thinking, or mental life generally, consisted simply of having certain perceptions, certain impressions and ideas in various combinations and sequences, then it would be plausible to equate believing with having a lively idea. What else, on these assumptions, could belief be? Hume is right in saying (as in *n*) that belief is not just another idea compresent with the idea of whatever we believe (or believe in). But as soon as we break free from these assumptions, this view becomes utterly implausible. At any time there are large numbers of things that I believe of which I have no idea at all, faint or lively. In so far as I can identify ideas and compare their degrees of vivacity, I seem to have very faint ideas of many things in whose existence I believe and some relatively vivid ones of what I class as fantasies. The theory that belief arises from association with a present impression is equally shaky. Some ideas of things I believe in are thus associated, but a great many are not. And some things the ideas of which are strongly associated with present impressions—for example, the events in a work of fiction that I am now reading, the printed words of which are before my eyes—are not believed. In so far as Hume's conclusions rest on this full-blown associationist theory of belief, then, they are ill founded. But he could fall back on the much more defensible thesis that human beings, and some other animals, have an innate or instinctive tendency to reason inductively, to expect a conjunction or sequence of events that they have noticed recurring a number of times—especially if it has recurred without exceptions—to be repeated in the future and to have occurred similarly in past unobserved cases. That there is such an inductive propensity can be confirmed experimentally for non-human animals (for example, the psychologists' rats) and can be taken as an empirical fact in its own

right, detached from the wider theory of the nature and causes
of belief in general; this proposition, which we may call f',
would be sufficient for some of Hume's purposes.

What I have called Hume's second line of thought has been
thoroughly analysed and criticized by Stove. Also, though this
problem-of-induction dilemma has tremendous importance for
other parts of philosophy, it is only marginally relevant to our
topic of causation. For both these reasons I shall deal with it
only briefly. Hume's argument is that if it were *reason* that leads
us, after the experience of a constant conjunction, to infer a
cause from an effect or an effect from a cause in a new like
instance, reason would be relying on the principle of the uniformity of nature, that unobserved instances must resemble
observed ones, but that this principle cannot be established
either by 'knowledge'—because its falsity is conceivable—or by
'probability'—because that would be circular. It would be
circular because 'probability' rests always on causal relations,
and so on a presumption of the very principle of uniformity the
support for which we are considering. Now Hume's premiss
that 'reason' would have to rely on the principle of uniformity
holds only if it is assumed that reason's performances must all
be deductively valid: if it were suggested that an observed constant conjunction of As with Bs *probabilifies* that this new A will
be conjoined with a B, in terms of some logical or relational
probability as proposed by Keynes and Carnap, that is, that
some non-deductively-valid argument is none the less rational,
that its premisses really support though they do not entail its
conclusion, then this possibility would not be excluded by
Hume's argument, because such a probabilistic inference would
not need to invoke the uniformity principle which produces the
circularity that Hume has exposed.

Reasonable but probabilistic inferences, then, have not been
excluded by Hume's argument, for the simple reason that Hume
did not consider this possibility. Modern readers are tempted
to suppose that he did consider, and refute, it because he calls
what the second horn of his dilemma discusses 'probable
reasonings'. But this does not mean probabilistic inferences; as
he tells us, he is using 'probable' in a wide sense, covering all
reasoning about matters of fact, as opposed to demonstrative
'knowledge' based on the comparison of ideas, and the only

reasonings that this second horn condemns as circular are deductively valid arguments in which the principle of uniformity is both a premiss and the conclusion. Hume can hardly be blamed for not having considered a possibility which was not clearly presented until 150 years after his death: but it is more surprising that modern philosophers like Ayer and Popper should suppose him to have refuted it.[18]

Proposition *e*, then, can be established only if we amend it, reading 'deductively valid' in place of 'rational', and interpreting 'necessity' in such a way that the denial that constant conjunction reveals necessity is equivalent to the denial that it furnishes the materials for deductively valid inferences about new instances. Let us call this amended version *e'*.

Returning to the first line of thought, we are forced to make a more complicated evaluation. Propositions *j*, *i*, *g*, and *h* are all clearly correct: neither the principle that every event has a cause, nor any specific causal law, nor any singular causal statement connecting particular events, is an analytic truth. Of

[18] See, for example, K. R. Popper, *Objective Knowledge*, p. 89, 'Hume's answer . . . as he points out, . . . remains negative even if our inference is merely to the probability of a connexion that has not been observed rather than to its necessity. This extension is formulated in the *Treatise*. . . . The argument against probabilistic induction is . . . purely formal.' Popper refers to Stove's article, but still has not grasped its point; 'since Hume's argument is formal . . . Stove cannot be right.' This ignores the fact that only a deductively valid 'induction' would require the uniformity principle, as well as misunderstanding Hume's use of the word 'probability'.

Similarly, A. J. Ayer in *Probability and Evidence*, p. 5, in what purports to be an exposition of Hume's argument, first correctly notes that the principle of uniformity is needed as an extra premiss to make the jump from 'All hitherto observed As bear the relation R to Bs' to 'This A will have the relation R to some B' *valid*, and correctly repeats Hume's claim that there can be no demonstrative argument for this principle. But he goes on: 'Even if the principle cannot be demonstrated, perhaps we can at least show it to be probable', and repeats Hume's circularity objection, without noting that to make it sound we must assume that what is being criticized is still an attempt to make the inductive jump *deductively valid*, and that 'probable' does not cancel this concern with validity, but merely means 'resting on empirical information'. He then adds what he has admitted (privately) to be his own extension and not a report of anything in Hume: 'The same objection would apply to any attempt to by-pass the general principle of uniformity of nature and argue that inferences from one matter of fact to another, though admittedly not demonstrative, can nevertheless be shown to be probable. Again, this judgement of probability must have some foundation. But this foundation can lie only in our past experience. . . .' To say this is simply to ignore the suggestion that there is a logical, *a priori*, relation of support or probabilification. Against *this* suggestion the same (circularity) objection does *not* arise.

course, we can find *descriptions* of causes and effects such that the description of a cause is analytically connected with the description of its effect, but this is a trivial point on which no time need be wasted. What matters is that there are no logically necessary connections between the events themselves, or between any *intrinsic* descriptions of them, however detailed and complete. On this Hume's argument is conclusive and beyond question. But difficulties begin with k. We can concede that the survey arguments of Section 14 in the *Treatise* and Section VII, Part I in the *Enquiry*, coupled with the signal lack of success of rationalist philosophers of science in taking up the challenge to produce examples of synthetic *a priori* physical laws or 'intelligible' explanations, provide a very strong, though not absolutely conclusive, case for the claim that we never observe a necessity$_2$ which would support a deductively valid *a priori* causal inference. But it has not been nearly so conclusively shown that no observations reveal a necessity$_2$ that might support a probabilistic *a priori* causal inference; for all that we have so far seen, observable features of one event, taken on its own, *might* probabilify a certain continuation or successor-event. And of course it has not been shown at all that no observations reveal what we have called necessity$_1$. If we then distinguish necessity$_{2.1}$ as something that would support a deductively valid *a priori* causal inference, necessity$_{2.2}$ as something that would support a probabilistic *a priori* causal inference, and apply subscripts to k to correspond with the kinds of necessity mentioned in it, we must conclude that k_1 is quite unsupported, $k_{2.1}$ is very strongly but not conclusively supported, while $k_{2.2}$ is a fairly open issue. Similar qualifications, with similar subscripting, must be applied to c and to d. In other words, d_1, the thesis that our knowledge of the distinguishing feature of causal as opposed to non-causal sequence arises purely from the experience of constant conjunction, is quite without support; $d_{2.1}$, the thesis that if there were any deductively valid inference 'from the impression to the idea' it would have to rest purely on the experience of constant conjunction, is pretty firmly established; but $d_{2.2}$, the thesis that a similar probabilistic inference would have to rest purely on this experience, is a moot point.

When we combine $d_{2.1}$, the only well-supported outcome of this first line of thought, with our amended propositions e' and

f', we can conclude that there are no deductively valid inferences 'from the impression to the idea', and that *if* we have an idea of a necessity that would support such inferences—*that* we have such an idea has not been shown—it may well be explained in Hume's manner as a projection of the inductive inferences that we instinctively make.

But in view of the relatively weak support for $d_{2.2}$, and the amendment (that Stove has shown necessary) of e to e', we must conclude that it is an open question whether, either before or after the experience of constant conjunction, there may be forceful probabilistic inferences from an observed cause to an unobserved effect or vice versa. What in Hume's way of speaking would come out as the corresponding kinds of necessity may, for all that he has shown, be discoverable 'in the objects'; there is *as yet* no need to explain them away in terms of instinctive tendencies to infer, transferred improperly to external reality as a result of the mind's propensity to spread itself upon objects.

And in view of the total lack of support for k_1 and the corresponding d_1, the question where and how we are to look for the distinguishing feature of causal sequences is wide open: it has not even been shown that anything in the area of constant conjunction or regular succession is required for this purpose. The search which Hume sacrificed to his argument must start again from scratch.

The conclusion that Hume has pretty well established about causal inferences—that the inference from an observed event to another event as its cause or effect is never deductively valid, even if we include in the premises the fact that a great many similar sequences have occurred—is not a surprising one; it may not have been clearly realized before Hume pointed it out, but it would now be accepted by most philosophers without dispute. The more sweeping conclusions about such inferences which he suggests but fails to establish—that these inferences are not even reasonable or probable, that they are to be ascribed to imagination, custom, and habit rather than to reason, that it is out of the question to try to justify them on any ground except that they are natural, instinctive, and unavoidable—are interesting and important. They raise those problems about induction, probable inference, and the confirmation of hypotheses which are still a major area of dispute and investiga-

tion for philosophers of science and inductive logicians. But to
pursue them directly would lead us away from the subject of
causation. I shall therefore now leave on one side what was,
as I have tried to show, Hume's main topic of inferences concerning matters of fact, and concentrate on what was for him
only a secondary subject, the nature of causation.

Hume's conclusions on this subject can be summed up under
three headings: the idea of causation, causation as it really is
'in the objects', and causation so far as we know about it in the
objects.

According to Hume, our idea of causation combines three
elements: succession, contiguity, and necessary connection.
When he includes contiguity he does not mean that we require
every cause to be contiguous with its effect, but merely that
where this is not the case, cause and effect are thought to be
joined by a chain of intermediate items, where each such item
is the effect of its predecessor and causes its successor, and is
contiguous with both of these. But, as I have said, he hesitates
about including contiguity even in this sense. I think he is right
to hesitate. While we are happiest about contiguous cause–
effect relations, and find 'action at a distance' over either a
spatial or a temporal gap puzzling, we do not rule it out. Our
ordinary concept of causation does not absolutely require contiguity; it is not part of our idea of causation in a way that
would make '*C* caused *E* over a spatial, or temporal, or both
spatial and temporal, gap, without intermediate links' a contradiction in terms. Hume did not hesitate about requiring
succession; I think he should have hesitated, but I shall discuss
this issue later.[19] But Hume is quite confident that our idea of
causation includes an idea of necessary connection. Sceptical
though he is about our ascription of necessity to the real world,
he is not sceptical about our having this idea; his problems
concern only its precise character and its origin. We can, it is
true, find such remarks as 'We never therefore have any idea
of power. . . . We deceive ourselves in imagining we can form
any such general idea . . . we have really no distinct meaning,
and make use only of common words, without any clear and
determinate ideas'[20] and 'the necessary conclusion *seems* to be
that we have no idea of connexion or power at all, and that

[19] In Chapter 7.   [20] *Treatise*, I, III, 14, Selby-Bigge, pp. 161-2.

these words are absolutely without any meaning . . .'.[21] Such remarks have led careless readers to think that Hume excluded necessity even from our *idea* of causation; but this is a mistake. These remarks express what *would* follow on a certain hypothesis, or what, at a certain stage of the investigation, *seems* to be the case; Hume goes on at once to explain that, and how, these conclusions can be avoided. The whole tenor of his thought is that we *have* this obscure idea, and that we must in the end find an impression from which it is derived. Admittedly even in stating his conclusion he says 'Either we have no idea of necessity, or necessity is nothing but that determination of the thought . . .';[22] but it is clear which alternative he prefers. Hume is very far from holding a regularity theory of the *meaning* of causal statements. His answer to the question 'What do we ordinarily mean by "*C* causes *E*"?' is that we mean that *C* and *E* are such that *E*'s following *C* is knowable *a priori*, in view of the intrinsic character of *C* and *E*, so that the sequence is not merely observable but intelligible. When at the conclusion of the discussion in the *Enquiry* he says 'we mean only that they have acquired a connexion in our thought', etc., he is telling us what we can properly mean rather than what we ordinarily mean. He thinks that the ordinary meaning is itself mistaken, and calls for reform.

On this crucial issue, I think that Hume is right to assume that we have what in his terminology, with my subscripting, would be an idea of necessity$_1$; we do recognize some distinction between causal and non-causal sequences, and what is more we are inclined to think that, whatever this difference is, it is an intrinsic feature of each individual causal sequence. But I have argued that Hume is quite wrong to assume that our idea of necessity$_1$ is also an idea of necessity$_2$, that we ordinarily identify the differentia of causal sequences with something that would support *a priori* inference.

About causation as it really is in the objects Hume usually says that it is regular succession and nothing more.

. . . we are led astray by a false philosophy . . . when we transfer the determination of the thought to external objects, and suppose any real intelligible connexion betwixt them . . . As to what may be

[21] *Enquiry*, Sect. VII, Pt. II, Selby-Bigge, p. 74.
[22] *Treatise*, I, III, 14, Selby-Bigge, p. 166.

said, that the operations of nature are independent of our thought and reasoning, I allow it; and accordingly have observed, that objects bear to each other the relations of contiguity and succession; that like objects may be observed, in several instances, to have like relations, and that all this is independent of, and antecedent to, the operations of the understanding. But if we go any further, and ascribe a power or necessary connexion to these objects, this is what we can never observe in them. . . .[23]

Sometimes, indeed, he speaks of secret powers and connections of which we are ignorant. 'We can never penetrate so far into the essence and construction of bodies as to perceive the principle, on which their mutual influence depends.' But he may well have his tongue in his cheek here, as he does when he speaks about the deity. At most he is 'ready to allow, that there may be several qualities, both in material and immaterial objects, with which we are utterly unacquainted; and if we please to call these *power* or *efficacy*, it will be of little consequence . . .'.[24]

It is about causation so far as we know about it in the objects that Hume has the firmest and most fully argued views. In effect, he makes three negative points, and one positive one. The first negative point is that there are no logically necessary connections between causes and effects as we know them, and Hume is clearly right about this. The second negative point is that what I have called necessity$_2$ is not known as holding between causes and effects. This second exclusion is of synthetic *a priori* connections, as the first was of analytic ones. It is this second exclusion that is vital and controversial. It is presupposed, for example, in Hume's very forceful argument (*Treatise*, Section 6) that we cannot get over the inductive problem by referring to powers which we infer to be present in causes (for even if we could infer that a certain power was associated with certain sensible qualities on one occasion, how are we to know that the same power will be associated with the same qualities on other occasions?). This assumes that the power needs to be inferred, that it cannot be observed ('it having been already prov'd that the power lies not in the visible qualities'). But this 'proof' was that 'such a penetration into

[23] *Treatise*, I, III, 14, Selby-Bigge, pp. 168–9.
[24] *Treatise*, II, III, 1 and I, III, 14, Selby-Bigge, pp. 400 and 168.

their essences as may discover the dependence of the one
[object] upon the other' would imply the 'impossibility of conceiving any thing different. But as all distinct ideas are separ-
able, 'tis evident there can be no impossibility of that kind.'[25]
Hume is here attempting to derive his second exclusion directly
from his first, that is, to derive k in our diagram from h (or
from g), and so to present c as having been established by g
alone. But of course this is invalid. Similarly, after explaining
'power' in the terms on which I have based my account of
necessity$_2$, Hume goes on to say that 'nothing is more evident
than that the human mind cannot form such an idea of two
objects, as to conceive any connexion betwixt them, or comprehend distinctly that power or efficacy by which they are
united. Such a connexion would amount to a demonstration,
and would imply the absolute impossibility for the one object
. . . to be conceived not to follow upon the other.'[26] Here, too,
Hume invalidly argues that there cannot be a synthetic *a priori*
connection because it would be an analytic one. Yet he also
takes the trouble to survey the various places where it might be
held that such connections are found, and uses a challenge
argument, saying 'This defiance we are obliged frequently to
make use of, as being almost the only means of proving a
negative in philosophy'.[27] This seems to show that he realizes
that he is now making a further point, which the separate con-
ceivability of causes and effects does not establish. If we discard
the arguments which confuse the second exclusion with the
first, we find that it is supported mainly by a series of assertions
that (in various fields) we do not in fact possess *a priori* knowledge of causal relationships, that we have to find, by experience
in each case—even in the cases of voluntary bodily movements
and the calling up of ideas at will—what effects each kind of
cause is actually able to bring about, together with a challenge
to anyone who disagrees to produce an example of *a priori*
causal knowledge. Again, there is the argument (already mentioned) that we could perceive necessity in the transition from
will to bodily movement only if we knew the whole process,
including 'the secret union of soul and body' and the succession

[25] *Treatise*, I, III, 6, Selby-Bigge, pp. 90–1 and 86–7.
[26] *Treatise*, I, III, 14, Selby-Bigge, pp. 161–2.
[27] *Treatise*, I, III, 14, Selby-Bigge, p. 159.

of events in muscles and nerves and 'animal spirits', which we
do not. These are strong but not absolutely conclusive arguments against a known necessity$_2$, if this is taken as necessity$_{2.1}$,
something that would support deductively valid *a priori* causal
inference. They seem less strong if it is taken as necessity$_{2.2}$,
something that would support probabilistic *a priori* causal inference. It may, indeed, seem that Hume underplayed his hand
here, that instead of looking for examples of observed necessity
and challenging his opponents to produce some he might have
asked what could conceivably count as a perception of necessity. How could we possibly perceive anything in one event
which would in itself point to anything else? Or how could we
perceive anything in one individual cause–effect sequence which
would tell us that any other event which resembled this cause,
however closely, was either certain or even likely to be followed
by an event which resembled this effect? Surely anything that
we *perceived* would be, as it were, enclosed within itself, and
could not point beyond itself in any way. This would have been
a very forceful argument for Hume's second exclusion. It is in
fact a variant of the strong basic case against synthetic *a priori*
knowledge of an objective reality. But we should not decide
whether to accept it without qualification until after we have
weighed the further considerations that will be introduced in
Chapter 8.

Hume's third negative point is that we find nothing at all in
causal sequences except regular succession and (perhaps) contiguity. This third sweeping exclusion is hardly supported at all;
but it is undeniably asserted. 'It appears that, in single instances
of the operation of bodies, we never can, by our utmost scrutiny,
discover any thing but one event following another. . . . All
events seem entirely loose and separate. One event follows
another; but we never can observe any tie between them.'[28]

---

[28] *Enquiry*, Sect. VII, Pt. II, Selby-Bigge, pp. 73–4: cf. *Treatise* I, III, 2, Selby-
Bigge, p. 77. Hume's view is endorsed and defended by Ayer in *Probability and
Evidence*, pp. 10–18: 'I think that we can make sense of this issue, . . . if we understand Hume to be denying that apart from relations of comparison there could be
anything more than spatio-temporal relations between events. This may sound
paradoxical at first hearing, but when we consider what it comes to we shall see
that it is at least very plausible. It amounts in fact to the claim, which is scientifically most respectable, that everything that happens in the world can be represented
in terms of variations of scenery in a four-dimensional spatio-temporal continuum . . .
there is nothing in the situation that calls for anything more than the identification

At the same time, Hume himself supplies examples which falsify this claim: 'the reason, why we imagine the communication of motion to be more consistent and natural, not only than those suppositions [that a body striking another might just stop, or go back, or be annihilated, etc.], but also than any other natural effect, is founded on the relation of *resemblance* betwixt the cause and effect, which is here united to experience, and binds the objects in the closest and most intimate manner to each other . . .'.[29] Of course, he is here arguing that such resemblance does not constitute an observed necessity$_2$, that it does not justify an inference but only aids the association of ideas. Still, it is something other than contiguity and succession that we observe in some causal sequences. This falsifies the third exclusion, which is made plausible only by its being confused with the second, just as the second received illicit support from confusion with the first. Again, Hume admits that when we set bodies in motion we experience 'a *nisus* or endeavour', and again that we have a special 'sentiment or feeling' when an object in motion strikes us.[30] These again are additional observed features in some causal sequences. Hume brushes them aside as 'sensations, which are merely animal, and from which we can *a priori* draw no inference'; that is, they cannot constitute necessity$_2$, but again this is only a confused reason for not admitting them as exceptions to the third exclusion. It is clear that both some sort of resemblance and some sort of *nisus* enter into the process by which will or desire or intention leads on to bodily movement; a pre-existing intention foreshadows the movement which fulfils it, and there is often some feeling of effort. Modern

of various objects and the specification of their changing spatio-temporal relations.' But it is worth noting that Ayer (i) allows relations of comparison, (ii) introduces, though with a hint that this is unnecessary, enduring identifiable objects, and (iii) like Hume, mixes up this third exclusion with the second: it is for the latter that he really *argues*: '. . . either this supposed relation is a phenomenal property, something detectable in the situation, or it is not. If it is, its existence will enable us to draw no conclusion with regard to any event occurring at any other time than the time at which it is manifested. If it is not . . . no terms could then be observed to stand in this relation . . . our uncertainty about what will happen cannot be removed by the introduction of this entirely spurious relation.' Ayer makes out a strong case for what I have called Hume's second exclusion, but not for the third. What this leaves room for, and why it is of interest, will be discussed in later chapters, particularly Chapter 8.

[29] *Treatise*, I, III, 9, Selby-Bigge, pp. 111–12.
[30] *Enquiry*, Sect. VII, Pt. II, footnote, Selby-Bigge, pp. 77–8.

philosophers sometimes on this account argue that intentional action cannot be a case of 'Humean' causation; but it is at least as reasonable to argue the other way round, that this is a case of causation and that Hume should therefore have withdrawn his third exclusion. Modern philosophers are, however, wrong if they think that intentions and actions are logically connected in a way that would conflict with Hume's *first* exclusion.[31]

In addition to these three negative points, Hume makes the positive assertion that causation as we know it in the objects involves regular succession. I have commented, right at the beginning of this chapter, on the vagueness and the prima facie implausibility of this claim. Whether all causal relationships that we discover involve some sort of regularity of succession, and if so what sort, are questions I must leave until a later chapter.[32] But in fairness to Hume it should be noted that he does *not* say that we can discover a particular causal relationship only by observing a number of sequences that instantiate it. On the contrary he admits that 'not only in philosophy, but even in common life, we may attain the knowledge of a particular cause merely by one experiment, provided it be made with judgement, and after a careful removal of all foreign and superfluous circumstances',[33] and his 'Rules by which to judge of causes and effects'[34] include fairly crude anticipations of Mill's methods of agreement, difference, and concomitant variation, which again allow the discovery of a causal relationship by the use of very restricted sets of observations. Of course, implicit in these methods is an appeal to some general uniformity assumption,[35] and Hume himself explains that the 'one experiment' is interpreted in the light of the principle—itself based on custom —that '*like objects, placed in like circumstances, will always produce like effects*'. In other words, he is content to let 'custom' provide a belief in certain general principles, but then to allow us to

[31] e.g. A. I. Melden, *Free Action*, p. 53; T. F. Daveney, 'Intentions and Causes', *Analysis*, xxvii (1966), 23; the view is criticized but also defended in a revised form by F. Stoutland, 'The Logical Connection Argument', *American Philosophical Quarterly Monograph* 4 (1970), 117–30 and by G. H. von Wright, *Explanation and Understanding*, pp. 93–4; it is discussed in Chapter 11 below.

[32] Chapter 3. [33] *Treatise*, I, iii, 8, Selby-Bigge, p. 104.

[34] *Treatise*, I, iii, 15, Selby-Bigge, pp. 173–4.

[35] Cf. my article, 'Mill's Methods of Induction', in *Encyclopedia of Philosophy*, ed. P. Edwards, also Chapter 3 and the Appendix to this book.

discover particular causal relationships by *reasoning* from those principles together with a few relevant observations. Belief, it seems, need not arise *immediately* from an associative link with a present impression, but can be produced by rational argument so long as the premisses include some to which the associative theory applies.

It is a curious fact that Hume's choice of regular succession as the one acceptable feature of causation as it is known in the objects may well be another result of his assumption that the differentia of causal sequence must be something that will justify causal inferences. For of course if we know that events of kind C are always followed by events of kind E, and events of kind E always preceded by events of kind C, then on observing a C we can validly infer that an E will follow, and on observing an E we can validly infer that a C has preceded. Regularity would do the job that Hume throughout assumes that necessity should do. But of course only genuine, unqualified regularity of succession will do this, whereas if Hume's doubts about induction are justified all that we can know is a regularity *in all the cases so far observed*. Only the latter could consistently figure in Hume's account of causation *as we know it in the objects*. The former, the unqualified regularity, might figure in an account of causation *as it is in the objects*; but, if he were consistent, this would fall under his condemnation of 'qualities, both in material and immaterial objects, with which we are utterly unacquainted'.[36]

We might, in other words, introduce a necessity$_3$, defined as something that would license causal inference—in both directions, from cause to effect and from effect to cause—but not, like necessity$_2$, as licensing such inference *a priori*, not, that is, supposed to be discoverable in each single cause or effect on its own. As I have shown, Hume undoubtedly sometimes assumes that our ordinary idea of necessity$_1$, our notion of what marks off certain sequences as causal, is the idea of a necessity$_2$. But at times he uses only the weaker assumption that our idea of necessity$_1$ is that of a necessity$_3$. Regularity (of some sort) is admirably suited for the role of necessity$_3$, and it is not as epistemologically objectionable as necessity$_2$. We can at least say what regular succession would be like, which is more than we can say about necessity$_2$. Presumably this is why Hume is prepared to use it in his reforming definitions, his account of what we can properly mean by 'cause'. But if his doubts about induction were well founded, not even necessity$_3$ could be known. We should be using a regularity in which we believed to license a causal inference about a particular case, but the belief in the regularity would itself be explained by Hume as a product of the association of ideas, and hence the causal inference in turn is never really justified, but only explained.

Modern philosophers frequently accuse Hume of having confused logic with psychology. His discussion certainly *combines* logical and psychological elements, but it is disputable whether they are confused. Admittedly his terminology can mislead us. If he ascribes a certain operation to, say, 'imagination' rather than 'reason', he may seem to be saying merely that it is performed by one mental agency or faculty rather than another, but in fact he will also be making a logical evaluation of the performance: whatever 'reason' does will be rationally defensible, what 'imagination' does will not. But we can, without much difficulty, learn to interpret such remarks as these. What is more important is that logical and psychological considerations can properly contribute to the same investigation. If it appears that we have a certain 'idea' or concept, but it is a moot point whether it is true of, or genuinely applicable to, the real things to which we are inclined to apply it, considerations which bear on the question whether those real things could conform to this concept will be relevant, so will considerations that bear on the question whether we could have observed such conformity, and so too will the possibility of giving an alternative account of how we could have acquired this concept if we did not in fact observe things conforming to it. In particular, anyone who, like Hume, casts sceptical doubts on ingrained everyday assumptions is committed to giving an alternative account of how these beliefs could have arisen if they were false. But such alternative accounts cannot fail to appeal to psychological principles or theories.

On the other hand, Hume's resort to psychology was premature. As we have seen, he looked for a psychological explanation of a very puzzling idea of necessary connection without having properly shown that the kind of necessity which he was about to locate in the mind really was the key element in our concept of causation. Before we look for a psychological explanation of an inappropriate idea, we should investigate more carefully what idea we actually have and use, and then inquire whether *it* is inappropriate.

Hume's discussion of causation, then, includes both strong points and weak ones. Accepting his exclusion of logically necessary connection and of necessity$_{2.1}$, and postponing consideration of necessity$_{2.2}$, we have still to consider what sort or sorts of regularity, if any, characterize causal sequences, what within our ordinary concept of causation differentiates causal sequences from non-causal ones, and what features—whether included in this ordinary concept or not—over and above 'regularity' are to be found in causal relationships. We may start with the job that Hume only pretended to be doing, of identifying what we naturally take as the differentia of causal sequences; that is, we may ask again what our idea of necessary connection (necessity$_1$) is in an open-minded way, without assuming that it must be the idea of something that would license *a priori* inferences.

2

The Concept of Causation—
Conditional Analyses

ONE of the many problems with which Hume's discussion leaves us is this: what is our concept of causal as opposed to non-causal sequences; what do we (rightly or wrongly) take to be their distinguishing feature? The obvious, naïve, way of tackling this question would be to compare two otherwise similar sequences, only one of which we recognize as causal, and see what distinctive comment we should make about the causal one. Let us, then, compare the following sequences A and B.

A: A chestnut is stationary on a flat stone. I swing a hammer down so that it strikes the chestnut directly from above. The chestnut becomes distinctly flatter than before.

B: A chestnut is stationary on a hot sheet of iron. I swing a hammer down so that it strikes the chestnut directly from above. At the very instant that the hammer touches it, the chestnut explodes with a loud pop and its fragments are scattered around.

I assume that we know or perceive enough about sequences A and B to be able to say that the chestnut's becoming flatter in A was caused by its being hit with the hammer, but that its exploding in B was not caused by its being hit with the hammer. (Among other things, the explosion was not due to the hammer's pushing the chestnut into closer contact with the hot metal, or anything like that.) I am not concerned, at the moment, with how we know this, but merely with what we mean, what we are *saying* when we say that the blow–flattening sequence was causal but that the blow–exploding sequence was not.

I suggest that the obvious answer, the one that pretty well

any intelligent but unprejudiced person would give to this question, is that in A the chestnut would not have become flatter if the hammer had not struck it, whereas in B it would have exploded even if the hammer had not struck it. It is tempting to say, then, that the contrast between these two contrary-to-fact conditionals is at least an initial indication of what we mean by calling the one sequence causal and the other not, that is, that to ascribe what we called necessity$_1$ is to assert such a contrary-to-fact conditional as the former. As Mill says, 'if a person eats of a particular dish, and dies in consequence, that is, would not have died if he had not eaten of it, people would be apt to say that eating of that dish was the cause of his death'.[1] They would indeed.

Curiously enough, Hume says this too. In the *Enquiry*, after giving the first, regularity, definition ('we may define a cause to be an *object, followed by another, and where all objects similar to the first are followed by objects similar to the second*'), he adds 'or in other words *where, if the first object had not been, the second never had existed*'.[2] Now of course this variant is *not* the regularity definition in other words. (It does not even follow from the regularity definition as given here, though on a certain interpretation of the conditional it might be held to follow from, and even to be equivalent to, a different regularity statement, namely 'where all the objects similar to the second are preceded by objects similar to the first'). But I shall not spend time on the questions why Hume asserted this implausible equivalence, or why he did not realize that this was a much better answer than the one he had given in all his previous discussion to the question 'What is our *idea* of necessary connection?', but consider directly the merits and the defects of this suggestion.

To simplify matters, I shall for the present be considering only singular causal statements, especially statements about individual event sequences, such as 'The hammer's striking the chestnut caused the flattening of the chestnut'. I shall speak of causes and effects (or results) as events, but 'event' is just a general term that stands in for such items as 'the hammer's

<hr>

[1] *System of Logic*, Book III, Ch. 5, Sect. 3. Conditional analyses of causal statements are defended and discussed by Ardon Lyon in 'Causality', *British Journal for the Philosophy of Science*, xviii (1967), 1–20.

[2] *Enquiry*, Sect. VII, Pt. II, Selby-Bigge, p. 76.

striking the chestnut'. (Anxieties about the exact ontology of causation may be postponed for later consideration in Chapter 10.) Such phrases are nominalizations of singular event-sentences or event-clauses; e.g. 'the flattening of the chestnut' is a nominalization of 'the chestnut became flatter'. The present suggestion, then, is that a statement of the form 'X caused Y' means 'X occurred and Y occurred and Y would not have occurred if X had not', it being understood that when we instantiate 'X' and 'Y' with particular event descriptions we can express the suggested meaning most neatly by going back from the nominalizations to the corresponding clauses or their negations: e.g. 'the striking of the match caused the appearance of the flame' would, on this suggestion, mean 'the match was struck and the flame appeared and the flame would not have appeared if the match had not been struck'.

But is the suggestion correct?

First, are there cases where we would say that X caused Y but would not say what is proposed above as the meaning of this claim? Well, clearly we cannot say that X caused Y unless both X and Y occurred, provided that we take 'occurred' in a fairly broad sense, to include the presence or persistence of standing conditions. But what about the counterfactual conditional? Might we not say that the striking of the match caused the appearance of the flame and yet admit that even if the match had not been struck the flame would have appeared if, say, this match had been touched by a red-hot poker? Certainly we might, so the suggestion needs some modification at least: let us insert 'in the circumstances', reading '. . . and in the circumstances the flame would not have appeared if the match had not been struck'. 'The circumstances' can be taken to include the fact that this match was not in fact touched by a red-hot poker at the critical time. And in general we can modify our suggestion to read '. . . in the circumstances Y would not have occurred if X had not', the qualifying phrase being interpreted in the sort of way indicated by our example. An objector, however, might say, 'But what if, for example, the match really was touched by a red-hot poker at the same instant that it was struck? Then even *in the circumstances* the flame would have appeared even if the match had not been struck.' True, but it is not clear whether in this case we would say that the striking of the match caused the appearance of the flame. What we would or should say in such cases of causal over-determination, of fail-safe causes, will be considered later: for the moment we need not take them as falsifying our modified suggestion.

Secondly, and more awkwardly, are there cases where we would *not* say that X caused Y but would say that X and Y both occurred and that in the circumstances Y would not have occurred if X had not? Would we not have to say the latter, trivially, if X and Y were identical? Provided that X occurred, we must admit that X occurred and X occurred and in the circumstances X would not have occurred if X had not. But events, unlike Spinoza's God, are not commonly said to cause themselves. Equally, the penny would not have fallen heads-up if it had not fallen tails-down; but we would not say that its falling tails-down caused its falling heads-up. Again, the driver would not in the circumstances have broken the law if he had not exceeded the speed limit; but we would not say that his exceeding the speed limit caused his breaking of the law. To exclude all such counter-examples, we must say that, in addition to the meaning suggested above, 'X caused Y' presupposes that X and Y are distinct events, and, as the last two examples show, this must be taken in a stronger sense than merely that 'X' and 'Y' are logically or conceptually independent descriptions. Indeed, it is not even necessary, any more than it is sufficient for this purpose, that these should be logically independent descriptions. It is legitimate, though trivial, to say that X caused every effect of X; again I can say that my meeting Tom on Monday caused my remembering, on Tuesday, my meeting Tom on Monday. And so on. Logically independent descriptions, then, are not called for; what is required is that the cause and the effect should be, as Hume says, distinct existences. It may be objected that this requirement is vague or obscure, but it is not, I think, necessary for me to aim at any great precision here. I am discussing only what causal statements mean, and for this purpose it is sufficient to say that someone will not be willing to say that X caused Y unless *he* regards X and Y as distinct existences. But are there really no limits to the possible descriptions of X and Y? What about *irrelevant* descriptions, ones that have, as we would say, nothing to do with the causal relationship? Some seem acceptable: 'the

incident in the tennis court advanced the French Revolution.'
But consider 'Jane's eating fishpaste in the pantry caused her
feeling ill' and the corresponding suggested expansion 'Jane ate
fishpaste in the pantry and felt ill and in the circumstances she
wouldn't have felt ill if she hadn't eaten fishpaste in the pantry'.
We are inclined to comment that she felt ill either because she
ate too much fishpaste or because the fishpaste was bad, and in
either case it wouldn't have mattered where she ate it. This
raises the question (which will be discussed in Chapter 10)
about the extensionality of causal statements. For the present
it is enough to say that the issue is in doubt: we might want to
reject or deny both the proposed singular causal statement and
its expansion, or we might want to say that so long as it was
eating the fishpaste that made Jane ill, and it was in the pantry
that she ate it, they are both true but merely misleading. But it
seems that whatever we decide to say, we can say about both
the singular causal statement and its proposed expansion, so
that examples of this sort do not tell against the suggestion that
the latter shows what the former means. Cases where X and Y
are collateral effects of a common cause create a more serious
difficulty. Labour's defeat at the election pleases James but
saddens John, who, as it happens, are quite unknown to each
other. Then James's being pleased does not cause John's being
sad, and yet we might well say that in the circumstances John
would not have been sad if James had not been pleased. Yet
there is a way of handling the words 'if' and 'in the circumstances' that will defeat this supposed counter-example. Construct a 'possible world' in the following way: take something
that is just like the actual world up to the point where, in the
actual world, James is pleased; keep out, from your possible
world, James's being pleased, but otherwise let your possible
world run on in the same manner as the actual world; only if
John does not become sad in your possible world can you say
'in the circumstances John would not have been sad if James
had not been pleased'. And if you *can* say this, then you can
also say that James's being pleased caused John's being sad (in
the actual world). But this special way of handling 'if in the
circumstances' runs a grave risk of circularity if we want to
use this conditional as an analysis of causal statements, since
in explaining this handling we have had to use the notion of

letting the possible world run on. Yet without this special interpretation of the counterfactual conditional, it seems that while
it may be required for the truth of the corresponding causal
statement, it is not sufficient for this.

Another difficulty is concerned with the distinction which we
are inclined to draw between conditions and causes. There may
be a set of factors which were, in the circumstances, jointly
sufficient and severally necessary for a certain result, and which
all occurred, as, consequently, did the result. Then we can say
of each of these factors that if in the circumstances it had not
occurred the result would not; but we may not be so willing
to say of each of them that it caused the result. Perhaps we
ought to say this, since they are all logically related to the result
in the same way: the situation as described is symmetrical with
respect to all the factors. But at present we are discussing not
what we ought to say but what our causal statements mean.
And there is no doubt that we tend to be a bit selective, to be
more ready to call some kinds of factors causes than others.
There are no firm rules governing this selection, but there are
some fairly systematic tendencies.

Thus we are more ready to say that an event caused a certain
effect than that a standing condition did: it was the spark
rather than the presence of inflammable material that caused
the fire. Even among events ones which are seen as intrusive
are picked as causes in preference to ones which occur within
some going concern: it was the severing of the artery rather
than the pumping of the heart that caused the loss of blood.
This preference shades into one governed by moral and legal
assumptions: what is normal, right, and proper is not so readily
called a cause as is something abnormal or wrong. This third
tendency may conflict with and override the first. Since it is
normal for people to be striking matches and lighting cigarettes
in a residential flat, but a gas leak is abnormal and should
not occur, we may well say that the explosion which wrecked
this block of flats was caused by the presence of a quantity
of gas rather than that it was caused by Jones lighting his
cigarette.

These matters may be clarified to some extent if we realize
that causal statements are commonly made in some context,
against a background which includes the assumption of some

CONDITIONAL ANALYSES   35

causal field.[3] A causal statement will be the answer to a causal question, and the question 'What caused this explosion?' can be expanded into 'What made the difference between those times, or those cases, within a certain range, in which no such explosion occurred, and this case in which an explosion did occur?' Both cause and effect are seen as differences within a field; anything that is part of the assumed (but commonly un-stated) description of the field itself will, then, be automatically ruled out as a candidate for the role of cause. Consequently if we take the field as being *this block of flats as normally used and lived in*, we must take Jones's striking a match to light his cigarette as part of the field, and therefore not as the cause of, or even a cause of, or as causing, the explosion. What caused the explosion must be a difference in relation to the field, and the gas leak, or the presence of the gas that had leaked out, is the obvious candidate.

What is said to be caused, then, is not just an event, but an event-in-a-certain-field, and some 'conditions' can be set aside as not causing this-event-in-this-field simply because they are part of the chosen field, though if a different field were chosen, in other words if a different causal question were being asked, one of those conditions might well be said to cause this-event-in-that-other-field. Any part of the chosen field is decisively ruled out as a cause; a more elusive point is that among factors not so ruled out which are still severally necessary for the effect, we still show some degree of preference on the grounds indicated above. But I think that this can be taken as reflecting not the meaning of causal statements but rather their conversational point, the sorts of use to which they are likely to be put. We often want to know what caused some event with a view to saying how it could, and perhaps should, have been prevented: pointing to the spark rather than to the presence of inflammable material indicates what would have been the last chance of preventing the fire. But it might be conceded that the state-ment that the presence of this material caused the fire would be

[3] This notion of a causal field was introduced by John Anderson in 'The Problem of Causality', *Australasian Journal of Psychology and Philosophy*, xvi (1938), reprinted in his *Studies in Empirical Philosophy*, and used to resolve difficulties in Mill's account of causation. I also used it in 'Responsibility and Language', *Australasian Journal of Philosophy*, xxxiii (1955), 143–59, to deal with problems of moral and legal responsibility.

as true as the statement that the spark caused it, and merely in some ways less interesting. We can and do indeed distinguish between triggering causes and predisposing causes, which shows that standing conditions are not prevented from being causes by the mere meaning of the noun, or of the verb, 'cause'. Similarly we may agree that the collision was caused just as much by Smith's driving straight ahead as by Brown's deviating to his right without warning, but say that it is more important, for moral and legal purposes, to draw attention to the second of the two causal relationships.

The supposed distinction between conditions and causes can be adequately accounted for in these two ways: an alleged condition which is not called a cause, although if in the circumstances it had not occurred the result would not, either is part of the field presupposed in the view taken by the speaker of the result (and so is not a cause in relation to this field) or is a cause, but mention of this fact happens to be irrelevant, or less relevant than mention of some other cause of the same result, to some current purpose.

There is admittedly some logical redundancy in the two treatments offered here of conditions which we are reluctant to call causes. We should get a neater account if, say, we assigned all such conditions to the assumed causal field, and said that anyone who withheld the title of cause from what he admitted to be one of a set of severally necessary and jointly sufficient conditions for some result was implicitly taking that condition to be part of the field. Again, we should get a neater account if we discarded the notion of a field, and interpreted the withholding of the title of cause from any such necessary factor as reflecting some conversational or other purpose of the speaker. But at present my object is not so much to give a logically neat account as to analyse our ordinary thinking about causal sequences, and I believe that this does contain the two separate elements I have tried to describe. On the one hand there is the implicit question, 'What caused such-and-such?', where 'such-and-such' is already thought of as a change in a certain material or background state of affairs; on the other hand, even among differentiae within this background, we tend to downgrade some and at least initially deny that they caused the result, though we might reluctantly concede, if pressed, that they helped to cause it.

Another sort of apparent counter-example is easily disposed of in the same way. It can be truly said of anyone now dead that if he had not been born he would not have died, and although it would here be pointless to insert 'in the circumstances', such an insertion would not make the statement false. Yet we would not say that being born caused his death—that is, not ordinarily: with sufficient ingenuity one can construct a case for saying this. But the reason is merely that when we look for a cause of someone's death, the event, this person's death, is a change in a field which centrally includes this person's being alive for a while, and hence (in the ordinary course of nature) his having been born. As before, his being born is part of the field, and therefore cannot be the cause of his death.

The suggested meaning for 'X caused Y' which we have been considering is 'X occurred and Y occurred and in the circumstances, Y would not have occurred if X had not'. A slightly different formula would run '. . . and there were circumstances such that in them Y would not have occurred if X had not'. To see the difference, suppose that the effect is that a certain part of a certain house catches fire, that the presence of oxygen, the absence of any extinguishing device, etc., are taken as parts of the field, and that in relation to this field the following three conditions, which were all present on the occasion in question, were severally necessary and jointly sufficient for the effect: an electric current in a certain wire (A), decayed insulation at a point on that wire (B), and inflammable material near that point (C). Then there were circumstances, namely B and C, such that in them the fire would not have occurred if the current, A, had not; equally there were circumstances, namely A and C, such that in them the fire would not have occurred if the faulty insulation, B, had not, and again circumstances, namely A and B, such that in them the fire would not have occurred if the inflammable material, C, had not. So by our modified formula, A, B, and C would each equally count as causing the fire. But someone who says that, for example, the faulty insulation, B, caused the fire, may be thinking of A and C as 'the circumstances', may be presupposing them rather than saying *that there are* circumstances in relation to which B was necessary. Before he will agree that A caused the fire, he will have to make a switch of presuppositions, and take B and C, rather than A and C, as 'the circumstances'. So whereas with our modified formula there is no conflict at all between the three statements that A caused the fire, that B did so, and that C did so—since the three existential statements are entirely compatible—there is, with our first formula, using the phrase 'in the circumstances', a contrast of approach and presupposition between those who assert these three statements, although no outright disagreement. And this surely is the case. If three speakers put forward these three alternative causal statements, they would be conscious of such a contrast of approach. I think, therefore, that our first formula is the better for catching the force of a causal statement in use. The modified formula might be said to yield more clearly marked truth conditions for causal statements; but I shall argue that what it yields are not, strictly speaking, truth (or falsity) conditions. Still, it may be conceded that the modified formula represents a perhaps desirable tidying up of the meaning of causal statements, whereas the original formula comes closer to displaying the meaning they actually have.

There is, however, something surprising in our suggestion that 'X caused Y' means, even mainly, that X was *necessary* in the circumstances for Y. Would it not be at least as plausible to suggest that it means that X was *sufficient* in the circumstances for Y? Or perhaps that it was both necessary and sufficient in the circumstances? After all, it is tempting to paraphrase 'X caused Y' with 'X necessitated Y' or 'X ensured Y', and this would chime in with some of the thought behind the phrase 'necessary connection'. But if 'X necessitated Y' is taken literally, it says that Y was made necessary by X or became necessary in view of X, and this would mean that X was sufficient rather than necessary for Y. Of course, an X which in ordinary discourse is said to cause a Y is practically never *in itself* sufficient for that Y, or even believed to be so; as before, we must add the qualification 'in the circumstances'. And then the suggested description seems to fit what we recognize as causes. Taking our last example again, and letting the circumstances include the electric current and the inflammable material, we can say that the faulty insulation (which on these assumptions caused the fire) was sufficient in the circumstances for it. And similarly in sequence A in our earlier example the hammer-blow was sufficient in the circumstances for the chestnut's becoming flatter. But is sufficiency sufficient, or is necessity necessary as well? Can we explain the fact that in sequence B the hammer-blow did not cause the explosion on the ground that it was not sufficient for it in the circumstances? In fact the circumstances in themselves, without the hammer-blow, were sufficient: does it not follow that the hammer-blow was trivially and automatically sufficient in the circumstances, since anything at all, or nothing, would have been so, provided that the relevant circumstances were not tampered with? If we argued that what is only thus trivially sufficient in the circumstances cannot be properly so described, and that that is why it cannot be said to cause the result, are we not covertly reintroducing the requirement that a cause should be necessary in the circumstances rather than sufficient? What there is any point in mentioning as sufficient in the circumstances will be necessary in the circumstances as well.

This point seems to be confirmed if we try to expand the phrase 'sufficient in the circumstances' into a conditional statement. 'X will be sufficient in the circumstances for Y' may be taken as saying 'Given the circumstances, if X occurs then Y will', and even as a non-material conditional this will count as true provided that the circumstances do not change, X occurs, and Y occurs also.[4] And then 'X was sufficient in the circumstances for Y' will be equivalent to 'Given the circumstances, if X occurred, then Y did', and provided that the circumstances referred to are the actual ones this will automatically be true of any sequence in which X and Y actually occurred. Sufficiency in the circumstances is, then, of no use for our present purpose of finding the distinguishing feature of causal sequences; every cause is sufficient in the circumstances for its effect, but so are many non-causes for events which are not their effects.

But this is a weak sense of 'sufficient in the circumstances'. Can we find also a strong, counterfactual sense which will not apply to the antecedent in every actual sequence? This would be that, given the circumstances, if Y had not been going to occur, X would not have occurred. This is a possible sense, and what we recognize as causes are in general sufficient in the

---

[4] I have discussed non-material conditionals, both open and counterfactual, and their truth conditions, in Chapter 3 of *Truth, Probability, and Paradox*.

circumstances in this strong sense as well as in the weak one. In the appropriate possible world in which the circumstances are the same as in sequence A, but the chestnut does not become flatter, the hammer-blow has not occurred. (In constructing this possible world, we are, of course, taking over laws of working from the actual world.) And we cannot say the corresponding thing about the non-causal sequence B. The statement 'If in the circumstances of sequence B the explosion had not been going to occur, the hammer-blow would not have occurred' is not true or even acceptable. The supposition implicit in its antecedent cannot be coherently considered in the light of the actual world's laws of working, for, given these laws, in the circumstances of sequence B the explosion was going to occur. And if we take the antecedent as inviting us to consider some change in those laws of working, there is still no reason why we should not combine, with whatever coherent interpretation we place on this supposition, the view that the hammer-blow still occurred. It looks, then, as if the strong counterfactual sense of 'sufficient in the circumstances' will distinguish causal from non-causal sequences, though the weak sense does not.

But granted that causes are in general sufficient in the circumstances, in this strong sense, as well as necessary in the circumstances, for their effects, while neither relation holds in non-causal sequences, we can still ask whether in calling something a cause we require both of these features or only one, and if so which.

To clear up this problem, let us consider three different shilling-in-the-slot machines, *K*, *L*, and *M*. Each of them professes to supply bars of chocolate; also each of them has a glass front, so that its internal mechanism is visible. But in other respects the three are different. *K* is deterministic, and conforms to our ordinary expectations about slot-machines. It does not always produce a bar of chocolate when a shilling is put in the slot, but if it does not there is some in principle discoverable fault in or interference with the mechanism. Again, it can be induced to emit a bar of chocolate without a shilling's being inserted, for example by the use of some different object which sufficiently resembles a shilling, or perhaps by poking at the mechanism with pieces of wire. Inserting a shilling is neither absolutely necessary nor absolutely sufficient for the appearance of a bar of chocolate, but in normal circumstances it is both necessary and sufficient for this. ('Necessary' and 'sufficient' are here being used with reference to the machine's laws of working, they describe general relations rather than relations between single occurrences. But it will be a consequence of these general relations that if on a particular occasion, in normal circumstances, a shilling is inserted, a bar of chocolate will come out, and further that the inserting of a shilling on this particular occasion was both necessary in the circumstances and sufficient in the circumstances in the strong sense for this result.) L, on the other hand, is an indeterministic machine. It will not, indeed, in normal circumstances produce a bar of chocolate unless a shilling is inserted, but it may fail to produce a bar even when this is done. And such failure is a matter of pure chance. L's failures, unlike K's, are not open to individual explanation even in principle, though they may be open to statistical explanation. With L, in normal circumstances, putting a shilling in the slot is necessary, but not sufficient, for the appearance of a bar of chocolate. M is another indeterministic machine, but its vagaries are opposite to L's. M will, in ordinary circumstances, produce a bar of chocolate whenever a shilling is inserted; but occasionally, for no reason that is discoverable even in principle, the mechanism begins to operate even though nothing has been inserted, and a bar of chocolate comes out. With M, in normal circumstances, putting a shilling in the slot is sufficient, but not necessary, for the appearance of a bar of chocolate.

Now on some occasion I put a shilling into K and a bar of chocolate comes out. As I have said, putting in the shilling was, in the circumstances, both sufficient in the strong sense and necessary for this result, and we have no hesitation in saying that it caused this result.

Again, I put a shilling into L and receive a bar of chocolate. Putting in the shilling was, in the circumstances, necessary for this result. It was also sufficient in the circumstances in the weak sense, but not in the strong, counterfactual, sense. A possible world, with the same laws of working as the actual world, can contain the same circumstances, can lack the result, and yet still contain the inserting of the shilling. The statement, 'Given the circumstances, if the chocolate had not been going to appear, the shilling would not have been inserted' is not now acceptable. But would we say in this case that the inserting of the shilling caused the appearance of the bar of chocolate? I think we would. Our ordinary causal concept seems to require that where the shilling is put in, the mechanism operates, and a bar of chocolate appears, and would not have appeared if the shilling had not been inserted, the insertion of the shilling caused the appearance of the chocolate despite the fact that in the circumstances even given that the shilling was inserted, the chocolate might not have appeared.

Similarly, I put a shilling into M and receive a bar of chocolate. Putting in the shilling was this time sufficient in the circumstances, in the strong sense as well as in the weak sense, for this result. In an appropriate possible world in which the chocolate did not appear, the shilling would not have been put in. But putting in the shilling was not, it seems, necessary in the circumstances. Not only generally but also on this particular occasion the chocolate might have appeared even if no shilling, or anything else, had been put in. But there is room for dispute here. Perhaps, it might be argued, the insertion of the shilling may have been necessary in the circumstances on this particular occasion, though not generally; it may be that on this occasion the mechanism would not have operated if the shilling had not been put in. Moreover, it may be possible to settle this issue. We can, by hypothesis, see the works of the machine. If on this occasion only the later stages of the mechanism operated, not those earlier ones which are normally actuated directly by the shilling, we can decide that the chocolate would have come out anyway, that the insertion of the shilling was not necessary in the circumstances. But if the whole mechanism operated, the issue cannot be settled. Since M is, by hypothesis, indeterministic, there is in principle no discoverable answer to the question whether the chocolate would on this occasion have come out if the shilling had not been put in, or, therefore, to the question whether the insertion of the shilling was on this occasion necessary in the circumstances for the result. And yet, it seems to me, it is just this question that we need to have answered before we can say whether the insertion of the shilling caused the result. If the chocolate would not have come out if the shilling had not been put in, then the insertion of the shilling caused the result. But if it would have come out anyway, the insertion of the shilling did not cause this. (This last ruling prejudges a question about causal over-determination that has still to be considered; but we shall reach an answer to this question which agrees with the present ruling.) And, consequently, if it is in principle undecidable whether the chocolate would on this particular occasion have come out if the shilling had not been put in, it is equally undecidable whether the putting in of the shilling caused the appearance of the chocolate.

The contrast between the comments we have made about the two indeterministic slot-machines L and M seem to show that 'X caused Y' entails 'X was necessary in the circumstances for Y' and also, trivially, 'X was sufficient in the circumstances for Y' in the weak sense, but *not* the latter in the strong counterfactual sense. This is not required, though in general it holds for what we recognize as causes, at least in the physical sphere. Indeterministic machines are pretty rare.

This conclusion is confirmed by what we are prepared to say about human beings without prejudging the question whether they are wholly deterministic or not. 'Tom's saying what he did caused Bill to hit Tom' is acceptable even if we suppose that Bill had free will, that in the circumstances even after Tom's remark Bill might have controlled himself, provided that we believe that in the circumstances Bill would not have hit Tom if Tom had not said what he did. In this respect we treat Bill in the way I have proposed to treat slot-machine L.

There are, however, several possible objections to the thesis that 'X caused Y' entails 'X was necessary in the circumstances for Y'.

The first of these concerns what we may call quantitative over-determination. In sequence A, the hammer-blow caused the chestnut's becoming flatter. But the whole of the blow was not necessary for this result, though it was more than sufficient: a somewhat lighter blow would have sufficed. Even if part of the hammer-head had been absent, this result would still have come about. And so on. But this difficulty is easily overcome. It is possible to go on to a functional dependence view of causation, which would relate exact quantities on the cause side with exact quantities on the effect side. This development will be considered in Chapter 6. But for the present we are dealing only with a fairly primitive causal concept, which treats events, states, and occurrences, as ordinarily recognized and described, as causes and effects. From this point of view we regard the hammer-blow as a unit, and simply do not consider parts or subdivisions of it or quantitative alterations to it. The alternatives considered are that I strike the chestnut in the way described and that I do not. In constructing possible worlds, in considering what might or would have happened, we either plug in the hammer-blow as a whole or leave it out as a whole. Reducing it a little bit is simply not an option at present under consideration. From this point of view the hammer-blow was necessary in the circumstances: leave it out as a whole from your possible world, and the chestnut remains round.

A much more serious objection concerns what we may call, by contrast, alternative over-determination, or what have been called fail-safe causes. Let us list some examples, some of which are favourites with writers on moral and legal responsibility.

(i) A man is shot dead by a firing squad, at least two bullets entering his heart at once, either of which would have been immediately fatal.

(ii) Lightning strikes a barn in which straw is stored, and a tramp throws a burning cigarette butt into the straw at the same place and at the same time: the straw catches fire.

(iii) '. . . conditions (perhaps unusual excitement plus con-stitutional inadequacies) [are] present at 4.0 p.m. that guarantee a stroke at 4.55 p.m. and consequent death at 5.0 p.m.; but an entirely unrelated heart attack at 4.50 p.m. is still correctly called the cause of death, which, as it happens, does occur at 5.0 p.m.'

(iv) Smith and Jones commit a crime, but if they had not done so the head of the criminal organization would have sent other members to perform it in their stead, and so it would have been committed anyway.

(v) A man sets out on a trip across the desert. He has two enemies. One of them puts a deadly poison in his reserve can of drinking water. The other (not knowing this) makes a hole in the bottom of the can. The poisoned water all leaks out before the traveller needs to resort to this reserve can; the traveller dies of thirst.[5]

[5] I touched on this problem in 'Causes and Conditions', *American Philosophical Quarterly*, ii (1965), 245–64, esp. 250–2. Examples (ii) and (iv) are borrowed from

In each of these five cases, we cannot say of either of the candidates for the role of cause that it was necessary in the circumstances for the effect. If either of the two bullets had not been fired, the man would still have died. If the lightning had not struck, the straw would still have caught fire; and equally if the tramp had not thrown the butt away. If Smith and Jones had suddenly abandoned a life of crime, the same crime would still have been committed by the other members of the gang; but equally if those other members had not been ready to act, the crime would still have been committed, as it was, by Smith and Jones. If the heart attack had not occurred, the stroke would have carried the man off at 5.0 p.m.; but if the conditions for the stroke had been absent, the heart attack would still have killed him as and when it did. If the can had not been punctured, the traveller would have died of poison, perhaps even sooner than he actually died of thirst; but if it had not been poisoned, he would have died just as and when he did.

But though they have this common feature, these examples fall into two groups. In (iii) and (iv) we have no hesitation in making specific causal statements, that the heart attack caused the man's death, and that the actions of Smith and Jones brought about the criminal result. In (v) also it seems clear to me that the puncturing of the can caused the traveller's death, but as Hart and Honoré say that 'it is impossible to give a satisfactory answer to this question in terms of either B or C or both causing A's death', and that 'their mutual frustration of each other's plan precludes us from saying that either caused A's death', I need to explain and defend my view of this case.

Where we have no hesitation in making causal statements we can tell some more detailed causal story: we can say how the heart attack caused the man's death, how Smith and Jones committed the crime. But the rival story about the alternative or reserve cause cannot be completed. The conditions for the stroke did not actually lead to a stroke, and since there was no stroke, no stroke led to death. The reserve members of the

K. Marc-Wogau, 'On Historical Explanation', *Theoria*, xxviii (1962), 213–33, the latter coming originally from P. Gardiner, *The Nature of Historical Explanation*, p. 101. Example (iii) is quoted from M. Scriven, review of E. Nagel, *The Structure of Science*, in *Review of Metaphysics* (1964). Example (v) is based on a modification by Hart and Honoré (*Causation in the Law*, pp. 219–20) of a hypothetical case devised by J. A. McLaughlin, *Harvard Law Review*, xxxix (1925–6), 149, 155 n. 25.

gang remained in reserve. What we accept as causing each result, though not necessary in the circumstances for that result described in some broad way, was necessary in the circumstances for the result *as it came about*.

This matter can be thoroughly clarified if we introduce here a distinction which will be discussed more fully in Chapter 10, between *facts* and *events* both as causes and as results or effects. In (v) the puncturing of the can brought it about that the traveller died of thirst, that is, it caused his dying of thirst (though it prevented his dying of poison). But we cannot say that the puncturing of the can brought it about that he died, or caused his dying—since he would have died anyway, if it had not been punctured. *That he died*, and *that he died of thirst*, are distinguishable facts, and hence distinguishable results. So, as long as we are dealing with fact-results, it is not surprising that the puncturing of the can should have brought about the second of these but not the first. But if we think of an effect as a concrete event, then the event which was the traveller's death was also his death from thirst, and we must say that the puncturing of the can caused it, while the poisoning did not. For a concrete event effect, we require a cause, or causal chain, that leads to it, and it is the chain puncturing-lack-of-water-thirst-death that was realized, whereas the rival chain that starts with poison-in-can was not completed. In this way I would defend my judgement that the traveller's death—that is, the concrete event—was caused by the puncturing of the can, but at the same time explain the doubts felt by lawyers (and others) about this case as due to the equally correct judgement that his dying —that is, the fact that he died on this journey—was not caused by the puncturing of the can.

These distinctions vindicate our general thesis that 'X caused Y' entails 'X was necessary in the circumstances for Y': apparently conflicting answers arise from some uncertainty or equivocation about what is to count as Y, whether it is a concrete event or a fact, and if so, which fact. If Y is the fact that the traveller died of thirst, then the puncturing of the can both caused and was necessary in the circumstances for Y. If Y is the fact that the traveller died on this journey, then the puncturing of the can neither caused Y nor was necessary in the circumstances for Y. If Y is the traveller's death qua concrete event, which was, among other things, a death from thirst, the puncturing of the can both caused and was necessary in the circumstances for Y.

In the dubious cases of alternative over-determination, such as (i) and (ii), it is natural to reject such statements as 'This bullet caused his death' and 'The lightning caused the fire'. In these cases even a detailed causal story fails to discriminate between the rival candidates for the role of cause, we cannot say that one rather than the other was necessary in the circumstances even for the effect *as it came about*. Even if we take the effect as a concrete event all that was clearly necessary for it in the circumstances was in (i) the volley and in (ii) the lightning/cigarette-butt cluster of events, and it is such clusters that we can confidently take as causing these effects. 'But which item in the cluster really caused (or "brought about") this effect (or "result")?' is a sensible question in so far as it asks for a discrimination between the alternative 'causes' by way of the filling in of a more detailed account. But if no more detailed correct account would provide the desired discrimination, this question has no answer.

For instance, if, as in an example mentioned earlier, a match is struck and touched with a red-hot poker at the same time, and a flame appears, we can say that the striking and the touching together caused the flame to appear, since if neither of them had occurred in the circumstances no flame would have appeared, but if the match was affected in both these ways simultaneously, we cannot say that either by itself caused this. Our ruling in these cases agrees with what we said about slot-machine M, where a shilling was put in and a bar of chocolate came out, but the bar might have come out even if no shilling had been put in: if on this particular occasion a bar of chocolate *would* (not merely *might*) have come out anyway, then the insertion of the shilling did not cause its appearance. This is a strange case of causal over-determination, because one of the rival factors is a null one: the bar would, on the present hypothesis, have come out spontaneously. But even a null alternative in a case of alternative over-determination is enough to prevent the other alternative from causing the result.

So far, then, we can defend the conclusion reached earlier: the statement that X caused Y entails that X was necessary in the circumstances for Y, but it does not entail that X was in the strong sense sufficient in the circumstances for Y. But the latter often holds as well.

Something very like this is the main negative thesis of Professor Anscombe's Inaugural Lecture: contrary to a long dominant philosophical tradition, causes need not be 'sufficient' for their effects, need not 'necessitate' them. Raymond Martin also has defended a 'necessity thesis' while criticizing a 'sufficiency thesis' which he finds in an earlier work of mine.[6]

But is there anything still to be said for the sufficiency thesis? A corollary of its rejection is that causal consequence is *not* formally analogous to logical consequence, legal consequence, and so on. If Q is a logical consequence of P, then P is logically sufficient for Q. If, given R, Q is a logical consequence of P, then, given R, P is logically sufficient for Q. Similarly if Q is a legal consequence of P, then P is, in the circumstances, legally sufficient for Q. And this holds in general for other sorts of consequences. But by our present account, Q may be a causal consequence of P without P being causally sufficient for Q even in the circumstances. This is strange, and yet it seems correct. There being a radon atom here now is a causal consequence of there having been a radium atom here a little earlier, but if radioactive decay is a non-deterministic process there are no circumstances such that in them the earlier presence of the radium atom was sufficient (in the strong, counterfactual sense) for the radon atom's being here now: the former might not have decayed, and even if it had the latter might also have decayed already. Similarly if Jim, who is colour-blind, and his wife Alice, who carries no gene for colour-blindness, have a daughter, Jane, who has a son, Tom, and Tom is colour-blind, then Tom's being colour-blind is a causal consequence of Jim's being colour-blind; but the latter gave only a fifty-fifty chance that any son of Jane would be colour-blind.

On the other hand, if P caused Q, we can surely say that Q occurred because P did; the latter is practically equivalent to 'Since P occurred, Q occurred'; a since-statement can be fairly

⁶ G. E. M. Anscombe, *Causality and Determination*; Raymond Martin, 'The Sufficiency Thesis', *Philosophical Studies*, xxiii (1972), 205–11; Martin, who criticizes my 'Causes and Conditions', *American Philosophical Quarterly*, ii (1965), 245–64, sent me an earlier version of his paper in 1969.

aptly described, in Goodman's terms, as a factual conditional, that is, as adding to the open non-material conditional 'If P occurred, Q occurred' the presupposition that P did occur (and hence that Q did so too). Putting these steps together, we seem compelled to take 'P caused Q' as entailing the non-material conditional 'If P occurred, Q occurred', which would commit its user to the counterfactual 'If Q had not been going to occur, P would not have occurred', that is to the strong counterfactual sufficiency of P for Q.

Another argument on the same side is that a future causal statement 'P will cause Q' or 'P would cause Q' seems to claim that P is sufficient in the circumstances for Q, that if P occurs, Q will occur also, and that if Q is not going to occur, neither is P. Even if we were right in saying that a past tense singular causal statement entails only that the cause was necessary, not also sufficient, in the circumstances for the effect, this may be characteristic of past tense uses rather than of causal statements in general.

It seems, then, that the analysis of a tenseless singular causal statement 'P causes Q' should include both the non-material conditionals 'If P occurs, Q occurs' and 'If P does not occur, Q does not occur', and therefore also their contrapositives, each of which will change into a counterfactual if the speaker takes its antecedent not to be fulfilled. But different parts of this concept will be stressed in different settings. When P and Q are both known to have occurred, it is natural to lay stress on the counterfactual form of the second conditional; but if their occurrence is problematic, it is natural to emphasize the open form of the first conditional, though the second is also in force. The general notion of a cause is of something which is both necessary and sufficient in the circumstances for its effect, but where the cause and the effect have both actually occurred we do not require that the cause should be sufficient in the strong counterfactual sense.

Some writers who have recognized that causes need not be sufficient for their effects have drawn the further conclusion that our ordinary concept is primarily probabilistic. Thus Patrick Suppes[7] argues that 'the everyday concept of causality is not sharply deterministic' from the evidence that we may say 'His

[7] *A Probabilistic Theory of Causality*, p. 7.

reckless driving is bound to lead to an accident', where ' "lead to" conveys the causal relation between the reckless driving and the predicted accident' and yet ' "is bound to" means [only] that the probability is high'. But this is a confusion. Saying that *A* is likely to cause *B* does not put likelihood into the causing itself: it could (though it does not) mean that *A* is likely to necessitate *B*, and I think it does mean that *A* is likely to be, in some particular case, necessary in the circumstances for *B*. What will fulfil this probabilistic prediction is an actual crash for which the man's reckless driving was necessary in the circumstances. Similarly Suppes is right in claiming that a mother who says that her child is afraid of thunder does not mean that a state of fright ensues whenever the child hears thunder, but rather that there is a fairly high probability of this; but when the child is actually frightened by thunder, the thunder is necessary in the circumstances for its state of fright.

Thus it may often happen that the only fully explicit causal generalization that a speaker is prepared to make is a probabilistic one, and yet he may still be taking it that the causal relation in any particular case that fulfils it is one of necessity, and perhaps also sufficiency, in the circumstances. To go straight from this evidence to a probabilistic theory is a mistake, and one that results from holding on to the Humean doctrine that causation is essentially general while admitting that causal claims need not involve *universal* generalizations. Against this I shall argue (in Chapter 3) for the primacy of singular as opposed to general causal statements.

These points seriously undermine Suppes's project of analysing causation as a whole in terms of probabilities. We can admit, none the less, that there may be probabilistic or statistical laws, and singular sequences of events which in some sense fulfil them, and that both of these can be called causal in a broad sense. These will be discussed in Chapter 9, with particular reference to problems about the form and content of statistical laws and the interpretation of the 'probabilities' associated with them—problems which Suppes does not bring out or resolve. For the present, however, we can affirm that a cause is ordinarily taken to be necessary in the circumstances for its effect, and perhaps sufficient in the circumstances as well.

We cannot, however, conclude that necessity-in-the-circumstances is *the* distinguishing feature of a cause. As we saw, one collateral effect may be necessary in the circumstances for another, but it is not said to cause the other. Also, if X caused Y, we have seen that X may be in the strong sense sufficient in the circumstances for Y. If it is, then Y will be necessary in the circumstances for X; but we shall not say that Y caused X.

Such counter-examples show that another relation, which we may call *causal priority*, is thought of as being required, along with necessity-in-the-circumstances, for causing. Of a pair of collateral effects, neither is causally prior to the other, and in our other example, since X caused Y, X was causally prior to Y, and Y was therefore not causally prior to X. But it seems that if any X is both necessary in the circumstances for and causally prior to Y, we shall say that X caused Y; also, wherever we are prepared to say that X caused Y we are prepared to say that X was necessary in the circumstances for and causally prior to Y. The distinguishing feature of causal sequence is the conjunction of necessity-in-the-circumstances with causal priority.

But this conclusion is rather hollow until we have said more about causal priority. A full discussion of this notion, and of the whole problem of the direction of causation, will be undertaken in Chapter 7; but a preliminary account will be in place here.

The core of the notion of causal priority is that the world has some way of running on from one change to another. But we can speak with any accuracy only when we associate causal priority with some kind of sufficiency or necessity. Thus X is sufficient in the circumstances in the weak sense for and causally prior to Y provided that if X is put into the world in the circumstances referred to and the world runs on from there, Y will occur. Similarly X is necessary in the circumstances for and causally prior to Y provided that if X were kept out of the world in the circumstances referred to and the world ran on from there, Y would not occur. And X is sufficient in the circumstances in the strong sense for and causally prior to Y provided that if X were put into the world in the circumstances referred to and the world ran on from there, Y would occur. Sufficiency-in-the-weak-sense plus causal priority is shown by an experiment on the actual world; but necessity and sufficiency-in-the-strong-sense plus causal priority involve counterfactual claims, and

therefore involve assertions about how the world would have
run on if something different had been done: they involve
thought about the independent running of a merely possible
world.

We have already illustrated this in suggesting a way out of
the difficulty about collateral effects. We thought of constructing a possible world which was just like the actual world up to
the point where, in the actual world, the proposed antecedent
occurs, of excluding this antecedent from the possible world and
then letting that world run on: if and only if the result did not
occur in that possible world were we prepared to say that the
antecedent was *in the special sense* necessary in the circumstances
for the result. That 'special sense' of 'necessary in the circumstances' is what we now recognize as the conjunction 'necessary
in the circumstances for and causally prior to'.

But this account needs some adjustment to make it generally
applicable. Our proposal to make the possible world just like
the actual one up to the point of time at which the proposed
antecedent X occurs in the actual world would have the un-
desired result of making temporal priority necessary, though
not sufficient, for causal priority. For if Y had occurred before
X in the actual world, it would already have been included,
by the above proposal, in the possible world: we should have
left no chance that the exclusion of X from the possible world
might, as that world ran on, exclude Y also. But temporal
priority is not conceptually necessary for causal priority. We
can coherently consider the possibility of backwards or time-
reversed causation. To leave room for this, we must modify the
suggested account. We must think of somehow excluding an X
from a possible world at a time t_3 (where X occurred in the
actual world at t_3) without prejudice to the question whether
a Y occurred in that possible world (as it did in the actual one)
at an earlier time t_2. But to combine this with the notion of
letting the possible world run on, we must think of excluding X
indirectly, by excluding some other possible event W which
actually occurred at a still earlier time t_1 and which is believed
to be necessary in the circumstances for X. Our possible world
is to have the same *circumstances* as the actual world, but to
diverge from it by the exclusion of W at t_1; from there on it is
allowed to run on by whatever laws of working the actual

world obeys. This leaves open the possibility that there should be among these laws a backward causal one such that this indirect exclusion of X would carry with it the non-occurrence of Y. If Y does occur in our possible world at t_2, then X is not necessary in the circumstances for and causally prior to it; but if Y does not occur in our possible world at t_2, X may be so, though there are other possibilities which it is not easy to exclude. (These details are discussed in Chapter 7.)

The notion of necessity-in-the-circumstances-plus-causal-priority, then, involves the thought of what would happen when a possible world, constructed by some appropriate alteration from the actual world, was allowed to run on. It presupposes that the actual world has some laws of working—not necessarily strictly deterministic ones—which can be carried over to the possible world. But it does not require that in order to use this notion we should know what those laws of working are.

I have explicitly added the notion of causal priority to that of being necessary in the circumstances. But I must admit that the terms 'necessary' and 'sufficient' are often so used as to include a suggestion of causal priority: even where a cause is sufficient in the circumstances in the strong sense for its effect we find it strange to say that the effect is necessary in the circumstances for the cause, just because the effect is not causally prior to the cause. However, there are senses of 'necessary' and 'sufficient' which do not include causal priority and which are exhausted by the appropriate conditional analyses, and I think it makes things clearer if we use 'necessary' and 'sufficient' in these simpler senses, and introduce causal priority as a further element.

In so far as we have used conditionals, especially counterfactual ones, in our analysis of the concept of causation, that analysis is incomplete until these conditionals have themselves been explained. A view of conditionals has probably been implicit in what I have already said; to make it explicit I want simply to take over conclusions that I have reached elsewhere.[8] A non-material conditional statement introduces a supposition (the antecedent) and asserts something (the consequent) within the scope of that supposition. The conditional 'If P, Q' can be paraphrased by 'Suppose that P; on that supposition, Q'; or

[8] In Chapter 3 of *Truth, Probability, and Paradox.*

again by 'In the possible situation that P, Q also'. This account holds for all non-material conditionals; a counterfactual adds to this the suggestion that the antecedent does not hold in the actual world. If so, there is liable to be a certain arbitrariness in the choice of '*the* possible situation that P', or in other words of the particular possible world of which the consequent is being asserted. It is a consequence of this analysis that only some conditionals are capable of being true or false. A conditional whose antecedent is fulfilled will be true if its consequent is true and false if its consequent is false. But if the antecedent of a counterfactual is, as its user believes, unfulfilled, it cannot be true or false in this way. A counterfactual whose antecedent entails its consequent can be allowed to count as true. But most counterfactuals cannot achieve truth in this way either, and will be neither true nor false, though they may be acceptable or unacceptable, well or poorly supported, and so on.

We are led, then, towards two conclusions which are similar to Hume's. Statements of singular causal sequence involve in their analysis counterfactual conditionals which on the present showing are not capable of being true; so the singular causal statements cannot be true either.[9] (They can still be false in rather obvious ways: 'X caused Y' will be false, for example, if either X or Y did not occur.) Also, whether they can be true or not, these counterfactual conditionals describe possible situations or possible worlds, they are concerned with suppositions and their consequences or accompaniments, they do not describe what actually occurred, let alone what was observed to occur, in the actual individual sequence. They state what would have happened, not what did happen. Necessity$_1$, then, the distinguishing feature of causal sequences, is not something that can be observed in any of those sequences. The case for saying this is even stronger than Hume's case for saying the same about necessity$_2$. Consequently a question analogous to one of Hume's arises here: how do we acquire the idea of necessity$_1$, since we do not derive it from anything we observe in the individual causal sequences to which we apply it? It looks as if a psychological account is called for; as I said at the

---

[9] A similar conclusion is reached by A. J. Ayer, *Probability and Evidence*, pp. 132–9. But for me this is only a tentative conclusion, which will be qualified at the end of Chapter 8.

end of Chapter 1, Hume's resort to psychology was not wrong in principle but merely premature.

The item for which we must seek a psychological explanation is not, as Hume thought, the idea of a support for *a priori* inferences from one distinct existence to another, but the sort of thinking that is expressed by the counterfactual conditional, 'If in these circumstances X had not occurred, Y would not have occurred either', coupled with the notion of X's causal priority to Y, the thought that the actual world ran on from X to Y, and that the appropriate possible world would run on from the exclusion of X to the non-occurrence of Y. Let us take the counterfactual first, leaving aside the priority. It can be paraphrased as 'Suppose that in these circumstances X did not occur; then Y did not occur either' or 'Given these circumstances, in the possible situation that X did not occur, Y did not occur'. For the general capacity and tendency to make suppositions, to consider possibilities that appear not to be realized, I can offer no explanation beyond the obvious evolutionary one; this capacity and tendency are of some value to their possessors and could have been fostered by the ordinary processes of natural selection. But it is worth stressing here that although we express this kind of thinking in words, its development need not have waited for the development of language. It is not essentially tied to verbal expression, and there is some reason to suppose that other, non-verbal, animals share this capacity with us. Possibilities can be literally envisaged rather than described.[10] But, given that we have this general tendency, can we explain the particular ways in which we employ it? That is, can we explain how, having supposed X not to have occurred in these circumstances, we decide what else to assert within the scope of this supposition, or how to fill out our picture of this merely possible situation? We can distinguish a sophisticated and a primitive way of doing this. The sophisticated way uses general propositions which we take to be confirmed by observations of the actual world, but which we feel justified in extending beyond the instances in which they are confirmed not only to other actual instances but to merely possible ones which are related to the confirming instances in

---

[10] Cf. *Truth, Probability, and Paradox*, p. 100.

the same way that other actual instances would be.[11] These are combined with the supposition, and consequences drawn by deductive reasoning from the combination are asserted within the scope of the supposition. This sophisticated way of developing a supposition anticipates a well-known procedure of 'natural deduction'. The primitive way of doing the same job relies not on this combination of inductive and deductive reasoning, but on imagination and analogy. I have observed another situation very like the present one, in which (unlike the present one) no event of the X type occurred. I borrow features from that other situation to fill out my imaginative picture of the possible situation that in the present circumstances X did not occur. In particular, if no event of the Y type occured in that other situation, I see the possible situation that X did not occur in the present circumstances as continuing without the occurrence of Y. The sort of observation that can be immediately used in this imaginative analogizing is that prescribed for Mill's Method of Difference: two otherwise very similar instances, in one of which both the 'cause' and the 'effect' occur, and in the other of which neither of these occurs. Such a pair of instances may be found in a number of different ways, but the most obvious, and presumably the most fruitful original source of the causal concept, is provided by the 'before and after' observation. In an otherwise apparently static situation, one striking change (X) occurs, followed shortly afterwards by another (Y). The situation before X occurred, when equally Y did not occur, provides the control case or negative instance, while the later situation, in which both X and Y occurred, provides the experimental case or positive instance. And in a quite primitive and unsophisticated way we can transfer the nonoccurrence of Y from the before situation to a *supposed* later situation in which, similarly, X did not occur, and form the thought which is expressed by the statement 'If X had not occurred, Y would not have occurred', or, in other words, 'X was necessary in the circumstances for Y'.

But this is only one part of our ordinary idea of necessary connection. We have also to account for the other element, the causal priority. It seems undeniable that this notion arises from our experience of our own active interventions in the world. If

[11] Cf. *Truth, Probability, and Paradox*, pp. 117–18, and Chapter 8 below.

I *introduce* the change X into an apparently static situation and then the other change Y occurs, I not only see X as in the weak sense sufficient in the circumstances for Y, but also see X as causally prior to Y. I see the actual world as running on from my introduction of X to the occurrence of Y. If, further, I think (for the reasons just outlined) of X as necessary in the circumstances for Y, I see the *possible* world in which I do *not* introduce X as running on without Y's occurring. I seem then to have introduced into the actual world not only X, but the whole X-Y sequence; but I seem to have done so by operating on the X end of it. The notion of the actual world's running on *from*—not *to*—X, and of a possible world's similarly running on from not-X, is derived from this complex experience of intervening and then waiting for results. Rightly or wrongly, I see myself as a free agent in introducing X, and therefore rule out the possibility that anything else in the objective situation is causally prior to X, that the world ran on to X; I therefore rule out also both the possibility that X and Y should be collateral effects of some common cause and the possibility that Y should have caused X, even if I see Y, as I well may, as being necessary in the circumstances for X.

We can, then, find natural and presumably instinctive ways of thinking which would be expressed by the counterfactual conditionals and assertions of causal priority which we have given as the analysis of necessity$_1$, of the distinguishing feature of causal sequence. But just as our analysis of necessity$_1$ differs from Hume's equation of it with necessity$_2$, so our account of the psychological mechanism involved is different. The key item is a picture of what *would* have happened if things had been otherwise, and this is borrowed from some experience where things *were* otherwise. It is a contrast case rather than the repetition of like instances that contributes most to our primitive concept of causation.

My main concern in this chapter has been to analyse our actual concept of causing, to formulate what we commonly take to be the distinguishing mark of causal sequences, and then, since this has turned out not to be an observed feature of those sequences, to sketch an explanation of our thinking in this way. In this analysis the major item is that a cause is thought to be both necessary and sufficient in the circumstances for its effect, but that the sufficiency is less firmly required than the necessity, particularly where the sequence is known to have occurred. But whatever our actual concept may be, it is obvious that we can construct causal concepts as we wish, which may be useful for particular purposes. We can speak, if we like, of *necessary causes*, and make it explicit that sufficiency is not required. Or we can speak of *sufficient causes*, and make it explicit that necessity is not required. Or we can make it plain that we are requiring both necessity and sufficiency in the circumstances. But the general pattern on which such concepts are constructed is that we combine the appropriate non-material conditional(s) with the notion of causal priority. But all such causal concepts are somewhat superficial: there may well be further backing for these conditional descriptions, further relations in the objects that encourage us to speak and think in these ways.

3

Causal Regularities[1]

ONE of Hume's legacies is the regularity theory of causation. In his definitions, which aim at reform rather than analysis of our ordinary concepts, he equates causation as it really exists in the objects with regular succession. Such regularity is, as we saw in Chapter 1, well fitted to play the role of necessity$_3$, that is, of something that would license causal inference but not *a priori*, not from a knowledge of the individual cause or effect on its own.

It was argued in Chapter 2 that an initial analysis, at least, of our ordinary causal concepts could be given in terms of certain conditional statements, especially certain counterfactuals; in asserting singular causal sequences we are talking, in part, not only about what has occurred but about what would or would not have occurred had things been different,

[1] The ideas underlying this chapter were originally presented in 'Causes and Conditions', *American Philosophical Quarterly*, ii (1965), 245–64. I have tried to take account of a number of discussions of this article, both published and unpublished, notably the criticisms made by Jaegwon Kim in 'Causes and Events: Mackie on Causation', *Journal of Philosophy*, lxviii (1971), 426–41. In particular, I have tried to clarify my account by maintaining, as I did not in the original article, a firm distinction between types of events ('generic events', 'properties') and the individual events that instantiate them, more or less as recommended in Part IV of Kim's article.

The account of eliminative induction used in this chapter was first presented in my article 'Mill's Methods of Induction', in *Encyclopedia of Philosophy*, ed. Paul Edwards, vol. 5, pp. 324–32. A fuller statement of it is given in the Appendix.

The ultimate credit for much of what is said here must go to J. S. Mill, but in recent years a number of philosophers have, independently of one another and using different approaches, produced improved accounts which are essentially alike even in respects in which they could not be derived from Mill. I have noticed particularly those of Konrad Marc-Wogau, 'On Historical Explanation', *Theoria*, xxviii (1962), 213–33, and of Michael Scriven, in a review of Nagel's *The Structure of Science*, *Review of Metaphysics*, xvii (1964), 403–24, and in 'The Logic of Cause', *Theory and Decision*, ii (1971), 49–66, but there are, I believe, more than a few others. Such a convergence of independent approaches suggests that we may be getting near to the truth.

that is, about some merely possible situations and events. We have, I suggested, two ways of doing this, a primitive one and a sophisticated one. The primitive one relies on imagination and analogy, but the sophisticated one uses general propositions, which sustain the counterfactual conditionals. If we have inductive reasons—reasons that carry us beyond the supporting observations—for believing that all situations of a certain kind develop in a certain way, we find plausible the counterfactual conditional statement that if this situation had been of that kind it too would have developed in that way. Regularity statements, if inductively supported, will sustain the conditionals which an initial analysis of causal statements brings to light. The meaning of causal statements is given by the conditionals, but their grounds may well include the corresponding regularities.

It is therefore appropriate to inquire how far a regularity theory will go as an account of causation as it exists in the objects. Regularity has at least the merit that it involves no mysteries, no occult properties like necessity$_2$. It is true that an unqualified regularity, holding for unobserved as well as observed instances, obviously cannot be observed: but we can say quite explicitly what it would be. And there is no need to introduce the mystery of a special *sort* of regularity, a 'nomic universal', to account for the ability of causal laws to sustain counterfactual conditionals.[2] Yet there is some obscurity in the notion of regular succession. Hume's account, as we noted, is careless and imprecise: if the regularity theory is to be given a fair trial we must begin by describing more accurately and in more detail the forms of regularity which might count as the whole or as part of causation in the objects.

Mill's account is a great improvement upon Hume's: he explicitly recognizes a number of important complications. 'It is seldom, if ever, between a consequent and a single antecedent that this invariable sequence subsists. It is usually between a consequent and the sum of several antecedents; the concurrence of all of them being requisite to produce, that is, to be certain of being followed by, the consequent.'[3] We may put this more

---

[2] I have argued this point in *Truth, Probability, and Paradox*, Chapter 3, pp. 114–19, but it is considered further in Chapter 8 below.

[3] *System of Logic*, Book III, Ch. 5, Sect. 3.

formally. There are certain *factors*—that is, types of event or situation—which we can symbolize as *A, B, C, etc.*, and the effect (Mill's 'phenomenon') *P* occurs whenever some conjunction of factors occurs—say the conjunction of *A* and *B* and *C*, which we shall symbolize as *ABC*—but not when only some of these conjuncts are present. All *ABC* are followed by *P*, but it is not the case that all *AB* are followed by *P*, and so on. (The references to 'sequence', to 'following', of course mean that the 'consequent' occurs, in each individual instance of the causal sequence, fairly soon after all the 'antecedents' are assembled, and in the appropriate spatial region. There is some looseness in these notions, which may reflect a real inadequacy in the regularity theory, but let us postpone this objection and assume that we understand well enough what counts as sequence.) Mill also points out that there can be what he calls a plurality of causes.

It is not true that one effect must be connected with only one cause, or assemblage of conditions; that each phenomenon can be produced only in one way. There are often several independent modes in which the same phenomenon could have originated. One fact may be the consequent in several invariable sequences; it may follow, with equal uniformity, any one of several antecedents, or collections of antecedents. Many causes may produce mechanical motion: many causes may produce some kinds of sensation: many causes may produce death. A given effect may really be produced by a certain cause, and yet be perfectly capable of being produced without it.[4]

In our symbolism, this means that we may have, say, not only 'All *ABC* are followed by *P*' but also 'All *DGH* are followed by *P*'. Now the conjunction of these two propositions is equivalent to 'All (*ABC* or *DGH*) are followed by *P*'. A plurality of causes is tantamount to a disjunctive antecedent, as an assemblage of conditions is to a conjunctive one: allowing for both, we have a disjunction of conjunctions. Now suppose that there is a finite set of assemblages of conditions that produce *P*, say *ABC*, *DGH*, and *JKL*. It may well be that *P* occurs only when at least one of these conjunctions has occurred soon before in the right region. If so, all *P* are preceded by (*ABC* or *DGH* or *JKL*). (There is, of course, no logical necessity that this should be so. Events might occur in a disorderly way: *P* might sometimes occur without there having occurred, just before in the right region, any assemblage of conditions which is always followed by *P*. But at present I am considering cases where this is not so. That is, we may have a pair of (roughly) converse universal propositions, 'All (*ABC* or *DGH* or *JKL*) are followed by *P*' and 'All *P* are preceded by (*ABC* or *DGH* or *JKL*)'.

In discussing such forms of regularity, it will be convenient to use the terms 'necessary condition' and 'sufficient condition' in senses different from, though related to, the senses in which these phrases were used in Chapter 2. There, a necessary condition, for example, was related to a counterfactual conditional; '*X* was a necessary condition for *Y*' meant 'If *X* had not occurred, *Y* would not', where '*X*' and '*Y*' stood for particular events. But we are now using letters to stand for types of event or situation, and '*X* is a necessary condition for *Y*' will mean that whenever an event of type *Y* occurs, an event of type *X* also occurs, and '*X* is a sufficient condition for *Y*' will mean that whenever an event of type *X* occurs, so does an event of type *Y*.

Then in the case described above the complex formula '(*ABC* or *DGH* or *JKL*)' represents a condition which is both necessary and sufficient for *P*: each conjunction, such as '*ABC*', represents a condition which is sufficient but not necessary for *P*. Besides, *ABC* is a *minimal* sufficient condition: none of its conjuncts is redundant: no part of it, such as *AB*, is itself sufficient for *P*. But each single factor, such as *A*, is neither a necessary nor a sufficient condition for *P*. Yet it is clearly related to *P* in an important way: it is an *insufficient* but *non-redundant* part of an *unnecessary* but *sufficient* condition: it will be convenient to call this (using the first letters of the italicized words) an *inus* condition.[5]

Mill includes in his assemblages of conditions *states*, that is, standing conditions, as well as what are strictly speaking *events*. He also stresses the importance of factors which we should naturally regard as negative, for example the absence of a sentry from his post. It may be the consumption of a certain poison conjoined with the non-consumption of the appropriate

---

[5] This term, 'inus condition', was introduced in 'Causes and Conditions', having been suggested by D. C. Stove; the term 'minimal sufficient condition' was used by K. Marc-Wogau in 'On Historical Explanation', *Theoria*, xxviii (1962).

antidote which is invariably followed by death. If a certain
type of event is symbolized as C, then not-C, or $\bar{C}$, will be the
absence of any event of that type. It may be that although AB
alone is not sufficient for P—because ABC is regularly followed
by not P—$AB\bar{C}$ is sufficient for P. Mill is reluctant to call such
a negative condition as $\bar{C}$ a cause, but speaks instead of the
absence of counteracting causes; if $\bar{C}$ is needed as a conjunct
in the minimal sufficient condition $AB\bar{C}$, then C itself is a
counteracting cause.[6]

A further complication, for which Mill does not provide, is
the recognition of a causal field in the sense explained in
Chapter 2. The 'antecedents' and 'consequents' will not, in
general, be events that float about on their own, they will be
things that happen to or in some subject or setting. In discussing the causes of death, for example, we may well be concerned
with the dying of human beings who have been living in an
ordinary environment. If so, human beings and this environment together constitute the field. We shall not then regard
the facts that these are human beings, or that they are in this
ordinary environment, as causal factors: these will not figure as
conjuncts in such a condition as $AB\bar{C}$. The causal field in this
sense is not itself even part of a cause, but is rather a background against which the causing goes on. If we sum up such
a field as F, and allow for the various points made by Mill,
we arrive at the following typical form for a causal regularity:

In F, all ($AB\bar{C}$ or $DG\bar{H}$ or $JK\bar{L}$) are followed by P, and, in F,
all P are preceded by $AB\bar{C}$ or $DG\bar{H}$ or $JK\bar{L}$).

For some purposes this may be simplified to

All F ($AB\bar{C}$ or $DG\bar{H}$ or $JK\bar{L}$) are P and all FP are ($AB\bar{C}$ or
$DG\bar{H}$ or $JK\bar{L}$).

That is, some disjunction of conjunctions of factors, some of
which may be negative, is both necessary and sufficient for the
effect in the field in question. But what then is the cause? Mill
says that 'The cause . . . philosophically speaking, is the sum
total of the conditions positive and negative',[7] in other words
such a conjunction as $AB\bar{C}$; but if we go as far as this there is
no good reason why we should not go further and equate 'the

cause, philosophically speaking' rather with the complete disjunction of conjunctions, such as ($AB\bar{C}$ or $DG\bar{H}$ or $\mathcal{J}\bar{K}\bar{L}$). It is this that is both necessary and sufficient for the effect (in the field) as causes have often been assumed to be. And when speaking from a regularity point of view, it will be convenient to call this the *full cause*. But what is ordinarily called a cause, or what is referred to by the subject of a causal verb, is practically never anything like this; rather, in general causal statements, like 'The consumption of more than such-and-such a dose of aspirin causes death', the cause is a factor such as is represented, say, by 'A' in our formula, and in singular causal statements like 'Taking this dose of aspirin caused his death' the cause is an instance of some such type of event as is represented by 'A'. That is, what is typically called a cause is an inus condition or an individual instance of an inus condition, and it may be a state rather than an event.

A regularity theory that is to have any chance of being defended as even a partial description of causation in the objects must deal in regularities of this complex sort. And such a theory has considerable merits. It seems quite clear that there are many regularities of succession of this sort, and that progress in causal knowledge consists partly in arriving gradually at fuller formulations of such laws. Also, even these complex regularities could play the role of necessity$_3$, they could license the sorts of causal inference that Hume thought so important. If ($AB\bar{C}$ or $DG\bar{H}$ or $\mathcal{J}\bar{K}\bar{L}$) is both necessary and sufficient for P in F, and this is known or believed, then if an instance of $AB\bar{C}$ in F is observed, an inference to the conclusion that an instance of P will follow is in order, while if an instance of P in F is observed, and there is reason to believe that neither $DG\bar{H}$ nor $\mathcal{J}\bar{K}\bar{L}$ (as a whole) has occurred at the right time and place, an inference to the conclusion that $AB\bar{C}$ has occurred and therefore that an instance of A has occurred is in order. Complex regularities still license inference from cause to effect and from effect to cause.

Moreover, they will sustain the various kinds of conditionals that come to light in the analysis of causal concepts. First, and most important, is the one which states that the individual cause-event was necessary in the circumstances for the effect, for example 'If he had not eaten of that dish, he would not have died'. Such a conditional, I have argued,[8] can be understood as saying 'Suppose that he did not eat of that dish; then (within the scope of that supposition) he did not die' or 'In the possible situation where he did not eat of that dish, he did not die'. Now if there is some regularity of something like the form suggested above—though no doubt with many more disjuncts—giving the 'full cause' of death of human beings in an ordinary environment, and one of the minimal sufficient conditions, say $A\bar{B}\bar{C}$, is the conjunction of consuming at least such-and-such an amount of a certain poison (which was in the dish in question, but nowhere else) with not taking the appropriate antidote and not having one's stomach evacuated within a certain time, and this minimal sufficient condition was realized on this occasion but none of the other minimal sufficient conditions was realized, then from the supposition that on this occasion he did not eat of that dish it follows that A did not occur on this occasion; from this, together with the second half of the regularity, of the form 'All FP are $(A\bar{B}\bar{C}$ or etc.$)$', and the information that none of the other disjuncts, summed up here as 'etc.', occurred on this occasion, it follows that P did not occur in F on this occasion; such an inference justifies the assertion, within the scope of the supposition that he did not eat of that dish, that P did not occur, that is, that he did not die, and hence sustains the conditional 'If he had not eaten of that dish he would not have died'.

Secondly, although I argued in Chapter 2 that we do not always require that an individual cause should be sufficient as well as necessary in the circumstances for its effect, I had to use rather odd indeterministic examples in order to discriminate between necessity and sufficiency in the strong sense. Most individual causes, it appears, both are and are taken to be sufficient in the circumstances in the strong sense: we can say that if in the circumstances he had not been going to die, he would not have eaten of that dish. This counterfactual conditional is sustained, analogously with the previous one, by the *first* half of the regularity 'All F $(A\bar{B}\bar{C}$ or etc.$)$ are P' together with the information that both B and C were absent on this occasion; for these together with the supposition that he did not die entail first that none of the disjuncts occurred on this

[8] *Truth, Probability, and Paradox*, pp. 92–108.

occasion, then that A did not occur (since $\bar{B}\bar{C}$ did), and hence that he did not eat of that dish. So 'He did not eat of that dish' can be asserted within the scope of the supposition that he did not die, and this is equivalent to the required counterfactual.

Thirdly, it is commonly held that a causal claim entails that if a sufficiently similar antecedent had occurred on other occasions (when in fact it did not) a similar consequent would have occurred. This means, in this case, that if $A\bar{B}\bar{C}$ had occurred in F on some other occasion, P would have, and it is clear that this counterfactual too is sustained, in much the same way, by the first half of the suggested regularity.

On the other hand, although such complex regularities may hold in the objects, we must admit that they are seldom, if ever, known in full. Even in a matter of such intimate and absorbing interest as the death of human beings, we cannot confidently assert any complete regularity of this kind. We do not know all the causes of death, that is, all the different closely preceding assemblages of conditions that are minimally sufficient for death. And even with any one cause, we do not know all the possible counteracting causes, all the factors the negations of which would have to be conjoined with our positive factors to make up just one minimal sufficient condition. Causal knowledge progresses gradually towards the formulation of such regularities, but it hardly ever gets there. Causal regularities *as known* are typically incomplete; they have rather the form

All $F (A \ldots \bar{B} \ldots$ or $D \ldots \bar{H} \ldots$ or $\ldots)$ are P, and all FP are
$(A \ldots \bar{B} \ldots$ or $D \ldots \bar{H} \ldots$ or $\ldots)$

where the dots indicate further as yet unknown conjuncts and disjuncts that have still to be filled in. What we know are certain *elliptical* or *gappy* universal propositions. We do not know the full cause of death in human beings, but we do know, about each of a considerable number of items, that it is an inus condition of death, that, as we ordinarily say, it may cause death.

The same knowledge that is expressed by such elliptical universal propositions can be expressed, alternatively, by propositions in which second-order existential quantifications precede the universal ones. Thus the knowledge that A is an inus condition of P in F may be formulated thus:

For some X and for some Y all $F(AX$ or $Y)$ are P, and all FP are $(AX$ or $Y)$.

The suggestion that causal regularities as known are commonly of this sort may provoke two questions. Of what use is such exiguous information? And how is knowledge of such a curious form acquired? We can show, however—surprising though this may be—that such knowledge can be of great value, and that it may be discovered in just those ways in which we do most commonly acquire causal knowledge.

First, this information still permits causal inferences (in both directions), but makes them more tentative. Knowing that something of the form $(AX$ or $Y)$—where A is known but X and Y are not—is both necessary and sufficient for P in F, we may well have reason to believe that the X, whatever it may be, is often present; if so, we can infer from an observed occurrence of A that P is fairly likely to follow. X will, of course, include the negations of all the counteracting causes, whatever they may be; and we may well have reason to believe that though there may be many as yet undiscovered counteracting causes they are absent, and their negations therefore are present, on this occasion. There may be many undiscovered antidotes to this poison, but this victim is unlikely to take any of them. Again, without being able to specify Y in any great detail, we may have some reason to believe that it is likely to be absent on this particular occasion. Y, of course, may be partly known; it may be known that some of the other disjuncts it covers are of the forms BZ, CW, etc., where B and C, say, are known, though Z and W are not. If so, we can check that these disjuncts at least are absent by discovering that B and C are; that is, we can check that none of the other known causes (that is, inus conditions) of P in F is present on this occasion. And then we can infer, still tentatively but with some probability, from the occurrence of P on this occasion that A has also occurred. Typically we infer from an effect to a cause (inus condition) by eliminating other possible causes.

Since we can often infer, with probability, an effect from a cause, we can similarly infer, in corresponding circumstances, the absence of a cause from the absence of an effect. And since we can often infer, with probability, a cause from an effect, we can similarly infer the absence of an effect from the absence of a cause. Consequently the gappy universal propositions, the incompletely known complex regularities, which contribute to such inferences will still sustain, with probability, the counterfactual conditionals that correspond to these inferences, that is, statements of the forms 'If A had not occurred, P would not' and 'If P had not been going to occur, A would not'. And the gappy universal in allowing inference from cause to effect will equally sustain the subjunctive conditional that if this cause occurred again in sufficiently similar circumstances, so would the effect, while leaving it open and unknown just what such sufficient similarity requires. Gappy universals, then, still sustain all the types of conditionals commonly associated with causal statements.

Moreover, exiguous though it is, this information allows us to engage, though of course with something less than complete confidence, in the production and the prevention of effects by way of causes. If X, whatever it may be, is often present, we may hope, by introducing an instance of A, to bring about a P. Equally, by eliminating a known cause, A, of P, we have done something to prevent the occurrence of P, and of course if there are several such known causes, say A, B, and C—that is, if the necessary and sufficient condition has the form (AX or BZ or CW or . . .)—then we do the best we can to prevent P by preventing the occurrence of A or B or C; just what X, Z, and W may be is then of no practical importance. And this, surely, is how in many fields intelligent practice goes on. We operate with, or on, factors about which we know only that they can, and perhaps often do, help to produce certain results. We take what precautions we can, but failure does not necessarily show that a plan was ill-conceived; and there is equally such a thing as undeserved success.

Secondly, the elliptical character of causal regularities as known is closely connected with our characteristic methods of discovering and establishing them: it is precisely for such gappy statements that we can obtain fairly direct evidence from quite modest ranges of observation. Of central importance here is what Mill called the Method of Difference; but we can improve on his formulation of it.

This is one of the set of methods of eliminative induction. Like any other such method, it can be formulated in terms of an assumption, an observation, and a conclusion which follows by a deductively valid argument from the assumption and the observation together. To get any positive causal conclusion by a process of elimination, we must assume that the result—the 'phenomenon' whose cause we are seeking—has *some* cause. While we can make some progress with the weaker assumptions that it has only a sufficient cause, or only a necessary cause, the most significant results emerge when we assume that there is some condition which is both necessary and sufficient for the occurrence (shortly afterwards and in the neighbourhood) of the result. Also, if we are to get anywhere by elimination, we must assume a somehow restricted range of possibly relevant causal factors, of kinds of event or situation which might in some way help to constitute this necessary and sufficient condition. Let us initially include in our assumption, then, a list of such *possible causes, possibly* relevant factors, say A, B, C, D, E, etc.— though as we shall see later, we do not in fact need a *list*. Even if we had specified such a list of possibly relevant factors, it would in most cases be quite implausible to assume that the supposed necessary and sufficient condition we are seeking is identical with just one of these factors on its own; we expect causal regularities to involve both assemblages of conditions and a plurality of causes. The plausible assumption to make, therefore, is merely that the supposed necessary and sufficient condition will be represented by a formula which is constructed in some way out of some selection from the list of single terms each of which represents a possibly relevant factor, by means of negation, conjunction, and disjunction. However, any formula so constructed is equivalent to some formula in disjunctive normal form—that is, one in which negation, if it occurs, is applied only to single terms, and conjunction, if it occurs, only to single terms and/or negations of single terms. So we can without loss of generality assume that the formula for the supposed necessary and sufficient condition is in disjunctive normal form, that it is at most a disjunction of conjunctions in which each conjunct is a single term or the negation of one, that is, a formula such as '($AB\bar{C}$ or $G\bar{H}$ or $\mathcal{J}$)'. Summing this up, the assumption that we require will have the form:

For some $\mathcal{Z}$, $\mathcal{Z}$ is a necessary and sufficient condition for the phenomenon P in the field F, that is, all FP are $\mathcal{Z}$ and all

$F\mathcal{Z}$ are P, and $\mathcal{Z}$ is a condition represented by some formula in disjunctive normal form all of whose constituents are taken from the range of possibly relevant factors A, B, C, D, E, etc.

Along with this assumption, we need an observation which has the form of the classical difference observation described by Mill. This we can formulate as follows:

There is an instance, I_1, in which P occurs, and there is a negative case, $\mathcal{N}_1$, in which P does not occur, such that one of the possibly relevant factors, say A, is present in I_1 but absent from $\mathcal{N}_1$, but each of the other possibly relevant factors is either present in both I_1 and $\mathcal{N}_1$ or absent both from I_1 and from $\mathcal{N}_1$.

An example of such an observation can be set out as follows, with 'a' and 'p' standing for 'absent' and 'present':

	P	A	B	C	D	E	
I_1	p	p	p	a	a	p	etc.
$\mathcal{N}_1$	a	a	p	a	a	p	

Given the above-stated assumption, we can reason as follows about any such observation:

Since P is absent from $\mathcal{N}_1$, every sufficient condition of P is absent from $\mathcal{N}_1$, and therefore every disjunct in $\mathcal{Z}$ is absent from $\mathcal{N}_1$. Every disjunct in $\mathcal{Z}$ which does not contain A must either be present in both I_1 and $\mathcal{N}_1$ or absent from both, since each of its constituents is either present in both or absent from both; so every disjunct in $\mathcal{Z}$ which does not contain A is absent from I_1 as well as from $\mathcal{N}_1$. But since P is present in I_1, and $\mathcal{Z}$ is a necessary condition of P, $\mathcal{Z}$ is present in I_1. Therefore at least one disjunct in $\mathcal{Z}$ is present in I_1. Therefore at least one disjunct in $\mathcal{Z}$ contains A. And it must contain A un-negated, if it is to be present in I_1 where A is present.

What this shows is that $\mathcal{Z}$, the supposed necessary and sufficient condition for P in F, must have one of these forms: (A), (AX), $(A$ or $Y)$, $(AX$ or $Y)$. That is, A is either an inus condition for P in F, if the necessary and sufficient condition is of the form $(AX$ or $Y)$—that is, if there are both other factors conjoined with A and other disjuncts as well as the one in which A figures—or, as we may say, better than an inus condition, if the necessary and sufficient condition has one of the other three forms. Our assumption and the difference observation together entail a regularity of the form

> For some X and for some Y (which may, however, be null), all F (AX or Y) are P, and all FP are (AX or Y).

This analysis is so far merely formal. To justify my suggestion that we can obtain fairly direct evidence for regularities of this form from modest ranges of observation I must show that it is sometimes reasonable to make the required assumptions and that we can sometimes make the corresponding observations. A number of points can be stated in support of this claim.

First, the actual listing of possibly relevant factors is not needed in practice: this was only a device for formal exposition. All that matters is that any features other than the one, A, that is eventually established as an inus condition (or better) should be matched as between I_1 and N_1, that there should be no other likely-to-be-causally-relevant difference between these two cases: *what* features they agree in having or in lacking is irrelevant. In a causal inquiry in a field in which we already have some knowledge we may, of course, already know what sorts of item are likely to be relevant, and so can check that these are matched between the two cases; but if an inquiry is starting from cold in a field in which little is known, the only available criterion of possible relevance is spatio-temporal neighbourhood: we simply have to see that things are, as far as possible, alike in the space-time regions where an instance of A is followed by an instance of P (our I_1) and where there is neither an instance of A nor one of P (our N_1).

Secondly, there are at least two well-known ways in which some approximation to the classical difference observation is often achieved. One of these is the before-and-after observation. Some change, A, is introduced, either naturally or by deliberate human action, into an otherwise apparently static situation. The state of affairs just after this introduction is our I_1, the state of affairs before it is N_1. If this introduction is followed, without any further intervention, by some other change P, then we can and almost instinctively do reason as the

Method of Difference suggests, concluding both that this instance of A helped to produce this instance of P, and that A generally is at least, in Mill's terms, an indispensable part of the cause of P. The singular causal judgement in such a case could, as I said in Chapter 2, arise in a primitive way from imaginative analogizing; but the corresponding general judgement requires something like the pattern of reasoning that we have just been trying to formalize; and of course once we have this general causal judgement, it could in turn sustain the counterfactual conditionals implicit in the singular judgement. The second well-known approximation to the difference observation is the standard controlled experiment, where what happens in the 'experimental case'—our I_1—is compared with what happens, or fails to happen, in a deliberately constructed 'control case' which is made to match the experimental case in all ways thought likely to be relevant other than the feature, A, whose effects are under investigation.

Thirdly, it may seem to be in general difficult to satisfy the requirement of the Method of Difference, that there should be only *one* point of difference between I_1 and N_1. But fortunately very little really turns upon this. Suppose that two possibly relevant factors, say A and B, had been present in I_1 but absent from N_1. Then reasoning parallel to that stated above would show that at least one of the disjuncts in Z either contains A un-negated, or contains B un-negated or contains both. This observation still serves to show that the cluster of factors (A, B) contains something that is an inus condition (or better) of P in F, whether in the end this turns out to be A alone, or B alone, or both these, or the conjunction AB. Similar considerations apply if there are more than two points of difference. However many there are, an observation of the suggested form, coupled with our assumption, shows that a cause—an inus condition or better—lies somewhere within that cluster of features in which I_1 differs from N_1. It does not, of course, show that the other features, those shared by I_1 and N_1, are irrelevant; our reasoning does not, as some misleading formulations of the method suggest, exclude factors as irrelevant, but positively locates *some at least* of the relevant factors within the differentiating cluster. This point rebuts a criticism sometimes levelled against the eliminative methods generally, that they presuppose and require a finally satisfactory analysis of causal factors into their simple components, which we never actually achieve. On the contrary, any distinction of factors, however rough, enables us to start using such a method. We can proceed, and there is no doubt that discovery has often proceeded, by what we may call *the progressive localization of a cause*. Using the Method of Difference in a very rough way, men discovered first that the drinking of wine causes intoxication. The cluster of factors crudely indicated by the phrase 'the drinking of wine' contains somewhere within it an inus condition of intoxication. Later, by distinguishing various possibly relevant factors within this cluster, and making further observations and experiments of the same sort, they located a cause of intoxication more precisely—the consumption of the alcohol contained in the wine. In a context in which the cluster of factors is put in or left out as a whole it is correct to say, of any particular case, 'He would not have become intoxicated if he had not drunk that wine'. But in a context in which alcohol and certain other constituents were put in or left out separately, it would be correct to say rather 'He would not have become intoxicated if he had not consumed that alcohol'. Did the wine make him drunk? At one level of analysis, of course it did; but in relation to a finer analysis of factors it was not strictly speaking the wine but the alcohol it contained that made him drunk. In different contexts, different specifications of a cause or inus condition may be equally correct.

Fourthly, it is instructive to contrast the Method of Difference as a logical ideal with any concrete application of it. If the assumption and the observation were known to be true, then the conclusion, asserting a typical causal regularity, would be established. No doubt the assumption and the observation are never known with certainty, but it may still be reasonable to accept them provisionally, and, if so, our formal analysis shows that it is equally reasonable to accept the regularity conclusion. In particular, once the assumption is accepted, we may well be in a position to say that we cannot see any other difference that might be relevant between I_1 and N_1, and consequently that we cannot see any escape from the causal conclusion.

Fifthly, we need not and in practice do not rely so heavily on a single observation (with just one I_1 and one N_1) as our

formal account might suggest. Of course there might, in such
a single pair of cases, be an unnoticed but relevant further
difference which undermined our reasoning. It might be that
our control case did not match our experimental case closely
enough, or, in a before-and-after observation, that some other
relevant change occurred at the critical time. But repeating the
experiment or the observation reduces this danger. If we can
add an I_2 and an N_2, and an I_3 and an N_3, and so on, and each
time the presence of A is the only noticed difference between
the two sets of antecedent conditions, it becomes progressively
less likely that any other relevant change occurred just at the
right moment on each occasion—unless, of course, this other
change is itself connected with A by what Mill calls some fact
of causation. But it is important to note that it is not the mere
repeated co-occurrence of A and P that supports the causal
conclusion; we are not moving over from the Method of Difference to the Method of Agreement; what we are relying on is
the repetition of a sequence which on each single occasion was
already, because of the Method of Difference pattern it appeared
to exhibit, prima facie a causal one. The repetition merely confirms this by greatly reducing the likelihood that some unnoticed
factor might be undermining this prima facie interpretation.

Sixthly, it is worth noting that the assumption required, while
it is of course a deterministic one, is much weaker than the
usual formulations of the uniformity of nature. We need not
assume that *every* event has a cause, but merely that for events
of the kind in question, P, in the field in question, F, there is
some, possibly very complex, necessary and sufficient condition.
It is true that we also need to assume that this condition is made
up from a range of possibly relevant factors that is restricted in
some way: if we have no previous causal knowledge in the
relevant sphere, we have to take spatio-temporal nearness as a
criterion of possible relevance. But this is not a final or absolute
assumption: if, using it as a working assumption, we reach some
conclusion, assert some causal regularity, but then this is dis-
confirmed by further observations, we can always relax this
working assumption and look a bit further afield for possibly
relevant differences. There is, no doubt, still a philosophical
problem about what justifies *any* such deterministic assumption,
however local and however weak. But at least this analysis

makes it clearer what precise form of assumption is needed to back up our ordinary detecting and establishing of causal regularities. In particular, I hope to have shown that while we can agree with von Wright that 'in normal scientific practice we have to reckon with plurality rather than singularity, and with complexity rather than simplicity of conditions', this does *not* mean, as he says, that 'the weaker form of the Deterministic Postulate . . . is practically useless as a supplementary premiss or "presupposition" of induction'.[9]

Towards the end of Chapter 2 I said that although necessity$_1$, the distinguishing feature of causal sequences, is not something that can be observed, we can explain how a certain sort of observation can set off a psychological process of imaginative analogizing that can yield a singular causal judgement. We can now add to this by explaining how a not implausibly strict assumption, coupled with that same sort of observation, can entail a causal regularity statement of the form we ordinarily use, and that this statement in turn will sustain the corresponding singular causal judgement.

It is a further merit of such an account of complex but incompletely known regularities that it disposes altogether of a type of objection that is sometimes brought against regularity (or 'Humean') theories of causation in general. Geach, for example, says that

. . . the laws that scientists aim at establishing are not *de facto* uniformities, either necessary or contingent. For any alleged uniformity is defeasible by something's interfering and preventing the effect. . . . Scientists do not try to describe natural events in terms of what always happens. Rather, certain natural agents . . . are brought into the description, and we are told what behaviour is proper to this set of bodies in these circumstances. If such behaviour is not realized, the scientist looks for a new, interfering agent. . . .

And he goes on to argue that 'interference just cannot be logically brought into a uniformity doctrine of causality'; criticizing some of Mill's statements, he says that Mill 'retreats into saying that physical laws do not state what *does* happen, but what *would failing interference* happen; but this is to abandon the Humian position'.[10]

9 *A Treatise on Induction and Probability*, p. 135.
10 *Three Philosophers*, by G. E. M. Anscombe and P. T. Geach, pp. 102–3.

It will be clear from what has been said above that though interference could not be brought into a doctrine of simple uniformities, it is easily accommodated in a doctrine of complex uniformities. Interference is the presence of a counteracting cause, a factor whose negation is a conjunct in a minimal sufficient condition (some of) whose other conjuncts are present. The fact that scientists rightly hesitate to assert that something always happens is explained by the point that the complex uniformities they try to discover are nearly always incompletely known. It would be quite consistent with an essentially Humean position—though an advance on what Hume himself says—to distinguish between a full complex physical law, which would state what always does happen, and the law as so far known, which tells us only what would, failing interference, happen; such a subjunctive conditional will be sustained by an incompletely known law. Moreover, the rival doctrine can be understood only with the help of this one. What it would be for certain behaviour to be 'proper to this set of bodies in these circumstances', what Aquinas's tendencies or *appetitus* are, remains utterly obscure in Geach's account; but using the notion of complex regularity we can explain that *A* has a tendency to produce *P* if there is some minimally sufficient condition of *P* in which *A* is a non-redundant element. (This is, indeed, not the only sense of the terms 'tend' and 'tendency'. We could say that *A* tends to produce *P* not only where *A* conjoined with some set of other factors is always followed by *P*, but also where there is an indeterministic, statistical, law to the effect that most, or some, instances of *A*, or some definite percentage of such instances, are followed by *P*, or perhaps where an *A* has a certain objective chance of being followed by a *P*.[11] These statistical tendencies are not reducible even to complex regularities: if they occur, as contemporary science asserts, then they constitute something different from, though related to, strict deterministic causation. But they have little to do with Geach's problem of interference.)

Does this improved and corrected account of causal regularities, with all its merits, constitute a defence of a regularity theory of causation? Can we identify causation with the holding

---

[11] See Chapter 9 below. Objective chance is also discussed in *Truth, Probability, and Paradox*, Chapter 5.

of regularities of this sort? No progress can be made with this problem unless we keep separate the three sorts of question, what do causal statements mean, what do we know about causation and how do we know it, and what constitutes causation as it is in the objects themselves.

It seems very clear that singular causal statements do not mean that the sequences about which they are made are instances of regularities of any sort. In the Humean tradition there is a doctrine that they *ought* to mean this, but Hume himself, as we have seen, did not claim that they do so. As I have argued in Chapter 2, the main part of our concept of the distinguishing feature of a causal sequence is expressible by a counterfactual conditional, or, what comes to the same thing, by the assertion that the cause was necessary in the circumstances for the effect, and the meaning of a singular causal statement will be analysable into the conjunction of this with, probably, some further claims or suggestions.

It is, however, sometimes said that causal statements are *implicitly* general. It is easy to refute the claim that a singular causal statement normally implies a simple regularity statement, of the form that instances of a certain kind of event are always, or even often, followed by instances of another kind of event: the taking of a contraceptive pill may cause one woman's death although millions of women have taken large numbers of exactly similar pills and survived. Nor can a singular causal statement imply a complex but complete regularity statement, since we commonly assert statements of the former kind when we are quite unable to formulate any corresponding complete generalizations. But perhaps singular causal statements imply our elliptical generalizations, or the equivalent forms with second-order existential quantifiers. It is not so easy conclusively to refute this suggestion, but since it is only in recent years that a number of philosophers have approached a correct formulation of the generalizations in question, we must say at least that this would be an implication of which most users of singular causal statements can be only very vaguely aware. In fact, I would go further and say, referring to what I called (at the end of Chapter 2) a primitive and unsophisticated way of arriving at counterfactuals and the associated causal judgements, that a singular causal statement need not imply even the vaguest generalization. This is true even of physical and mechanical examples. One can judge that this (very hot) stone was cracked by water being poured over it without being committed to any generalization, meaning only that the stone would not in the circumstances have cracked had the water not been poured on, and that this pouring was causally prior to the cracking in the sense explained in Chapter 2. It is, of course, even more obviously true of mental examples; I can judge that Bill's warning shout made me stop short of the precipice without generalizations of any sort being involved.

On the other hand, I have argued that there is a sophisticated way of arriving at causal and counterfactual statements which does involve elliptical generalizations: one can use something like the Method of Difference to establish such a generalization, which will then sustain the counterfactuals involved in the singular causal judgement. But even here it is the generalization that supports the causal statement, rather than the causal statement that implies the generalization. Also, it is worth stressing that the generalization here is of the elliptical universal form, it does not say what always or normally or generally or even often happens—for example, careful checks might make it probable that a certain pill had caused someone's death even if this was the very first time such a pill had had any ill effect (though further cases of the same sort would confirm this conclusion), but the doctor who reached this conclusion would say that the victim must have been unusually susceptible, that she had some as yet unknown combination of characteristics which, in conjunction with the consumption of the pill, would regularly lead to death. Again, it is worth stressing that the generalization need not be known in advance: it may be discovered and (tentatively) established by the observation of the very sequence of events about which the causal statement is made. Not even the vaguest foreknowledge about what often happens is needed to smooth the way even for a physical causal discovery. The doctor (Sir Norman Gregg) who discovered that German measles in pregnancy had caused eye defects in a number of children had no previous reason for regarding this as anything but the mildest of ailments, with no lasting effects. It is true that previously known generalizations may contribute to a causal conclusion, but they do so by supporting the belief that

the *other* features present on this occasion would be unlikely to
have produced the observed result. If someone eats of a certain
dish, and then becomes ill, what helps to show that (something
in) this dish made him ill is the fact that everything else that
he ate and drank on the same day, and everything else that he
then did, were of kinds and in quantities that he regularly ate
and drank and did without becoming ill. Such previously
known generalizations work, indeed, in the way explained by
what Mill called the Method of Residues: in effect, they are
used to *construct* a negative instance, corresponding to our N_1,
instead of *observing* one, as in the classical form of the Method
of Difference.[12] Even these previously known generalizations,
then, are only useful, not essential: an observed negative
instance that resembles sufficiently closely the positive one makes
them superfluous. No specific generalization, however vague,
then, needs to be known in advance in order to support the
interpretation of an observed sequence as causal: even for the
sophisticated way of handling this observation all that is required
is the assumption that what has happened is an instance of
some, probably complex, regularity, that some perhaps as yet
quite unknown and unsuspected uniformity is instantiated here.
The singular causal statement says that without A, on this
occasion (our I_1), P *would* not have occurred; this is very often
supported by the observation that without A, on some other
similar occasion (our N_1), P *did* not occur. In the sophisticated
procedure, this 'did not' supports the 'would not' because it is
assumed that there is *some* underlying regularity of behaviour;
it is this assumption that justifies the transfer of the non-
occurrence of P from N_1 to the suppositional reconstruction of
I_1. In the unsophisticated procedure, the transfer is made
imaginatively, by analogy; but one could say that to be prone
to make such imaginative moves is somewhat like having an
unconscious belief that there is some underlying regularity
in the world. Even my judgement that I would not have stopped
if I had not heard Bill's shout involves a similar transfer from
what I know of my own thoughts and movements before he
shouted to the hypothetical situation in which, a moment later,
I did not hear his shout. But it is only in these very tenuous
senses that singular causal statements, sophisticated or primitive,

[12] See Appendix.

physical or mental, are implicitly general, that they necessarily assert or presuppose regularities of any sort.

But what about general causal statements? The statements that heating a gas causes it to expand, that hammering brass makes it brittle, and such related dispositional statements as that strychnine is poisonous and that lead is malleable, can indeed be interpreted as assertions that the cause mentioned or indicated is an inus condition of the effect. But even here it would be more appropriate to take the general statements as quantified variants of the corresponding singular ones, for example, as saying that heating a gas always or often or sometimes causes it to expand, where this 'causes' has the meaning that 'caused' would have in a singular causal statement. However, the essential point is that singular causal statements are prior to general ones, whereas a regularity theory of the meaning of causal statements would reverse this priority.

The question whether regularities enter into what we know about causation and into our ways of learning about it has been answered incidentally in this discussion. The crucial and outstanding question is to what extent such complex regularities as we have described constitute causation as it is in the objects.

It is undeniable that we ordinarily suppose both that there are some such regularities underlying many of the sequences that we take to be causal and that in scientific inquiries, at least in the physical and the biological sciences, we make progress towards fuller formulations of them. Whether these suppositions are correct can still be questioned. The methods so far examined for establishing them rest upon assumptions of uniformity which those methods cannot themselves establish: to ask whether such success as they seem to have achieved can be taken to have confirmed their assumptions, or whether those assumptions can be justified or vindicated in some other way, is to raise the fundamental philosophical problem of induction which I cannot pursue further here; though I noted in Chapter I (following Stove) that the reasons given by many of Hume's successors for supposing it to be insoluble are poor ones.* But assuming that this problem can be somehow solved or dissolved, that we are justified in placing some reliance upon our ordinary methods of induction or of the confirmation of hypotheses, it seems very likely that there are in fact regularities of this complex sort. The only plausible alternative view is that the physical world works merely by statistical laws (which we shall consider in Chapter 9), and that these generate only approximations to regularities of the form discussed here.

Even if we grant, provisionally, that such regularities are involved in at least some cases of causation, we must still question whether all cases of causation involve them, and whether causation ever consists only in the holding of such regularities.

The stock argument for a negative answer to this last question is that we can point to regularities of succession that are not causal: day regularly follows night, but night does not cause day, and is not even a partial cause of day;[13] the sounding of factory hooters in Manchester may be regularly followed by, but does not cause, London workers leaving their work.[14] Mill, being aware of this problem, tried to solve it by saying that causal sequences are not merely invariable but unconditional: night is not unconditionally followed by day, because we can describe changed conditions in which there would be night but day would not follow. But this suggestion is in the end fatal to the theory which it was designed to save. In the first place, Mill himself has stressed that no ordinary causal sequences are unconditional: what we commonly accept as causes are only members of assemblages of conditions, positive and negative, and only such a complete assemblage is unconditionally followed by the effect. But this is a fairly superficial criticism. There is a problem, to which we shall return, why some conditional regularities should be not accepted as cases of the earlier item causing the later, while other regularities, no less conditional, are accepted as cases of causation. But there are more fundamental objections to Mill's way out. We must distinguish *de facto* unconditional regularity from counterfactually unconditional regularity. If night in, say, Glasgow is always in fact followed by day in Glasgow (it is evening in Glasgow when the earth eventually blows up), then this regularity is *de facto* unconditional; Mill's protest that we know of conditions in

[13] T. Reid, *Essays on the Active Powers of Man*; Mill, *System of Logic*, Book III, Ch. 5, Sect. 6.

[14] C. D. Broad, *The Mind and its Place in Nature*, pp. 455-6. Broad's actual example is of workers going *to* work, but the reverse is in some ways more convenient.

which night *would not* be followed by day (for example, those in which the earth blows up just before daybreak in Glasgow) means only that this regularity is not counterfactually unconditional. Mill is claiming, then, that to be causal a regularity must be counterfactually unconditional. But while this may throw some light upon our concept of causation, it cannot apply directly to our present question whether regularity constitutes causation *in the objects*. For the holding of a counterfactual conditional is not a fully objective matter: we must go back from the conditional to whatever grounds make it reasonable to assert it or to suppose it to hold. Now if we find some 'causal mechanism', some continuous process connecting the antecedent in an observed conditional regularity with the consequent, we may be able to sort out some counterfactually unconditional regularities which underlie the conditional one. (This will be discussed and illustrated in Chapter 8.) On the other hand, even if we can find no mechanism, no continuous connecting process, and even if we believe that there is none to be found, we may still assert, and have reason for asserting, that there is some counterfactually unconditional regularity. Russell at one time postulated, though he later rejected, 'mnemic' causation, in which an earlier event (an experience) is the *proximate* cause of a later one (a memory).[15] This would not mean that experiences are unconditionally followed by rememberings, but it presumably would mean that in an appropriate field (which would have to include the survival, and the consciousness, of the subject) some assemblage of conditions, including an experience, was unconditionally followed by the corresponding memory, but without any specific linking mechanism over and above the mere survival of the intermittently conscious subject. This hypothesis may well be false and is indeed, as Russell admitted, extravagant, but it is not incoherent, and we could fairly easily describe experiments and observations which might confirm it by disconfirming alternative explanations of remembering. Such a regularity, then, could be reasonably asserted to be counterfactually unconditional; its instances would then fall under our concept of genuine causal sequences, but all that was present in the objects would be that pattern of regularities and

---

[15] *The Analysis of Mind*, pp. 78–9; *An Inquiry into Meaning and Truth*, p. 297; 'Reply to Criticisms' in *The Philosophy of Bertrand Russell*, ed. P. A. Schilpp, p. 700.

irregularities, 'agreements' and 'differences', which we reasonably took as confirming this hypothesis and as disconfirming its rivals. Of course, this and all similar hypotheses may well be false; it may be that causation in the objects always does involve continuous processes, but we cannot say that it must do so, that such continuity must be added, even to those regularities which we reasonably take as counterfactually unconditional, in order to make them causal.

However, even if Mill could so far defend the claim that counterfactually unconditional regularity is sufficient for causation, we can refute this claim by using, in a slightly different way, the stock counter-examples to the regularity theory. Typically, these are cases of branched causal patterns.[16] A common cause, the rotation of the earth relative to the sun, is responsible for night in Glasgow, that is, for a period of, say, twelve hours of darkness there, and also for the ensuing day, that is, for a period of, say, twelve hours of light. A similar, though more complicated, account can be given of the Manchester hooters and the London workers. Generalizing, we have the sort of causal pattern that is roughly indicated by this diagram:

Diagram (iv)

Here C is the common cause, A one effect, and B the other; the pattern is repeated over and over again, but each instance of A occurs just before the associated instance of B. But of course this linear diagram is only rough: in fact other conditions will be conjoined with C to produce A, and others again to produce B: C is presumably only an inus condition of A and of B. We can concede to Mill that the A–B sequence is not unconditional. But it is not this that prevents A from being the (or a) cause of B; for we can find, underlying this, an unconditional sequence which is still not causal. Suppose that the full cause

[16] But these are not the only counter-examples. More thoroughly accidental regularities will be discussed in Chapter 8.

of A is $(CX$ or $Y)$, and the full cause of B is $(CZ$ or $W)$, X and Z being present whenever this whole pattern is instantiated. Then clearly $A\bar{Y}$ is *unconditionally* preceded by C, while CZ is *unconditionally* followed (after a longer time interval) by B; hence $A\bar{Y}Z$ is *unconditionally* followed by B, though $\bar{Y}Z$ presumably is not. There is an unconditional sequence in which the antecedent is an assemblage of conditions of which A is a non-redundant member, and the consequent is B. In more concrete terms, the sounding of the Manchester factory hooters, plus the absence of whatever conditions would make them sound when it wasn't five o'clock, plus the presence of whatever conditions are, along with its being five o'clock, jointly sufficient for the Londoners to stop work a moment later—including, say, automatic devices for setting off the London hooters at five o'clock, is a conjunction of features which is unconditionally followed by the Londoners stopping work. In this conjunction the sounding of the Manchester hooters is an essential element, for it alone, in this conjunction, ensures that it should *be* five o'clock. Yet it would be most implausible to say that this conjunction causes the stopping of work in London. So the antecedent in even an unconditional sequence may fail to cause the consequent. (And this is not because the sequence is logically necessary, though our description may have suggested this. Though I have spoken of whatever conditions are sufficient for this or that, this is only a way of indicating the concrete conditions Y and Z, whatever they may be; Y and Z are not themselves logically related to A, B, and C, though our descriptions of them are; the sequence in which $A\bar{Y}Z$ is followed by B is logically contingent though unconditional.)

Nor can this sort of counter-example be undermined by saying that to be causal a sequence must be such as to be reasonably taken to be counterfactually unconditional. For if the $(CX$ or $Y)$–A and $(CZ$ or $W)$–B sequences are counterfactually unconditional, so is the $A\bar{Y}Z$–B one. This sort of counter-example shows, too, that adding a causal mechanism, a continuity of process, is not enough; for if there are such mechanisms or continuities between C and A and between C and B, there will inevitably be a set of mechanisms, a resultant continuous process, linking A with B.

But it is not too difficult to begin to see what the key additional feature is that marks off genuine cause–effect sequences, and that is lacking in this *A–B* counter-example. It is what we spoke of in Chapter 2 as causal priority. In the branched pattern, each instance of *A*, or of $A\tilde{Y}\tilde{Z}$, is not causally prior (though it is temporally prior) to the associated instance of *B*. Each *A* is indeed related to its *B* by 'some fact of causation', by what is roughly indicated by the arrows in the diagram; but the *C–A* arrow is pointing the wrong way. The $A\tilde{Y}\tilde{Z}$–*B* sequence is causally maintained, but $A\tilde{Y}\tilde{Z}$ does not cause *B*. Admittedly this is only a schematic answer, since we have not yet discovered in what causal priority in the objects consists: the account sketched at the end of Chapter 2, in terms of conditionals and possible worlds, may help to identify *our notion* of causal priority, but it falls far short of anything that could be an objective description. But though it is elusive, causal priority can hardly be non-existent. The regularity theorist could rebut this last criticism only if he were prepared to say that there is no difference in the objects between the causal pattern represented, however crudely, by the above diagram and that which would be represented thus:

Diagram (v)

—in other words, that there is no difference between a means (or intermediate link in a causal chain) and a side-effect. But this would be most implausible.

We can now return to our first criticism of Mill's suggestion, to the point that some *conditional* regularities are accepted as cases of the earlier item causing the later, while others are not. While a number of considerations (of which some were mentioned in Chapter 2, and others will be touched upon in Chapter 5) restrict the application of the term 'cause' to some inus conditions in preference to others, what is most important in the present context is again the absence of causal priority. The sounding of a hooter in Manchester is not causally prior to Londoners stopping work, while the sounding of a hooter in London is, although both these hooter–stopping regularities are equally conditional, both *de facto* and counterfactually.

In conclusion, then, regularity of the sort we have elucidated, even if it is of a kind that can be called counterfactually unconditional, is not the whole of what constitutes causation in the objects. Some causal mechanism or continuity of process *may be* an additional and distinguishing feature of sequences in which the earlier item causes the later, but whether it is or not it seems certain that something which we can call causal priority is such an additional distinguishing feature. The regularity theory, even in its improved form, is not a complete account of causation in the objects, and as we saw earlier it is not adequate either as an account of what causal statements mean or of what we know about causation. But to say this is by no means to deny that causal regularities, complex and only partly known, contribute something to the answers to all three of these questions.

Those who find regularity theories inadequate commonly insist on some intrinsic necessity in causal relations, or suggest a 'genetic' view of causation, according to which causes produce or generate their effects and are not merely followed by them, or both.[17] But it is not enough to reiterate such words as 'necessity' and 'production' and 'generation'; we need some clear account of what this necessity is, or of what producing or generating can be. Moreover, this account must be able to resist Hume's criticisms, to take up his challenges, to explain how these key relations escaped his notice. Logical necessitation between distinct occurrences or their features is ruled out, and Hume's challenge to his opponents to point out anything like what we have called necessity$_2$ is not easy to meet. Nor, I think, is it at all helpful to say that things have causal *powers*: the concept of powers needs to be elucidated in terms of causation rather than causation in terms of powers.[18] Since what was called, in Chapter 1, Hume's third exclusion or third negative point was poorly supported, there is no serious obstacle to the

[17] For example, A. C. Ewing, *Idealism*, pp. 151–87; W. Kneale, *Probability and Induction*, pp. 70–103; R. Harré, *The Principles of Scientific Thinking*, Chapters 4, 10, and 11.

[18] I have discussed powers and dispositional properties in Chapter 4 of *Truth, Probability, and Paradox*.

description of some empirical relations that might be called producing and generating; but the description needs to be given and, if possible, related in some way to the counterfactual conditionals that are at the heart of the ordinary notion of causing. In Chapters 5 and 8 I shall try to resolve these problems, by both borrowing from and criticizing the work, in particular, of Ducasse and Kneale, while in Chapter 7 I shall investigate that other essential supplement to regularity, the direction of causation.

4

Kant and Transcendentalism

HUME's treatment of causation, as is well known, led on to
Kant's, indeed it provoked Kant's whole critical philosophy.[1]
Should we retrace this historical path, and consider whether,
despite Hume's arguments, there is some important *a priori*
element in causation? Some of our discoveries may have
diminished this temptation. In criticizing Hume's arguments,
in Chapter 1, we saw that the notion of a necessity$_2$, of something that would justify or support *a priori* inference from cause
to effect and vice versa, is not really part of our ordinary concept of causation; consequently the failure to find any empirical
basis for such a notion need not drive us to search for an *a priori*
basis. We also saw in Chapter 1 that while Hume has shown
that experience and 'demonstration' together cannot establish
in a deductively valid way the principle that every event has a
cause, or any particular causal law, or even the conclusion of
any single causal inference, he has not excluded the possibility
that there might be forceful probabilistic inferences from an
observed cause to an unobserved effect or vice versa, or from
experience to particular causal laws, and even perhaps to the
general causal principle. Hume's empiricism has not after all
led to a scepticism so extreme that we should be strongly
tempted to abandon the empiricism. And having brought out
in Chapter 2 the patterns of conditional thinking that really
constitute the main part of necessity$_1$, of what we ordinarily
take to differentiate causal from non-causal sequences, we found
it fairly easy to suggest a psychological source for them. On the
other hand, we also studied in Chapter 3 a more sophisticated
way of arriving at and handling the key conditional statements,
and this, we found, could be formulated in terms of methods

[1] Kant, *Prolegomena*, 257–60.

which involved, among their premisses, almost totally unsupported assumptions which, while not quite equivalent to the old universal causal principle, yet had some affinity with it. For these assumptions, at least, it is still tempting to seek an *a priori* foundation or justification. Besides, there are two further aspects of our ordinary idea of causation for which our discussion so far has not adequately accounted: the notion of some intimate tie between an individual cause and its effect, and that of the direction of causation, the priority of cause to effect.

As Kant saw it, Hume

challenged Reason . . . to . . . say with what right she thinks: that anything can be of such a nature, that if it is posited, something else must thereby also be posited necessarily; for this is what the concept of cause says. He proved irrefutably: that it is wholly impossible for reason to think such a conjunction *a priori* and out of concepts. For this conjunction contains necessity; but it is quite impossible to see how, because something is, something else must also necessarily be. . . . From this he inferred that Reason completely deceives herself with this concept, in falsely taking it for her own child, whereas it is nothing but a bastard of the imagination fathered by experience.[2]

But Kant claimed that his own critical philosophy solved Hume's problem not just for the special case of causation but for a whole system of metaphysical concepts, showing that they have, after all, their origin in 'pure understanding'.

But as an escape from the difficulties Hume encountered in trying to find an 'impression' from which to derive 'the idea of necessary connexion', Kant's treatment is disappointing. He says practically nothing about what the concept of causation contains. The Metaphysical Deduction hints that the 'pure concepts of the understanding', the categories, correspond to the logical forms of judgement, and in particular that the category of cause and effect has something to do with the hypothetical (conditional) form of judgement. But this, though correct, is only a hint, and requires the sort of development attempted in Chapter 2; Kant himself says that he purposely omits the definitions of the categories.[3] In the passage quoted above he tells us that what the concept of cause says is that

2 *Prolegomena*, 257, trans. P. G. Lucas.
3 *Critique of Pure Reason*, A 82 = B 108.

something is 'of such a nature, that if it is posited, something else must thereby also be posited necessarily'. But this is ambiguous as between necessity$_2$ and necessity$_3$. It says that causation must be something which licenses an inference from cause to effect, but not whether this inference must be based wholly on something in the cause itself, on its own, or whether it is enough that there should be some rule or law from which, in conjunction with the cause, the effect could be inferred. However, when Kant comes to a detailed discussion and defence of something *a priori* about causation, this ambiguity is resolved in favour of necessity$_3$: in the Second Analogy, his concern is only with the principle that 'All alterations take place in conformity with the law of the connection of cause and effect';[4] in the first edition he was even more explicit: 'Everything that happens . . . presupposes something upon which it follows according to a rule.'[5] Surprisingly, in view of the importance which it would appear to have for his thesis that objective time-order depends upon causation, Kant has little to say about causal priority, and he has nothing to say about any intimate tie between an individual cause and its effect. Causation in the (phenomenal) objects is, for Kant no less than for Hume, just regularity. All that is *a priori* is that there should be some regularity covering every case. Nor did he have anything to say (as Mill did) about what sort of regularity it was, about assemblages of conditions and plurality of causes. His account bears only upon the status of such regularity: it purports to show that, and why, the rules in accordance with which changes are seen as occurring are strictly universal, are not merely of the form 'All *C*s so far observed have been followed by *E*s' with inductive extrapolations forever plagued by sceptical doubts. But, as Kant says, the question is not merely 'whether the concept of cause is correct, useful, and in respect of all knowledge of nature indispensable': even Hume did not doubt or deny this. The question raised by Hume was whether this concept 'is thought *a priori* by reason, and in this way has an inner truth independent of all experience and hence . . . [is] not limited merely to objects of experience',[6] and what Kant claims to have shown is that 'these concepts' (including those of substance and community as well as that of cause) 'and the principles drawn from them' (for example, that everything that happens 'presupposes something upon which it follows according to a rule') 'stand *a priori* before all experience and have their undoubted objective rightness, though admittedly only in respect of experience'.[7]

I shall examine this claim; but also, since modern commentators like Bennett[8] and Strawson,[9] after pointing to many fallacies and obscurities in Kant's own arguments, have offered other arguments in their place which are still Kantian in spirit, use Kantian materials, and purport to establish conclusions which are at least close to part of what Kant tried to establish, I shall also consider whether any such replacement arguments yield important conclusions about causation.

There is a preliminary puzzle about the apriority of concepts as opposed to principles. Even if a concept were *a priori* in the sense of not being derived from experience, it is hard to see how this would help. How would being 'thought *a priori* by reason' give it an 'inner truth'? Surely the crucial question is whether the concept is *applicable*, either to experience or to some kind of non-experienced entities, and it will be some *principle* that states that it is so applicable. On the other hand it is conceivable that such a principle should have some *a priori* justification without being itself universal in form: there might be good *a priori* reasons for expecting some alterations to take place in accordance with some, possibly only approximate, regularities, even if there were not good *a priori* reasons for expecting all alterations to conform to strict laws. This would not have suited Kant, both for temperamental reasons and because it would not have supplied the desired foundation for Newtonian science; but it is a live option for modern thought.

But *how* could such a principle be *a priori*? Not by being demonstrable as an analytic or logical truth: that is a possibility which Hume has, as Kant admits, conclusively ruled out. What we need is a transcendental argument, to show that the principle is necessarily presupposed in our experience. But this can itself be taken in either of two ways, with or without Kant's transcendental idealism. With the idealism, we could say that the principle was necessarily true of the content of our experience

[7] Ibid., 311.   [8] Jonathan Bennett, *Kant's Analytic*.
[9] P. F. Strawson, *The Bounds of Sense*.

because that content itself had somehow been constructed in accordance with it, and was proved by Kant's system to have been so constructed. Without the idealism, on Strawson's 'austere interpretation', the principle, or the corresponding concept, would be merely 'an essential structural element in any conception of experience which we could make intelligible to ourselves'.[10] Its being true of the world we know, the world of science and common sense, would not be guaranteed by anything we knew or could prove about that world itself. For once we reject the transcendental idealism and say that the world we are concerned with is genuinely objective, completely real and not merely 'empirically real but transcendentally ideal', nothing founded solely upon presuppositions of our experience can be authoritative about it. All that would be shown would be that it was idle for us to speculate about the possible falsity of the principle in question, since a world for which it was false would lie, for us, beyond the scope of investigation and beyond the scope of coherent detailed speculation.

If such a principle were known *a priori*, how would this help? Would this put any necessity into individual causal sequences, or allow us to infer a particular effect from a particular cause? For this would we not require *a priori* knowledge of particular causal laws, such as Newton's law of gravitation? Yet Kant explicitly denies, in the *Critique*, that these are known *a priori*. An answer which Kant does not give explicitly, but to which he seems to be committed, is that the *a priori* knowledge of the general principle that every change is covered by some regularity would somehow help us to discover and establish particular causal laws. Such an answer could be developed and defended by constructing something like Mill's methods of induction (or the improvements on them suggested in Chapter 3 and in the Appendix) and showing how particular causal laws can be *deduced* from limited observations taken in conjunction with an appropriate general assumption. In this way empirical causal laws could be given a strict universality that enabled us to apply them with certainty to unobserved instances, whereas

[10] *The Bounds of Sense*, p. 68. The passage in *Prolegomena*, 259, partly quoted on p. 90 above, shows that Kant himself would have been thoroughly dissatisfied with such an austere interpretation: it would leave him saying no more than that, in his view, Hume had already admitted.

observation and truly inductive reasoning alone could not give them such strict universality. But Kant nowhere develops such an answer. All he does is to argue for the apriority of the general causal principle itself.

Arguments relevant to this problem are to be found in two places in the *Critique of Pure Reason*, the Transcendental Deduction and the Second Analogy. Let us consider them in turn.

The Transcendental Deduction is, as Strawson says, not only an argument but also 'an explanation, a description, a story'.[11] In the latter respect it belongs to what he unkindly calls 'the imaginary subject of transcendental psychology'.[12] As Bennett remarks,[13] this chapter in the first edition was 'desperately ill-written', and the second edition version 'is only marginally clearer'. Nevertheless, we can sort out at least the main drift of the argument as distinct from the 'story', though its precise interpretation is much more difficult. Kant himself provides a summary:[14]

The manifold given in a sensible intuition is necessarily subject to the original synthetic unity of apperception, because in no other way is the *unity* of intuition possible (§ 17). But that act of understanding by which the manifold of given representations . . . is brought under one apperception, is the logical function of judgement (cf. § 19). All the manifold, therefore, so far as it is given in a single empirical intuition, is *determined* in respect of one of the logical functions of judgement, and is thereby brought into one consciousness. Now the *categories* are just those functions of judgement, in so far as they are employed in determination of the manifold of a given intuition (cf. § 13). Consequently, the manifold in a given intuition is necessarily subject to the categories.

This is none too clear; but a paraphrase might run as follows:

(1) Any experience must include some plurality of sensory elements, and it must be possible for all these elements to be seen as owned by a single consciousness, by a self which is able to be self-conscious. (2) Only judgements bring elements together in a kind of experience that is thus potentially self-conscious. (3) Any experience, then, must be united by some form of judgement (some propositional form). (4) To fit into such a propositional form is to be subject to one of the categories. (5) Therefore, any experience is subject to the categories.

[11] Op. cit., p. 86. [12] Op. cit., p. 97. [13] *Kant's Analytic*, p. 100.
[14] B 143.

Kant explains that this conclusion, that the categories are valid *a priori* for all objects of experience, is meant to hold for any experience based on sensible, not intellectual, intuition, whether that sensible intuition is like ours or not; but (for us) 'only *our* sensible and empirical intuition can give [the categories] body and meaning'.[15]

It is clear that any categories for which this line of argument is to yield a deduction must be closely linked with the forms of judgement; that is, any determinate conclusion here would be parasitic not only upon the Metaphysical Deduction as stated but also upon that detailed development of it which Kant purposely omitted. But, what is far worse, the conclusion could at most be merely that every chunk of experience must be subject to *at least one* category, must be unified in at least one propositional form. There is nothing here to guarantee that any chunk, or even any larger body, of experience should be subject to *all* the categories, or even that every category should find some employment within experience. For all that this line of argument could show, a certain category, say that of cause and effect, might have no application at all within our experience. This argument, then, fails completely to establish or illuminate the status of causation.

Kant does, indeed, argue in the Metaphysical Deduction that since judgements of all twelve kinds can be made about any object, it must be subject to all the twelve categories. But 'can' is not enough. Unless all twelve forms of judgement are actually and necessarily used in uniting each item of experience, there is nothing to show that every experience must incorporate each of the categories.

This criticism would stand even if we accepted steps (1) to (3). In fact, they too are open to question. But this area of discussion becomes more important when we leave Kant's explicit argument and consider some of the other lines of thought which commentators have either found implicit in what Kant says or themselves constructed in a Kantian spirit.

Thus Bennett concedes to Kant the premiss that 'all suppositions about possible experience must concern experience which is owned and which is accompanied by self-consciousness'. He argues that although a non-reflective animal might have

[15] B 148–9, B 161.

experience, and consciousness, without self-consciousness, we could not envisage ourselves as having such experience.[16] This is too close for comfort to Berkeley's notorious argument that we cannot without contradiction conceive trees existing unconceived.[17] On the contrary, we can quite coherently envisage, that is, contemplate the possibility, *that we might have* consciousness without self-consciousness; though if we tried actually to imagine ourselves being unselfconscious there would be a contradiction between the imagining and the prescribed unselfconsciousness. But even if we, unnecessarily, follow Bennett and give Kant this premiss, how can he argue that 'if I am self-conscious I must have a mental history which I can bring under concepts'?[18] Bennett first tries to illustrate Kant's notion of intellectual synthesis by such examples as these: 'I am aware of the presence of something cold, and of something which hums; I consider the criteria for one thing's having two properties . . . and conclude that the cold thing is the humming thing, perhaps by identifying both with the tuning-fork which I see in my hand.' Or again, I synthesize two book-appearances by connecting them as appearances of a single book. In cases like these, as Bennett says, there is or may be something that could be described as an (empirical) act of synthesizing. But, he insists, nothing like this is involved in one's awareness of the unity of mental states in one's own mind. Kant seems to say that where a unity is not produced by an empirical act of synthesizing it must depend on a transcendental one, but Bennett, like Strawson, finds this sort of transcendental psychology totally unacceptable. Rejecting this 'genetic' interpretation of transcendental synthesis, he suggests that there is a better, 'analytic' interpretation: 'when someone is aware of a unity without having reasoned his way to this awareness, there is still a "transcendental synthesis" in the sense that the unified items must satisfy certain criteria for unity or identity, and the person concerned must have a grasp of those criteria',[19] and he argues that this applies even to being aware of mental states as one's own. Bennett suggests that on this analytic interpretation,

---

[16] *Kant's Analytic*, pp. 105–6.

[17] *Principles*, § 23, and First Dialogue: I have examined the fallacy in 'Self-Refutation; a Formal Analysis', *Philosophical Quarterly*, xiv (1964), 193–203.

[18] *Kant's Analytic*, p. 124. [19] Ibid., p. 113.

' "transcendental synthesis" refers to a conceptual complexity the grasp of which consists in a capacity for . . . empirical synthesis'.[20] He argues against Kant that the making of judgements does not *require* such a capacity: a dog, for example, can make judgements about the present without having 'the kind of intellectual capacity Kant needs for the later stages of his argument in the "Principles" chapter'.[21] But he says that a capacity for empirical synthesis is required for any awareness of a unity which involves judgements about the past, and that this is enough for Kant's argument, since 'Self-consciousness . . . entails a capacity to judge about the past, and so—by my argument in *Rationality*—entails the possession of a concept-exercising language'.[22]

We can summarize this argument: (1) Coherently conceivable experience requires self-consciousness. (2) Self-consciousness requires the capacity to judge about the past. (3) This capacity entails a command of concepts. (4) Therefore, any coherently conceivable experience would involve the use of concepts.

I have already queried the first step. The second, I think, when used in conjunction with the first, involves an equivocation about self-consciousness. There is a difference between the minimal self-consciousness, the reflective contemplation of an experience that one is having as an experience, which is the most that the (fallacious) Berkeleian argument for (1) would even purport to show to be required, and the full-blooded consciousness of a persisting self which would require judgements about the past.

These criticisms may be reinforced by a general doubt about the kind of argument proposed. The steps are intended to be progressive, to constitute an advance. The various premisses of the form 'X requires Y' are therefore not meant to be analytic. And yet if they are not analytic, by what are they supported? Presumably by a kind of thought-experiment: one tries to imagine coherently what it would be like to have X without Y, but fails. I suggest that such failures (if not due to analytic impossibilities, which will build up to a progressive argument only with the help of equivocations) can result from, and reveal, nothing more than the limitations of our imagination,

[20] *Kant's Analytic*, p. 115.   [21] Ibid., p. 116.   [22] Ibid., pp. 116–17.

the difficulty that we find in going far beyond the forms of our actual experience. I want to suggest that there are various possible forms of experience, to our coherent conceiving of which there are only contingent, psychological, barriers. As Bennett admits, there could *be* consciousness without self-consciousness. Indeed even Kant admits this possibility, though he disparages it: 'merely a blind play of representations, less even than a dream'[23]—which, he says, would not then 'belong to any experience'. As Bennett admits, though Kant does not, there could be judgement without self-consciousness. Again, there could be minimal self-consciousness without awareness of oneself as a being with a past. And so on, in opposition to the various synthetic but allegedly transcendental premises of whatever argument of this sort we are examining. Whereas the aim of a transcendental argument (as Strawson, quoted above, has said) is to reveal 'an essential structural element in any conception of experience which we could make intelligible to ourselves', I suggest that it will succeed in revealing only a very pervasive structural feature of our actual experience. Only the limits of our imagination, along with equivocations which allow the same verbal formulations to express now analytic truths, now synthetic claims, and into which it is all too easy to fall in a complex, highly abstract, and obscure discussion, make what is pervasively actual seem essential.

It is, of course, obvious that even if we waived all these objections and accepted Bennett's conclusion (4) above, that any coherently conceivable experience would involve the use of concepts, we would not have shown that any specific concept, such as that of cause and effect, is applicable to any, let alone to all, of our experience. That task is reserved for the Analytic of Principles, in particular for the Second Analogy.

Strawson explores and develops, more fully than Bennett, Kant's anti-Cartesian notion that I can be aware of myself as a single subject of experience only by being aware of a unified world. Considering the Transcendental Deduction as an argument, he says that 'its fundamental premise is that experience contains a diversity of elements (intuitions) which, in the case of each subject of experience, must somehow be united in a single consciousness capable of judgement, capable, that is, of

23 *Critique*, A 112.

conceptualizing the elements so united' and that 'its general conclusion is that this unity requires another kind of unity or connectedness on the part of the multifarious elements of experience, namely just such a unity as is also required for experience to have the character of experience of a unified objective world, and hence to be capable of being articulated in objective empirical judgements'.[24] This formulation seems to me to mingle intermediate steps with both the premiss and the conclusion. The intended argument may be set out more distinctly as follows, using others of Strawson's formulations: (1) Any coherently conceivable experience must contain elements, experiences, which are 'subject to whatever condition is required for it to be *possible* for [the subject] to ascribe them to himself as *his* experiences'.[25] (2) 'Unity of diverse experiences in a single consciousness requires experience of objects';[26] 'for a series of diverse experiences to belong to a single consciousness it is necessary that they should be so connected as to constitute a temporally extended experience of a unified objective world'.[27] (3) If we ask 'How in general must we conceive of objects if we are to be able to make judgements, determinable as true or false, in which we predicate concepts of identified objects of reference, *conceived of as related in a single unified spatio-temporal system*?' or equivalently 'What in general must be true of a world of objects, so conceived, of which we make such judgements?', we shall in answering these questions 'simultaneously find our *a priori* concepts or categories and the guarantee of their application'. But these 'will be the schematized categories we actually employ in the spatio-temporal world', not the unschematized ones which Kant 'envisaged as discoverable with the help of the clue provided by formal logic',[28] that is, as in the Metaphysical Deduction, and as applicable to *any* sensible intuition, however unlike our own. (4) Therefore, any coherently conceivable experience must be such that the schematized categories are applicable to it.

Or, sacrificing accuracy to brevity: (1) Coherently conceivable experience requires unity in a single consciousness. (2) What is united in a single consciousness must be experience of a unified objective world. (3) Experience of a unified

[24] *The Bounds of Sense*, p. 87.   [25] Ibid., p. 98.   [26] Ibid.
[27] Ibid., p. 97.   [28] Ibid., p. 83.

objective world must be of a world seen as subject to the categories. (4) Therefore (as above).

(The remarks quoted in the fuller statement of (3) above occur in what Strawson describes as a sketch of an over-hasty argument. But his main comment is that it is undesirable that the argument should *immediately* follow these lines, and that 'a major part of the role of the Deduction will be to *establish* that experience necessarily involves knowledge of *objects*, and hence to displace that thesis from the status of prior definition, or premised assumption, of the inquiry'.[29] Given that under-pinning, these remarks can represent a step in a line of argument which Strawson thinks respectable, though it is not one which Kant actually completed in the Transcendental Deduction.)

But are these premisses (1), (2), and (3) true? Strawson's (1) is weaker than Bennett's, and might therefore be more defensible: Strawson does not say that each item of experience must be accompanied by self-consciousness, but only that it must be possible for the subject to ascribe them to himself. Yet I can see no convincing reason for accepting this. Admittedly if there were (are?) creatures who had successive experiences but were incapable of self-consciousness, then as Strawson says 'We seem to add nothing but a form of words to [this hypothesis] by stipulating that [these experiences] all belong to a single consciousness';[30] still, we have no difficulty in conceiving that there should be such successions of experiences, even though the attempt to conceive *ourselves* as having them is self-refuting. But this issue is elusive; (2) gives rise to a much plainer dispute. Surely there could be a kind of experience which consisted of a sequence of impressions, with some memory, some recognition of similarities, but which gave no ground for any distinction between those impressions and their objects. Strawson considers this objection carefully. 'Certainly concepts, recognition, some span of memory would be necessary to a consciousness with any experience at all; and all these would involve one another. But why should the concepts not be simply such sensory quality concepts as figure in the early and limited sense-datum vocabulary? . . . The claim is that it is quite conceivable that experience should have as its contents...

[29] Ibid., pp. 85, 87.   [30] Ibid., p. 100.

impressions which neither require, nor permit of, being "united in the concept of an object".'[31] But he replies that 'it must be possible, even in the most fleeting and purely subjective of impressions, to distinguish a component of recognition'; and 'Recognition implies the *potential* acknowledgement of the experience into which recognition enters as being one's own'.[32] I am afraid that I simply cannot see this implication. Strawson adds that the fact that this potentiality is implicit in recognition 'saves the recognitional component . . . from absorption into the item recognized . . . even when that item cannot be conceived of as having an existence independent of the particular experience of it'.[33] I would agree that the recognizing that an experience is of a certain sort, or resembles some remembered earlier experience, must be something other than the experience itself: this recognizing, we might say, has the experience as its object even where the experience itself has no object. It thus introduces an awareness/object distinction where at first none was allowed. But I cannot see that this has anything to do with the potential *acknowledgement* of the experience as one's own. But the crucial step is the next.

The minimum implied [by the potentiality of such an acknowledgement] is that some at least of the concepts under which particular experienced items are recognized as falling should be such that the experiences themselves contain the basis for certain allied distinctions: individually, the distinction of a subjective component *within* a judgement of experience (as 'it seems to me as if this is a heavy stone' is distinguishable within 'this is a heavy stone'); collectively, the distinction *between* the subjective order and arrangement of a series of such experiences on the one hand and the objective order and arrangement of the items of which they are experiences on the other.[34]

Now this has some plausibility. The acknowledgement 'This is mine'—that is, my experience, my idea, my impression—can have point only where a contrast with what is not-mine—an objective reality, or perhaps the experience of some other subject—is implied and can at least occasionally be implemented. But as soon as we realize that this is what the 'acknowledgement' involves, we must be more reluctant than ever to concede the previous claim that recognizing that an experience is of a certain sort, or resembles some earlier one, carries with it the possibility of acknowledgement of the experience as one's own. Whereas Strawson says that 'the thesis of the necessary unity of consciousness can itself be represented as resting on a yet more fundamental premise—on nothing more than the necessity, for any experience at all to be possible, of the original duality of intuition and concept',[35] I think that this last-mentioned necessity cannot bear the weight of the superstructure Strawson erects upon it.

Strawson sums up his criticism of 'the sense-datum theorist's conception of a possible experience' as follows:

> If such an experience were possible, then a series of corresponding judgements of experience would be possible. But a set of such judgements would yield no picture of a world of objects the relations of which are distinct from the relations of experiences of them. Hence it would provide no basis either for the conception of an experiential route through such a world or for the isolation of the subjective, experiential component in individual judgements. Hence it would provide no basis for the necessary self-reflexiveness of experience, which is in its turn the essential core of the possibility of self-ascription of experiences. Hence the theorist has not succeeded in producing a description of a possible experience.[36]

The first three sentences here can be accepted as merely spelling out the sense-datum theorist's hypothesis. We can agree, too, that the hypothetical experience would provide no basis for self-ascription in the sense in which this involves a contrast between 'mine' and 'not-mine'. But we must hesitate over 'necessary self-reflexiveness'. Granting that any conceivable experience will somehow include the duality of intuition and concept—or, more simply, particular items being, and being seen as being, of certain sorts—that it must be reflexive in the sense of containing a 'component of recognition', it does not follow and it is not true that it must be reflexive in the sense of making self-ascription possible.

There is, I believe, a fundamental flaw in Kant's argument which survives in Strawson's reconstructions. Even though the various 'representations' must *in fact belong* to a single consciousness in the sense that they are remembered, compared, and so on, it does not follow that they must be *seen as belonging* to a single consciousness in the sense in which this carries with it the contrast between 'mine' and 'not-mine', subjective and objective, and methods of at least sometimes implementing this contrast.

But what has all this to do with causation? Directly, very little. As Strawson says, 'for anything detailed or specific by way of conclusion, [Kant's argument] depends entirely on the derivation of a list of categories from the forms of judgement. We can place no reliance on this derivation.'[37] Even if we could rely on this derivation, Kant's argument, as we have seen, would at best prove that every experience embodies some category, and does not guarantee any application at all for any specific category, such as causation. The conclusion which Strawson says we are left with reason for entertaining favourably is 'that any course of experience of which we can form a coherent conception must be, potentially, the experience of a self-conscious subject and, as such, must have such internal, concept-carried connectedness as to constitute it (at least in part) a course of experience of an objective world, conceived of as determining the course of that experience itself'.[38] This is still a long way from a vindication of the category of causation. Even if we accepted what Kant, or Bennett, or Strawson hopes to extract from the Transcendental Deduction, the vindication of any such specific category would be left for the Analytic of Principles. Yet it is not quite beside the point to draw attention to weaknesses in the preliminary argument. If Kant or Bennett or Strawson were right, the Transcendental Deduction would at least set the stage for the Second Analogy: it would lead us to suppose that the transcendental method had already yielded some general requirements, and that a further pursuit of the same method might well yield some more specific ones. But if my criticisms of these preliminary arguments are correct, the prospect for detailed successes is much less promising.

Kant's argument in the Second Analogy is very repetitive, the same point being made over and over again in various forms, sometimes directly and sometimes by way of a *reductio ad absurdum*, but unlike the Transcendental Deduction it is not tortured or tortuous, and there is no great difficulty in under-

---

[37] *The Bounds of Sense*, p. 117.   [38] Ibid.

standing what he says. He sets out to prove that all alterations
(in the phenomenal world, the world of science and of common
sense) take place in accordance with causal laws: 'Everything
that . . . begins to be, presupposes something upon which it
follows according to a rule.'[39] His proof may be summarized
as follows: If I see a ship move downstream, I have a succession
of subjective impressions. But if I survey the various parts of a
house I also have a succession of subjective impressions. What
makes the difference between those sequences of impressions
which I interpret as representing an objective process or
sequence of events and those which I interpret as representing
the coexisting parts of a persisting object? It is that the order
in which the impressions succeed one another is in the one case
determined and irreversible, it is a *necessary* order, whereas in
the other case the order in which the impressions succeed one
another might well be reversed. That is, a sequence of impressions which I interpret as representing an objective succession
must conform to some rule which prescribes an objective order
from which the subjective order is derived. Consequently, it is
only conformity to such a rule which enables me to establish
an objective succession; hence all alterations in the phenomenal world, which we take to be objective, must take place
in accordance with rules.[40]

   This argument as stated provokes some objections, by
examining which we can bring out its substance more clearly.
There is what Strawson calls the simple-minded objection that
the subjective order of impressions in Kant's ship example is
not in fact irreversible: ships move upstream as well as downstream, and even a ship which is pointing downstream may be
carried upstream by the tide or towed upstream by a tug which
I cannot see. Kant must reply that all he means is that when
on a particular occasion I do see a ship move downstream I am
not *then* free to have the impression of its lower position before
I have the impression of its higher one. But there are cases
where I do have such freedom. There is what Strawson calls
the more sophisticated objection that if I am, say, watching a
man chopping through a log on the far side of a valley from
me, I shall see the halves of the log fall apart before I hear
the last stroke of the axe, whereas if I had been close by I

[39] A 189.   [40] Précis of A 189–94, B 233–9.

should have received these impressions of sight and sound in the reverse order. To meet this Kant must, as Strawson suggests, reply that the order of perceptions will be irreversible provided that they are equally direct and in the same sensory mode.[41] But even if these cracks can be papered over, the argument seems to proceed, as Strawson says, 'by a *non sequitur* of numbing grossness'.[42] The fact that the order of impressions (on a particular occasion) was not one which I was free to reverse does not imply that either they, or an objective sequence of which they are perceptions, took place in accordance with a rule. Kant's argument turns upon a blatant fallacy of equivocation, a play upon two different senses of the word 'necessary'. An order which is necessary as not being reversible in the particular case need not be necessary as in accordance with some universal rule or law.

The fallacy is indeed so gross that we may wonder how Kant can have been guilty of it. There are several things that help to explain, if not to excuse, it.

First, the fallacy stands out only when, in response to the 'simple-minded objection', we have pinned down the kind of irreversibility involved in such an example as that of the ship. Another kind of irreversibility may have clouded the issue, though it would not really help Kant's case. Kant may have been thinking vaguely of the kind of sequence where one *always* has a perception of one sort before, not after, one of another sort: the perception of a spark, say, precedes and does not follow that of an explosion. Of course, as we have noted in Chapter 3, we do not really encounter such unqualified simple regularities. But even if we did, the key step in the argument would still be unsound. Kant would be saying, in effect: it is only where my perceptions of *A*s have so far been regularly followed, not preceded, by my perceptions of *B*s that I can interpret each (perception-of-an-*A*)–(perception-of-a-*B*) sequence as a perception of an objective *A*–*B* sequence, therefore it is only because there is a rule which ensures that *A*s are followed by *B*s with strict universality (not just so far) that I can see each *B* as following its *A* in an objective time-order. And even if the premiss were true, this would still be a *non sequitur*. The problem of how to distinguish an objective from a subjective succession contributes nothing to the bridging of the inductive gap between regularity-so-far and an unqualified universal rule.

Secondly, if on some particular occasion a ship has moved downstream, so that (given the stipulations that exclude our simple-minded and sophisticated objections) I had to have the impression of its higher position before having the impression of its lower one, this necessity-for-me arises indeed from 'some fact of causation', namely from the causal links between the ship's being in each position and my impression of it in that position, conjoined with the simple fact that its higher position is earlier than its lower one. But although causal necessity thus comes in somewhere, it does not come in where Kant wants it, namely between the ship's occupancy of its higher and of its lower position, or between some events that underlie and determine this sequence. Even if the sequence of these two situations were the purest accident, the necessity-for-me, the irreversibility of the order of my impressions (given our stipulations) would be no less rigid.

But thirdly, and most significantly, there is at least a hint of a second argument on which Kant may be relying. Suppose that I am presented with a sequence of impressions; they come in a subjective time-order, but I have not even a prima facie reason for interpreting this subjective order as a copy or even an indication of an objective order; how then can I put them together in something that I can treat as an objective order of events, either the same as or different from the subjective order of the impressions? Surely I can do so only if there is some intrinsic rightness about one possible order as contrasted with any other. It is as if I were handed the pieces of a linear jigsaw puzzle in some order which might or might not be that in which I was to put them together. Surely I could put them together with confidence in one order rather than another only if either their shapes, or the bits of pictures on them, indicated which piece would join on to which, and which way round. And if I were presented with several sequences of impressions, each sequence in a subjective order, I could put together as representing objective sequences of events only those sequences of impressions among whose members I could detect some intrinsic rightness of some possible order.

This clearly is a different argument from the one we have been discussing, and it does not incorporate the *non sequitur* that Strawson finds so shocking. But it has other fatal flaws. The story told obviously misrepresents our empirical intellectual history. We are, fortunately, not confronted in infancy with sequences of impressions whose subjective order is out of all relation to the objective time-order of events: while some are indeed successive perceptions of coexisting parts of persisting things, others are successive perceptions of the successive phases of processes in the right order. And we are helped in deciding which are which—or rather, in fairly automatically arriving at a view of the world in which such a decision is implicit—by the fact that the impression-sequences that belong to coexisting parts are reversible in the simple sense that impressions of recognizably the same parts often come in different orders (wall–window–door, window–wall–door, door–wall–window, and so on) while at least some impression-sequences that belong to processes exhibit a fair degree of repetition of similar phases in the same order, they are 'irreversible' in the sense considered three paragraphs back. To save the present argument, Kant would have to retreat from empirical into transcendental psychology, claiming (as he would be very willing to do) that the human mind—not in infancy but somehow out of time altogether—is confronted with a task analogous to that of our jigsaw puzzle, of constructing a world of objects from a manifold of representations, and for all we know it may get no help in this from any initial subjective time-order. But then this argument requires the transcendental psychology, the 'genetic' interpretation of intellectual synthesis, about which modern commentators are so sceptical. But even if we waived this scepticism, the argument would still fail. For clearly it requires that there should be some intrinsic rightness about particular sequences, in other words, that particular causal laws should be knowable, indeed known, *a priori*. They would constitute the design in accordance with which we had (transcendentally) constructed the phenomenal world. But this conflicts with the actual procedures of science, especially with the Newtonian science whose foundations Kant thought that he was making secure, and with what he explicitly says in the *Critique*. 'Certainly, empirical laws, as such, can never derive their origin from pure understanding.'

'To obtain any knowledge whatsoever of these special laws, we must resort to experience.' It is true that he says also that 'all empirical laws are only special determinations of the pure laws of understanding', and that 'The laws of nature, indeed, one and all, without exception, stand under higher principles of understanding. They simply apply the latter to special cases [in the field] of appearance.'[43] These last remarks are unclear, and they might mean that particular causal laws are only applications of higher pure laws to concrete situations, that a particular law—perhaps of the form 'There are As and they are regularly followed by Bs'—is a logical consequence of the conjunction of a pure law with the proposition that there are As, so that the latter is the only information for which we need to resort to experience. If this were so, then the pure laws would in themselves be sufficient to constitute the design in accordance with which we had (transcendentally) constructed the time-order of events. But even if Kant meant this, it could not be reconciled with the actual procedures of science. A more defensible interpretation, to which, as I have said, Kant seems to be committed, would be illustrated by our account of the Method of Difference and of the other eliminative methods of induction.[44] A particular law of nature 'stands under' a general principle of uniformity if it can be inferred from such a principle in conjunction with the empirical fact that certain related groupings of features occur, such as those set out as I_1 and N_1 in our classical difference observation. But now the law of nature is not even knowable *a priori*, and Kant's argument would again fail.

This second argument, then, will not do. Neither it, nor the previous one, nor the conjunction of the two, will really serve Kant's purpose, but the deficiencies of each may have been partly concealed from him by the simultaneous operation of the other within his thinking.

Bennett distinguishes two arguments in the Second Analogy, 'the object/process argument', which is our first, and 'the ordering argument', which is roughly equivalent to our second.[45]

---

[43] A 127, B 165, A 159, B 198; cf. Strawson, op. cit., p. 116. Bennett, op. cit., pp. 157-9. In the *Opus Postumum* Kant says that some particular laws are knowable *a priori*, but this is not his view in the *Critique*.

[44] Chapter 3 and Appendix.   [45] *Kant's Analytic*, pp. 222-9.

He says that the latter 'occurs in fragments, just below the surface of Kant's text', that 'several parts of the text become more intelligible if they are seen to be coloured by a subliminal awareness of the ordering argument'. I would agree, but since it is below the surface, the precise interpretation of this argument is open to dispute. Bennett frees it from dependence upon transcendental psychology, upon a 'genetic' interpretation of intellectual synthesis, and also from implausible empirical claims about the intellectual achievements of infants, by relating it to memory: how am I to recollect digging in the garden *before* having a bath? The suggestion is that to do this 'I must be able to appeal to objective considerations' such as 'the behaviour of clocks, or the fact that I always have a bath after gardening, or the fact that the mud which I recall washing off in the bath could only have come from my digging in the garden'. As an interpretation of Kant, I find this implausible (though I accept Bennett's point that the ordering argument, unlike the object/process one, applies as much to the order of experiences as to the order of objective events); but how good is it as an argument in its own right? As Bennett says, the thesis that remembered temporal order depends on such objective considerations does not hold without exceptions: he mentions three ways in which the order of a pair of events can be *simply recalled*. First, we may 'recall a specious present containing both'. Secondly, we may recall a sequence of happenings, $A–B–C–D–E$ say, where each contiguous pair is recalled as belonging to one specious present. Thirdly, 'One may simply recall that X preceded Y by recalling a time when one experienced Y while recalling X.' Still, as he says, these exceptions leave a lot of work to be done by the objective, causal considerations. But, Bennett rightly concludes, this thesis will not suffice to establish Kant's principle that all alterations take place in accordance with laws. It merely illustrates what Hume would have been happy to admit, that causation in addition to being 'to us, the cement of the universe', constitutes, to us, the reinforcing rods as well.

Most of what Kant says in the later paragraphs of the Second Analogy merely restates the same two basic arguments though with some picturesque touches. 'Now since absolute time is not an object of perception, this determination of position cannot be derived from the relation of appearances to it. On the contrary, the appearances must determine for one another their position in time, and make their time-order a necessary order.'[46] That is, the Newtonian time-axis is not visible, with a series of dates marked off along it, nor do events come to our perception with their dates stamped on them. But this only raises the question how we arrive at an objective time-order: to get an answer Kant must use one or other, or both, of the arguments already discussed.

Kant does, however, mention a difficulty which is of some interest.[47] How is he to reconcile his thesis that causation supplies objective time-order with the fact that causes are sometimes simultaneous with their effects, indeed that 'the great majority of efficient natural causes' are so. Kant's reply that it is the *order*, not the *lapse*, of time that matters, and that the order can persist even where the interval between cause and effect is a vanishing quantity, is unconvincing. He correctly illustrates the sort of experiment that reveals a direction of causation: 'if I lay a ball on the cushion, a hollow follows upon the previous flat smooth shape; but if (for any reason) there previously exists a hollow in the cushion, a leaden ball does not follow upon it'. This shows, indeed, how causal priority is established between simultaneous cause and effect (the ball *resting* on the cushion, and the *hollow*) where these are as it were continuations of events between which there is a temporal succession (the ball *being placed* on the cushion and the cushion *sinking* in the middle). But such examples still falsify the thesis that causal order is what constitutes objective temporal order.

Kant also discusses 'the law of the continuity of all alteration', and attempts an *a priori* deduction of it. What he actually says is of little value, but this point and the previous one show that he was aware of certain aspects of causation that call for further attention, such as I shall attempt to give in Chapters 7 and 8.

Strawson points out the crucial fallacy in the object/process argument; he does not bring out any version of the ordering argument; but he does make 'another attempt' at an *a priori* vindication of causality. 'If the direct arguments of both second and third Analogies fail, . . . it does not follow that the problem of the Analogies cannot be advanced at all, and advanced in something like a Kantian direction, with the help of materials

<hr>

[46] A 200 = B 245.   [47] A 202-3 = B 247-9.

which Kant puts at our disposal.'[48] The argument which Strawson suggests may be summarized as follows: (1) If there were no currently unperceived, but perceivable, objects co-existing with objects of actual perception, there would be no effective distinction between objective and subjective time-orders.[49] (2) There can be such unperceived coexisting objects only if we perceive some things as relatively persistent things of certain kinds, in some spatial or quasi-spatial framework of relations.[50] (3) If we also have the idea of perceived objective succession or change (that is, if we can sometimes conceive a change in our perceptions as the perception of a change) our concepts of persistent objects must be concepts of objects which are capable of changing without changing out of all recognition: there may be some random changes, but only against a background of regular persistences and alterations.[51] (4) Some changes in perceptions 'exhibit a regular correlation with change of the observer's position and his sense-orientation . . . Without some such correlation it is impossible to see how notions of enduring and reidentifiable objects of changing perception could secure application in the observer's experience. But the possibility of this correlation in turn seems to depend upon changes and persistences in the world of objects being themselves subject to some kind and degree of order and regularity.'[52] (5) Our concepts of objects, therefore, '[are] necessarily compendia of causal law or law-likeness, carry implications of causal power or dependence. Powers, as Locke remarked . . . make up a great part of our idea of substances. More generally, they must make up a great part of our concepts of any persisting and re-identifiable objective items. And without some such concepts as these, no experience of an objective world is possible.'[53]

My fundamental unease about this argument is the same as that which I expressed about the Transcendental Deduction. Is not Strawson misreading pervasively actual features of our experience as essential? On (5), for example, we can concede that powers, dispositional properties, *do* make up a great part

---

[48] *The Bounds of Sense*, p. 140.   [49] Ibid., p. 141.   [50] Ibid., p. 142.
[51] Ibid., pp. 143–4.   [52] Ibid., p. 144.
[53] Ibid., pp. 145–6; Locke's actual words (*Essay*, Book II, Chapter 23, Sections 8, 10) are: '. . . powers make a great part of our complex ideas of substances . . .'.

of our concepts of objects: but *must* they do so? Could not our experience of an objective world have been one of objects each of which persisted for a while, with little change, then ceased to exist, which did not interact much, and whose changes and ceasings to be were unpredictable? A Lockean would reply that if these are *perceived* objects, they must at least have regular powers to produce 'ideas', 'impressions', or something of the sort, in us. But many philosophers have tried, however perversely, to get along without a causal theory of perception: it would be strange if it now turned out to be an *a priori* truth. It may be a quibble, and it certainly would not affect the general outcome of Strawson's argument, but is even (2) strictly true? Could not a sufficient degree of regularity in successive phases of continuous processes enable us to dispense with persistent *things*? And if my criticisms of Strawson's reconstruction of the Transcendental Deduction have any force, we cannot now use as a premiss the penultimate conclusion of that argument, that any coherently conceivable experience must be of a unified objective world.

But what is perhaps most worth noting is how little of Kant's grand scheme would be left even if Strawson's arguments went through. Strawson offers only 'the necessary but loosely woven mesh of our concepts of the objective'. Kant's 'two absolute thoughts—of *strictly sufficient* conditions for *every* objective change'—are not necessary thoughts but only natural hopes, 'a pressing to the limit of those truly indispensable but altogether looser conditions' for which Strawson has argued.[54] We have not perfect conformity to a precisely derivable set of schematized categories, but just *some* persistence and *some* regularity in a world that we can treat as objective.

But perhaps this is not so bad. We do not feel, as Kant did, the need to lay philosophical foundations for Newtonian physics. Modern science, in some of its aspects, would be positively embarrassed by an *a priori* proof of strict universal determinism, and yet might welcome a presumption of some regularity, some persistence.

More serious is the change in the status of the conclusion. Having rejected Kant's transcendental idealism, Strawson can claim that even these modest regularities are necessary only

[54] Ibid., p. 146.

in the sense that we cannot coherently conceive a mode of experience without them. But is this any sort of safeguard, any defence against scepticism? For example, does it protect us against Hume's scepticism about induction? Surely not. The Humean sceptic can still say 'Induction seems to have worked all right so far, some inductive conclusions have been further confirmed, many of our more carefully reached predictions have been fulfilled; but that only shows that the world so far has shown a degree of regularity that matches the Strawsonian requirements; from now on, perhaps, everything will go wrong.' And it is not much comfort to be able to reply: 'You can't say in detail, or even imagine, what it would be like if everything went wrong.' It is true that sceptics are commonly unjustifiably selective in their scepticism: they are liable to suppose that the regularities which are involved in the continued existence and broad relative location of things, in our own existence, and in our perceiving of what is there, will survive, but that those which we more immediately classify as causal may go wrong. If so, they can be convicted of arbitrariness; but the thorough-going sceptic is not so easily defeated.

There is, nevertheless, some point in the exposure of selective scepticism. Since we can show that presumptions of some degree of regularity are involved in our ordinary concepts of things and of their largely dispositional properties, we can criticize as arbitrary any unwillingness to grant a similar presumption in favour of what we need as the assumption in some particular application of the Method of Difference or of one of the related methods. For, as we have seen in Chapter 3, such an application does not require the complete uniformity of nature, but only some local regularity, and we can use this as a working assumption so long as there is some initial reason for adopting it, without needing to claim that it is certain and indeed while being prepared to give it up if the empirical evidence is hostile. But it seems to me that to make this point one needs only to bring out the extent to which causal regularities are involved in our actual picture of a world of objective persisting things, not to add Strawson's disputable claim that the conditions for which he has argued are indispensable in the sense that any coherently conceivable experience must satisfy them.

I conclude that neither Kant's explicit arguments nor the

KANT AND TRANSCENDENTALISM

general Kantian approach contribute much to our understanding of causation. The attempt to establish the general causal principle as valid *a priori* for the objects of experience (and so to vindicate the universality of particular causal laws in a way that would be proof against Humean doubts about induction) has failed, and the claim that weaker principles of regularity can—without invoking transcendental idealism—be shown to be still in some way necessary turns out to be questionable and in any case not very useful. And, as we noted, Kant does not even attempt a transcendental deduction of those other still puzzling features of our ordinary concept of causation, the notions of causal priority and of an intimate tie between individual cause and individual effect, nor do his recent commentators.

There is, indeed, one clue—no more than that—which might be worth following. Kant's chapter on Schematism offers an obscure solution to an equally obscure problem, namely how the pure categories, which are supposed to have been generated by the forms of judgement, can apply to sensory appearances. The solution is that time somehow mediates between the intellectual and the sensible and produces the schematized categories of substance, causation, and the like. These are the categories which we actually use, and these, because they essentially involve time, will fit on to the objects of sensory experience. But related to Kant's obscure problem there is, for us, a more pressing question. We have found that certain conditional statements are prominent in the analysis of causal beliefs—these are the counterpart to Kant's attempt to derive the pure category from the hypothetical form of judgement. We have been able to relate these to certain psychological processes and also to certain (complex and incompletely known) regularities. But we have not yet linked them with the notion of a continuous closely knit process, with our spatio-temporal picture of a bit of causing going on. Perhaps if we did so link them we should have a counterpart to Kant's schematism.

Another point of some interest might be developed from Kant's suggestion in the Second Analogy that time is somehow dependent upon causation. As we have seen, he is concerned only with time-*order*; but a much stronger relation can be shown with respect to duration, to the metrical aspect of time.

Newton, in a famous passage, claimed that absolute time flows
equably;[55] but as Newton himself admitted, we cannot see it
flowing and cannot therefore measure it directly. If we observe
three successive instantaneous events A, B, and C, we cannot
directly inspect the durations between A and B and between
B and C, and so decide whether these intervals are equal or
whether one is longer than the other. So of course we have to
use what Newton calls relative time;[56] in other words, consult
a clock. Keep a pendulum swinging continuously and count
the swings between A and B, and between B and C, and compare these numbers. Another, perhaps better, clock is the rotating earth. See how often it rotates, or through what angle it
rotates, relative to the sun or to a fixed star, between A and B
and again between B and C. But of course the swinging of the
pendulum, or the rotating of the earth, is (in a broad sense) a
causal process. The presumption that if, and only if, the absolute
time intervals A–B and B–C are equal, our clock will go through
equal numbers (or quantities) of its characteristic performances
is one example of our general presumption of uniformity. But
causation also plays a further role. Our actual clocks are only
prima facie clocks; some of them, as Newton says, are certainly
inaccurate, and all of them may be.[57] But then do we just
arbitrarily choose one prima facie clock rather than another as
our criterion of the equality of durations? Certainly not. Or
do we take votes, and rely on majority verdicts, or average the
measurements supplied by all available prima facie clocks?
Not quite, though we may give the consilience of a number
of clocks some provisional, interim authority. Rather, if two
clocks disagree about the relative length of two durations, we
look for a causal explanation of the changed behaviour of at
least one of them—for example, if clock X measures A–B and
B–C as equal, while clock Y measures A–B as shorter than B–C,
we might explain this by finding that the pendulum of Y has

[55] *Principia* (1st edition), p. 5: Tempus absolutum verum et Mathematicum,
in se et natura sua absque relatione ad externum quodvis, aequabiliter fluit,
alioque nomine dicitur Duratio.

[56] Ibid.: relativum apparens et vulgare est sensibilis et externa quaevis Dura-
tionis per motum mensura, (seu accurata seu inaequabilis) qua vulgus vice veri
temporis utitur.

[57] Ibid., p. 7: Possibile est ut nullus sit motus aequabilis quo Tempus accurate
mensuretur.

contracted because it became colder round about time *B*, or that *X*, which is driven by a mainspring, was fully wound at *A* and has since been running down. We correct the measurements supplied by a clock where we find a causal explanation for a change in its behaviour; that is, we no longer take its rotations or oscillations or whatever it may be as simple and direct indications of the equable flow of absolute time.

This is what we in fact do. It is not, indeed, the only thing that we could do. It has a more plausible claim than any alternative procedure I can think of would have to give us progressive approximations to accurate measurements of absolute duration. There are admittedly still problems about the philosophical interpretation of what we thus achieve. But this procedure illustrates, far more strikingly than anything to which Kant draws attention, the way in which causal notions and causal discovery compensate for the lack of a visibly graduated Newtonian time-axis. But this too, it seems to me, shows not that causation is in any worthwhile sense *a priori* or transcendentally guaranteed, but only that it is a very important pervasive structural feature of our actual experience.

We might make one other small move in a Kantian direction. Though I insisted that Kant's second or ordering argument, taken empirically, misrepresents our intellectual history, and that in that history we are helped in arriving at our view of the world, in discriminating between processes and persisting complex objects, by the actual 'subjective' order of impressions, we may concede that we are helped also by certain innate tendencies or propensities in favour of some kinds of simplicity and regularity. An infant looking round a room has, it is plausible to suppose, some inborn reluctance to interpret what it sees as disorderly sequences—sometimes window followed by wall followed by door, sometimes door followed by wall followed by window, and so on. If the impressions come like this, they are more readily interpreted as showing one door, one window, and so on, each persisting much as it is; but if the infant has impressions that fit into the pattern of the same sort of process, the same type-sequence of phases, repeated on different occasions, then it will interpret these impressions as of processes. There may well be something, then, that could be described as *a priori* forms in terms of which empirical impressions are interpreted and ordered. But this kind of apriority is no guarantee of necessary truth. The causal beliefs that result when our actual sequences of impressions are interpreted in accordance with these *a priori* forms might still be 'bastards of the imagination fathered by experience'. Before we can say whether we can add to such innate propensities any genuine presumption in favour of some kind and some degree of regularity we must pay attention to those aspects of the causal relation which Kant brushed aside: how, if at all, causal laws differ from other universal truths; the link between individual cause and effect; and the direction of causation. When we have thus clarified the concept whose applicability is at issue we shall be better able to decide whether it is only an arbitrary prejudice, a quirk of our imaginations, to suppose that such relations actually hold.

5
Common Sense and the Law

ONE of the best studies that have been made of ordinary causal concepts is that by Hart and Honoré in *Causation in the Law.* Their discussion deals not only with legal applications of causal notions, but also with the common-sense concepts and their ordinary use, concentrating particularly on singular causal statements. It will therefore be a good test of the account which I have tried to develop in Chapters 2 and 3 to see how well it can either accommodate the points made by these authors or defend itself against them.

Hart and Honoré stress 'the possibility that the common notion of causation may have features which vary from context to context, that there may be different types of causal inquiry, and that there may not be a single concept of causation but rather a cluster of related concepts';[1] they argue, in fact, that these possibilities are realized.

In this cluster, the fundamental division is between those ordinary causal statements which assert 'that one physical event was caused by another such event or by a human action', and 'statements of interpersonal transactions [which] involve the notion of a person's reason for acting'. For the first class (which I shall refer to as *physical*) Mill's analysis is often at least approximately correct, but for the second (which I shall call *interpersonal*) something radically different is needed. However, there are also 'cases where causal language is used to indicate relationships different from either of these two main types but with important affinities to them'.

Where Hart and Honoré find only a cluster of related concepts, I would rather say that there is a single basic concept of causing to which various frills are added: there is one common

---
[1] *Causation in the Law*, p. 17.

kind of causing but with different accompaniments. Since we
have no well-established rules for counting concepts, this may
seem to be a dubious distinction; but we shall find that it
covers some substantial differences.

Hart and Honoré recognize Mill's improvements on Hume—
in admitting standing conditions, as opposed to events, as
causes, and in allowing for assemblages of conditions and for
plurality of causes, with the resulting complexity of generalizations. But they insist, rightly, that 'Mill's standard of "invariable
and unconditional sequence" cannot be met', that his doctrine
'presents an idealized model' even for the physical causation to
which it is more or less appropriate.[2] Our account has allowed
for this by noting, first, that causal regularities *as known* are
elliptical, and, secondly, that Mill's requirement of uncondi-
tionality was a misguided attempt to deal with the difficulty
that regularities of succession may fail to be causal, the correct
resolution of which involves the direction of causation.

Hart and Honoré say that 'Mill's description of common
sense "selecting" the cause from a set of conditions is a *suggestio
falsi* so far as . . . simple causal statements are concerned; for,
though we may gradually come to know more and more of the
conditions required for our interventions to be successful, we do
not "select" from them the one we treat as the cause. Our
intervention is regarded as the cause from the start before we
learn more than a few of the other necessary conditions. We
simply continue to call it the cause when we know more.'[3] This
is at least part of the truth; it is allowed for both by the analysis
suggested in Chapter 2, that a cause is 'necessary (and perhaps
also sufficient) in the circumstances' whatever those circumstances may be, and by the thesis of Chapter 3 that causal
regularities as known are elliptical, but in varying degrees.
They also argue that 'The line between cause and mere condition' (whose philosophical importance Mill denied) 'is . . .
drawn by common sense on principles which vary in a subtle
and complex way, both with the type of causal question at
issue and the circumstances in which causal questions arise . . .
two contrasts are of prime importance . . . [those] between what
is abnormal and what is normal in relation to any given thing

2 *Causation in the Law*, pp. 21, 41.
3 Ibid., p. 29; the point is also made more fully on pp. 42–3.

or subject-matter, and between a free deliberate human action and all other conditions'.[4] Developing the first of these they say that '. . . normal conditions (and hence in causal inquiries mere conditions) are those . . . which are present as part of the usual state or mode of operation of the thing under inquiry: some . . . will also be familiar, pervasive features of the environment, . . . present alike in the case of disaster and of normal functioning'. By contrast, 'What is abnormal . . . "makes the difference" between the accident and things going on as usual.'[5] Features which are normal in this sense are the ones which in Chapter 2 above were relegated to the causal field, and therefore not allowed to count as causes. Hart and Honoré stress the relativity to context of this contrast between the normal and the abnormal.[6] 'If a fire breaks out in a laboratory or in a factory, where special precautions are taken to exclude oxygen during part of an experiment or manufacturing process, since the success of this depends on safety from fire, there would be no absurdity at all in *such* a case in saying that the presence of oxygen was the cause of the fire. The exclusion of oxygen in such a case, and not its presence, is part of the normal functioning.' Again, 'The cause of a great famine in India may be identified by the Indian peasant as a drought, but the World Food authority may identify the Indian government's failure to build up reserves as the cause and the drought as a mere condition.' As I have put it, different fields may be chosen for causal accounts of the same event. What is normal may depend upon man-made norms: the gardener's failure to water the flowers caused their dying, being a deviation from a routine practice as well as a duty, but the failure of other people to water the flowers was normal and hence not a cause.[7] Hart and Honoré also show that 'A deliberate human act is . . . most often a barrier and a goal in tracing back causes . . . it is something *through* which we do not trace the cause of a later event and something *to* which we do trace the cause through intervening causes of other kinds.'[8] The presence of arsenic in a man's body caused his death, but someone's putting the arsenic in his food (which caused this cause) also caused his death, though causing is not always taken as transitive. (If lightning caused a

---

[4] Ibid., p. 31.   [5] Ibid., pp. 32–3.   [6] Ibid., p. 33.
[7] Ibid., pp. 35–6.   [8] Ibid., p. 41.

fire, the atmospheric conditions which caused the lightning are not said to have caused the fire.) On the other hand, even if something caused the poisoner to act as he did, we would not say that this something caused his victim's death.

Now these are quite real distinctions, and they are important for an analysis of the ordinary uses of causal terminology, which in turn may be, as Hart and Honoré argue,[9] rightly relevant to legal decisions, though they are not the only considerations that affect the limits of responsibility. But I would stress that though our account has not developed them, it has left room for them, in noting that 'an alleged condition which is not called a cause . . . either is part of the field presupposed in the view taken by the speaker . . . or is a cause, but mention of this fact happens to be irrelevant, or less relevant than mention of some other cause of the same result, to some current purpose'.[10] Deliberate human actions are particularly relevant as causes just because they are the focus of interest with respect to responsibility and various forms of control. But since even the choice of a field is relative to a purpose or a point of view, and since even apart from this what we recognize as a cause, rather than a mere condition, commonly depends on what we know— or what we knew first—or what is closely related to our interests, there is much to be said for Mill's refusal to distinguish 'philosophically speaking' between causes and conditions. As an analysis of ordinary language, this would be wrong; but from a theoretical point of view, as an account of causal processes themselves, it would be right. What is not a cause in relation to one field may be so in relation to another. A deliberate human act is related to a physical result that it helps to bring about in just the same way that other factors may be, namely as 'necessary (and perhaps sufficient) in the circumstances', as an instance of an inus condition, and as being causally prior to that result.

Of much greater moment is the claim made by Hart and Honoré that statements of interpersonal transactions, involving the notion of a person's reason for acting, incorporate a quite different causal concept from that of which Mill's analysis is approximately correct. But their main ground for this claim is that generalizations play a different role in physical and in

⁹ Especially in their Chapters 3 and 4.   ¹⁰ Chapter 2, above.

interpersonal cases '. . . the assertion that one person, for example, induced another to act is not "covertly" general even in the modified sense discussed in Section IV. Generalizations have a place here but a less central one.'[11] I think, however, that this is a false contrast, and that it is due to their having conceded too much to Mill in the physical sphere. Singular causal statements in this sphere are not, I shall argue, covertly general even in the modified sense allowed by Hart and Honoré.

Criticizing Hume, Hart and Honoré say that 'the lawyer approaches the general element inherent in causal statements in a different way, which disguises it: when it is suggested that A is the cause of B he is apt to ask as the first question, would B have happened without A? And though in fact, in order to answer this question, we have . . . to use our general knowledge of the course of nature, it looks as if this general knowledge were just part of the *evidence* that a particular event was the cause of another, and not constitutive of the very meaning of the particular causal statement.'[12] Yes; but it is not only the lawyer who is apt to ask this first question, but also the ordinary man, and (as we have seen) even Mill, and even, in an unguarded moment, Hume himself. It is the negative answer to this question, and nothing either explicitly or implicitly general, that I have put at the centre of the analysis of singular causal statements. I have shown (in Chapter 3) that it is only in very tenuous senses that any singular causal statements are implicitly general. Also, granted that general knowledge may somehow be part of the evidence that this particular event of type A caused that particular event of type B, *what* general knowledge plays this role, and just how does it work? I have argued in Chapter 3 that an elliptical generalization, saying that A is an inus condition (or better) of B, will sustain the counterfactual conditionals involved in this singular causal statement. *If* an appropriate elliptical generalization is known, it will indeed make it easier for us to interpret this particular A–B sequence as causal, and I grant that in physical cases such generalizations are often known in advance. As Hart and Honoré say, 'When we assert that A's blow made B's nose bleed or A's exposure of the wax to the flame caused it to melt, the general knowledge used here is knowledge of the familiar "way" to

---

[11] *Causation in the Law*, p. 48.   [12] Ibid., p. 14.

produce . . . certain types of change.'[13] But, as I have shown, even in physical cases no such generalization *need* be known in advance: the elliptical generalization can be discovered and (tentatively) established by the observation of the very same individual sequence the conditionals about which it may be said to sustain. We do not, then, need it as *evidence*. The generalizations that are far more vital as providers of evidence are those which inform us of the *irrelevance* of various other changes in the spatio-temporal neighbourhood of the observed sequence, for example, that *B*'s nose is unlikely to have been made to bleed by *C*'s whistling or by the cold draught as *D* opened the door, or that the wax is unlikely to have been melted by the mere movement that brought it near to the flame. This distinction is vital, because general knowledge related in the same way to the singular causal judgement is relevant even in the interpersonal cases. How do we know that it was *A*'s threat that induced *B* to open the safe? It is not enough that *A*'s gesture with a loaded revolver *gave B a reason* for opening the safe; we want to say that this *was his reason* for doing so. This causal statement too will have an analysis that includes the counterfactual '*B* would not have opened the safe on this occasion, in these circumstances, if *A* had not threatened him'. To be able to say this, we need to know that *B* is not prone to open the safe gratuitously in the presence of strangers or in response to an unauthoritative request. This is general knowledge that we probably have about *B*, and that *B* almost certainly has about himself, and both *B* himself and we as spectators are implicitly relying on such knowledge when we say that it was the threat which induced him to open the safe. It may be objected that *B* himself, at any rate, has no need to appeal even to *this* general knowledge, that he knows that until *A* produced the revolver he had no thought of opening the safe, and so knows directly that on this occasion he would not have opened it if the revolver had not been displayed, whatever he may or may not have done, or might or might not do, on other occasions. We can concede this; but this is no more than an example of the imaginative analogizing, the automatic transfer from an earlier situation to a reconstructed later

[13] *Causation in the Law*, p. 29.

one, which we have already recognized as an unsophisticated way of arriving even in physical cases at the counterfactual conditional 'If in these circumstances X had not occurred, Y would not'. Not only B himself but we as spectators can think in this way in an interpersonal case; but so can we in a physical case. And just as we may need, in a physical case, to back up this unsophisticated imaginative performance by reliance on the general knowledge that regularly when in similar circumstances no event of type X occurs, no event of type Y occurs either, so in the interpersonal case B himself, and *a fortiori* we as spectators, might need to back up our immediate imaginatively based judgement with the general knowledge that B does not open safes gratuitously. It is true that we need no generalization *about B's regularly opening safes when threatened*; but equally we do not *need* the corresponding generalization in the physical case. The general knowledge that a blow can make a nose bleed *facilitates* our interpretation that on this occasion A's blow made B's nose bleed, but we *can* interpret a quite novel sequence as causal if we have the general knowledge which with the help of observation rules out rival explanations. Hart and Honoré themselves concede that 'what we recognize as a possible reason is not independent of how in a very broad sense most people act . . . we recognize as a reason for action . . . something which is relevant to some purpose known to be pursued by human beings'.[14] Indeed, I think they concede too much here. Given appropriate evidence, we *could* recognize a novel human purpose, and hence could recognize something quite bizarre as giving someone a reason for acting. The correct point is merely that our general knowledge of human purposes *facilitates* interpersonal causal interpretations of what we observe, and this is strictly analogous to what we can say about physical cases. Once we see just how general knowledge of different sorts may or may not come in, we find no systematic difference between physical and interpersonal types of case which would justify us in speaking of two different causal concepts. In both spheres, the elliptical generalizations which tell us that Xs can cause Ys, that the X event-type is an inus condition of the Y event-type, *aid* the interpretation that this X caused this Y; in neither sphere is advance knowledge of such a generalization *required*. In both

[14] Ibid., p. 53.

spheres the general knowledge of the other sort, that which tells us that the *other* features of the situation were *not* sufficient to produce an event of type Y, may be needed to back up the causal interpretation; yet in both spheres an initial causal judgement is often made in an unsophisticated way, without actual use of such general knowledge, the 'Y would not have occurred' being reached by transfer, by imaginative analogizing, from like, especially immediately preceding, states of affairs. In other words, once we complete the job of refining and correcting Mill's account of causal statements and causal relations in the sphere in which that account is recognized by Hart and Honoré to be appropriate to some degree, we enable it to cover also causal statements and causal relations in the interpersonal sphere, where Hart and Honoré think that something radically different is required.

I am, of course, here verging upon a well-known group of controversial topics, whether desires and other 'motives' can be said to cause the correlated actions, whether an explanation of an action in terms of the agent's reasons is a causal explanation, and so on. I think the affirmative answer to these questions is correct, and that the popular arguments for the opposite view are inadequate, and indeed often rest on an inadequate account of causation. That is, I think that these arguments will be indirectly weakened, undermined, by the account of causation which I have been developing. However, I am now directly concerned not with these questions, but with the rather different question whether if A induces B to do something by offering him a reward or a bribe, or by threatening him, A's doing what he does causes B's doing what he does *in the same sense* in which a blow causes a nose-bleed. For the rival view of Hart and Honoré is not that such inducing is non-causal, but merely that it exemplifies a different causal concept. In rejecting their view, I am not of course saying that there are no systematic differences between 'physical' and 'interpersonal' cases. In any variety of inducing, the result comes about by way of the second agent's desires and choices, and some desire or at least readiness to desire and some capacity in this agent to understand the offer or threat must be either part of the field or conjoined factors in the assemblage of conditions, and nothing like these will be operative in ordinary physical causation. What I am saying is that inducing is still causing in the same basic sense, but with these additional features.

Hart and Honoré mention, as another kind of exception, even in the 'physical' sphere, to the Millian account of causation, 'cases . . . where an *omission* or failure to act is identified as the cause of some (usually untoward) event'. As they say, 'Our concern here is to show that the omitted precaution would have averted the harm, not that when it is omitted harm always results.'[15] But this is an exception only to the way that we have already rejected of incorporating generalizations in the analysis. An omission that is recognized as a cause is 'necessary in the circumstances' in just the same way that a positive act or event or state is: to say that the precaution would have averted the harm is to say that if the omission had not occurred, the harm would not have occurred either.

Hart and Honoré discuss another kind of interpersonal transaction, the giving of opportunities. 'A man who carelessly leaves unlocked the doors of a house . . . has provided the thief with an opportunity to enter and steal the spoons though he has not caused him to steal or made him steal.'[16] The leaving of the doors unlocked may well have been necessary in the circumstances for the stealing of the spoons, and causally prior to it, it will then be a (partial) cause of the latter in terms of our analysis; is this not, then, a difficulty for our view? I should reply that this is another instance of the same basic causal relationship; in a philosophically interesting sense it *is* causing, the problem is merely why we are reluctant to use causal language here. In fact we should be happy to say that the stealing of the spoons was a (causal) consequence of the leaving of the doors unlocked, though we should not say that it was an effect of this, or, as Hart and Honoré point out, that it caused the thief to steal or made him steal. Surely these last expressions are avoided because they too strongly suggest inducement or coercion or overwhelming impulse, whereas in this case the thief had, presumably, already set out to steal something when he came upon the unlocked door. And there are, as Hart and Honoré point out, fine distinctions between 'consequence', 'effect', 'result', and so on. 'The use of the term "effect" is . . . fairly definitely confined to cases where the

15 *Causation in the Law*, p. 47.   16 Ibid., p. 55.

antecedent is literally a *change* or *activity* . . . and where the event spoken of as the effect is a change brought about in a continuing thing or person. . . . "Consequences" has a much wider application, . . . [but] it is not normally used of the terminus of a very short series of physical . . . changes.'[17] Along these lines we may perhaps be able to account for the differential use of particular causal words and phrases. It would be possible to speak of distinct sub-concepts of effect, consequence, and the like, but unless these differential usages showed a fair degree of persistence through time and over a multiplicity of dialects, and had close counterparts in a number of languages, to speak even of sub-concepts would be misleading and not very useful. But however we describe these fine distinctions, what matters is that they rest upon features which are additional to the basic causal relationships, and do not replace these: How long was the series of physical changes? How hard would it have been for the agent to do otherwise? Did the interpersonal cause start what we see as a single course of action or feed into it some way along? The only trouble is that the very word, 'cause', which we most naturally adopt for the common basic concept, tends to be already used for what is at best a sub-concept. But this is merely linguistically embarrassing, not philosophically significant.

However, in trying to formulate this basic concept I have used such phrases as 'necessary in the circumstances'. Hart and Honoré argue that there are (at least?) 'three different ways, hidden by the general expression "necessary", in which a cause may be said to be a necessary condition of the consequence'.[18] If so, perhaps my phrase gives a misleading impression of unity. The three senses are, first, that a condition may be 'one of a set of conditions jointly sufficient for the production of the consequence: it is necessary because it is required to complete this set'; secondly, it may be 'a necessary member of every set of sufficient conditions of a given type of occurrence'; thirdly, it may be necessary on the particular occasion, whereas what is necessary in the first sense may, through over-determination (fail-safe causes), not be necessary on the particular occasion. The second sense is not relevant: a type-event which is a (partial) cause of some other type-event may in fact be necessary for it in this stronger sense, but it is never required to be

<hr>

[17] *Causation in the Law*, pp. 25–6.   [18] Ibid., pp. 106–7.

so, in any established concept of a cause. I have argued, in effect, in Chapter 2 that the third is the key sense of 'necessary in the circumstances', that the first is not strong enough, and I have shown how we càn accommodate those cases of over-determination where we do regard one factor rather than another as the cause. This plurality of senses of 'necessary', therefore, does not undermine the unity of my account.

There is a major issue in legal theory with which Hart and Honoré are concerned. Granted that not everything which would count as a (partial) cause of some outcome in terms of what I have called the basic common concept is actually recognized as a cause, or still less as a 'proximate' as opposed to a 'remote' cause, is such an item's being recognized as a (proximate) cause prior or posterior to a legal decision? The traditional view is that there is some genuine issue, prior to any legal decision or policy, about whether something that was admittedly a condition *sine qua non* of the outcome *caused* it or not, or was or was not a proximate cause. The 'modern' view is that whether a condition *sine qua non* counts as a (proximate) cause is always a matter of legal policy. The difference is brought out by two examples. 'In the State of New York . . . if a fire negligently started spreads to buildings, damages may be recovered only in respect of the first of the buildings affected.' But the claim of the owner of even the first house against the negligent fire-starter would be rejected if 'it transpired that just as the fire was flickering out a third party deliberately poured paraffin on the embers'.[19] On the modern view, the rejection of a house-owner's claim on either of these two grounds (that it was the second house to which the fire had spread, or that a third party had intervened with the paraffin) is simply a matter of legal policy, the fire-starting being a condition *sine qua non* of the actual damage in either case. But on the tradi-tional view, while a New York court's rejection of a claim on the first ground would be a matter of legal policy, a claim would be rejected on the second ground because in the case described the original fire was not the cause of the damage (the paraffin-pouring was). While they recognize that modern criticism has produced 'advances towards simplicity and clarity',[20] Hart and Honoré still find some merit in the

---

[19] Ibid., p. 84.   [20] Ibid., p. 103.

traditional view. And clearly there are differences between the two kinds of case. Though we can see the point of the New York doctrine, it would be in no way surprising if other jurisdictions followed different rules, and allowed damages to be claimed in respect of buildings other than that first affected. But it would be somewhat more surprising if courts anywhere awarded damages against a man who negligently started a fire which would have died out harmlessly unless someone else had deliberately poured on paraffin. Yet is this not still to be explained in terms of a policy, though one that is broader, more fundamental, and more widely embraced? In any such case we are looking for someone to blame (and to bill) for the damage, and a deliberately harmful act, being both more open to deterrence and seen as worse than a negligent one, attracts to itself blame that might initially be shared between them. The negligent starting of the fire was in the actual course of events a non-redundant factor, and hence undeniably, by our account, a (partial) cause of the damage. But we cannot ignore the fact that it could easily have been replaced: if the paraffin-pourer had not found some convenient embers, he would presumably have struck a match. Though the negligent act and the deliberate one were both partial causes of the damage, very natural and widespread human purposes will lead us to pin the cost upon an act which, if it had not occurred, would not have been likely to be replaced in the causal network rather than upon one for which a substitute would almost certainly have been found.

We can in this way resolve the question whether one cause or causal factor can have more *weight* than another.[21] If two factors are each necessary in the circumstances, they are equally necessary; one inus condition cannot be more of an inus condition than another. But, as the last example shows, one can be more easily replaceable than another. The elimination of one

---

[21] In 'Causes and Conditions', *American Philosophical Quarterly*, ii (1965), 253, I said: 'Each of the moments in the minimal sufficient condition, or in each minimal sufficient condition, that was present can equally be regarded as the cause. They may be distinguished as predisposing causes, triggering causes, and so on, but it is quite arbitrary to pick out as "main" and "secondary" different moments which are equally nonredundant items in a minimal sufficient condition, or which are moments in two minimal sufficient conditions each of which makes the other redundant.' This view has been criticized but it can be defended in the sense explained here.

might have diminished the likelihood of the result (as seen from some ordinary point of view incorporating less than complete knowledge of the situation) more than would the elimination of the other. Also, time differences may well be important for some purposes: the 'last clear chance rule' has been used in law to assign responsibility for negligence to 'the party who failed to take the last clear chance of avoiding the harm'.[22] Hart and Honoré rightly argue that this rule, as applied by the courts, does not embody any common-sense principle of causation; it goes beyond the principle that a later voluntary or reckless act, or gross or extraordinary negligence, 'negatives' a causal connection between someone else's prior conduct and subsequent harm. But all such judgements can be seen as the expression of various purposes and policies: in themselves all actual causal factors are equally causes of the result for which each was necessary in the circumstances, but from some human point of view one such factor may be selected as the more important cause, or even as the sole cause.[23]

But other examples where the courts have, with some reason, distinguished between a condition *sine qua non* and a cause require a different treatment. Hart and Honoré quote a case where the owners 'in breach of a Hongkong ordinance sent a ship to sea without duly certificated officers. The master, though uncertificated, was a perfectly competent man of long experience, but the ship was in fact involved in a collision when he was the officer of the watch and guilty of negligent navigation.' The judge held that the owners' breach of the ordinance was a cause of the collision 'in the sense of it being a *causa sine qua non* . . . because . . . Sinon, the uncertificated officer, was in fact the officer of the watch at the time . . .', but that since he was,

[22] Hart and Honoré, op. cit., pp. 201–7.

[23] On the other hand quantitatively measurable effects and the functional dependence concept, to be discussed in Chapter 6, do allow a more objective weighting of causes. It could be that three-quarters of the increase in the cost of a product was due to a rise in the price of raw materials and only one-quarter to a rise in wages.

Less coherent selective judgements can also be found. Thus a psychiatrist who discovered that 'a widely used anti-depressant drug could cause temporary loss of speech in some patients' is reported (*Guardian*, 20 December 1972) as saying: 'All but one of the patients recovered when treatment was stopped . . . reports of patients being "struck dumb" are alarmist and sensational. . . . It is not the fault of the drug but idiosyncrasies of certain patients. Vast numbers of people have the drug without any effect at all.'

by all the evidence, competent, there could not be 'any causal connection between the fact of his not having a certificate and the fact of his negligent navigation'.[24] What this amounts to is that Sinon's being in charge caused the collision, and he was an uncertificated officer; but it was not an uncertificated officer's being in charge that caused the collision. His being uncertificated would have been causally relevant if it had meant that an incompetent man was in charge, and this had caused the collision, but on the evidence this was not so. We are here verging upon the question (to be examined in Chapter 10) of the extensionality of causal statements and the related question whether the phrases that identify events or states which enter into causal relationships are to be read as perfect or as imperfect nominalizations of the corresponding verbal forms. A concrete event describable by the perfect nominalization 'an uncertificated officer's navigating' *did* cause the collision, but it was not its being an event of this type that caused it, as would be asserted if we said, with an imperfect nominalization, 'an un-certificated officer's having navigated caused the collision': the event's being of *this* type was causally irrelevant. But it is quite misleading to draw a distinction here between a cause and a condition *sine qua non*. The actual man's, Sinon's, navigating was both a cause and a condition *sine qua non*; that this concrete event was of the type *an uncertificated officer's navigating* was neither a cause nor a condition *sine qua non*; the judge's reasonable decision drives no wedge between a factor's being necessary in the circumstances and its being recognized as a cause either by common sense or by the law.

Another such wedge is suggested by Hart and Honoré in their discussion of accidents caused by a motorist's excessive speed.[25] Where the speed leads through traceable stages to the driver's losing control and hence to a collision, or where it accounts for the great violence of the impact and so for the amount of injury or damage, there is no difficulty: the speed is said without qualification to have caused the accident or the harm. But it is different where a driver's excessive speed was a condition *sine qua non* of an accident only because, if he had driven more slowly, he would not have arrived at the critical time at the place where this particular accident occurred. Here

[24] *Causation in the Law*, pp. 112-13.   [25] Ibid., pp. 114-16.

we do not want to say, for legal purposes, that the speeding caused the accident; yet in terms of our basic analysis, it did. Hart and Honoré quote the view of the American courts that in these problematic cases the earlier speeding was not causally connected with the accident, sometimes backed up by the argument that there would have been no accident if the driver had gone faster still! It is true that in a case of this sort it is not exceeding the speed limit as such which has caused the accident, but exceeding it to just that particular degree; but to deny a causal connection here is absurd. However, I find equally unsatisfactory the view of Hart and Honoré that the right distinction between the causally necessary condition and the mere condition *sine qua non* is that in the problematic, mere *sine qua non*, cases 'We could not show that the sequence of events, even when broken down into stages, exemplified some traceable general connexion between speeding and [accidents]'. Admittedly these cases do not exemplify any general connection between speeding and accidents; but each stage of the process does exemplify some general connection, for example between being at one place at one time, moving at eighty miles an hour, and being at a place four miles distant three minutes later, and again between one car's meeting another at an intersection and both cars, and their occupants, being damaged. But in any case I have argued that the exemplifying of a broad generalization is not an essential feature of even physical causal connections. What Hart and Honoré themselves describe as a sensible way of dealing with the matter, but then unaccountably leave on one side, is to say that 'the purpose of rules against speeding is to protect persons from injuries arising in certain familiar ways which would normally be regarded as the risks attendant on speeding'. In other words, although a statute may verbally prescribe special penalties (and perhaps special rights) in cases where accidents and injuries are caused by excessive speed, it is intended only to guard against (or to compensate for) damage and injuries that arise from speeding in the direct and familiar ways. In the bizarre cases the speeding is still a cause, as well as a condition *sine qua non*, of the damage, but not in the way with which the statute is concerned.

Hart and Honoré may well be right, as we saw earlier, in drawing attention to ways in which ordinary usage restricts the term 'cause' more narrowly than our basic analysis, and in saying that the law should take some account of these ordinary restrictions. But while these restrictions will not, of course, be relative to specific local legal policies, they still depend upon the broader human interests and purposes that commonly give point to causal statements, and they seem not to drive any philosophically important wedge between a cause and what is necessary in the circumstances, over and above the refinements of that notion that we considered in Chapters 2 and 3.

One further matter of interest is the contrast that Hart and Honoré draw between the use of the general verb 'cause' and such simple transitive verbs as 'push, pull, bend, twist, break, injure'. We use simple verbs where the process 'consists of an initial immediate bodily manipulation of the thing affected and often takes little time', but we speak of 'cause' and 'effect' where the effect is a secondary change brought about by some primary change in what we directly manipulate: 'we cause one thing to move by striking it with another'.[26] It may be true that we tend not to use the words 'cause' and 'effect' of these immediate manipulations, but the converse thesis would not hold: there are plenty of simple transitive verbs which describe the indirect bringing about of 'secondary' changes: 'kill', 'poison', 'cure', 'calm', 'bake', 'clean', 'water', and a host of others. I can see nothing wrong in saying that whenever any of these simple verbs is applicable, some causing is going on or has gone on, and that this is causing in accordance with our basic analysis. If A kills B, A does something which causes B's dying; if A waters the garden, A does something which causes the garden's becoming wetter; if A bends a twig, he makes a movement which causes the twig's ceasing to be straight. We have simple verbs for some of these transactions but not for others, and where we have a simple verb it will usually be clumsy and pedantic to use the word 'cause'. But nothing vital turns upon these linguistic differences.

Simple transitive verbs may, however, throw light on philosophical questions about causation in another way. Problems that have been with us since Hume include these: What is the intimate tie between an individual cause and an individual effect? Where and how, if at all, can we perceive causation?

[26] *Causation in the Law*, pp. 26-7.

It may be argued that these problems evaporate, or admit of
startlingly simple solutions, if we attend to the use not of the
general verb 'cause' but of the simple transitive verbs, especially
those of which Hart and Honoré were speaking. What need is
there to look for a further 'tie' or 'link' between my hand and
the cup it pushes? The coupling between the railway engine
and the truck it pulls is clearly visible. Hume has taught us to
look in vain for the power and necessity in causing, but is it
so hard to see a stone break a window? Thus R. F. Holland
says: 'Our understanding, then, of "the link between cause and
effect" is basically an understanding of physical contacts in all
their various kinds—jolting, pushing, gashing, rubbing, gnaw-
ing, scooping, severing, grappling, getting entangled with,
absorbing, falling on top of, crushing, mixing, irradiating, and
so on (it is to be noticed that our words for the various sorts
of contact mostly indicate a pattern of motion and a degree of
force).'[27] There is no doubt that it is in and from observations
and experiences of this sort that we get at least part of our
understanding of causation, but we can still ask just what
understanding we get, and how. If I see someone else peel a
potato, I see the relative movement of the potato and the knife,
I see the gradually lengthening strip of peel come up from the
surface of the potato, each new portion coming up just as the
leading edge of the knife reaches it; but as Hume would still
rightly protest, I don't *see* the knife *making* the peel come up.
And what I most obviously fail to *see*, though I do *judge*, is
that each bit of the peel would not have come up if the knife
had not moved in there. But what if I peel the potato myself?
Then in addition to seeing all that has been mentioned, I feel
my fingers pressing on the knife and on the potato, and I may
guess that the knife is also pressing on the potato and the potato
on the knife. As Holland says, there is force here as well as
motion. But to feel forces, and even to transfer them, in thought,
from one place to another (from the finger–knife and finger–
potato surfaces to the knife–potato surface) is still not to perceive a counterfactual conditional. To arrive at this we still
need either the sophisticated or the unsophisticated procedure
discussed in Chapters 2 and 3, and the shift of attention from

[27] From an unpublished paper. Similar points are made by G. E. M. Anscombe, *Causality and Determination*, pp. 8–9.

causing in general to the various processes described by simple transitive verbs has not diminished this need. It sounds absurd to say, in the spirit of Hume, that I do not perceive myself peeling a potato, but only imagine this, even in the most favourable circumstances. But it is not absurd, but true, to say that an element either of imagining or of discursive thinking enters into what we would ordinarily call my knowledge that I am peeling a potato. We should not fall back from the correct parts of Hume's critical analysis to a mere acceptance of common sense.

Admittedly we can, in the most ordinary sense of 'see', see a stone break a window. But this seeing, like almost all seeing, includes an element of interpretation. And, of course, we *might* be wrong. It might be that a vacuum somehow suddenly produced on the inside of the window made it collapse a tenth of a second before the stone arrived. The point of mentioning such fantastic possibilities is not to promote scepticism, not to recommend the conclusion 'Perhaps the stone did not really break the window' on some perfectly ordinary occasion, but merely to bring out the fact that something which we can call interpretation is involved, and to leave room for a further inquiry into its nature, which the simple adherence to the common-sense judgement or the ordinary use of language might preclude.

Whereas Holland deprecates the search for a general analysis of causal statements and insists that understanding is to be found in the *variety* of ordinary physical contacts, a general theory of causation that incorporates some of the same principles has been advocated by Ducasse.[28] His main themes are 'that the correct definition of the causal relation is to be framed in terms of one single case of sequence, and that constancy of conjunction is therefore no part of it, but merely, under certain conditions, a corollary of the presence of the causal relation', and that this relation 'when correctly defined, is as directly observable as many other facts, and that the alleged mysteriousness of the causal tie is therefore a myth due only to a mistaken notion of what a tie is'.[29]

[28] C. J. Ducasse, *Truth, Knowledge and Causation*, Chapters 1 to 4. The first of these chapters reprints a paper 'On the Nature and the Observability of the Causal Relation', which was originally published (in *Journal of Philosophy*, xxiii) in 1926.

[29] *Truth, Knowledge and Causation*, p. 1.

Ducasse assumes that 'if the occurrence of a particular change sufficed to the occurrence of [another] it is then said to have caused that other', and suggests that this 'sufficing' is to be defined as follows:

Considering two changes, *C* and *K* (which may be either of the same or of different objects), the change *C* is said to have been sufficient to, i.e. to have caused, the change *K*, if:

1. The change *C* occurred during a time and through a space terminating at the instant *I* at the surface *S* [the limit of a change of a solid being a surface, not a point].

2. The change *K* occurred during a time and through a space beginning at the instant *I* at the surface *S*.

3. No change other than *C* occurred during the time and through the space of *C*, and no change other than *K* during the time and through the space of *K*.

More roughly, but in briefer and more easily intuited terms, we may say that *the cause of the particular change K was such particular change C as alone occurred in the immediate environment of K immediately before*.[30]

Several things are to be noted about this definition. Ducasse's first thesis, that causation is to be defined first for the singular sequence, and that any constancy or regularity is a secondary matter, anticipates what I have argued in Chapter 3. He is also right in arguing that causation can be *detected* in a single sequence: 'one single experiment is sufficient in principle to make evident that [one particular change] did cause [another]. For repetition of the experiment is called for, if at all, only to make sure that the experiment was conducted strictly and its outcome observed accurately.'[31] Ducasse's definition is, of course, an

[30] Ibid., pp. 3–4.
[31] Ibid., p. 27. This quotation comes from a chapter which reprints an article published in 1965 (in *Philosophy and Phenomenological Research*, xxvi). In my own 'Causes and Conditions', published (later) in the same year, but written without knowledge of Ducasse's account, I said, about my analysis of the Method of Difference: 'The importance of this is that it shows how an observation can reveal not merely a sequence but a causal sequence', and, about the repetition of experiments, 'it is not the repetition as such that supports the conclusion that the dipping causes the turning red, but the repetition of a sequence which, on each single occasion, is already *prima facie* a causal one. The repetition tends to disconfirm the set of hypotheses each of which explains a single sequence of a dipping followed by a turning red as a mere coincidence, and by contrast it confirms the hypothesis that in each such single sequence the dipping is causally connected with the change of colour.' These points are echoed in Chapter 3 above.

account of what it is for one change *immediately* to cause another;
but there would be no difficulty in covering indirect causation
by defining cause as the 'ancestral' of the relation analysed by
Ducasse. As Ducasse says, he has in effect turned Mill's Method
of Difference into a definition of cause, whereas for Mill it is a
roundabout method of ascertaining something beyond what is
observed. But he is so using what from Mill's point of view is
only one of the possible ways of finding suitable 'instances' (our
I_1 and N_1); for Ducasse, the before-and-after observation is
radically different from the comparison of an experimental case
with a control case, and it is only the former that is taken up
into his definition.[32] Also, he has tightened up and made
explicit what I called in Chapter 3 the use of spatio-temporal
neighbourhood as a criterion of possible causal relevance.
What may be more surprising is that Ducasse has dispensed
with what I call the *assumption*: it is only (in a refined form)
the difference *observation* that he has turned into a definition.
No doubt this is because he does not want a conclusion in the
form of a generalization, for which an assumption would clearly
be required. Another way of looking at his definition would be
to say that he has equated causation with contiguity and succession, dispensing with Hume's third factor, necessity; but
strictly speaking his replacement for Hume's necessity is the
requirement that C be the *only* change contiguously preceding
K and that K be the *only* change contiguously succeeding C. It
is a consequence of Ducasse's definition that he can reinstate
the sharp distinction between a cause and a condition which
Mill denied: only an event, not a state or standing condition,
can be a cause. (He does not, indeed, restrict causes to changes,
for he allows what, following Dr. Charles Mercier, he calls
unchanges, that is a state's enduring for some time unchanged,
also to be causes.)[33] But the clear and simple distinction thus
drawn will not coincide with that which, as Hart and Honoré
say, 'is . . . drawn by common sense on principles which vary
in a subtle and complex way . . .'.[34]

What might seem to be a difficulty for Ducasse is raised by
the question, 'What if several changes take place in the same
spatio-temporal region, say that of C in the definition?' For

[32] *Truth, Knowledge and Causation*, pp. 7–8.   [33] Ibid., pp. 5, 29.
[34] See above, pp. 118–19.

COMMON SENSE AND THE LAW

example (his own example) 'at the instant a brick strikes a
window pane, the pane is struck . . . by the air waves due to
the song of a canary near by'.[35] Consistency forces him to say
that the cause of this particular breaking of this pane is the
total change contiguously preceding it, including the air waves
as well as the brick's impact. He admits our reluctance to say
this, but explains it as a confusion between the questions *'What
did cause, i.e., what did then and there suffice to, the occurrence of that
concrete individual event?'* and *'which part of what did suffice would
be left if we subtracted from what did suffice such portions of it as were
unnecessary to such an effect?'* This second question, Ducasse
admits, 'is usually that which we mean to ask when we inquire
concerning the cause of an event'; but he argues that 'it is not,
like the first, really an inquiry after the cause of one individual
concrete event strictly as such. It is, on the contrary, an inquiry
concerning *what is common to it and to the causes of certain other
events of the same kind.* This much of a generalization, indeed, is
indissolubly involved in the mere assigning of *a name* to the
cause and to the effect perceived; although *it is not involved in
the merely perceiving them.*'[36] But there is a tangle of problems
here. We can indeed perceive that the total contiguously preceding change *C* 'sufficed'—was sufficient, given the standing
conditions—for *K* in what I called in Chapter 2 the weak sense
of 'sufficient in the circumstances', just because *K* did occur.
But whether it was also sufficient in the circumstances in the
strong, counterfactual, sense, that if *K* had not been going to
occur, *C* would not, is not so easily decidable. And yet an answer
to this counterfactual question need not involve any generalization. Similarly, an answer to Ducasse's second question, which is
equivalent to my 'What was necessary in the circumstances for
K', that is, 'What occurred such that if it had not occurred *K*
would not?' need not involve any generalization. I rely on the
discussion in Chapter 2 for a proof that an answer to the latter
(and perhaps also to the former) counterfactual question is
involved in the meaning of an ordinary singular causal statement, and on that in Chapter 3 for a proof that this counterfactual element is not, as Ducasse holds, an infection from a
general inquiry about what is common to a number of causal
sequences. Ducasse's contrary argument rests upon a refusal to

[35] *Truth, Knowledge and Causation*, p. 11.   [36] Ibid.

consider counterfactual conditionals: 'to say that the song of the canary was unnecessary . . . is to say only that in *another* case, otherwise similar, where the song did not occur, an effect of the *same sort*, viz., breaking, nevertheless did occur'.[37] Another actual case, that is: he eschews possible or imaginary cases, and hence what is necessary or unnecessary can only be a matter of general truths, of universally or existentially quantified statements.

Another serious difficulty concerns the uniformity of causality, which Ducasse discusses with Professor Richard M. Gale.[38] Gale questions Ducasse's thesis 'that *every* event of *necessity* must have a cause from which it follows in a uniform manner'; quoting from another work by Ducasse a definition which is formulated a little differently from that quoted above, but essentially equivalent, he says that 'the crucial question is whether this definition either includes or entails that causality is uniform'.[39] Ducasse argues that his definition does entail that causality is both uniform and universal. Distinguishing 'causally sufficient' and 'causally necessary' from 'logically sufficient' and 'logically necessary', he explains that if in a completely determinate state of affairs S a change C occurs at moment M, and immediately afterwards there occurs in S another change E, these being the only changes that occur in S during the period that contains them both, then C was both *causally sufficient* and *causally necessary for E*, and (what is equivalent to this) E was both *causally necessitated by* and *causally contingent on C*.[40] If the italicized terms are thus defined, it does indeed follow that every event has a cause which is both sufficient and necessary for it, by which it is necessitated and on which it is contingent: something, some total change or unchange, must have been going on in the spatio-temporal region contiguously preceding any event (with the possible exception of the beginning of the universe in time). Causality (so defined) is thus universal; the key question is whether it must also be uniform. Gale argues that it need not.

---

[37] *Truth, Knowledge and Causation*, pp. 12–13.

[38] Gale's paper is in *Philosophy and Phenomenological Research*, xxii (1961), 92–6; Ducasse's reply appeared in the same volume and is reprinted as Chapter 4 of *Truth, Knowledge and Causation*.

[39] Op. cit., p. 92, reported by Ducasse, op. cit., p. 29: the definition used is from *Nature, Mind, and Death*, p. 106.

[40] *Truth, Knowledge and Causation*, p. 32.

Suppose that there is, at some other time and place, a state of afiairs S' just like S, and at some moment M' a change C' occurs in S' which is quantitatively and qualitatively identical with C; Gale says that this supposition, together with what we have already said about S, C, and E, does not logically necessitate that there will occur, immediately after M', an only change E' quantitatively and qualitatively identical with E.[41]

Gale is surely right in this. Ducasse's reply is so curious that it must be quoted in full:

> I submit, however, that this contention is self-contradictory and therefore invalid, for it supposes that the requirements for *causal* necessitation of E in S, as these were defined, *are* strictly met, and yet that this *does not logically necessitate* that occurrence of E in S is then *causally necessitated*.
>
> More explicitly, the fact which *logically* necessitates that causation of E in S by C in S, as defined, is uniform, is that the definition of such causation makes no reference at all either explicitly or implicitly to any particular date or point in space. Hence the supposition that C in S did, in the sense defined, cause E in S yesterday, and yet that identical occurrence of S and of C in S today might not, in the sense defined, cause identical occurrence of E in S is incongruous exactly as would be the supposition, for instance, that a prime number is defined as one divisible without remainder only by itself and unity and that 7 is such a number, and yet that 7 might be prime today but perhaps not tomorrow. In both cases alike, particular date or place in space, merely as such, is totally irrelevant.[42]

Something is very wrong here. If *causally sufficient* and the other three relations are defined strictly as holding between the concrete individual events C and E in S in the way suggested, then the quantitative and qualitative identities between these three items and C', E', and S' will *not* logically necessitate that C' is causally sufficient for an event E' in S', and so on. Ducasse seems, inconsistently, to be using 'C', 'E', and 'S' as names for *types* of events and a *type* of state of affairs—he does not here use such distinctive symbols as 'C'', 'E'', and 'S''. But then the statement that C is causally sufficient for E in S will already be a generalization, asserting that *any* event of the (fully determinate) type C in any state of affairs of the (fully determinate) type S will be contiguously followed by an event of the (fully determinate) type E; and this is clearly not something that can be observed on a single occasion. Or perhaps he is influenced by the strong, counterfactual, sense of 'sufficient', though this would be inconsistent with his definitions. Alternatively, as the end of the passage quoted suggests, he is simply *assuming* that space and time are causally indifferent; but this is equivalent to the traditional principle of the uniformity of nature, and (however natural) it is an additional assumption, which again goes beyond what can be observed on any occasion or in any finite collection of events. If, in whatever way, we incorporate the uniformity into the definition of cause, the proof given above of its universality at once becomes invalid; though any event must be contiguously preceded by something, there is nothing to show that whatever contiguously precedes it here will be contiguously followed by like events elsewhere. Ducasse's argument in this passage seems to be another member of the family of invalid proofs of the causal principle so decisively criticized by Hume.

It would, then, be better if Ducasse went back to the interpretation of his definition as one strictly for the single sequence, and abandoned the view that 'constancy of conjunction' is even 'a corollary of the presence of the causal relation'.

Even so, we could not accept his account as an analysis of the ordinary concept of cause and effect for the reasons brought out by the example of the window pane and the canary: the element of counterfactual conditionality, of the cause's being necessary in the circumstances for the effect, is part of our ordinary notion of a singular causal sequence, and it cannot be brushed aside as an intrusion of the general into the singular, as involving a concealed comparison of this individual sequence with others.

But though this account fails as an analysis, might it be defended as a proposal for reform? Is it a *better* concept than our ordinary one? Its merits are undeniable. By eliminating the counterfactual element, it removes the essential (though only partial) subjectivity of the ordinary concept, the feature which, near the end of Chapter 2, led us towards the conclusion that singular causal statements cannot be true, do not describe what actually occurred, let alone what was observed to occur. Causa-

tion as Ducasse defines it is a relation which does literally occur
and can be observed. (It is, of course, no part of his case to
claim that such observation is infallible. We may think that
some change *C* was the only one that occupied the right spatio-
temporal region when some other, unnoticed, one occurred
there too. All he claims, and all he requires, is that causation
should be as observable as many other facts, that it should not
be essentially mysterious or inaccessible.) His account gives us
at once a link between individual cause and effect which other
approaches left obscure. It also preserves in an overwhelmingly
simple way the centrality of the Method of Difference in causal
discovery: 'although sequence is not *eo ipso* consequence, yet,
when sequence occurs under the special conditions distinctive
of what is properly called *an experiment*—whether one performed
by man or by Nature—then, *eo ipso*, the sequence is *causal
sequence*'.[43] It also builds upon the fact that the clearest cases of
causation are most naturally described, not by the word 'cause',
but by simple transitive verbs.

But it also has serious demerits. What it offers may be all
right as far as it goes, but something more seems to be needed.
Now that we have shown that it does not have constancy of
conjunction even as a corollary, the causal relation suggested
by Ducasse cannot in itself serve as the foundation for causal
inference: it could not be, 'to us, the cement of the universe'.
Equally, it would not be a basis for recipes and precautions.
A connected but perhaps even more serious point is that it is
insufficiently *selective*. We should like to have a concept that
allowed us to say that, even in this individual case taken on its
own, it was the brick and not the air waves from the canary's
song that broke the window, that if a copper wire conducts
heat and electricity at once, it may be the electricity, not the
heat, that rings a bell, but the heat, not the electricity, that
makes some piece of metal expand. It is easy to see how we
get this selectivity once we bring in counterfactual conditionals
and generalizations and comparisons of one sequence with
another, for example, the 'experimental case' and 'control case'
form of the difference observation as opposed to the before-
and-after one. It is not so easy to see how we can get it while
remaining strictly within the bounds of the single sequence as

[43] Op. cit., p. 27.

it is (not as it might have been). Yet there is something to be found even here. The breaking of the pane—that is, the actual movements of the glass and of the fragments of glass—is a continuation of the movement of the brick in a way in which it is not a continuation of the air waves. But where a delicate glass bowl is shattered by a loud musical note of just the frequency at which that bowl naturally vibrates, the movements of the glass *are* a continuation of the air waves. The processes involved in the ringing of the electric bell are a continuation of the flow of electrons in the wire, but not of the molecular acceleration which we recognize as a flow of heat. At least in such favourable cases, then, we can find a tie which binds an individual cause and an individual effect together more closely and more selectively than does the relation defined by Ducasse, and which is still in principle observable. We have still to consider how widely applicable, among what we ordinarily regard as cases of causation, this notion is, and also whether there is any connection between it and the counterfactual element in our ordinary causal concepts.

This final suggestion, that a modification of Ducasse's account may yield an observable link between an individual cause and its effect which is also selective, which allows for a distinction between the causally relevant antecedent features and the rest, is a hint for further inquiry. In the main this chapter has been devoted to testing the accounts developed in Chapters 2 and 3 by comparing them with those given or suggested by Hart and Honoré, Holland, and Ducasse. I have argued that a unitary basic analysis of causal judgements can be defended, that failures of coincidence between this analysis and the use of explicitly causal terminology, and some of the complications of that terminology, can be explained without sacrifice of this basic unity, but that this analysis has to retain the puzzling counterfactual element which is an obstacle to our saying that causal relations can be simply and directly observed in single sequences.

6

Functional Laws and Concomitant Variation

'The law of causality . . . is a relic of a bygone age, surviving, like the monarchy, only because it is erroneously supposed to do no harm.'[1] Already in 1912 Bertrand Russell was arguing that the concepts of causation and of causal law, to which we have been paying such close attention, were from the point of view of science out of date, perhaps even incoherent, and had been or should be replaced by the notions of functional relation and of differential equations.

Russell's lively, brief, rather dogmatic discussion makes a large number of points against what he regards as current misconceptions, by no means all of equal importance or of equal merit. Some of them contribute to 'soft determinism', to the 'reconciling project' first advanced by Hume,[2]* the thesis that the conflict between free will and determinism is largely illusory. Some are negative claims about the direction of causation: past and future do not differ in principle with respect to determination; it is merely by definition that an effect is subsequent to its cause; there would be one-way determination only if there were a many–one correlation, various alternative causes being correlated with exactly the same effect—for example, if various alternative mind-states went with exactly the same brain-state, there would be a one-sided dependence of brain on mind. These views will be considered in Chapter 7. But first I shall examine Russell's criticisms of the view that science either is or should be concerned with regular sequences of distinct

---

[1] 'On the Notion of Cause', *Proceedings of the Aristotelian Society*, xiii (1912–13), 1–26; reprinted in *Mysticism and Logic*, to which all page references are given: the passage quoted is on p. 180.
[2] *Treatise*, II, III, 1 and 2, and *Enquiry*, Sect. 8.

events, and the theory of functional relations with which he would replace it.

One main criticism has the form of an antinomy, though it is not explicitly so presented. The thesis is that, if there were causal sequences of events, there would have to be a finite time-interval between cause and effect. For, if they were contiguous,

either the cause or the effect or both must . . . endure for a finite time [presumably, because two instantaneous items, if contiguous, would be simultaneous, so that the one would not *succeed* the other]; indeed . . . it is plain that both are assumed to endure for a finite time. But then we are faced with a dilemma: if the cause is a process involving change . . . only the later parts can be relevant to the effect, since the earlier parts are not contiguous to the effect, and therefore (by the definition) cannot influence the effect. Thus we shall be led to diminish the duration of the cause without limit, and however much we may diminish it, there will still remain an earlier part which might be altered without altering the effect, so that the true cause, as defined, will not have been reached . . . If, on the other hand, the cause is purely static . . . then, in the first place, no such cause is to be found in nature, and, in the second place, it seems strange—too strange to be accepted, in spite of bare logical possibility—that the cause, after existing placidly for some time, should suddenly explode into the effect. This dilemma, therefore, is fatal to the view that cause and effect can be contiguous in time; if there are causes and effects, they must be separated by a finite time-interval . . .[3]

To prove the antithesis, that there can be no time-interval, Russell argues that however short we make it,

Something may happen during this interval which prevents the expected result. I put my penny in the slot, but before I can draw out my ticket there is an earthquake which upsets the machine and my calculations. In order to be sure of the expected effect, we must know that there is nothing in the environment to interfere with it. But this means that the supposed cause is not, by itself, adequate to insure the effect. And as soon as we include the environment, the probability of repetition is diminished, until at last, when the whole environment is included, the probability of repetition becomes almost nil.[4]

But both these arguments are unsound. In the thesis argument, contiguity without simultaneity would require only that

Op. cit., pp. 184–5.   4 Op. cit., p. 187.

either cause *or* effect should endure for a finite time, and the most that Russell's dilemma could show is that the cause cannot so endure. But, more significantly, the first horn of the dilemma fails. There is nothing in the definition he has quoted, and certainly nothing in the general notion of causation as regular contiguous succession, to show that the 'earlier parts' of the cause-process are irrelevant or 'cannot influence the effect'. On the hypothesis considered, it is not true that an earlier part might have been altered without altering the effect, for there will be, as he mentions, 'causal relations between its [the cause-process's] earlier and later parts'. It is true that smaller and smaller final bits of this process could be taken as the cause, but there is no need to say that there is a 'true cause' which has not been reached until the trimming off of earlier parts of the cause-process, and its diminution to its final phase, have been carried to the limit.

The antithesis argument also fails. Russell's 'environment', which is our 'causal field', needs only to be described generally and largely negatively in order to ensure that the effect will regularly follow the proposed cause. For the penny in the slot regularly to produce a ticket, we need the *absence* of earthquakes, bombs, and intrusions from outer space, but it does not matter in the least what in detail the non-intrusive surroundings are like, and there is no improbability about repetitions of the suggested cause within this broadly defined field.

For all that Russell's arguments show, then, there could be regular causal sequences of events either with or without a time-interval. Without a time-interval, at least one, and presumably both, of the cause and the effect would be processes having duration, contiguous in the way that Ducasse's definition[5] explains. With a finite time-interval, the freedom from intervention is secured by the fact that it is only within some broadly defined field that the regularity of sequence holds. And in fact there are regularities of succession, as we noted in Chapter 3, though our knowledge of them is almost always incomplete.

But Russell has a second, and more telling, criticism, namely that science is not much concerned with such regularities. They belong to 'the infancy of a science'; 'every advance in a science

[5] Above, p. 135.

takes us away from the crude uniformities which are first
observed into greater differentiation of antecedent and consequent, and into a continually wider circle of antecedents
recognised as relevant'.[6]

The last phrase here refers only to the point which we have
already taken over from Mill about conjunctions of factors,
'assemblages of conditions'. But Russell's main point is that the
laws of an advanced science take a form different even from
that of the complex regularities we discussed in Chapter 3, a
form which is illustrated by Newton's law of gravitation. 'In
the motions of mutually gravitating bodies, there is nothing
that can be called a cause, and nothing that can be called an
effect; there is merely a formula. Certain differential equations
can be found, which hold at every instant for every particle of
the system, and which, given the configuration and velocities
at one instant, . . . render the configuration at any other earlier
or later instant theoretically calculable.' And he unkindly suggests that philosophers have remained faithful to the old 'law
of causality' only because most of them are unfamiliar with the
mathematical idea of a function. We should replace 'same
cause, same effect' with 'sameness of differential equations'.[7]
The nearest approach we could find, in non-mathematical
language, to a 'law of causality' that is actually discoverable
in the practice of science would be: 'There is a constant relation
between the state of the universe at any instant and the rate of
change in the rate at which any part of the universe is changing
at that instant, and this relation is many–one, i.e. such that the
rate of change in the rate of change is determinate when the
state of the universe is given.'[8]

Nothing turns, of course, upon the particular Newtonian
gravitational form that Russell has chosen as an illustration,
but it will be simplest to continue to use this to illustrate our
discussion. In it, certain second derivatives with respect to
time, namely the acceleration of each particle, have, at any
moment, values which are functions of the distances and masses
at that moment of all other bodies in the system. Given the
masses and distances, the accelerations are fixed and calculable,
but not vice versa.

[6] Op. cit., p. 188.   [7] Op. cit., pp. 194–5.
[8] Op. cit., p. 195; Russell has a strange idea of non-mathematical language.

Now there is no doubt that science has formulated quite a number of laws of this general kind. It is, perhaps, only for Newtonian gravitation that the reference to the state *of the universe* is in order; as Russell himself points out, what scientists actually deal with is rather some 'relatively isolated system'. But with this qualification it is plausible to suggest that as sciences leave their infancy and become 'advanced', they come to be concerned more with laws of this functional sort, or come nearer to being 'reduced' to sciences which already deal in such functional laws. Let us call what such laws describe *functional causation*, and, in contrast, let us call what we have been dealing with so far *neolithic causation*, so as to maintain Russell's analogy with the institution of monarchy. I have already argued, against Russell, that neolithic causation can be coherently presented. But I would argue also that neolithic and functional causation are much more closely related than Russell's account might suggest, and that this makes it natural to extend the old term 'causation' to cover the subject of functional laws.

First, I shall show that Russell's causation can be seen as a limiting case of causal sequence of distinct events as described, for example, by Ducasse. In the gravitational illustration, the analogue of the effect is the acceleration of each particle. Mathematically, this is represented as acceleration at an instant. But 'acceleration at an instant' makes sense only as a limiting description of changes of velocity over periods of time. Talking about the acceleration-effect at the instant t amounts to a special way of talking about changes in velocity over longer or shorter periods of time starting at t. A Russell type effect, then, is just the limit approached by a Ducasse type effect—a process starting at the instant where cause and effect are contiguous—as the time-length of this process is decreased towards zero. It is obvious that this holds not only for the gravitational example but wherever the functional analogue of a neolithic effect is a derivative, of whatever order, with respect to time.

A second, closely related, point is that a functional law will entail the holding of neolithic laws in appropriate fields. A differential equation containing time-derivatives, of whatever order, can in principle be integrated with respect to time, and will then tell us what later states of the system will regularly follow such-and-such earlier ones. Galileo's law of terrestrial gravitation is a functional law, but it entails such neolithic laws as that stones thrown up into the air in an ordinary 'empty' environment will subsequently fall to the ground. If functional effects could not be thus integrated with respect to time to yield actual *changes*, functional laws would be of little interest or use.

Thirdly, a neolithic causal regularity of the complex form discussed in Chapter 3 can be seen as a special case of a functional law where the variables take only one of the two crude values 'present' and 'absent', which we could write as '1' and '0'. If the presence at t of some disjunction of conjunctions of actually relevant factors or their negations, such as ($AB\overline{C}$ or $DG\overline{H}$ or $J\overline{KL}$), is both necessary and sufficient in the field F for the presence at a slightly later time $t+\delta t$ of P, then we could say that the change of value of P between t and $t+\delta t$ was a function of the values at t of A, B, C, D, G, H, J, K, and L.

This last point may look like a mere formality, but it leads on to a fourth and much more significant link between neolithic and functional causation. The Method of Difference is, as we have seen, the principal method for discovering and establishing neolithic causal regularities, while variants of it, such as Mill's Method of Residues, and related devices like the Method of Agreement and some of the things covered by the name of the Joint Method, can also play some part.[9] What Mill calls the Method of Concomitant Variation is pretty clearly a device of the same general sort as these; but I shall show that it is not one method, but several, including counterparts of the Methods of Difference, Agreement, and so on, that it works with the functional concept of causation very much as they work with the neolithic concept, and hence that reasoning closely analogous to that which identifies neolithic causes does some, but only some, of the work of identifying functional causes.

The 'Fifth Canon' by which Mill introduces this method is far too loose to be helpful: '*Whatever phenomenon varies in any manner whenever another phenomenon varies in some particular manner, is either a cause or an effect of that phenomenon, or is connected with it*

[9] See Appendix.

through some fact of causation.'[10] In fact by an equivocation in the use of 'whenever' between 'whenever without restriction' and 'whenever within the observation' it mixes up a new, functional definition of 'cause' with the principle of a method, or methods, for discovering such causes. The definition hinted at is, of course, a development of a regularity definition, and like others of this class leaves on one side the question of the direction of causation. We must now think of the various 'phenomena' as items that have some kind of magnitude. Carrying over from our previous discussion the notion of a field (F) and the expectation that causes will in general be complex, we obtain, as the typical form of a functional causal regularity, the statement that the magnitude of P in the field F is always such-and-such a function of the magnitudes of the factors, say, A, B, C, and D, which we can write

$$P_F = f(A, B, C, D).$$

Where such a regularity holds, we may say that the complete set of actually relevant factors, A, B, C, D, together with the function f which shows in what way they are relevant, constitutes the *full cause* in this functional sense of P in F, while we may call each of the various actually relevant factors, A, B, C, and D, a *partial cause*. The full cause will be that function of the magnitudes of the various relevant factors on which the magnitude of P in F wholly depends, while a partial cause will be a factor on whose magnitude that of P in F partly depends. (Since we are leaving aside the problem of direction, 'depends' has here a purely mathematical sense.)

But this says only what concept of a cause is now being used: where does the method of discovery or proof come in? Clearly, what is required is an ampliative method, one in which we argue from a covariation *in some cases* or *over some limited period* to a regularity of the kind just indicated, which is believed to hold for unobserved cases as well. We argue from 'whenever within the finite range of observations' to 'whenever absolutely'. As we saw, Mill obscured this argument with an equivocation. It is also clear that there are two distinguishable tasks, that of identifying the various partial causes and that of determining the functional relation f, of deciding just how the partial causes

[10] *System of Logic*, Book III, Ch. 8, Sect. 6.

affect the magnitude of P. The completion of the first task would yield a mere list of terms, that of the second a mathematical formula. It is in the performance of the first task that we can find the closest analogy with the other eliminative methods.

If an ampliative method is to be formally valid it will, of course, require an assumption as well as an observation. The general pattern of reasoning will be this: we assume that there is *some* regularity of the kind indicated, relating the magnitude of P in the chosen field F to the magnitudes of some members of a range of possibly relevant factors (we can work formally with a list of such possibly relevant factors, but as before this is only an expository device, in practice no *list* is needed); we observe over some limited period certain patterns of variation and non-variation of P and the possibly relevant factors; and we infer that certain of the possibly relevant factors are actually relevant, that they are in fact partial causes in the sense defined.

A counterpart of the Method of Difference would identify a certain factor, say A, as actually relevant by observing cases in or between which P varies while A varies but all other possibly relevant factors remain constant. The assumption would be that the magnitude of P in the field F wholly depends in some way on the magnitudes of one or more factors X, X', X'', etc., where each of these is identical with one of the possibly relevant factors A, B, C, D, E, etc. Then if it is observed that over some period or range of cases (in the field F) P varies while A varies but B, C, D, E, etc. all remain constant, it follows that one of the factors X, X', X'', etc. is identical with A. It is not shown, of course, that B, C, D, E, etc. are irrelevant; but it is shown that the full cause cannot be made up of them alone, for, if it were, the magnitude of P would have remained constant over that period when the magnitudes of all of B, C, D, E, etc. remained constant. That is, this assumption and an observation of this form together entail that A is *an* actually relevant factor, a partial cause. A series of experiments, in each of which one possibly relevant factor is varied at a time, the others being held constant, could in accordance with this method pick out partial causes one by one.

A counterpart of the Method of Agreement would identify a certain factor, say A, as actually relevant by observing cases in or between which both P and A remain constant while other possibly relevant factors vary. Like the original Method of Agreement,[11] this requires a stronger assumption than does its Difference counterpart if any conclusion is to be entailed. If we assume that (in the field chosen) the magnitude of P depends on that of just *one* of the possibly relevant factors A, B, C, D, E, etc., and that it is *responsive* to all changes in that actually relevant factor, then the observation indicated will show that this one actually relevant factor must be A: it cannot be B, or C, or D, or E, and so on, because each of these has varied while P has not. But if we make the weaker and in general far more plausible assumption that the magnitude of P depends upon those of one *or more* of the possibly relevant factors, nothing follows from the observation indicated. For although B and C, say, have varied while P has remained constant, it is still possible that the magnitude of P is a function of those of B and C, since the function might be such that the variations in B and C compensated for one another, adding up to a zero result. And sets of more than two partial causes are similarly not ruled out.

Suppose, on the other hand, that the magnitudes of P and of A both remained constant over some considerable period, during which the magnitudes of all the other possibly relevant factors varied *independently*. Then if we could say that these other factors had varied in all conceivable ways, it would follow that no function of any set of them would have remained constant, and therefore that they must all be irrelevant, that the magnitude of P must be correlated with that of A alone— all the time, of course, in the field in question. This would be another counterpart of the Method of Agreement, it would require only our weaker and more plausible form of assumption, and it would have the great merit of providing a way of *closing* the set of actually relevant factors, whereas our counterpart of the Method of Difference only picked out relevant factors one by one, and did not positively exclude any as irrelevant. Unfortunately the proposed observation is, speaking strictly, an unattainable ideal; there must in principle, for any finite range of observed variations in B, C, D, E, etc., be functions of their magnitudes which remain constant: no actual pattern of

[11] See Appendix.

variation can include variation in all conceivable ways. However, we can have a probabilistic method which approximates to this ideal. If P and A are observed to remain constant while there is a great deal of apparently random and independent variation in all the surrounding conditions—other, of course, than what has been taken as included in the field F—then in effect all functional hypotheses that we can actually think of to relate P to combinations of these surrounding factors are ruled out, and by contrast it is at least probable that the magnitude of P depends, in F, on that of A alone. And it is obvious that a similar argument could be used to show the irrelevance of, say, D, E, and so on if they vary randomly while, say, A, B, and C, as well as P, remain constant: the probabilistic evidence for the closure of the set of actually relevant factors can operate after any number of partial causes have, by repeated appeals to our counterpart of the Method of Difference, been included in that set.

It is, I think, undeniable that many actual investigations contain parts which could be regarded as applications of these methods to the task of picking out (all) the partial causes, in this functional sense, of some phenomenon in some field. In practice this task is likely to be mixed up with the different, second, task of determining just what the functional relationship is, which will be a matter of testing hypotheses and fitting curves to data. When we note *that* P and A vary while all other possibly relevant factors remain constant, we shall naturally try to say also *how* P varies as a function of A, and if we find that B, and C, say, are also actually relevant factors, we shall look for a formula that covers all the observed covariations. Nevertheless, these two tasks can be distinguished, and when we study the logic of such investigations it is appropriate to distinguish them, and to attend separately to the different devices that aid their fulfilment. And when we do so, we find close formal and logical analogies between the assumptions, observations, and conclusions of the original Methods of Difference and Agreement which establish neolithic regularities and those of their Concomitant Variation counterparts which identify functional causes.

The Method of Concomitant Variation, then, is not, as Mill seems to have thought, just a second-best way of discovering the same old sorts of causal relationship in situations where, for some reason, it was difficult to secure the total absence of this or that factor: it implicitly introduces a new, though systematically related, form of causal connection; it is a bridge between neolithic and functional causation.

This fact, together with the three other links we found earlier between neolithic and functional causes, makes it plausible to regard the functional notion as a refinement and extension of the neolithic causal concept rather than as an entirely new concept: the magnitude of each partial functional cause is necessary in the circumstances for the magnitude of the effect. (The sovereignty of parliament is perhaps an analogous refinement of the neolithic institution of monarchy, and one for which the Newtonian age was also responsible.) It is worth noting that this refinement resolves a difficulty which we encountered in Chapter 2, that, for example, a hammer-blow is said to have caused a chestnut's becoming flatter although quite so hard a blow was not necessary in the circumstances. Working, as we were in Chapter 2, with the fairly crude neolithic concept, we could explain this by saying that we were there regarding the hammer-blow as a unit, something which was either present as a whole or absent as a whole. Now, with our refined functional concept, we can take account of the quantity of momentum, of how hard the blow was and of how hard it needed to be, and we can say either that the actual momentum was necessary (and sufficient) in the circumstances for the actual degree of flattening, or that what caused such-and-such a flattening was the occurrence of a blow of at least so much force. The supposed difficulty arose from a confusion between these different correct comments, that is, from an attempt to speak in neolithic and functional terms at once.

Russell's first criticism, then, does not show the neolithic causal concept to be incoherent, and while his second criticism may show that that concept *on its own* is likely to be left behind by the advance of science, we can see that what that advance calls for is a development and extension of that concept, not its replacement. The old concept—allowing, of course, for complex and incompletely known regularities—will continue to be applicable in many spheres, even if neolithic causation is to be seen as ultimately resting upon laws of the functional sort; and even where we are dealing with functional relations, very similar patterns of thought and inquiry are in order. It is, indeed, very plain that whereas Russell thought that causality was out of date in 1912, causal concepts are, sixty years later, constantly being used in our attempts to understand perception, knowledge, and memory, and to clarify our thought about action, responsibility, legal claims, purpose, and teleology.

As Bunge points out,[12] Russell's view that functional dependence should replace causation was widely shared. It was put forward by Mach, and adopted by Schlick and the Vienna Circle. Bunge remarks that 'functional dependence is poorer than causation, since it does not include the concept of genetic connection through a process'.[13] This could be misleading. It is true that functional relationships *need* not be genetic, that functions can express inert uniformities of coexistence: but, as we have seen, those that include time-derivatives yield, by their integration, laws of change and succession. Functional formulae can neatly express the interdependence of quantities and magnitudes, the results of two-way causation between persisting things or features of things, but of course neolithic causation allows for this too. The asymmetrical relation of causal priority, the unique direction from cause to effect, does not preclude the state of A at t helping to bring about a change in the state of B between t and $t+\delta t$, while the state of B at t helps to bring about a change in the state of A between t and $t+\delta t$. In other respects, the functional dependence view is only a variant of a pure regularity theory of causation, and appealed to positivists for that reason. And what it crucially leaves out is what regularity theories in general leave out: the direction of causation and any adequate treatment of the problems of necessity and the 'causal tie'. But if the functional concept is interpreted non-exclusively, as neither abolishing the neolithic concept nor precluding all non-regularity aspects of causation, it can be welcomed as a refinement and extension of older notions.

But having recognized the need for this extension of the concept of cause and effect, we may be led to consider two others.

[12] M. Bunge, *Causality*, pp. 91–8.
[13] Ibid., p. 98. Bunge is, no doubt, referring to the fact that functional dependence does not conceptually require the sort of continuity of process that is discussed in Chapter 8 below.

One concerns the relation between an earlier and a later phase
in a continuous self-maintaining process. A top, or the earth,
say, rotates continuously, whether at a changing or at a constant rate, from t_1 through t_2 to t_3. Having been spinning between
t_1 and t_2, it goes on spinning after t_2. Why? Because nothing,
or nothing much, interfered or tended to stop it. Given that it
was spinning, the cause of its continuing to spin was the absence
of interference. But in relation to some wider field, can we not
say that it went on spinning after t_2 because it was already
spinning before t_2? Can we say, then, that the rotation from t_1
to t_2 caused the rotation from t_2 to t_3? We would, it is true, not
ordinarily say this, whereas we would say that the friction
between the top and the air, and between its point and the
ground, caused its slowing down, and that tidal friction is
similarly changing, very slowly, the earth's speed of rotation.
We ordinarily look for and recognize a cause of a change in a
process, rather than for the mere continuance of the process.
And yet, as we saw, we can speak of a negative cause, an
absence of interference, as causing its continuance. Also, where
a process needs some sort of input to keep it going we are ready
to speak of a cause: the pull of the engine causes the continued
movement of the trucks. If we include the various frictions in
'the circumstances', the pull of the engine is necessary and
sufficient in the circumstances for the train's not slowing down;
conversely, if we include the engine's pull in 'the circumstances',
the frictions are necessary and sufficient in the circumstances
for the train's not speeding up; these two partial causes together
are responsible for the constancy of the train's velocity. Similarly, where there is (practically) no friction, the absence of
friction and of various other interferences is necessary and sufficient in the circumstances for the earth's continuing to rotate
at (practically) the same speed. But all these causes, even where
their effect is some constancy of behaviour, and even where the
cause is itself negative, are in an obvious sense intrusive or
transeunt: they come in, or refrain from coming in, from outside, in a way that an earlier phase of the same rotation (or
other movement) does not. However, while it seems strange to
call this earlier phase a cause, and while our reluctance to do
so reveals something about our actual concept of causing, there
are analogies which would justify our extending the existing

concept to cover this. If we do not include the rotation between t_1 and t_2 in the field, it is quite clear that, in 'the circumstances' which include neither any appreciable friction nor any new impulse to rotate, the rotation between t_1 and t_2 was necessary and sufficient for the rotation between t_2 and t_3. Besides, the relation between earlier and later phases of a continuous self-maintaining process is very like that between cause and effect as defined by Ducasse. A very minor difference is that successive phases make contact with one another over a three-dimensional volume, whereas his cause and effect make contact only over a two-dimensional surface. The earlier phase of a self-maintaining process surely brings about, or helps to bring about, the later phase. If the concept of cause and effect does not yet cover them, it should: we can recognize immanent as well as transeunt causation.

But if this extension is accepted, can we reasonably stop there? Should we not extend the concept still further to include the relation between the earlier and later phases of the existence of any material object? Is not any physical object a self-maintaining process or a cluster of such processes, helped to some extent by a balance of inputs and outputs, of interactions with neighbouring things? Is its continued existence not very like the continued movement of the train, which is largely self-maintaining but is also kept up by the balance between friction and the pull of the engine? It is very easy to find circumstances such that the existence of a pen here from t_1 to t_2 is necessary and sufficient in the circumstances for the existence of a pen here from t_2 to t_3.

No doubt if we thus stress the analogies which justify these extensions of the existing concept we should also try to explain why the existing concept is so restricted, in much the same way that in Chapter 4 we noted and tried to explain restrictions on the use of the term 'cause' even among events and states that are undeniably inus conditions of some result.

I suggest that the explanation lies in the associations between 'cause', 'because', and 'why'. It is especially where we are inclined to ask why-questions that we will be ready to accept because-statements as answers to them, and we are particularly ready to call causes those items that can be described by clauses introduced by 'because'. Now the persistence of many sorts of object is something that we take very much for granted. Without going all the way with Strawson, we can admit that this is a very pervasive and fundamental structural feature of the world as we know it. We are little inclined, then, to ask why this pen (in ordinary circumstances) continues to exist. We might well ask why there is a pen here now if there had not been one anywhere in the neighbourhood immediately before, or, even if there had been one here immediately before, if it had survived, say, an atomic explosion, but not if such a pen had been here immediately before and no catastrophes had intervened. Such persistences are assumed and used in answering other why-questions rather than made the subject of why-questions themselves. The earlier phase of a thing's existence is not, then, looked upon as causing the later phase because the later phase is not something for which an explanation seems to be required when we know, or assume, that the thing has just continued to exist.

The continuance of a process, for example a rotation, is, indeed, neither so familiar nor so thoroughly built into our ordinary world picture as is the persistence of objects. Our experience suggests that many processes quickly run down and stop when left to themselves, and if anything keeps on working we look for a sustaining cause. Even if we know that the top has been spinning from t_1 through t_2 to t_3, we can therefore still ask why it has been spinning from t_2 to t_3. But if we do ask this, the answer 'Because it was spinning from t_1 to t_2', is still likely to appear disappointing. It will merely provoke us to ask further, 'But why was it spinning then?' We are not satisfied until we come to an impulse that started the process off or to an input of energy that keeps it going. This is another case rather like that to which Hart and Honoré drew our attention, that we trace causes back through intermediate causes *to* a deliberate human act, but not *through* that act to *its* causes. Here we are in so much of a hurry to trace the cause of the later phase of a process back *through* the earlier phase *to* some energy input that we do not recognize the intermediate cause, the earlier phase of the self-maintaining process, as a cause at all.

But all such attempts at an explanation of the restrictions of our existing concept of cause and effect point to fairly superficial

differences, to respects in which the same basic pattern of
relations may present itself differently to our knowledge, beliefs,
expectations, and practical interests. If we attend rather to
what is there 'in the objects', it is the common pattern that
impresses us, and it is this that justifies the extension of causal
terms and causal concepts to cover not only all event and state
inus conditions (or better) but also functional causes and the
earlier phases of persisting objects and self-maintaining processes.

On the other hand, if we accept both the kinds of development and extension of causal concepts that have been considered in this chapter, we should also take note of the differences
between them. According to our second sort of extension, what
something is next or does next depends upon what it has been
or upon what it has been doing; according to the first, a change
in what one thing does depends upon how other things are.
This contrast carries others with it. In the second case the
effect typically resembles the cause, being indeed some kind of
continuation of it; in the first case it may well not. In Russell's
gravitation example, there is no resemblance between the
acceleration of one body and the distances and masses of the
surrounding bodies. This example can, indeed, be used to
bring out both sides of the contrast. The almost equal *velocity*
of a body just before and just after *t* illustrates our second kind
of extended 'cause' and 'effect', while the body's *acceleration* at
t, as a function of the distances and masses of other bodies,
illustrates our first. The two problems which I have mentioned
from time to time take different forms in these different contexts. The tie between individual cause and individual effect is
obvious in the cases covered by our second extension: it is
simply the continuity of activity or existence between arbitrarily
marked off phases. But in the cases covered by our first extension it is not clear what sort of link we could even hope to find.
The problem of the direction of causation, to which I shall turn
in the next chapter, arises in both cases, but in the one case
there is, while in the other case there is not, an obvious temporal
sequence of events.

And yet this contrast may have been pushed too far. There
is nothing in functional relationship as such to preclude resemblance or continuity. The Newtonian gravitational example,

in which the function holds instantaneously between utterly disparate factors, may be an unusually extreme one. There is certainly a difference between interaction and the mere continuance of some self-maintaining process, but interaction can itself involve continuous but intersecting processes. Transeunt causation can share a feature which immanent causation most clearly displays: this will be of interest when we return, in Chapter 8, to the problem of the necessity of causes.

7

The Direction of Causation[1]

THE relation between cause and effect is commonly taken to be asymmetrical: a cause is related to its effect in some way in which the effect is not related to its cause. We have been using the term *causal priority* as a name for whatever it is that marks this distinctive direction; but so far this phrase has been little more than a name for an unknown somewhat. To make it much more than a mere name we must try to answer the two questions, 'What is our concept of causal priority, of the direction of causation?' and 'What, if anything, constitutes causal priority in the objects? In what real respects, if any, is the causal relation asymmetrical?'

On a simple regularity theory, a cause is both necessary and sufficient for its effect in such a sense that it follows automatically that the effect is equally sufficient and necessary for its cause: whenever an event of type B occurs an event of type A has preceded it and whenever an event of type A occurs an event of type B will follow. This symmetry is unaffected by the improvements and complications in the account of causal regularities given in Chapter 3. A full cause, as there defined, is still both necessary and sufficient for its effect in some field, and in that same field the effect will be both necessary and sufficient for the full cause—all these statements of necessity and sufficiency being translatable into the appropriate universal propositions. But what about the relation between a partial cause, or inus condition, and its effect? This relation is not symmetrical: it is logically possible that A should be an inus condition of B while B is not an inus condition of A. But neither

[1] I discussed this problem in Section 8 in 'Causes and Conditions' *American Philosophical Quarterly*, ii (1965), and more fully in 'The Direction of Causation' *Philosophical Review*, lxxv (1966), 441–66, but the present chapter embodies considerable changes of view.

is it asymmetrical, and in fact where A is an inus condition of B, B is usually also an inus condition of A. If (in the field F) there is some X and some Y such that all $(AX$ or $Y)$ are B and all B are $(AX$ or $Y)$, it follows at once that all $B\bar{Y}$ are A, and there will usually be some Z such that all $(B\bar{Y}$ or $Z)$ are A while all A are $(B\bar{Y}$ or $Z)$. So this relation will in general fail to introduce any asymmetry, any distinctive direction.

It is not surprising, then, that regularity theorists tend to rely on time to supply the asymmetry: if the type of event A is necessary and sufficient for the type of event B, and vice versa, or again if each type is an inus condition of the other, then events of whichever type the events of which regularly precede the associated events of the other type are the causes. Causal priority is just temporal priority under another name.

But this view is at variance at least with our ordinary concepts.

For one thing, we seem ready to accept causes that are simultaneous with their effects—for example, Kant's leaden ball resting on a cushion and being causally responsible for a hollow, or, in a Newtonian gravitational set-up, the acceleration of one body at t depending causally upon the masses and distances of other bodies at that same t. We even seem able to conceive that there might be backward causation, with the effect preceding its cause in time. Certainly many people have speculated about the possibility of some sort of direct precognition, of a literal foreseeing of future events, and some have believed that they, or others, have had this power. But such a literal seeing of the future would mean that the future event was already *affecting* the precognizer. We need not, of course, defend the view that precognition, or any other form of backward causation, or even simultaneous causation, actually occurs. It is enough for our present purpose that they have been conceived, for this would show that our concept of causal order is not simply that of temporal order, that we have some notion of a relation of causal priority which can be variously directed with respect to time.

A possible reply to this argument is that while we can talk and speculate vaguely about these possibilities, we cannot conceive them coherently. Backward causation, it might be said, is like time travel. The concept, which we have, of just a single time dimension makes literal time travel conceptually impossible; but this has not prevented novelists from telling stories about it. However, I shall argue later that we can dispose of this reply by describing in some detail conceivable experimental results which, if they were obtained, would be coherently interpreted as evidence for backward causation.[2]

Another reason for insisting on a conceptual distinction between causal and temporal priority is that these relations seem to have different logical structures. The direction of time characterizes the dimension as a whole, whereas the direction of causation characterizes each process or sequence on its own. Suppose, for example, that events A, B, C, D, E form a series in this order in time, but perhaps not in this temporal direction —I mean that it may be that A comes first and E last, but again it may be that E comes first and A last; what is settled is that B comes between A and C, C between B and D, and so on. Suppose further that events D' and E' are simultaneous with D and E respectively. Then as soon as we fix the time direction between any two of these events, we fix it for every pair. If B comes before C, then A comes before B, D before E, and D' before E'; but if C comes before B, then all the other relations are correspondingly reversed. Once a time-direction has been given to any pair of events, it has been given to the system as a whole. Not so with causal direction. It belongs, if it belongs

[2] There has been a vigorous controversy about the possibility of backward causation, started by the symposium between M. Dummett and A. Flew 'Can an Effect Precede its Cause?' in *Proceedings of the Aristotelian Society*, Supplementary Volume XXVIII (1954), 27–62. See also Max Black, 'Why Cannot an Effect Precede its Cause?', *Analysis*, xvi (1955–6), 49–58, reprinted in *Models and Metaphors*; A. Flew, 'Effects before their Causes?—Addenda and Corrigenda', *Analysis*, xvi (1955–6), 104–10; M. Scriven, 'Randomness and the Causal Order', ibid., xvii (1956–7), 5–9; D. F. Pears, 'The Priority of Causes', ibid., xvii (1956–7), 54–63; A. Flew, 'Causal Disorder Again' ibid., xvii (1956–7), 81–6; R. M. Chisholm and R. Taylor, 'Making Things to have Happened', ibid., xx (1959–60), 73–8; W. Dray, 'Taylor and Chisholm on Making Things to have Happened', ibid., xx (1959–60), 79–82; A. J. Ayer, *The Problem of Knowledge*, pp. 170–5; M. Dummett, 'Bringing about the Past', *Philosophical Review*, lxxiii (1964), 338–59; S. Gorovitz, 'Leaving the Past Alone', ibid., 360–71; R. M. Gale, 'Why a Cause Cannot be Later than its Effect', *Review of Metaphysics*, xix (1965), 209–34. I have drawn freely on points made by all those who have contributed to this controversy, though my main purpose is not to consider whether causes could be later than their effects, or could be found to be so, but simply to discover what concept we have of causal priority and what, if anything, constitutes causal priority 'in the objects'.

at all, to each ordered pair of events on its own. *B* may be causally prior to *C*, and yet *D* and *E* may be causally irrelevant to one another, or again *E* might be causally prior to *D*. It seems conceivable that although *D* and *D'* are simultaneous, and *E* and *E'*, the direction of causation might be from *D* to *E* and yet from *E'* to *D'*. Of course this suggestion that causal direction characterizes processes separately is a direct denial of the view that it is simply temporal direction in disguise. An adherent of the latter view would say that when it is settled that *D* is temporally prior to *E*, although they may be causally unrelated, it follows at once that *if* they are causally related, *D* is the cause and *E* the effect. But what I am maintaining is that this seems not to be how we ordinarily see this matter.

This apparent difference of logical structure would also be a difficulty for a view which is the reverse of that which we have been considering, and which makes temporal priority causal priority in disguise. (This second view is implicit in discussions which are ostensibly about the direction of time, time's arrow, or temporal asymmetry, but whose detailed concern is with asymmetries in specific kinds of causal process.)[3] It is hard to see how the pervasive directedness of the whole time dimension, which is undoubtedly part of our concept of time, could be constituted by the local asymmetries of particular processes. This view would have to be seen as involving a revision of our concept of time, as saying that time does not really have the pervasive directedness we ascribe to it. All that is pervasive is its unidimensionality; given this, we can borrow an asymmetry from particular processes and impose it upon the whole dimension.

How are these two views related to one another? We are tempted to say that they cannot both be right: we cannot, without vicious circularity, analyse the concept of causal priority wholly in terms of temporal priority and also analyse the concept of temporal priority wholly in terms of causal priority. Yet it would be possible, however implausible, to say that direction is imposed on the time dimension by a borrowing from some special sorts of causal process, and that the supposed direction of causation in all other sorts of causal process is

³ For example, H. Reichenbach, *The Direction of Time*; K. R. Popper, 'The Arrow of Time', *Nature*, clxxvii (1956), 538; A. Grünbaum, 'Temporally-asymmetric Principles, etc.', *Philosophy of Science*, xxix (1962), 146–70.

merely that of time. This would mean, in effect, that there is an essentially causal priority of some causes to their effects, but that the causal priority we ascribe to other causes consists merely in their lying, as we might say, on the same side of their effects in the time dimension as do those special causes whose relation to their effects is intrinsically asymmetrical.

A third reason for insisting on a conceptual distinction between causal and temporal priority is that we regard causes as explaining their effects in a way in which effects do not explain their causes, and the mere fact of temporal priority would not account for this. A corollary is that if two events occur close together this may be explained by their being collateral effects of a common cause, but not by their being joint causes of a single effect. The same principle applies if two features, or two kinds of event, tend frequently to occur together. A tendency for white hair and pink eyes to go together may be explained by these features being both produced or encouraged by a single gene; but we could not explain a tendency for high humidity and falling barometric pressure to go together by their being joint causes of the falling of rain. It may be objected that such joint causes are not really time-reversed images of collateral effects. Since, given some of the circumstances, the common cause is necessary and probably also sufficient for one effect, and given others of the circumstances, it is necessary and probably also sufficient for the other effect, the time-reversed image of this situation would be one where, given some circumstances, one cause was sufficient and probably also necessary for the common effect, while, given others of the circumstances, the other cause was sufficient and probably also necessary for that same effect. The nearest we could come to this would be a case of causal over-determination. And we could still use this example to make our point: we do not regard the co-occurrence of a pair of over-determining causes—say the flash of lightning and the throwing of the cigarette butt in example (ii) in Chapter 2—as being explained by the fact that they do between them over-determine their common effect—the fire in the straw. But, the objector may say, the cases are still not parallel. Given all the circumstances, the common cause, C, may be sufficient—in the strong, counterfactual, sense—for each of its collateral effects, E_1 and E_2, and it is only when it is so that it explains their co-occurrence. But the common effect, E, cannot in this sense be sufficient for each of its over-determining causes, C_1 and C_2. For if it were, each of them would be necessary in the circumstances for it; but neither of them is necessary in the circumstances just because the other also occurs. (The letters C, E_1, etc. here refer to individual events.)

But the extreme difficulty which we encounter in setting up a time-reversed image of the commonplace pattern of events in which one cause has two collateral effects itself illustrates the point that we work all the time with a concept of causal direction that is not reducible to temporal direction. We are happy to say that, given the circumstances, C was sufficient for E_1 and for E_2: if E_1 had not been going to occur, C would not have occurred, and so, since C was necessary in the circumstances for E_2, E_2 would not have occurred either. And the same holds with E_1 and E_2 exchanging places. We are willing to accept the claim that there is no causally possible world which includes all the circumstances and E_1, but not E_2, or vice versa. But in the proposed time-image of this case, we are not prepared to say that C_1 and C_2 were each necessary (as well as sufficient) in the circumstances for E. If C_1 was sufficient for E, then C_2—even if it was in fact simultaneous with C_1—could not also be necessary for E, in the circumstances. We are convinced that there *must* be possible worlds which include the relevant circumstances and C_1, but not C_2, and vice versa. C_1 and C_2 cannot be tied to co-occurrence by their relationships to a later event E, whereas E_1 and E_2 can be tied to co-occurrence by logically analogous relationships to an earlier event C. But if we cannot keep the rest of the conceptual pattern while reversing the time-direction, we must be using a notion of some other asymmetry which we believe to be somehow linked with the asymmetry of time. And this must be something other than the corresponding regularities, for these are time-reversible. We cannot plausibly lay it down, *a priori*, that C_1 and C_2 cannot be both necessary, as well as sufficient, in the circumstances for E in the regularity sense of 'necessary' and 'sufficient'. It must be possible that C_1, C_2, and E and the relevant circumstances should be such that whenever in those circumstances an event of the C_1 type occurs an event of the E type follows, and that whenever an event of the E type occurs, an event of the C_2

type has preceded, so that an event of the C_1 type never occurs without one of the C_2 type occurring also, and vice versa.

These arguments show that we have some concept of a causal priority that is something more than temporal priority, and that is not constituted by regularities; but they do not yet tell us what this concept is. Does Russell's suggestion that one-way determination can be nothing but many–one correlation help us here? The suggestion is that if we have a law which says that whenever an event occurs of any one of several types, say A, B, C, D, an event of type E occurs also, and that whenever an event of type E occurs, an event occurs either of type A or of type B or of type C or of type D, then if an event of type A, say A_1, and one of type E, say E_1, occur appropriately together, satisfying both halves of the law, we shall say that it is A_1 that is causally prior to E_1; and it is suggested that only a relation of this form will fulfil our concept of causal direction. Now it is true that in such a case we can say not only that A_1 was sufficient for E_1, in a strong, counterfactual, sense, but also that A_1 was necessary in the circumstances for E_1, since no event of type B or C or D occurred; equally we can say that E_1 was necessary for A_1; but we cannot say in the strong sense that E_1 was sufficient for A_1, since E_1 might well have been associated not with an A but with a B or a C or a D. So there is a sense in which we can agree with Russell that the occurrence of A_1 determines that of E_1, but not vice versa. But this has nothing to do with our ordinary concept of causal priority. Any attempt to base causal priority on such a relationship would, for instance, be at once overruled by temporal order. Suppose that the law ensured that any E would be closely followed by either an A or a B or a C or a D, and that any one of these would be closely preceded by an E; none the less when E_1 occurred and was closely followed by A_1, we should say that E_1 had brought about A_1, despite the known fact that Es could bring about Bs or Cs or Ds as well as As. This case would in fact be analogous to that of our partially indeterministic slot-machine L in Chapter 2. The existence of a law of this form does not in the least tempt us to talk of backward causation, of the later A_1 bringing about the earlier E_1. So Russell's one-way determination does not produce a corresponding assignment of causal priority; and on the other hand we are often ready to assign causal priority when we have no thought of anything like Russell's relationship. No doubt we are at least dimly aware of Mill's plurality of causes, of the fact that the effect, described in whatever, perhaps fairly broad, way we are thinking of it, could have been brought about by alternative causes instead of the actual one; but equally we are aware not only that this same cause would have had alternative outcomes in other circumstances, but that even in the same circumstances a cause which would still fall under the description under which we are thinking of this one might well have other effects. And where, in scientific contexts, we describe the relevant field, the cause, and the effect so accurately that there is no room left either for alternative effects of this cause or for alternative causes of this effect, we still confidently assign causal priority to the earlier event. It may be true that if we were thinking of causation purely in terms of regularities, but had advanced from neolithic to functional regularities, and had adopted the special feature of Russell's Newtonian example that the function related simultaneous and instantaneous values of the relevant quantities, then we could find nothing but Russell's one-way determination to mark off causes from effects; but this procedure would have even less to do with our ordinary concept of causal priority than Hume's idea and impression of necessity$_2$ have to do with our ordinary concept of what marks off causal from non-causal sequences; Russell, like Hume, would be advocating a conceptual reform.

In order to express the strong, counterfactual, sense in which a cause may be—though it need not be—sufficient for its effect I have used statements of the form 'If E had not been going to occur, C would not have occurred'—for example, 'If the chestnut had not been going to become flatter, the hammer-blow would not have been struck'. But this, even where it is acceptable, where we are prepared to expand it into the claim that in the appropriate possible world in which the chestnut does not become flatter the hammer-blow is not struck, is obviously much less natural than the converse counterfactual, 'If the hammer-blow had not been struck, the chestnut would not have become flatter'. This contrast in naturalness is clearly connected with the fact that the hammer-blow is causally, not merely temporally, prior to the flattening. If we were entertaining a precognition hypothesis, we should find it quite natural to say that if the later, target, event had not been going to occur the foreseer would not have had the experience he did. But we can hardly use this contrast in naturalness as an analysis of the notion of causal priority: we must go further and try to understand why we find one antecedent–consequent order in a conditional linking two (possible) events more natural than the other.

A more promising approach is by way of the notions of control and 'effectiveness': the direction of causation is connected with the way round in which we might use a causal law as a recipe. A cause is *effective* as a means of bringing about its effect. The striking of a match on a matchbox is an inus condition of the appearance of a flame, and vice versa. But I can use the striking as a means to the flame (if the other conditions are right), whereas although I can produce a closely similar flame independently (say, by applying another, already lighted, match to this one) I cannot use the flame as a means to the previous striking of the match on the box.

But this brings out one of the queerest aspects of the hypothesis of backward causation. One might suppose that if there were a time-reversed exact analogue of causation, with causal priority opposite to temporal priority, then one could use a later event as a means to the bringing about of an earlier one: in one of the stock examples, putting up a particular picture on Tuesday would be a way of bringing it about that a precognizer *had had* a corresponding experience on Monday, and even *had made*, on Monday, a drawing that resembles this picture. And this seems absurd.[4] If there were such a thing as backward causation, it would somehow have to stop short of offering us means of bringing about the past.

The causally prior item, then, seems to be the one which we can directly control, and by way of which we can indirectly control the other. Causes are effective, effects are not.

---

[4] This point is used, by Flew, in *Analysis*, xvii (1956–7), 81–4, to argue that what Scriven offers as an example of backward causation would not be causation because it leaves out 'effectiveness'. Gale similarly (op. cit., p. 217) takes 'effectiveness' to be an essential feature of a cause, saying that 'a cause is that which can be used for the purpose of making, or bringing it about that, something else happens', and concluding from this that 'the ordinary concept of causality is anthropomorphic'.

actions give us our primary, direct, awareness of causal priority. It is not unlikely that something that belongs essentially to them is at least the core of our concept of causal priority. Nevertheless, there may be something of which we are then at least dimly aware, something objective and not essentially tied to human agency and intervention.

Von Wright has adopted just such an analysis of causal priority.[6] 'I now propose the following way of distinguishing between cause and effect by means of the notion of action: p is a cause relative to q, and q an effect relative to p, if and only if by doing p we could bring about q or by suppressing p we could remove q or prevent it from happening.' To the objection that causation holds outside the scope of human action he gives two replies. Though the eruption of Vesuvius was the cause of the destruction of Pompeii, and men cannot make volcanoes erupt, there are distinguishable events within the complex event, the destruction of Pompeii—stones hitting men on the head, roofs collapsing under loads, and so on—which are of kinds with which we are familiar from experience 'and which are such that the cause-factor typically satisfies the requirement of manipulability'. Action-conferred priority in *analogues* of the component events somehow constitutes the priority in the complex, non-manipulable event of which they are components. And although causation 'operates throughout the universe— also in spatial and temporal regions forever inaccessible to man', von Wright insists that 'to think of a relation between events as causal is to think of it under the aspect of (possible) action'.

This analysis raises all the problems I have mentioned, and, as von Wright's subsequent discussion shows, other difficulties as well. To explain the asymmetry of the causal relation in particular cases, he says that '*In the cases* when I bring about q by doing p, p is the cause and not q', even if on other occasions an event of the same type q causes an event of the type p, namely when I bring about p by doing q; but this distinction (if p and q are simultaneous) 'requires that there is some *basic* action, i.e. an action which we can do "directly" and not only by doing something else'. If p were a basic action, such as raising my arm, it would be the cause and q the effect even if p and q were simultaneous. But this assigning of causal priority to basic

6 *Explanation and Understanding*, pp. 70–81.

actions has paradoxical consequences. There may well be neural events or processes which are both necessary and sufficient for any muscular activity, and which slightly *precede* in time the rising of my arm. Then, if raising my arm is the basic action, it must *cause* the associated necessary and sufficient neural processes: by raising my arm I can bring it about that these neural events have occurred. Von Wright accepts this as a genuine case of 'causation operating from the present towards the past',[7] and of course this makes backward causation extremely common. But he also admits that a neurophysiologist might produce or suppress neural events in such ways as to make my arm rise or to prevent me from raising it. He reconciles these facts by saying that there are different 'closed systems', in one of which the rising of my arm, when I raise it, is causally prior to the neural events, and in the other of which the neural events, manipulated by the neurophysiologist, are causally prior to the rising of my arm. But it is very tempting to say that on an occasion when I actually raise my arm, so that by von Wright's account the neural events are the effect, they are causally prior in that a neurophysiologist *could have* interfered with them and could *thereby* have prevented my arm from rising. The talk of closed systems allows von Wright to say that only one direction of causation is actually operated in any single case, but he has obviously abandoned the assumption that a specific direction of causation holds between the objective events. Such an objectivist assumption would require that if the neurophysiologist could have brought about not-*q* by suppressing *p*, then *p* was in fact causally prior to *q*, and it would then be contradictory to say that since I actually brought about *p* by doing *q*, *q* was also in fact causally prior to *p*.

These further difficulties, the acceptance of frequent backward causation and the abandonment of objective causal order, should make us even more dissatisfied with the proposed analysis of causal priority. Surely von Wright has mistaken the experience which gives us our primary awareness of causal priority for the relation of causal priority itself. It is no doubt by performing 'basic actions' and seeing what they bring about that we originally detect the asymmetrical relation between

[7] The argument is due to R. M. Chisholm, 'Freedom and Action', in *Freedom and Determination*, ed. K. Lehrer.

individual effects and causes, but there is no need to say that this relation just *is* being-brought-about-by-means-of, or that to think of a relation between events as (unidirectionally) causal 'is to think of it under the aspect of (possible) action'. This analysis, promising though it appeared, is only a first attempt; we must try to go beyond it. If we succeed, we may be able to conclude that the neural events are objectively causally prior to my arm's rising, even though my raising of my arm is 'basic' within my experience, since it is what I see myself as just doing, and not as bringing about by way of doing something else. It is as misleading to say that I bring about these neural events by raising my arm as it would be to say, when I am driving my car, that by going round a corner to the left I bring it about that the track-rods move to the right.

Let us try another approach, examining a type of experiment that could conceivably be used to provide evidence for backward causation.[8] By so doing, we may not only defend the claim made earlier that this possibility can be coherently conceived but also, by discovering *what* would count as evidence for it, find out more about our concept of causal priority.

On Monday a person who claims to have powers of precognition is asked to draw a copy of a pattern that is going to be displayed in a certain place the next day; on Tuesday the pattern is produced by some randomizing device and duly displayed; and, let us suppose, the precognizer's drawing turns out to be exactly like the random pattern which it was intended to copy. Prima facie, this result is evidence that this person really has precognized the pattern. Of course, several precautions will have to be taken if this evidence is to have any weight. We must check that the drawing has not altered or been altered to bring it into agreement with the pattern, that it still is on Tuesday just as it was drawn on Monday. We must exclude various possible ways in which the supposed precognizer, or his drawing, might have controlled, or fed information into, the alleged randomizing device. Again, a single favourable result, however surprising, might be written off as an accident; but if the experiment were repeated a number of

---

[8] This is based on Scriven, op. cit. An important feature of Scriven's experiment, the use of *several* precognizers, is temporarily omitted but will be brought in later, to make a distinct point.

times with all the appropriate precautions and continued to yield favourable results, then this would begin to constitute weighty evidence that precognition was occurring. And if we conclude that it is precognition, we are not merely saying that if the pattern had been different the drawing would have been correspondingly different in a sense in which the converse counterfactual—that if the drawing had been different the pattern would have been correspondingly different—would have been equally true. We are saying also that the pattern is responsible for the details of the drawing being as they are, that it has determined the drawing and not vice versa; in other words, that the pattern is causally prior to the drawing.

In this experiment, nothing depends essentially upon the use of a human precognizer. We could describe a conceivable experiment a favourable result of which might give evidence of backward causation without precognition by replacing the supposed precognizer by a machine which included, say, a photographic film. If the film, when developed, regularly showed a picture that closely resembled the pattern subsequently produced by the randomizing device, then, given all the appropriate precautions, we should have evidence that this photographic machine was being affected by the subsequently produced pattern. In particular, we need not make any use of the fact that a human precognizer would be *trying* to draw on Monday a pattern that was to be shown, in some place known to him, on Tuesday, that he was directing his attention in a specific way. Nor need we even make use of the fact that a photographic plate, though itself devoid of purpose, is commonly intended, by those who make and use it, to record things. We could replace the plate by, say, iron filings on a flat sheet of glass, which are found to exhibit, on Monday, a pattern very like that which is displayed nearby on Tuesday. However, I shall continue to discuss this form of experiment with reference to a precognizer's drawing, though it is to be understood that nothing turns upon this special feature.

But *how* would a successful experiment of this sort provide evidence for backward causation? It is not the randomness of the pattern, in the sense in which this is an intrinsic feature of the pattern, which tends to show its causal priority; for the drawing, being very like the pattern, will share this sort of randomness with it. This sort of randomness, in both items, is important only because it makes it unlikely that two similar random figures should have come into existence close together but independently. Reduced to essentials, all that we have here is a surprising degree of agreement in detail, so good that it is hard to set even a single case aside as a coincidence. In each single case there is prima facie evidence of some sort of causal connection, and this is made much stronger by repetition. But this evidence is in itself symmetrical. How then do we go from 'some sort of causal connection' to backward causation? Only by ruling out explanations in terms of forward causation.

There are two different methods by which the defender of the experiment may try to achieve this. First, he could take care to exclude various specific ways in which the drawing might have influenced the pattern—locking the drawing up as soon as it is made, making sure that no photograph or description of it gets around, putting the precognizer into a twenty-four hour coma as soon as he has made his drawing, and so on. But these specific exclusions may not be enough. They leave us with a choice between some mysterious, hitherto unknown, variety of forward causation and the equally hitherto unknown and even more mysterious possibility of backward causation. The former would seem to be the lesser evil. The defender gives his hypothesis more initial plausibility by speaking of precognition, that is, by assimilating his hypothesis to the familiar process of visual perception which, as we know, can reproduce a complicated pattern in much of its detail. But since precognition would have to be utterly different from ordinary seeing, which uses normal causal mechanisms, this analogy does not really support the precognition hypothesis against its rival; foreseeing would be too unlike seeing to be prima facie any better an explanation than 'some mysterious forward causal connection'. And in any case even the initial plausibility disappears if we replace precognition, as suggested above, by something like our iron filings on a glass sheet.

Secondly, the defender of the experiment may try to exclude all forms of forward causation, even unknown ones, either by making the pattern that appears on Tuesday the product of one or (preferably) more than one free human choice, or by making it the product of what is in a very strong sense a random device, something which operates indeterministically, by objective chance. Its nucleus, say, is something like a Geiger counter with some radioactive material nearby. In either case he is claiming to have terminated the regress of causal antecedents of the pattern so that it cannot reach back to the drawing.

Of course the fact that there is *something* indeterministic in the pattern's causal antecedents would not prevent the drawing from being causally prior to it. A grandfather's genes help to determine his grandchild's character even if it is only by way of various free, indeterministic, choices that the grandchild comes into existence at all. Similarly the drawing might influence the pattern even if something indeterministic allowed the pattern to be produced. What is wanted is an indeterministic source for the pattern's having just those features, rather than others, which constitute its too-close-to-be-fortuitous resemblance to the drawing. The defender's argument then has this general form:

A and *B* are too alike for their resemblance to be coincidental; so there is *some* causal connection between them. Therefore either *A* is causally prior to *B* or *B* is causally prior to *A*. But *B*'s origin is indeterministic in a way that precludes the tracing back to *A* of the causation of the features relevant to this resemblance. So *A* is not (in the relevant respect) causally prior to *B*. Therefore *B* is causally prior to *A*.

Thus set out, the argument has an obvious flaw. The resemblance might be explained by *A* and *B* having, in the respects relevant to their surprising resemblances, a common cause rather than by either being causally prior to the other. But this possibility is also blocked by the tracing of *B*'s possession of the relevant features to an indeterministic source. This prevents not only the tracing back of their causation to *A*, but also the tracing back of their origin to any *C* which could also be causally responsible for *A*.

Spelling out the argument in this way reveals two further things. First, the argument assumes that where there is an explanatory causal connection between any two items there must be some causal priority relation(s), either one item being causally prior to the other or some third item being causally prior to both. Secondly, it assumes that we already know the direction of causation between one or more free choices and their outcome or between an indeterministic device and its product. This experiment, then, cannot be claimed to yield a primary awareness of causal priority; it cannot purport to contain what Hume would call an impression of causal priority; so it does not, after all, throw much light on this idea. Even if it can be defended, this experiment does not in itself reveal what our concept of causal priority is or what is our fundamental way of recognizing it. But it has made one small contribution: we have seen that any indeterministic device would do instead of a free agent; there is some hope after all of detaching causal priority from human agency and 'effectiveness'.

Can we say, then, that the basic notion of a causally prior item is of something that *just happens*: something pops up from nowhere and events run on from there? (Of course not everything to which we ascribe causal priority is itself seen as such a sheer beginning. If X is causally connected with Y, and Y with Z, then if X is a sheer beginning, it is causally prior to Y, but for this very reason Y is also prior to Z. Relative causal priority is transmitted linearly from items that are seen as having absolute causal priority, that is, causal primacy.) This would seem to agree with our preliminary sketch of the notion of causal priority in Chapter 2. But an objection is that we seem to be trying to define causal priority in terms of causal primacy, and causal primacy in terms of the negation of causal priority: the item which just happens, which pops up from nowhere, is simply something to which nothing is causally prior. And it is not, of course, something to which nothing is causally linked: it is typically the beginning of a chain of causation. Can we then ascribe causal primacy to something merely because it is at one end, and not in the middle, of a chain of causation? No, because it is quite conceivable that a causal sequence should die out, that there should be a last event in the chain rather than, or as well as, a first, but the last event would not be seen as having causal primacy or as transmitting causal priority to its neighbours. This line of thought, then, seems to yield nothing new. We are driven back to agency and 'effectiveness'. We seem to have to say just that X is causally prior to Y where, if an intervention had been applied to X, Y would have been different, and if we are asked what an intervention is we can only say that it is the sort of thing we are sometimes aware of making: we can give instances which will indicate the relevant sort of experience.

If this were all that we could say about the concept of causal priority it would be profoundly disappointing. Let us, then, see if anything more can be extracted from discussion of the precognition experiment. Something may be revealed by an important objection to the claim that any result of such an experiment, however favourable, could support a hypothesis of backward causation.

Suppose that the first part of an experiment has been performed, and a certain drawing has been made on Monday. According to the precognition hypothesis, this is literally a copy of a pattern that is to be produced on Tuesday. But then suppose that someone decides to stop or destroy the device that would have produced the pattern, so that no pattern is produced after all. The drawing cannot be a copy of a pattern which never comes into existence, and thus on this occasion the precognition hypothesis is false. But on every occasion, after the drawing is made, it is possible that someone or something should intervene so that the corresponding pattern fails to be produced. Consequently, it cannot on any occasion be the pattern that is responsible for the details of the drawing: the precognition hypothesis must be false even for those occasions when the device is not stopped, when the pattern actually is produced and turns out to be just like the drawing.[9]

This objection rests on the assumption that past and present events and states of affairs are fixed and settled and unalterable, whereas at least some future ones are still to be fixed, as yet undecided. The argument is that if at any time A is fixed while B is still unfixed, B cannot be causally prior to A, because at this time things might still be so decided that B does not occur. Can this objection be countered in any way? We may dismiss the fantastic suggestion that past events may be not fixed but still subject to decision; but the reply is still available that some future events may already be fixed, and that these alone can be precognized or have other effects in the present. The objection tells only against (and indeed is fatal to) a supposed case of backward causation where the occurrence of the

    [9] Cf. Flew's three articles and Black's article mentioned p. 162, n. 2 above. This is what Flew calls the 'bilking experiment'.

supposed cause is still undecided at a time when the supposed effect has already occurred. But this undermines the argument used above in attempting to extract a positive conclusion from the experiment. Its defender was there using the assertion that B was produced (on Tuesday) by free human choices or by an indeterministic device to preclude any tracing of B's causal origins back to A or to any earlier cause of A, say C. But we now see that what was there used to show that neither A nor C was causally prior to B can equally be used to show that B is not causally prior to A. If B really is undecided on Monday then its resemblance to A must be fortuitous, however implausible this may seem: we have ruled out the possibility of causation in either direction between them or to both from a common cause.

The defender of the experiment might try to meet this objection by saying that B could (already by Monday) be fixed in something stronger than the trivial logical sense that if, as it turns out, it does occur on Tuesday it was, on Monday, already going to occur. He could suggest that B may be fixed in a sense strong enough to block the bilking experiment without having deterministic causal antecedents. I do not think that this can be reconciled with B's being, in the relevant respects, the product of a genuinely free choice as we conceive such choices; but it might be reconciled with B's being the product of an indeterministic device. The full freedom of choice seems to require a metaphysical non-fixity in its object that goes beyond the mere absence of causal determination. Alternatively, the defender might fall back from the second to the first of the two methods mentioned above, abandoning the requirement that B should be produced, on Tuesday, by something indeterministic, allowing B's occurrence on Tuesday, with the relevant features, to have been already fixed by Monday by some sufficient cause C, and merely trying to check that C does not affect A by any kind of forward causation and that A does not affect the chain of causes by which C brings about B. He is then, as we saw, left with a choice of hypotheses, and that of some mysterious forward causation may be the lesser evil; but as we shall see later the defender of the experiment has one further resource.

However, the possibility of precognition, or of backward causation generally, matters less to us than what the arguments for and against this possibility reveal about the concept of causal priority. The defender's difficulties arise from his trying to meet two requirements at once: that the causally prior item should lie, in some line of causation, between the causally posterior item and some intervention, and that the causally posterior item should not be fixed at a time when the causally prior one is not fixed. The second is required for the priority itself, the first for any detection of the priority; the difficulty lies in securing that both requirements should be known, or even reasonably believed, to be met when the causally prior item comes later in time than the causally posterior one.

But let us attend for the moment to the second requirement. It is, so far, just that an effect cannot be fixed at a time when its cause is not fixed. But this has the corollary that if A and B are causally connected in a direct line, then if B is fixed at a time when A is not fixed, it must be A which is the effect and B the cause. It is a point in favour of this account that while it clearly relates causal order to temporal order—the easiest way of getting B fixed while A is unfixed is to have B occur before A, with room for some indeterminacy between them—it does not simply reduce one to the other, but mentions this further feature of fixity. Moreover, it leaves open at least the logical possibility of backward causation, however difficult it might be to acquire firm evidence for this: it is possible that, although A occurs at t_2 and B at the later time t_3, B should have already been fixed at the earlier time t_1 by the occurrence then of a sufficient cause for B, while A was still unfixed at t_1. We leave room for backward causation but not for bringing about the past: we cannot at t_3 bring about A at t_2, since B must already have been fixed before t_3 if it is to be a cause of A. But it is conceivable that we might at t_1 bring about A at t_2 by way of B at t_3 and the backward link from B to A: we might bring about something in the future by means of a line of causation *part* of which is time-reversed.

This account of causal priority in terms of fixity and unfixity is closely related to that in terms of effectiveness and interventions. We said that X is causally prior to Y where, if an intervention had been applied to X, Y would have been different, but not vice versa. Now if Y had been fixed at a time when X was not, an intervention could in principle have been applied to X at that time; but if it had been, Y, being fixed already, would *not* have been different. That is, the fixity/unfixity pattern which rules out a certain direction of causation rules out automatically the corresponding effectiveness. Conversely, if at a time when X is not fixed Y is not fixed either, and X is necessary in the circumstances for Y, then intervening to prevent X, or failing to intervene to bring about X, will prevent the occurrence of Y.

But does the account in terms of fixity add anything to that in terms of effectiveness? In particular, does it free us from the deplorable anthropocentricity of talk about interventions? Or is our notion of unfixity simply that of something's being in principle open to being brought about or prevented by a deliberate act? Not quite. If events have preceding sufficient causes in the strong, counterfactual, sense then they are fixed as soon as these causes have occurred; and this will hold if there are regularities of the form 'Whenever in the field F the conjunction $AB\bar{C}$ occurs, P follows'. If, on the other hand, there are events which occur but not in accordance with such regularities, not as necessitated by any preceding sufficient causes— though they may have had preceding necessary causes, and again may have had causes in the sense defined by Ducasse, 'such particular change as alone occurred in the immediate environment . . . immediately before'—then it is natural to regard these events as unfixed until they occur. While it would be very difficult to obtain *conclusive* evidence that a certain event lacked any preceding sufficient cause, it would not be difficult to find *some* evidence for this, and the hypothesis that events of certain kinds commonly occurred without sufficient (or 'necessitating') causes would be as much open to confirmation as scientific generalizations usually are. In other words, there could be knowledge about a class of (presumptively) unfixed events which was not derived purely and directly from our experience of free choices and interventions. Radioactive disintegrations are a case in point.

It is true that an event which was thus unfixed until it occurred could not be the cause in a bit of backward causation: for if it were necessary in the circumstances for some preceding event, that preceding event would be sufficient in the circumstances—in the strong, counterfactual, sense—for it, so that it would have been fixed as soon as that earlier event occurred. (This is another variant of the argument about the bilking experiment: it was for this reason that we had to choose, as a conceivable backward cause, an event which was unfixed not right up until its occurrence (at t_3) but only much earlier, at t_1.) In any instances of causal priority that we identified directly with the help of these unfixed events the causes would also be temporally prior to their effects.

It may be objected to this account of causal priority in terms of fixity that it would make it impossible for a sufficient cause to be causally prior to its effect: if X is a sufficient cause of Y, then Y is fixed as soon as X is (unless the relevant circumstances are still unfixed). Whether this is so depends on how we clear up a vagueness that has so far been left in this account. We have said that if X causes Y, there cannot be a time when X is unfixed and Y is fixed. But do we want to add that if X causes Y there must be a time when X is fixed and Y is unfixed? It is the latter that would deprive sufficient causes of causal priority. Since our notion of causal priority seems not to exclude sufficient causes, we should not add this second condition to our analysis. But then how do we detect the priority of a sufficient cause? The unfixity of the relevant circumstances may reveal it. Otherwise we must fall back either on our experience of interventions, or on the continuity of causal processes. Even if X is sufficient for Y, it may be plain enough that it was to X, not to Y, that the intervention was applied; although a spark was sufficient in the circumstances for an explosion, it was the spark that I fairly directly made, say by striking flint and steel together. Or again, even if X was sufficient for Y, it may be plain that some continuous process of movement or change, starting from some other event Z that was unfixed until it occurred, led on to X and only through X to Y. But 'basic actions' as we see them are not an infallible guide to the direction of causation. In the example discussed by von Wright, though my raising of my arm is a 'basic action', there can be no doubt that the associated neural processes were fixed at a time when the rising of the arm was still unfixed: there was a (very short) stretch of time into which interferences of various sorts might have intruded, so it was the neural processes that were causally prior to the rising of the arm.

We seem to have found, then, in this notion of fixity a basis for the concept of causal priority which does not reduce it merely to temporal priority, which leaves a small gap into which backward causation (but not the bringing about of the past) might conceivably be fitted, but which will not (as an account solely in terms of effectiveness would) proliferate very brief displays of backward causation, and which frees causal priority from complete anthropocentricity, while still allowing us to explain both why it is our active interventions that mainly give rise to this concept and why temporal and causal priority tend so strongly to go together. But let us now leave this account aside, and consider some other suggestions that have been made about asymmetries in causal processes.

There is a class of processes, pointed out by Popper as being temporally asymmetrical, of which an example is the system of circular waves spreading out from a centre, as when a stone is dropped into a pool. The reverse process, with circular waves contracting to a centre, would be equally compatible with the laws of physics, but it never, or hardly ever, occurs, whereas expanding wave systems are extremely common.[10] As Popper says, the reverse process with contracting waves 'would demand a vast number of distant coherent generators of waves, the coherence of which, to be explicable, would have to be shown . . . as originating from one centre'. That is, we have here a situation in which A is a single event (the disturbance at the centre of the pool), B is an occurrence which involves a sort of coherence between a number of separated items (a wave motion all round the circumference of the pool), and there are causal laws in accordance with which A could lead to B, but B could equally lead to A. B, however, is here in need of explanation in a way in which A is not; consequently A could satisfactorily explain B, whereas before B could explain A the coherence in B itself would need to be explained by reference to some other single event C. (We could explain the contracting wave pattern easily enough if it arose from the reflection, at the edge of a circular pool, of a wave that had previously spread out from a stone dropped at the centre, or if a flat circular ring, just inside the circumference of the pool, were connected with a handle

[10] K. R. Popper, 'The Arrow of Time', *Nature*, clxxvii (1956), 538, also *Nature*, clxxviii (1957), 382, and clxxix (1958), 1297.

and moved up and down as a whole.) Examples of this kind establish a direction of explanation, *from* some central occurrence *to* the coherence of a number of separated items: explanation runs to situations involving dispersed order from ones which do not. Let us say that the central disturbance as compared with the expanded wave is *prior with respect to the dispersal of order*. If we add the principle that a cause explains its effect in a way in which the effect does not explain the cause, it follows that there can be a satisfactory causal explanation only if the causally prior item is also prior with respect to the dispersal of order. If the opposite were the case, if the item exhibiting dispersed order were causally prior to the only related central one, the two requirements for explanation would be in conflict with one another. These points are, however, not directly relevant to the direction of *time*. It is clear that it is logically possible that a particular process which is the reverse of a normal one—that is, one in which what is prior with respect to the dispersal of order comes later in time, in which the order-dispersal direction is opposite to the order-dispersal direction of most processes in the same time-continuum—could occur without there being any normal process available to explain its starting point. This must be so, since to get such a reversed process we need only take something like a contracting wave that in fact results from the reflection, at a circular edge, of a previously expanding one, and wipe out the earlier, expanding, phase. Nor would such a reversed process be intrinsically inexplicable. To explain it we need only to establish, or assume, that the item which was prior with respect to the dispersal of order was also causally prior, despite the fact that it came later in time; that is, such a process would be explained in terms of backward causation. If in fact such a reversed process never occurs without a previous normal process to set up its initial conditions, this merely exemplifies the general truth that processes which would call for explanation in terms of backward causation do not actually occur, though they are not logically ruled out.

But why is it so plausible to say that a cause explains its effect, but not vice versa? Surely this is due to the link between causal priority and fixity. The explanatory account retraces the order in which the effect was either brought, or allowed, into existence, the way that it came to be fixed. Although we may be able to *infer* a cause from a previously known effect, this would show only *that* the cause occurred: it would smooth the way to our knowledge of the cause, but not to its existence, whereas if we explain an effect by reference to a cause we see how the way was smoothed to the existence of the effect. And above all, if the effect was unfixed when the cause was fixed, we cannot explain the cause's actually being there by reference to something which still might not have happened; what is explained must depend upon what explains it, so the latter cannot have been ontologically less solid than the former.

An example of dispersed order, then, such as the outer circular wave, is a set either of collateral effects or of joint causes of the central event. Because of its complex coherence, it is intrinsically improbable and in need of explanation. Since causes explain effects, and not vice versa, the central event will explain the dispersed order only if it is its cause, not if it is its effect. But the central event could still in principle explain the dispersed order as the co-occurrence of its effects even if the central event occurred later in time, provided that we could say that the central event was fixed at least as soon as the scattered effects were, that they came to be fixed by way of it. And this points to what could be another kind of evidence for backward causation.

In many cases what is, or could be, a set of collateral effects is an example of dispersed order, and therefore is in need of the explanation that is provided by the tracing of them to a common cause. But we might find them all related, by continuous processes which conformed to time-indifferent physical laws, to some *later* central event, and we might fail to find any similar relation to any earlier central event, even after looking very hard for one. Then, unless there were some strong reason for saying that that later central event could not have been fixed by the time the dispersed order items were, it would be tempting to speculate that the central event was causally prior to the dispersed order and so explained it, by a time-reversed causal process. Indeed we can greatly strengthen our precognition experiment by adding this feature to it.[11] Suppose that instead of just one alleged precognizer we have a number,

[11] Scriven, op. cit., makes use of this feature.

all making drawings on Monday of the pattern that is to be displayed on Tuesday, and suppose that all the drawings closely resemble the pattern that is later produced. Then the mutual resemblances between the drawings of this set are themselves in need of explanation; the set of drawings is itself an example of dispersed order. If there was no communication between the precognizers, and no other common cause occurring earlier in time can be found, then there is a case for taking the subsequently produced pattern as the common cause, and it is plausible to say that a successful experiment of this modified form would give strong support to a hypothesis of precognition. Not, of course, overwhelming support: there is always the possibility of some other, unknown, earlier central event influencing all the precognizers. But the introduction of dispersed order, of the set of many separate precognizers, makes forward causation *from the drawings to the pattern* useless as a rival hypothesis: such joint or over-determining causes might explain the resemblance of the pattern to the drawings, but it would be powerless to explain the resemblances of the drawings to one another.

But if we found—as we do not—many examples of the sort illustrated by a contracting wave pattern without any discoverable earlier central event to explain the coherence of the many dispersed 'generators', these would be even better evidence of backward causation than the precognition experiment, just because they would display, as it does not, continuous processes conforming to time-indifferent laws and connecting the dispersed order items with the later central event.

We find, then, not that priority with respect to the dispersal of order *is* causal priority, but that it is *evidence* for causal priority, and we can see why it should be so. If the two coincide, if the central event is also the causally prior event, the situation is explicable, whereas if they fail to coincide it is bewildering: we have a situation which is in need of explanation, but no explanation can be given.

This resolves what would otherwise have been a difficulty. If, as I have argued, causal priority is not to be simply identified with temporal priority, it becomes a synthetic proposition that they always (so far as we know) coincide, that all, or at least most, causation is forward causation. But where do we find the data for this inductive conclusion? If our detection of causal priority had been limited to experience of our own voluntary actions, then even if causal priority always coincided with temporal priority here, it would be rash to conclude that they coincide in processes of all other kinds as well. But since priority with respect to the dispersal of order is evidence of causal priority, we can and do have far more extensive evidence that the directions of time and of causation normally coincide.

It is often suggested that the increase in entropy in any isolated system constitutes a general temporal asymmetry in causal processes. But this is not so.[12] Let us consider the stock example of a rigid chamber containing gas, initially with part of the gas, at a higher temperature than the other part, concentrated at one end of the chamber; the two parts gradually mix and the gas approaches a uniform temperature throughout the chamber. If we consider this chamber as persisting for a very long time, with no loss of energy from the chamber as a whole, we must say that there is an enormous number of possible arrangements of the gas molecules, and that of these the overwhelming majority will be *disordered*—that is, will represent fairly uniform distributions of temperature. *Ordered* arrangements with a distinctly higher temperature at one end of the chamber than the other will be extremely improbable; nevertheless, given a sufficiently long time they will occasionally occur. It follows that among the (rare) occurrences of order, the change from order to disorder will be practically universal, whereas among the (very common) occurrences of disorder, changes from disorder to order will be extremely rare. Yet in this very long run changes from disorder to order will occur, and will occur with the same absolute frequency as changes from order to disorder. Examples of this sort, then, do not yet exhibit any asymmetry of causal pattern in relation to the direction of time. Given a record of the statistical behaviour of any closed system over a very long period, one could not infer which was the forward time-direction.

What is true, however, is that if such a system is put into a low entropy state by some intervention from outside and is then left to itself, if it is in effect a closed system from then on, it is overwhelmingly likely that its entropy will increase with time.

---

[12] Cf. A. Grünbaum, *Philosophical Problems of Space and Time*, Chapter 8, esp. pp. 241–2.

But this seems to have nothing to do with our concept of causal priority. It is a mathematical fact that, of all the possible distributions of molecular positions and velocities in what would count as a relatively low entropy state, most will lead to states with higher entropy and very few to states with still lower entropy. Then if, by and large, such low entropy states as are actually set up (by interventions) are fairly representative of the range of possible distributions, it is a consequence that most of them will in fact display subsequent increases in entropy. This consequence is not itself a mathematical truth, but neither is it utterly contingent; it is in an obvious sense very much to be expected. Yet I can find no indication that this expectable truth about statistical closed systems is incorporated in any way into our concept of causal priority. Even when we extend the notion of cause, as I argued in Chapter 6 that we should, to include the successive phases of self-maintaining processes, we have no tendency to see the cause-phase as distinguished from the effect-phase by greater intrinsic orderliness or lower entropy. The Second Law of Thermodynamics seems not to have been built into our causal concepts, either traditional or innate.

A complication, however, is that the dispersal of order also enters into the sort of example used to illustrate the increase of entropy. The state of the gas a short time after the two parts have begun to mix will be, with respect to the general distribution of temperature, and hence with respect to the availability of energy for external work, a fairly disordered one; nevertheless it will be different from most equally disordered distributions of molecular positions and velocities in that if each velocity were simultaneously reversed, the gas would return in a short time to the very unusual, highly ordered arrangement with the part at one end of the chamber at a higher temperature. In other words, this is a rather special sort of disorder, and while the occurrence of disorder in general is intrinsically highly probable and calls for no special explanation, the occurrence of this special sort of disorder does call for explanation, and is indeed to be explained as the outcome of a recently-previous ordered state. In fact, this special sort of disorder is another example of what we have been calling dispersed order. The coherence is now concealed within what superficially looks like any other disordered arrangement of molecules; but there is still an intrinsically improbable coherence between the positions and velocities of the various molecules, which is brought out by considering what would happen if all the velocities were reversed; this requires explanation and is explained by the lawful descent of this from the recent obviously ordered state. Once again, then, we have a definite direction of explanation, *to* a dispersed order *from* a non-dispersed order to which it is related by laws. The mixing process, then, is explicable on its own, in terms of ordinary forward causation, because the temporally prior state is also prior with respect to the dispersal of order, so that a coherent explanation can be given if we assume that this earlier state is also causally prior. But a change in the opposite direction, a process of separation into two parts at different temperatures, because of the initial improbability of its initial state, its dispersed order constituting a sort of position and velocity distribution that is very rare among states of equal entropy, could not be explained *on its own* without assuming backward causation; yet since this initial state is only improbable, it could be explained, going outside this process itself to the whole history of our closed system, as something that occurs very infrequently in a long period of time; and this explanation would not require backward causation. In other words, we can find an asymmetry of Popper's type in the sort of example that is used to illustrate the increase of entropy; but this asymmetry is quite different from the entropy increase itself, and, unlike the latter, has the conceptual links already traced with explanation, fixity, and the direction of causation. The general principle is that otherwise improbable concomitances and co-occurrences can be explained as collateral effects of a common cause, as dispersed order lawfully related to a causally prior non-dispersed order; but it must be a common cause, not a shared effect, and the collateral effects must not be fixed at a time when the proposed common cause is still unfixed.

I have made a number of attempts to come to grips with and to clarify the concept which we undoubtedly have of causal priority. What seems to emerge from this long and often frustrating survey is this.

Our concept of causal priority is not merely that of temporal priority; nor does it reduce to any asymmetry in the form of causal regularities—it is not, for example, Russell's concept of many–one correlation; nor is it the concept of increasing entropy or of anything like that. A first approximation to an analysis of 'X was causally prior to Y', where X and Y are individual events, is 'It would in principle have been possible for an agent to prevent Y by (directly or indirectly) preventing, or failing to bring about or to do, X'; if we speak instead of types of event, X-type events are causally prior to Y-type events if in circumstances where an X-type event is necessary for a Y-type one, it is in principle possible for an agent to prevent the occurrence of a Y-type event by preventing the occurrence of any X-type one, or if in circumstances where an X-type event is sufficient for a Y-type one, it is in principle possible for an agent to bring about a Y-type event by means of an X-type one.

However, we can carry the analysis a stage further and reduce its dependence on the notion of agency, as follows. Suppose that X and Y are individual events, and X is seen as necessary (and sufficient) in the circumstances for Y, so that the basic requirement for the judgement that X caused Y is met. Then, despite this, X was not causally prior to Y if there was a time at which Y was fixed while X was unfixed. If, on the other hand, X was fixed at a time when Y was unfixed, then X was causally prior to Y. Again, if X was not fixed until it occurred, then even if Y also was fixed as soon as X occurred (given, of course, that X was necessary in the circumstances for Y), X was causally prior to Y. And further, if there is some line or chain of causation, some continuous causal process, linking X and Y and some other event Z so that X was between Y and Z, and if Z was not fixed until it occurred, then X was causally prior to Y.*

Again, if there is some central event A, and somehow causally connected with it some dispersed order item B—that is, some collection of separate events B_1, B_2, B_3, etc., whose co-occurrence is intrinsically improbable and calls for explanation—so that A is prior to B with respect to the dispersal of order, and there is no other central event that can be related to B_1, B_2, B_3, etc., so as to explain their co-occurrence, then this is evidence that A is causally prior to B; the reason being that A is apparently the only available explanation for the co-occurrence, but it can explain this only if it is the causally prior item.

This, then, or something like this, is our concept of causal priority. But does it have any application? Does any such directedness actually belong to objective causal processes? As I have said, the counterfactual conditionals into which we initially analyse singular causal statements cannot be literally true of the objective sequences, but these can be replaced by regularities which would sustain them. Similar difficulties undermine the objective applicability of our first approximation to an analysis of the priority itself. But the further analysis, in terms of fixity and unfixity, could have objective application provided only that there is a real contrast between the fixity of the past and the present and the unfixity of some future events, free choices or indeterministic physical occurrences, which become fixed only when they occur. Now we certainly do not know that there are no such events; we do not know that strict determinism holds; but neither do we know that it does not hold, though the balance of contemporary scientific opinion is against it. So we had better be content with hypothetical judgements here: if determinism does not hold, the concept of causal priority which I have tried to analyse will apply to the objects, but if determinism holds, it will not. If you have too much causation, it destroys one of its own most characteristic features. Every event is equally fixed from eternity with every other, and there is no room left for any preferred direction of causing.

This conclusion will not, indeed, follow from a popular slightly mitigated, only almost total determinism. If

> . . . the first Morning of Creation wrote
> What the Last Dawn of Reckoning shall read[13]

then that first creation or coming into existence was presumably an event which was not fixed until it occurred, and causal priority will be linearly transmitted from it: X will be causally prior to Y, in terms of our analysis, if X lies between creation and Y in a continuous line of causation. But although on this hypothesis causal priority would indeed belong to the objects, all the experiences in and through which we have acquired the concept would in this respect be spurious.

But if *total* determinism holds, and there was not even a first creative event, our present concept of causal priority will not

[13] E. FitzGerald, *Rubáiyát of Omar Khayyám.*

be true of the real world. Of course, we can go on applying it, basing such applications on our false beliefs about the previous unfixity of human choices and perhaps of some physical events; but it will be a widespread, systematic, error. Other directional concepts, however, will still have application. There will be the direction of entropy increase from most low-entropy states of what are, for a time, closed systems. There will be, in some (especially functional) regularities, Russell's one-way determination based on many–one correlations. Neither of these, I have argued, has anything to do with our present concept of causal priority. Again, obviously, there will still be the direction of time, which we see (but on the present hypothesis wrongly) as almost perfectly correlated with the direction of causation. And there will still be the direction of the dispersal of order, which we now take as evidence for something else, but which, if that something else is a fiction, will remain as an interesting directional feature of causal processes in its own right.

8

The Necessity of Causes

WE may now come back to what Hume called 'one of the most sublime questions in philosophy', namely that of the power or efficacy of causes, of the necessity that has been thought to reside in the causal relation. We may begin by reminding ourselves of the different jobs that necessity has been expected to do.

It has been thought of, both by Hume and by some of his critics, as something that would either justify or replace induction, something which, if only we could detect it, would give us knowledge of how nature works even in unobserved and future cases. In this sense, Russell's principle of the permanence of laws[1] does the work of necessity. Closely related to this is the notion, in Hume, of what we have labelled necessity$_2$, something which if it were detected in one (cause) event would license *a priori* the inference that a certain other (effect) event would follow, with perhaps a counterpart which if detected in an effect event would license *a priori* the corresponding inference to its cause. This is closely related to the former notion, since knowledge of such a property would entitle us to assert the universal hypothetical that if a property of either sort occurred anywhere at any time, the appropriate effect would follow (or the appropriate cause would already have occurred). Thirdly, there is the weaker notion of what we have labelled necessity$_3$, of something which would license causal inference in new cases but perhaps not *a priori*; it is in this sense that Hume was prepared to redefine necessity as 'the constant union and conjunction of like objects'.[2] Necessity in this sense neither justifies nor replaces induction; rather, knowledge of it, or belief in it, is the typical product of a piece of inductive reasoning. Fourthly, there is the notion of what we have called necessity$_1$,

---

[1] *Mysticism and Logic*, p. 196.   [2] *Treatise*, II, III, 2.

of something that marks off causal from non-causal sequences. Fifthly, especially under the title of 'natural necessity', there is the thought of something that distinguishes causal or nomic regularities (or universal propositions or generalizations) from merely accidental ones. Sixthly, though this is closely linked with the fourth notion, is the idea of an intimate tie that joins each individual effect to its individual cause. Seventhly, there is the belief that it is in some sense necessary that every event should have a cause, which Hume contrasts with the belief that such particular causes must have such particular effects.[3] The necessity of causes in this sense would be something that required there to be a causal law behind any event. This, of course, joins hands with the first notion in so far as a general causal principle, once established, might help to validate or justify the drawing of particular inductive conclusions from appropriate observations or bodies of evidence. And, finally, there is always in the background the concept of logical necessity. This will not do any of the seven jobs, though it plays a part in association with necessity$_3$; an unrestricted statement of regularity or constant conjunction along with an adequate description of initial conditions will logically necessitate the assertion that such-and-such an effect will follow.

I shall examine first regularity-type theories of necessity and then theories of a radically different kind in an attempt to reach a defensible view of this subject.

The conclusion reached at the end of Chapter 3 was that the meaning of causal statements (singular or general) could not be analysed in terms of regularities, but that the complex regularities there examined constituted *part* of causation in the objects, and (in their elliptical form) constituted part of causation as we know it in the objects; what we there found to be needed, over and above complex regularity, to constitute causation in the objects was causal priority and perhaps some underlying causal mechanism. We have now dealt with causal priority; what remains to be considered is whether objective causation includes anything *more*, anything over and above both (complex) regularity and what we have found to constitute the direction of causation, perhaps something indicated by talk about an underlying mechanism, perhaps not.

---

[3] *Treatise*, I, III, 2.

How well can a regularity theory cope with the seven jobs for necessity listed above? It does not help with the first, that is, it does not in itself justify or replace induction. The second job was that of necessity$_2$, and of course any regularity approach simply denies that there is any such thing, and it thus excludes something that might have been able to justify induction. Yet it would be wrong to say that a regularity theory makes the problem of induction insoluble.[4] In Hume's argument, what makes this problem *seem* insoluble is quite a different step, his misleading use of the problem-of-induction dilemma, and as our analysis of his argument in Chapter 1 shows, that dilemma does not in any way rest on the regularity doctrine, but instead that doctrine is ultimately supported, in part and at several removes, by the dilemma. Regularity is, as we have noted, well fitted for the third job, that of necessity$_3$, and we have seen in Chapter 3 that even complex and incompletely known regularities can still do this job. It will also do the fourth job, that of necessity$_1$, of marking off causal from non-causal sequences: according to a regularity account, a single sequence is causal if and only if it instantiates a regularity. But does it do this job properly? Does it draw the line in the right place? If we use both halves of such complex regularities as we have formulated it will admit as causal only those sequences in which the earlier item is both necessary and sufficient in the circumstances for the effect. To allow for the point made in Chapter 2, that we do not always require strong, counterfactual, sufficiency, we should have to read the regularity account as admitting, as causal, sequences which instantiate the second half of such complex regularities as we have formulated—that which has such a form as 'In the field F, all P are preceded by ($AB\bar{C}$ or $DG\bar{H}$ or $JK\bar{L}$)'—even if no corresponding first half, of such a form as 'In the field F, all ($AB\bar{C}$ or $DG\bar{H}$ or $JK\bar{L}$) are followed by P', is in force. On the other hand, it is this first half of a regularity that would perform the more frequently mentioned task of necessity$_3$, that would, in conjunction with some description of the cause, logically necessitate the effect; the second half of a regularity would perform only a less popular task; it would, in conjunction with some description of the effect,

4 Or even that it is a regularity theory that gives rise to this problem. Cf. H. R. Harré, *The Philosophies of Science*, p. 117.

logically necessitate the previous occurrence of the cause. There is tension here between the ordinary requirements for causal sequence and the philosophical tradition: once it is assumed that causation has something to do with logical necessitation it is tempting to make the causally prior item at least part of the logically prior item, to put the cause on the logically necessitating side. But then it will be different halves of a regularity that do the more frequently mentioned task of necessity$_3$ and supply the most vital part of necessity$_1$. Even apart from this, in order to get the right sequences marked off as causal we must add the proviso that there should be the right relation of causal priority and also allow, as in Chapter 2, for the fact that *some* members of over-determining sets of causal factors are causes while others are not. These are minor and not particularly troublesome adjustments. But the major issue is whether, even after they have been made, the regularity account picks out the right sequences as causal. This depends on its success in doing the fifth job. For if there are or can be regularities which are altogether accidental (and do not merely have the causal priority arrows wrongly placed), it seems that their instances will count as causal by the regularity definition, while they would be intuitively set aside as non-causal. This is a problem which we must discuss at length. A purely regularity theory simply refuses to do the sixth job; it denies that there is any tie between the individual cause and effect over and above their instantiating of the right sort of regularity; again, we shall consider whether it is right to do so. The regularity approach is also unhelpful in connection with the seventh job: there seems to be no reason why the instantiating of regularities should pervade the universe, and we have examined and rejected, in Chapter 4, both Kant's arguments for the strong thesis 'Everything that happens . . . presupposes something upon which it follows according to a rule' and arguments of a Kantian type put forward by modern thinkers in support of similar but weaker conclusions. We shall consider whether some other (or further) account of what causation in the objects *is* lends more weight to the expectation that events *should* have causes.

The problem raised by the fifth job for necessity, that of distinguishing causal from accidental regularities, is the great difficulty for any regularity theory of causation. We can distinguish a general and a specific form of this difficulty. In his classic discussion of the character of natural laws[5] Kneale considers four possible views, that such laws are 'principles of necessitation', that they are restricted universals, applying only to limited regions of space and time, that they are unrestricted but still only contingent universals, describing what always and everywhere actually occurs, and that they are prescriptions, maxims, or rules. The third of these is the Humean regularity view; against it Kneale brings what he regards as the conclusive objection that laws of nature entail counterfactual conditionals, while contingent, actual universals do not. For example, if there had been a law of nature that all dodos have a white feather in their tails, this would have entailed the counterfactual conditional that if there had been any dodos other than those that actually existed, they too would have had a white feather in their tails, whereas the contingent universal proposition that all actual dodos had a white feather in their tails does not entail this counterfactual conditional.[6] But even if this specific difficulty were resolved, there would still be a more general difficulty: we want to draw *some* distinction between laws of nature on the one hand and merely accidentally true universal propositions on the other (even if it is not the entailing of counterfactuals that distinguishes them), and it is hard to see how a regularity theory can explain this. In a later article[7] Kneale gives examples of conceivably true but only accidental universals which we should not count as even derived laws of nature: 'there has never been a chain reaction of

[5] W. C. Kneale, *Probability and Induction*, pp. 70–103.

[6] Ibid., p. 75. Kneale speaks of *contrary-to-fact* conditionals: others have suggested that nomic universals are distinguished by their entailing *subjunctive* conditionals. This is less apt, for the term 'subjunctive conditional' is ambiguous between counterfactuals, that is, those whose form indicates that the speaker takes their antecedents to be unfulfilled ('If there had been any . . .', 'If there were any . . .') and those which merely indicate that the speaker takes their antecedents to be unlikely ('If there were to be any . . .'). The latter are only a species of open conditionals, and even an accidental universal will entail all the corresponding open conditionals. If it is a cosmic accident that all past, present, and future As are Bs, it still follows that if there is an A (in such-and-such a place) it is a B and that if there were to be an A—however unlikely—then this too would be a B. It is only the conditionals whose antecedents are unfulfilled that even look like the exclusive property of nomic universals.

[7] 'Natural Laws and Contrary to Fact Conditionals', *Analysis*, x (1950), reprinted in *Philosophy and Analysis*, ed. Margaret Macdonald, pp. 226–31.

plutonium within a strong steel shell containing heavy hydro-
gen and . . . there never will be' and 'no human being has ever
heard or will ever hear this tune' (said by a musician who has
just composed an intricate tune on his deathbed).

A Humean might respond in either of two ways to this
general difficulty: he might try to draw, in his own terms, the
required distinction between nomic and accidental universal
truths, or he might, heroically, maintain that it was only an
unwarranted prejudice that there should be any such distinction. He might argue that in a deterministic universe everything
that happens happens in accordance with causal laws, so that
any allegedly accidental universal truths like those suggested
by Kneale hold, if they hold at all, in consequence of laws, and
should therefore be regarded as laws themselves, but derived
laws. This is not a very good argument, but we need not bother
about its other weaknesses since it is completely destroyed by
the reflection that we have no right to assume that the universe
is deterministic. Suppose that we manufacture a number of
atomic bombs, all alike in all relevant respects, each of which
will explode if and only if a nuclear disintegration of a certain
kind A occurs spontaneously before a nuclear disintegration of
some other kind B occurs within the same core—a reaction of
type B will in effect defuse the bomb. Some of the bombs
explode and some do not, but it is a matter of pure chance
which do, that is, whether in each bomb an A-reaction occurs
before a B-reaction. Suppose further that it just happens that
a red spot has been painted on all and only the bombs that in
fact explode. Then we have a true universal proposition of just
the right form to count as a causal regularity making the having
of a red spot painted on the outside an inus condition of such
a bomb's exploding, and therefore necessary and sufficient in
the circumstances for this: whenever there are the other conditions, and the red spot, the bomb explodes, but whenever
there are only the other conditions, without the red spot, it
does not. Also the fixity relations are right to allow the spot-
painting to be causally prior to the explosion in each case.

Our heroic Humean will, then, say that this is a causal
regularity, a law of nature. But, *ex hypothesi*, its truth is not a
consequence of the truth of any other laws: it was a matter of
pure chance, at least so far as all the laws of atomic disintegra-

tion are concerned, that just those particular bombs blew up. If the red-spot/explosion universal is a law, it is a new fundamental law of nature in its own right. Well, the Humean could still *say* this, defending it on the ground that nothing can be found in those other universal truths which we happily accept as fundamental laws of nature that relevantly distinguishes them from this one. But most Humeans would prefer, if they could, to find some grounds, compatible with their system of ideas, which would draw a line between regularities like this one, which could be called accidental, and those which would be counted as causal laws or laws of nature.

But let us go back to the specific difficulty, to Kneale's argument that laws of nature entail counterfactuals while contingent universal truths do not. If a counterfactual conditional were merely the conjunction of a material conditional with the denial (or a hint of the denial) of the antecedent, then indeed this problem would not arise: contingent universal truths of the most accidental sorts would entail counterfactuals too. But then all counterfactuals, if their antecedents were in fact unfulfilled, would be trivially true; this analysis of counterfactuals removes the objection only by missing the point of the discriminating use of some counterfactuals but not others: we want to say 'If this bit of potassium had been exposed to air it would have burst into flame' but not 'If this bit of potassium had been exposed to air it would have turned into gold'. I have argued instead for a 'suppositional' analysis of conditionals, including counterfactuals.[8] The first of the two just given is seen as saying: 'Suppose that this bit of potassium has been exposed to air; then (within the scope of this supposition) it has burst into flame.' An almost equivalent way of treating it would equate it with 'In the possible (but not actual) situation that this bit of potassium was exposed to air, it burst into flame'; but I have insisted that such talk about possibilities (or possible worlds) must not be taken too literally: to talk about them is still only to talk about our supposings and how we develop them; possible worlds other than the actual one have no fully objective existence. It is a consequence of this analysis that counterfactuals whose antecedents are, as the speaker suggests, unfulfilled, and whose antecedents do not entail their consequents,

[8] *Truth, Probability, and Paradox*, Chapter 3.

cannot be true in a strict sense; I would therefore not want to
say that even the most respectable counterfactual was *entailed*
by a law of nature. Nevertheless I would say that it was reasonable to assert some counterfactuals, notably those that could be
said to be *sustained* by laws of nature, and not at all reasonable
to assert others. Since it is a law of nature that potassium when
in contact with oxygen ignites, it is reasonable to assert the
first of our two counterfactuals above; the law sustains this in
that when we combine the supposition that this bit of potassium
was exposed to air with the law and with the fact that air contains a fair proportion of oxygen we can validly infer from their
conjunction the conclusion 'This bit of potassium burst into
flame', corresponding to the consequent of our conditional. But
why does not the truth of the singular material conditional
'(This bit of potassium was exposed to air) ⊃ (it turned into
gold)'—which is true just because its antecedent is false—
equally sustain our second counterfactual? The conjunction of
it with the supposition that this bit of potassium was exposed
to air equally entails the conclusion 'This bit of potassium
turned into gold'. The obvious answer is that it is not reasonable to combine, with that supposition, a proposition which we
believe to be true only on the ground that that supposition is
false, and attempt to draw any conclusion from their conjunction. To reason in that way would amount, in effect, to
using a statement and its denial as joint premises in a serious
argument, and though according to the rules of the classical
propositional calculus such a pair of contradictory premises
validly *entails* any conclusion at all, no one supposes for a
moment that this is a sensible way of *arguing*. Again, an example
of an accidental universal truth that does not sustain counterfactuals would be 'All the coins in my pocket are shiny', which
seems neither to entail nor to sustain the counterfactual 'If that
other coin had been in my pocket it would have been shiny'.
The reason why it fails to do so is plain: it is not reasonable to
retain, along with the contrary-to-fact supposition that that
other coin is in my pocket, a universal proposition which is
believed solely on the strength of a complete enumerative check
of all the coins actually in my pocket. The required argument,
'Suppose that that other coin is in my pocket; all the coins
in my pocket are shiny; so that other coin is shiny', though

formally valid, is not one that can be sensibly used in the circumstances envisaged: the second premiss is accepted about the actual world on grounds that make it absurd to retain it within the scope of the supposition of the first premiss, and so apply it to a certain possible situation, for that first premiss totally undermines our reason for accepting the second. The accidental universal, accepted solely on the strength of a complete enumeration, therefore fails to sustain a counterfactual for a reason rather like (but still a little different from) the reason why the material conditional mentioned fails to sustain the counterfactual that if this bit of potassium had been exposed to air it would have turned into gold.

This explanation[9] shows why accidental universals do *not* sustain counterfactuals; but we must still explain why laws of nature do so. Clearly, it must be because it is reasonable to retain a law of nature along with a contrary-to-fact supposition. But how can it be, if the law of nature itself does no more than describe a contingent and actual state of affairs? If the supposition takes us to a merely possible world, how can it be reasonable to carry with us, in our baggage for this journey, a statement that merely describes the actual world? The answer lies not in any peculiar content of the law of nature, any stronger-than-contingent link which it reports between its antecedent and its consequent, but in the sort of reason we have for believing it. Either this law itself, or some higher law or set of laws from which it is derived, or perhaps, indeed, both this law itself and one or more higher ones, will be supported by some sort of inductive evidence: or, what comes to the same thing, it or they or both will be confirmed or corroborated by some observations or experiments. We need consider only the simplest case, where this law itself is either directly confirmed or inductively supported. If it is, say, the law that potassium when in contact with oxygen ignites, the evidence will be that other samples of potassium, in contact with oxygen under varying conditions, have ignited, that experiments have been made in which potassium has at first been kept away from oxygen and has not ignited, and then, some oxygen having been brought

---

[9] Which I gave originally in 'Counterfactuals and Causal Laws', in *Analytical Philosophy*, ed. R. J. Butler, pp. 66–80, and again in *Truth, Probability, and Paradox*, pp. 114–19.

into contact with it, but nothing else, so far as we can tell, that could possibly be relevant having changed, the potassium has burst into flame, and so on. Now consider how this body of evidence is related to the following other cases: first, some potassium will be brought into contact with oxygen tomorrow; secondly, some potassium was brought into contact with oxygen yesterday, but we have not heard what happened on that occasion; thirdly, someone may be bringing some potassium into contact with oxygen just now in the next room; fourthly, suppose that this bit of potassium, which has not in fact been exposed to oxygen, had been so exposed. The evidence does, by hypothesis, support the proposed law. It does, therefore, give us some reason to believe that the potassium in the first case will ignite; equally, that the potassium in the second case did ignite; and equally that if in the third case the potassium in the next room is now being exposed to oxygen, it is igniting. But that body of evidence bears the same logical relation to the fourth, the counterfactually supposed case, as it bears to the other three. It therefore makes it reasonable for us to assert, within the scope of that counterfactual supposition, that the potassium ignited. And it therefore makes it reasonable for us to use the counterfactual conditional, the use of which is merely an abbreviation of the performance of framing the supposition and asserting the consequent within its scope: if this bit of potassium had been exposed to oxygen, it would have ignited.

Despite the fact, then, that a counterfactual conditional of the kind that emerges in the analysis of singular causal statements cannot be true and cannot be entailed by the merely actual regularity which can be true, it can be as well supported by the *evidence* for that unrestricted regularity as are the conditionals about actual but unobserved cases.

This explanation rests on just three assumptions: that what we regard as laws of nature are supported by evidence which makes it in some degree reasonable to believe that unobserved cases will obey the law; that such making reasonable depends upon some formal relations between the body of evidence and the new propositions which it supports; and that conditionals, especially counterfactual ones, are to be understood in the way I have suggested. The first two of these are very difficult to deny; for the third I have argued at length elsewhere.

If this explanation is correct, then it is somewhat misleading to say even that laws of nature sustain, let alone entail, counterfactuals. Strictly speaking, it is not the laws themselves that do this but the evidence by which they are ultimately supported—a curious latter-day vindication of Mill's thesis that it is reasoning from particulars to particulars that is important.[10] The evidence has not done all its work when it has warranted our acceptance of the law as an unrestricted but contingent universal truth about the actual world: it continues to operate separately in making it reasonable to assert the counterfactual conditionals which look like an extension of the law into merely possible worlds. But they only look like this; since what is really going on is what I have set out above we should resist the temptation to take uncritically the suggestion that the counterfactual describes one or more possible worlds.

But once we have understood what is going on, could we after all concede Kneale's point and recognize natural law statements, or nomic universals, as a queer special type of statement, taking the 'statements' here to incorporate the (reasonable) readiness to assert counterfactual applications of these generalizations? 'A asserts a nomic universal' will then be shorthand for 'A asserts a contingent actual universal statement on (ultimately) inductive evidence and is also ready to assert the counterfactuals which are related to that evidence in the same way as are (actual) instances of the universal statement'. If we could adhere to this understanding of the phrase, it would be harmless. But for that very reason, it would no longer justify Kneale's further claim that laws of nature are principles of necessitation, that in asserting them we are somehow claiming that there is, in what goes on in the world, something like a logical requirement (although we do not know enough to be able explicitly to see it as such or to know it *a priori*). Moreover, the natural law statements, thus understood as incorporating counterfactual applications, could no longer be held to be, in a strict sense, *true*. Their function would be not only to describe the world—certainly not only the actual world, and there are not really any merely possible ones—but also in part to express an admittedly reasonable way of handling suppositions: quite a creditable performance, but still something that *people do*.

[10] *System of Logic*, Book II, Ch. 3, Sect. 3.

This specific difficulty, then, can be completely resolved so that it no longer tells against the thesis that natural laws, in so far as they have any claim to truth, are contingent unrestricted universals. But, as we have seen, this still leaves us with the corresponding general difficulty: there still seems to be *some* line to be drawn between such laws and those other contingent universals which we say are, if they are true, only accidentally true.

Some light may be thrown on this problem by the distinction Mill draws between uniformities of succession and uniformities of coexistence.[11] If not only all the coins in my pocket but all the coins in every pocket were shiny, that is if, among coins, the properties of being in a pocket and being shiny uniformly coexisted, this would still not be a causal law; for causal laws, Mill thought, are uniformities of succession, they describe regular ways in which events, or states, follow one another in time. But, first, the sort of functional relationship stressed by Russell between, for example, accelerations and masses and distances would appear to be a uniformity of coexistence, and yet it would be a law and, in the sense defended in Chapter 6, a causal law. Secondly, Mill does not and could not claim that the distinction between sequence and coexistence coincides with any distinction between laws and non-laws. In rather subtle and careful discussions he argues that the uniform co-existence of the effects of a common cause can be regarded as a derivative law, but that the uniform coexistence of the effects of different causes cannot, since they will depend on the *non-lawful* coexistence of their causes.[12] Keeping to our example, we may say that if the going together of the properties of being in a pocket and being shiny could be causally explained, say by the fact that the owners of pockets always chose shiny coins to put in them, together with the fact that a coin if shiny when put into a pocket, would remain so, then this uniformity of coexistence would be a derivative law; but if the causal histories of these two properties were independent, so that *this* uniformity was derived, via two separate causal chains, from a mere going together of some ultimate cause of shininess with some ultimate cause of pocketing, itself not explainable as the

---

[11] *System of Logic*, Book III, Ch. 5, Sect. 9, also Ch. 22.
[12] Ibid., Book III, Ch. 5, Sect. 9 and Ch. 22, Sect. 3.

coexistence of joint effects of any further cause, then our uniformity of coexistence would not be a law. And Mill argues that
though many of the coexistences of properties of natural kinds,
for example of chemical elements, may in this sense be derivative laws, there must be some ultimate, unexplainable, coexistences of properties. But he admits that among these
ultimate coexistences of properties there may be some invariable uniformities—the ultimate particles of which the universe
is composed may exhibit invariable, but just because they are
ultimate, unexplainable, combinations of properties. These Mill
will allow to be 'a peculiar sort of laws of nature',[13] but he
insists that they are very different from causal laws: there is
'one great deficiency, which precludes the application to the
ultimate uniformities of coexistence of a system of rigorous
scientific induction, such as the uniformities in the succession
of phenomena have been found to admit of. The basis of such a
system is wanting; there is no general axiom, standing in the
same relation to the uniformities of coexistence as the law of
causation does to those of succession.'[14]

Forceful and illuminating as these comments are, they have
in one way only deepened the problem. For we now seem to
have three classes of contingent universal truths: purely accidental ones, such as 'All the coins in my pocket are shiny' is
and as 'All the coins in every pocket are shiny' might be;
fundamental laws of the coexistence of properties in the ultimate
material constituents of things; and causal laws. And though
we have distinguished these, we have not seen clearly just how
they differ from one another. Even if Mill is right in saying
that causal laws are partly supported by a universal law of
causation, and that this makes them easier to discover by such
experimental procedures as those formalized by the Method of
Difference, whereas the fundamental laws of coexistence have
no such support, and can be established only by simple enumerative inductions, we have not yet found any intrinsic difference
between the laws of these two classes that would explain this
epistemological inequality; nor have we yet seen what marks
off both classes of what Mill is willing to call laws from purely
accidental generalizations.

[13] Ibid., Book III, Ch. 22, Sect. 3.
[14] Ibid., Book III, Ch. 22, Sect. 4.

Regularity theorists are naturally tempted to say that what marks off a nomic generalization from an accidental one is its being explainable by, that is derivable from, higher or more fundamental laws. To say this is, of course, to use again the same sort of move that they have used to distinguish causal from non-causal individual sequences. A single sequence is causal if and only if it is an instance of some law; similarly a generalization is nomic if and only if it is derivable from some higher laws. But, as our example of coins in pockets showed, what is still only an accidental uniformity may be derivable from some laws in conjunction with another accidental uniformity of coexistence (the going together of the ultimate causes of shininess and of pocketing). So we would have to say that a generalization is nomic if and only if it is derivable from some higher laws *alone*. This has the surprising but perhaps tolerable consequence that Kepler's Laws are not laws: that the planets move (approximately) in ellipses is not a consequence of Newton's gravitational laws alone, but only of those in conjunction with what Mill calls collocations, here the fact that the parts of the solar system started off with just such initial positions and velocities, or that they have just such positions and velocities at any particular moment from which we start our calculations. Different initial conditions combined with Newton's laws would make the planets move in, say, hyperbolas rather than ellipses, or, if they were too large or too close together, in paths that did not even approximate to any conic sections.

But the fundamental objection to this move is that it explains the lawfulness only of derived or derivable laws. Unless we postulate, quite gratuitously, an infinite regress of possible derivations, we shall have to say that there are some basic laws which, just because they are basic, are not derivable from anything else, and yet which must be laws if derivation from them is to make other things laws. The regularity theorist may at this point be tempted to turn his criterion upside down and say that these basic laws are laws not because they are derivable from laws, but because other laws are derivable from them. But will this leave us with any discrimination? Any true universal proposition at all will entail others, and pairs of universal propositions so related as to be joint premises of syllogisms will together entail more: will they not then count as laws by this definition and confer the same status on the conclusions derived from them? A possible reply is that the basic laws of a system must be of very wide application; if we take this way out we shall say that what makes basic laws laws is their being contingently true universal propositions of very wide application, and what makes derived laws laws is their being derivable from such widely applicable universal truths alone. It is presumably this line of thought that makes Mill willing to recognize the ultimate uniformities of coexistence of properties as laws, though of an inferior kind.

This connects with the suggestion that an accidental universal truth is one which holds only for some limited region of space and time, or in the formulation of which proper names occur non-eliminably. It can be no more than an accidental generalization that all the coins in John Smith's pocket on 19 November 1972 are shiny. Yet this criterion is easily undermined; we can presumably find uniquely identifying descriptions of John Smith, and of this date, using only general terms; and yet if the original statement about John Smith is only accidentally true, so surely is its artificially generalized translation. Can we then make the distinction turn not upon the kinds of words used but upon the sort of fact that makes the universal statement true? It has been pointed out that there is a general strategy, traceable in Comte, Mill, Reichenbach, and Popper among others, of 'distinguishing universals which are true generally from those which are true by virtue of what is the case locally'.[15] But it seems that no definition based on this strategy will capture our intuitive distinction between laws and accidental generalizations. It will not do to say that something is not a law if it is made true by what is locally the case, by what goes on within some closed space–time region. It might well be that life occurred only on earth, and only over a period of time closed at both ends. If so, any laws about living organisms that are true would be made true by what goes on in this closed region; yet we would want to count them as laws. Might we say instead that something is not a law if it is made true *only* by what is locally the case, defending the law status of organic laws on the ground

[15] W. Suchting, 'Popper's Revised Definition of Natural Necessity', *British Journal for the Philosophy of Science*, xx (1969), 349–52.

that though they *could* in principle be established by a survey of this closed region, they do not *need* to be, they are in principle derivable from physico-chemical laws to whose instantiation there are no spatio-temporal limits. But then if there were any 'emergent' laws about organic life, any universal truths about how living things proceed and develop which were not reducible without remainder to physico-chemical laws, these would still be denied the status of laws; but it is far from clear that there could not be such emergent general truths, and if there were we should, I think, want to call them laws. And on the other hand, could there not be cosmic accidents, propositions whose universal truth could not be ascertained by a survey of any closed region, but which none the less only happened to be true? Consider any occurrence which is in fact unique, which has no exact replica anywhere in the universe. (Each of us likes to suppose that he himself, or some of his activities, is or are such, but even if this is inexcusable vanity there must be plenty of other examples.) Since it *has* occurred, it is not excluded by any natural law or conjunction of laws. But equally this occurrence *might* not have occurred, in all its unique detail, and it seems plain that it *would* not have occurred if some initial conditions had been a bit different, or if some uncaused events, if there are such, had gone differently, without any change in the laws of nature. And the elimination of this unique occurrence need not have ensured the emergence, somewhere else, of an exact replica of it. Then it might have been true that *no occurrence of just this sort ever occurred*, and yet, by hypothesis, that there was no conjunction of laws alone that ensured this. That is, there might have been a cosmic accident of the form 'Nothing of exactly such and such a sort ever occurs anywhere'; but it would be only how the universe as a whole was that made this true, not the state of any closed space–time region. Not being made true only by what is locally the case is therefore neither necessary nor sufficient for a contingent universal's having what we intuitively recognize as the status of a law.[16]

But alongside and intertwined with this vain attempt to equate accidentality with spatio-temporal limitation there is another and more fruitful idea. Conceding Kneale's point that

---

[16] This is the conclusion reached also by Suchting in the discussion quoted above, on slightly different grounds.

'there may be *true, strictly universal statements* which have an accidental character rather than the character of . . . laws of nature', and that 'the characterization of laws of nature as strictly universal statements is logically insufficient and intuitively inadequate', Popper suggests that the natural or physical necessity in laws 'imposes *structural* principles upon the world' while leaving 'initial conditions' free.[17] Whereas on Kneale's view, or Descartes's, a God who was limited by logical necessities was free to choose the initial conditions of the world but not its structure, on Popper's view such a God would have two different choices to make, the first of 'structure', that is, of how the world was to work, and the second of initial conditions. He offers this definition (but with considerable reservations both about its accuracy and about the importance of definitions anyway, as contrasted with ideas): '*A statement may be said to be naturally or physically necessary if, and only if, it is deducible from a statement function which is satisfied in all worlds that differ from our world, if at all, only with respect to initial conditions.*' This idea is illustrated by an example: we may assume that the biological structure of the moa organism is such that under favourable conditions it might live for sixty years or more, but the actual conditions under which all moas in fact lived were far from ideal—perhaps some virus was present—so that no moa ever reached the age of fifty. So, Popper says, 'All moas die before reaching the age of fifty' will be a true universal statement, but not a law of nature: the laws of nature would allow moas to live to sixty, and only the accidental or contingent conditions, such as the co-presence of the virus, prevented this. This co-presence counts, presumably, as an initial condition or as an outcome of some initial conditions. Still, the distinction between structural principles and initial conditions is not yet clear: just why does the biological structure of moas contribute to laws, but the presence of a virus only to an accidental universal? Perhaps the answer is that the term 'moas', defined just by that structure, is the subject of the laws and non-laws under consideration; if their biological structure condemned moas to a life span of, say, less than seventy years, 'All moas die before reaching the age of seventy' will be a (derived) law, but 'All moas die before reaching the age of fifty' will not. But if we

[17] *The Logic of Scientific Discovery*, Appendix *x*, pp. 426–41.

change the subject we can turn the latter too into a derived law: 'All moas in the presence of virus *x* die before reaching the age of fifty.'

We may be able to get a firmer grip on the important distinction if we contrast *laws of working* with what Mill called *collocations*,[18] and consider another, simpler, example. We have, fixed on the surface of the earth, a plane inclined at an angle θ to the horizontal, several feet long from top to bottom. Near the top (left) edge are placed six similar balls, three red (R_1, R_2, R_3) and three blue (B_1, B_2, B_3) spaced a few inches apart in the order $R_1\, B_1\, R_2\, B_2\, R_3\, B_3$ from left to right. They are released simultaneously, and all run down the plane in accordance with Galileo's law, and pass in turn a point P near the bottom of the plane. Let us consider the following statements about this system:

(1) Wherever there is a red ball there is a blue ball immediately to its right.

(2) Whenever a blue ball passes P a red ball passes P shortly afterwards.

(3) Whenever a ball is released on this plane it runs down it in accordance with the law $a = g \sin \theta$.

(4) Whenever an object of mass m is near the surface of the earth it is subject to a force mg in the direction of the centre of the earth.

(5) Whenever an object of mass m is subject only to a force f it has an acceleration f/m in the same direction as that of the force.

(6) Between any two objects there is a force proportional to the mass of each and inversely proportional to the square of the distance between them.

How are we to characterize these various statements? (1) is a pure collocation statement. It is a true contingent universal statement about this small system. Its application is spatio-temporally limited, but this is not the point. Even if something similar were true of the whole universe, it would be no more than a cosmic accident. (2) is a derived law of this system; it is derived from the conjunction of (3) with the collocation statement (1)—and a little further description of the set-up. But (3)

[18] *System of Logic*, Book III, Ch. 12.

also is a derived law; it follows from (4) and (5), along with some principles about the resolution of forces, and so on, in conjunction with some collocation statements, especially that the plane is inclined at the angle θ. And even (4) is in turn a derived law, following from (6) together with a collocation statement about the mass of the earth and the solution of the mathematical problem of integrating the gravitational effects of all the portions of a sphere. Of the statements listed, (5) and (6) alone represent a system of basic laws of working, in this case the Newtonian theory of motion and gravitation. But also, of those listed, only (1) is a pure collocation statement (though other relevant collocation statements have been hinted at). (2), (3), and (4) are all mixed products, the result of combining laws of working with collocations. But each of these can be turned into a pure, though derived, law of working by generalizing it, by replacing references to the individual set-up with descriptions of its *relevant* features. Thus if we substitute, in (4), 'a sphere of such-and-such a radius, mass, and so on' for 'the earth', it becomes a mathematical consequence of the basic laws alone. The same can be achieved with (3) if we insert both this relevant general description of the earth and a description of the relevant features of the plane, and with (2) if we add to all this a description of the initial placing of the balls. That is, we purify the mixed laws of their collocation component by putting it explicitly into the antecedents of the general conditionals. Thus we can sort out pure laws of working—some basic, some derived—from both mixed laws and collocation statements. We can do this in practice only where we take it that we fully understand how the system in question works, as we do with a Newtonian mechanical system.

Let us try to apply these distinctions to Popper's moa example, where we do not actually know the relevant laws. That all actual moas lived in the presence of virus x we can take as a fact of collocation. 'All moas die before reaching the age of fifty' will be a mixed law; so is 'All moas die before reaching the age of seventy', since it is presumably the product of some more basic biological laws along with facts about how moas are actually built. But the latter could be turned into a pure though derived law of working by replacing the subject 'moas' with 'creatures of such-and-such a structure' *including in this description all the features that are relevant to their life span*.[19] And then the former too can be turned into a pure though derived law by adding to this detailed description of the subject a further clause, 'in the presence of a virus with such-and-such characteristics'. But here the notion of laws of working, basic or derived, is that of a theoretical ideal: we do not actually know these laws, and for that reason we do not know the relevant features whose explicit mention could purify the mixed laws that we actually deal with. But it is reasonable to suppose that there are some, as yet unknown, pure laws of working, and that there is a real objective distinction between these and collocations or initial conditions, although we are not in a position to implement it. We can read Popper's definition, then, as calling naturally or physically necessary all pure laws of working, basic or derived, and all singular conditional statements which these entail.[20]

Equipped with these distinctions, we can now say that in our atomic bomb example the presence of a red spot on every bomb in which an *A*-reaction occurred before a *B*-reaction was only a (locally) universal collocation, as contrasted with the probabilistic laws of working in accordance with which these reactions occurred.

But given that we can draw this distinction, that we can leave a post-Newtonian God with his two choices rather than the Cartesian single choice, what is the point of the distinction? Why should the laws of working be said to have natural *necessity*? The analogy that Popper draws with Tarski's definition of logical necessity, that while what is logically necessary holds in all possible worlds, what is physically necessary holds in all worlds that differ from ours, if at all, only with respect to initial conditions, seems not very illuminating. Since 'initial conditions' are simply what we contrast with laws of working, this means that what is physically necessary holds in all worlds

[19] This is, I think, how Popper intends this statement to be taken, since he speaks of using 'moa' as 'a universal name of a certain biological structure'; but he does not emphasize the need to mention all the relevant features.

[20] I think that this treatment preserves the idea behind Popper's definition while avoiding the objections raised by G. C. Nerlich and W. A. Suchting to its literal formulation in 'Popper on Law and Natural Necessity', *British Journal for the Philosophy of Science*, xviii (1967), 233–5. Popper replied to this, in the same volume, pp. 316–21, but later in *Logic of Scientific Discovery*, 2nd English edn., Addendum (1968), on p. 441, expressed dissatisfaction with his reply.

that have the same laws of working as our own, and any actual feature could be turned into its own variety of necessity by a similar device. For example, the existence of just such minds as there are is spiritually necessary in that it holds in all worlds that differ from ours, if at all, only in non-spiritual respects. In the end Popper himself decides to rest no weight on this analogy: he regards 'necessary' as 'a mere word'; 'there is not much connection here with logical necessity'; the only connection between causal connection and logical necessity is that the material conditional $a \to b$ follows with logical necessity from a law of nature.[21]

One point that the distinction may have is that laws of working will typically be discovered by inductive and hypothesis-confirming procedures, whereas initial conditions will be discovered by complete surveys and will not be inductively supported. (Of course initial conditions may be inferred from subsequent conditions, themselves ascertained by survey, with the help of inductively supported laws, but that is another matter.) In particular, experiments interpreted with the help of the assumption that there are *some* laws of working seem to be needed to sort out pure laws of working from mixed laws that

---

[21] Op. cit., p. 438. Similarly in 'Two Faces of Common Sense' printed as Chapter 2 in *Objective Knowledge*, Popper says:

'At any rate, in the light of a conjecture we can not only explain cause and effect much better than Hume ever did, but we can even say what the "necessary causal link" consists of.

'Given some conjectural regularity and some initial conditions which permit us to deduce predictions from our conjecture, we can call the conditions the (conjectural) cause and the predicted event the (conjectural) effect. And the conjecture which links them by logical necessity is the long-searched-for (conjectural) necessary link between cause and effect.' (p. 91.)

That is, the only necessity involved is what we have called necessity₃: the conjunction of the regularity-statement with the description of the cause entails the prediction of the effect.

As a solution to the problem of 'the long-searched-for . . . necessary link' this is laughable: it leaves out everything that is difficult and interesting—the detailed form of causal regularities, causal priority, and all the jobs mentioned at the beginning of this chapter except the third and fourth. It explains cause and effect not better than Hume did, but almost exactly as Hume did (e.g. 'Necessity . . . consists either in the constant conjunction of like objects or in the inference of the understanding from one object to another', *Enquiry*, Sect. VIII, Pt. II, Selby-Bigge, p. 97). As I suggested in Chapter 1, Hume was probably attracted to constant conjunction by its suitability for the role of necessity₃. Philosophers after Hume have gone on searching for the causal link just because they could not believe that this was all there was to it.

depend partly on collocations: we check that something is independent of collocations by changing the collocations and seeing if it still holds. If so, these laws of working will have the right sort of backing to allow them to sustain counterfactuals, whereas statements of collocations or initial conditions will not. (Reichenbach, who realized that 'inductive verifiability' was the key to counterfactual force, tried to define nomological statements by requirements that would indirectly ensure inductive verifiability, but his requirements seem too formal to achieve what is wanted, in particular to exclude cosmic accidents and to include laws whose application is in fact limited to a closed space–time region.)[22]

However, mixed laws no less than pure ones are discovered and supported by inductive and hypothesis-confirming procedures, and they also can therefore be said to sustain counterfactuals. These will not be distinctive features of the pure laws of working which we should like to mark off as naturally necessary.

But is there anything more about laws of working that would justify their being singled out as necessary? Here we may turn to a theory of necessity which is radically different from the regularity-type views we have been examining, namely that which Kneale presents and defends against Humean criticisms, while using both what I have called the specific and the general difficulties to attack the regularity theory.

The view which Kneale defends he tentatively ascribes to Locke: it is that natural laws are 'principles of necessitation', necessary in the same way in which necessary connections that we are able to comprehend—for example, that redness and greenness are incompatible—are necessary, although we are not able to comprehend the natural laws, not simply because our intellects are too feeble, but rather because 'our experience does not furnish us with the ideas which would be required for an understanding of the connexions we assert'.[23] The essential idea is that the things that enter into causal transactions, and hence also the events that are their doings, have insides which

[22] H. Reichenbach, *Nomological Statements and Admissible Operations*, especially pp. 12–13, 40, 48; see also p. 94 for an account of 'relative nomological statements' which correspond to our 'mixed laws'.*

[23] *Probability and Induction*, p. 71.

we do not and perhaps cannot perceive; the necessary connections hold between these internal features. We cannot in fact comprehend their necessity, but we could if we could perceive the features between which the connections hold, and what we would then comprehend would be something like the incompatibility of redness and greenness. When we assert a natural law we do not claim to know it as necessary, but we conjecture *that there is* a necessary connection holding unperceived between kinds of events which we identify by their external features.

Kneale thinks that the Humean objection to this view is based on a mistaken doctrine of perception, on the theory of impressions and ideas, or of sense-data, and the various phenomenalist systems erected on this basis. Only on this assumption, he argues, would the fact that we can *conceive* a cause without its effect, or vice versa, refute the suggestion that they are necessarily connected in the sense proposed. We can conceive these external features without those, and if the 'objects' in question were wholly constituted by their external features that would be the end of the matter. Consequently Kneale's main reply to the Humean objections consists of a criticism of phenomenalism and a defence of realism about 'truths concerning perceptual objects which are not open to inspection'. This vindication of realism is, perhaps, less necessary now than it was twenty-five years ago; I, at any rate, would accept this conclusion without question. But I do not think that this takes all the force out of Hume's doubts about objective necessities of the kind proposed. As I have said in Chapter 1, the main weight of Hume's argument bears upon *causation so far as we know about it in the objects*, and he explicitly (though perhaps ironically) leaves room for 'several qualities, both in material and immaterial objects, with which we are utterly unacquainted' but which may be *called* power or efficacy.[24] But he *could* have argued that whatever qualities there may be in the cause-event, however unperceived and unconceived, they cannot *logically*-necessitate the occurrence of an effect at all, let alone an effect with such-and-such correlated qualities, just because the cause-event and the effect-event are distinct existences. As I said in Chapter 1, there can be no logically necessary

[24] *Treatise*, I, III, 14, Selby-Bigge, p. 168.

connections between the events themselves or between any *intrinsic* descriptions of them, however detailed or complete, and, we may now add, however internal and closed to inspection. But this argument bars only logical necessity, entailment: Kneale might be content to claim a necessity that falls short of logical necessity but is illustrated by the incompatibility of redness and greenness. Of course, there is no agreement about how this incompatibility is to be analysed; but we need not go into this question because this analogy, too, is inappropriate. Anything like this can be only an impossibility of two features occurring at the same place and time, in the same subject, or, if it has a positive counterpart, a necessity of one feature occurring at the same place and time as another, in the same subject. Nothing in this example helps us to see even what could be conjectured about a necessity linking two distinct occurrences.

To find anything worthy of the name of necessity in laws of working, then, we must turn to what Kneale says about the explanation of natural laws, not merely by their being derived from 'higher' laws—the characteristic regularity-theory move which, as we have seen, is unhelpful—but by their association with *transcendent hypotheses*, such as wave or particle theories in physics. These hypotheses introduce new terminology, they are 'concerned with things which are not observable even in principle', and they concern only 'structures' which can be expressed in the language of mathematics. Since the translations between this new terminology and the ordinary language of material objects are contingent, there is no prospect of our being able to derive laws of nature about material objects from self-evident truths alone. 'Although the connexions *within* the world of transcendent entities posited by a theory may all be self-evident, the relations *between* this world and the world of perceptual objects remain opaque to the intellect, and it is only by assuming these relations that we can explain our laws about observables.'[25] It is the concessive clause here that is vital; and a few lines earlier Kneale has said that 'attempts are . . . made to specify the hypothetical entities of the system in such a way that any connexions between them required for the purposes of the theory are intrinsically necessary'.

The suggestion, then, is that we advance beyond a view of

[25] *Probability and Induction*, p. 97.

causation as mere regular succession when we conjecture that there really is some causal mechanism underlying the succession and explaining it. But must this be a matter of conjecture, of *transcendent* hypotheses? Would it not be even better actually to uncover and observe the mechanism? And yet, if we did so, would not Hume's criticisms again have force: what, in the operation of a mechanism, however delicate and ingenious, could we see except the succession of phases? It may be to avoid this reply that Kneale stresses the transcendent character of the hypotheses; but whether the mechanism is observable or not, the question must still be answered: what *is* there in it except the succession of phases?

For Kneale, it is the 'structures' and the possibility of mathematical description of them that are vital. The cause-event is identical with something unobservable that has a certain mathematically describable structure. The latter develops, necessarily, into something else which is also unobservable and also has some such structure. The latter something is identical with the effect-event. The necessity of the development of the one structure into the other would be self-evident to us if we knew those structures (and, presumably, if we were mathematically competent enough). Science can help to conjecture what these structures are, though not the correlative contents, not the substances of which these are the structures. And the statements identifying observable things and occurrences with unknowns with such-and-such structures can never be more than contingent conjectures, which are not themselves intelligible, but are confirmed by their success in relating observed regularities to intelligible structure-developments.

But how is a structure-development intelligible or necessary? Physically it will be, say, a certain wave-pattern changing into a certain other wave-pattern, or one assembly of particles, each with a certain mass and position and velocity at one time, changing into another arrangement of the same particles, each retaining its mass but changing its position and perhaps its velocity. Mathematically there will be some *form* of description applicable to both the earlier and the later phases of the developing structure; the two particular descriptions of this form will have identical values for some of the quantities (for example, the total energy of the wave system may be conserved, or the number of particles and also perhaps their mass and energy, or at least the sum of both) while the values for *other* quantities in the later phase will be derivable from the earlier values with the help of the integration over time of some differential equation, that is, some law of the functional dependence variety. We may speculate, then, that what could count as necessity or intelligibility here is some *form of persistence*.

Let us consider the simplest of all cases, a single particle, free from interference, moving in a straight line in accordance with Newton's first law (see diagram).

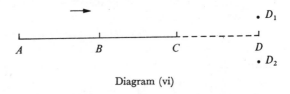

Diagram (vi)

There are several things we can say about this.

First, if the particle moves continuously from A to B, from B to C, and from C to D, these being all equal distances, in equal times, it is in a very obvious sense keeping on doing the same thing. It is not of course logically or mathematically necessary that if it moves a distance d in a time t between A and B it should move an equal distance d in the succeeding interval t and in the same direction, from B to C. But it may well seem expectable that it should go on doing as nearly as possible the same thing (of course, it *has* to do it at a different place) if nothing intervenes to make it do anything else.

Again we can argue, on the assumption that there has been and will be no interference, that the motion from A to B has produced the motion from B to C; but the motion from B to C is just like the motion from A to B; so, if like causes produce like effects, the motion from B to C will produce something just like itself, that is, the motion from C to D; if we knew that it had gone smoothly from A to C in a period $2t$, we could expect it to go from C to D in the next period t, all the time on the assumption of no interference, of a constant uniform background.

Such an argument was given by d'Alembert, and has been

criticized by Nagel,[26] whose criticisms have been widely accepted. They are, however, unsound in part, and for the rest are easily met by a modification of d'Alembert's argument. Thus he says, 'D'Alembert simply assumes that a force is required to account for changes in the *uniform velocity* of a body (where the state of rest is a special case of uniform velocity), but that none is required to account for changes in the mere *position* of a body. But this is to beg the entire question at issue.' But d'Alembert doesn't *assume* this. He *argues* that 'a body cannot be brought into motion by itself, since there is no reason why it should move in one direction rather than another': that is, he uses the same sort of symmetry considerations here as in the argument below against a deviation from the straight line (say to our D_1). Nagel asks, 'Why should uniform velocity be selected as the state of a body which needs no explanation in terms of the operation of forces, rather than uniform rest or uniform acceleration (such as motion along a circular orbit with constant speed) or, for that matter, some still different state of motion of the body (for example, the constancy of the time-rate of change of the acceleration)?' The answer is that *a priori* there would be no reason for such a preference, but that d'Alembert needs no reason, since he is not committed to an *a priori* preference. He could ask, in our terms, what is the nearest that something can be to keeping on doing the same thing? If it is at rest, staying at rest is clearly the answer. But if it is already moving, that is ruled out, and uniform motion is the next best possibility. Or he could confine himself, as I have done in the text above, to a case where the body has already moved uniformly from A through B to C. If there has been and is no interference, d'Alembert can then argue that what produced the B–C movement was the A–B one, and that the B–C one, being just like the A–B one (except for position), will produce something exactly alike. This argument involves no prejudice in favour of uniform velocity. We could argue equally well that if a spherical body has rotated uniformly over a certain period it will go on rotating, though this will involve a persistence of various accelerations towards the centre. On the other hand, a body's moving uniformly in a circular orbit is not *in itself* intelligible

[26] *The Structure of Science*, pp. 175–8, quoting d'Alembert's argument from *Traité de dynamique*, Paris, 1921, vol. i, pp. 3–6.

in the same way as rectilinear motion is. Any small segment of the orbit is obviously asymmetrical, in a way that would cry out for some further explanation—for example by the presence of another body at the centre, or on the opposite side of the centre, of the circular orbit. Nagel suggests that if a body has been moving in a circular orbit subject to a central force, and that force is then eliminated, d'Alembert's considerations of symmetry could lead to the expectation that the circular movement would continue, rather than to the Newtonian expectation of tangential movement. But this is clearly wrong. As long as whatever force has so far maintained the circular motion is present, d'Alembert's reasoning would lead us to expect that motion to be continued; but if the conditions are changed by the elimination of the central force, they no longer point to any conclusion at all. Nagel concludes that d'Alembert's argument 'is worthless simply because one can always exhibit in a given state of motion of a body a variety of distinct symmetries and asymmetries' with no logical grounds for preferring one to another; but in the cases considered this judgement is simply false, and only excessive devotion to empiricism has made it palatable. Nagel's further suggestion that Newton's axiom can be construed as 'a concealed definition, a convention which specifies the conditions under which one will *say* that there are no impressed forces acting on a body' is therefore gratuitous. Nagel does, indeed, mention what is a serious problem for d'Alembert: he has assumed a Newtonian framework that allows one to speak of absolute rest, motion, and so on of one body at a time. D'Alembert would need either to vindicate this assumption, or to recast his argument so that everything was done in terms of relative motions. But the latter at least could be done, at the cost only of some loss of simplicity.

Another comment of the same kind is that if after going from A to B and from B to C the particle had then gone not to D but, say, to D_1, this would have been prima facie surprising: since D_1 is placed asymmetrically with respect to the line ABC, we might say that if it were to go to D_1 it might as well go rather to D_2, similarly placed on the other side of the line; since it cannot go to both, it ought not to go to either, but should confine itself to the continuation of its straight path through D.

Of course none of these arguments shows that the particle

logically must continue to obey Newton's law. Innumerable other sequences are conceivable, none is ruled out even by the most complete, most 'internal', intrinsic description of the motion from A to C. Yet they cast some doubt on Hume's claim that 'If we reason *a priori*, anything may appear able to produce anything' or even that 'Any thing may produce any thing'.[27] Perhaps it *may*; but at least in some cases some outcomes are less intrinsically surprising than others; and yet this is a matter of *a priori* considerations, it does not depend on any appeal, either open or covert, to our actual experience of or familiarity with processes of the kind in question.

What holds for this simplest case holds to some extent for some less simple ones too. If we have several particles near one another, each moving initially in some straight line at some speed, it may be prima facie expectable that each will go on as it is going, if they can do so without colliding. Of course, this case is not as clear as the last: the different particles might influence one another (as in fact, of course, they would): still, it would be expectable that whatever they did to one another would as it were be built on to a foundation of the continuance of the separate motion of each. The persistence of a wave motion is no doubt more complicated and less obviously intelligible than that of the motion of a particle; but it has one great advantage, that different waves can pass through one another, adding up and cancelling out so far as their local effects are concerned, but without damaging one another permanently.

We may suggest, then, that basic laws of working are, in part, forms of persistence. In Chapter 6 I argued for extensions of the concept of causing to include both the persistence of objects and the persistence of self-maintaining processes, saying that in both of these we could regard an earlier phase as a cause and a later phase as an effect. I am now suggesting that this sort of causing plays a larger part, underlying processes that at the perceptual level are cases of unrelieved change, of a cause being followed by an utterly different effect. A match is struck on a matchbox and a flame appears: on the face of it this effect has nothing in common with its cause. But if we were to replace the macroscopic picture with a detailed description of

---

[27] The more guarded claim is from *Enquiry*, Sect. XII, Pt. III, the less guarded from *Treatise*, I, III, 15.

the molecular and atomic movements with which the perceived
processes are identified by an adequate physico-chemical
theory, we should find far more continuity and persistence.
And this is part of the point of micro-reduction, of the transcendent hypotheses of which Kneale speaks. Charles's Law
tells us that if the temperature of a quantity of gas in a container of constant volume rises, the pressure on the walls will
rise proportionately; but there is no immediately obvious homo-
geneity between temperature and pressure. But if temperature
is identified with the average kinetic energy of molecules, and
pressure with their change of momentum in elastic collisions
with the walls of the container, both acquire a relation to the
mean speed of the molecules, and we can begin to see a continuity between them. A more obvious example is Fajan's Law
for radioactive disintegration, that emission of an alpha particle
moves an atom to a position two places lower in the periodic
table of elements. The heterogeneity of cause and effect disappears when an alpha particle is identified as one with two
units of positive electrical charge and occupying a certain place
in the periodic table with having a certain charge on the
nucleus: the emission of this particle simply carries this amount
of charge away. What is called a causal mechanism is a process
which underlies a regular sequence and each phase in which
exhibits qualitative as well as spatio-temporal continuity.

On the other hand, there can be no question of reducing a
process of change *wholly* to some persistence: if the earlier and
later phases on the macroscopic level are different, there must
be equally real differences between the micro-states with which
they are identical; the most we can expect is that there should
be more persistence mixed with the differences than there
appears to be. Also, wherever there is interaction (say gravitational or electro-magnetic attractions or repulsions) it seems in-
escapable that there should be a law of working which is not
just the persistence of anything: it is worth recalling that in
Chapter 6, along with the extension of the causal concept to
cover the persistences of objects and processes, where 'causes' and
'effects' resembled one another, we found appropriate another
sort of extension to cover functional dependences of which
the paradigm case was the gravitational law, in which the 'effect'
was an acceleration while distances and masses were the 'cause'.

I have strayed rather far from the sort of theory Kneale proposes. In relating natural to logical necessity and to the incompatibilities of colours he is adhering to a rationalist tradition; instead of anything of this sort I find that his transcendent hypotheses reveal only continuities and persistences; these are an empirical counterpart of the rationalists' necessity. But we can agree with Kneale that we can only conjecture that actual laws of working will exhibit whatever this natural necessity turns out to be. If laws of working are identified in the way indicated by our discussion of Popper's theory, it is clearly a synthetic claim, and not one that can be called *a priori* in any strong sense, that they will also be forms of persistence.

We may weave in here some notions that have cropped up earlier in our discussion. In Chapter 3 we considered the possibility that some causal mechanism or continuity of process might help to constitute causation in the objects; we have now found a place for it, particularly as constituting a sort of necessity that may belong to basic laws of working. In Chapter 1 we noted Hume's hesitation over contiguity, and suggested that he was right not to include this as an essential part of our ordinary concept of causing. Yet contiguity, that is, a merely spatio-temporal continuity of processes, may have a place in causation as it is in the objects, not so much for its own sake but rather as making possible qualitative or structural continuity as well.

Although I am offering this notion of persistence or of qualitative or structural continuity as a hint of a kind of necessity that may belong objectively to basic laws of working, it is worth noting that something of the sort is to be found also in our concept of causing. Michotte, investigating this concept from the point of view of experimental psychology, found that we have in certain cases an immediate perception or impression of causation. His two basic cases are these. In one, an object A approaches another object B; on reaching B, A stops and B begins to move off in the same direction; here the observer gets the impression that A has 'launched' B, has set B in motion. In the other, A continues to move on reaching B, and B moves at the same speed and in the same direction; here the observer gets the impression that A is carrying B with it. In both cases observers typically report that A has caused the movement of B.

Michotte argues that it is an essential feature of observations that give rise to this causal impression that there should be two distinguishable movements, that of the 'agent' *A* and that of the 'patient' *B*, but also that it is essential that the movement of the patient should in some degree copy or duplicate that of the agent.[28] Where the effect is in this sort of way a partial continuation or extension of the cause—Michotte speaks of *l'ampliation du mouvement*—it is, as Hume himself pointed out,[29] particularly easy for us to see them as belonging together, to form, imaginatively, the arrangement of ideas that is expressed by the judgement that if the cause had not occurred, the effect would not. This source of such thinking and judgement involves only the intrinsic features of the single observed sequence; it does not, like the Method of Difference reasoning, require any general assumption. It is also different from, but can reinforce, the sort of imaginative analogizing that we took in Chapters 2 and 3 to be a primitive counterpart of the use of the Method of Difference followed by a sophisticated sustaining of a counterfactual. Our ordinary concept of causation does not require this qualitative or structural continuity, but such perceived continuity does contribute to the formation of that concept, it is one among several sources of the counterfactual conditional thinking which is the core of the ordinary concept.

It is worth noting, also, that those cases of alternative over-determination which nevertheless allowed us to pick out one rather than another of the over-determining factors as the cause were ones in which we could tell some more detailed causal story, in which we could find links in a continuous chain connecting the preferred factor, but not its rivals, with the result.

Qualitative or structural continuity of process, then, may well be something in the objects, over and above complex regularity, which provides some backing for the conditional and especially counterfactual statements that emerge in the analysis of our ordinary causal concept. We can, as I suggested in Chapter 4 that we might, thus relate the logical forms associated with causal beliefs to our spatio-temporal picture of a bit of causing going on—a connection which bears some resemblance

---

[28] A. Michotte, *La perception de la causalité* (translated by T. R. and E. Miles as *The Perception of Causality*), Introduction, pp. 17–19; Chapter 14, esp. p. 214.

[29] *Treatise*, I, III, 9, Selby-Bigge, pp. 111–12 (quoted in Chapter 1 above, p. 24).

to Kant's schematism of the categories, an embodiment of forms of judgement in a spatio-temporal pattern of sensory appearances.

Remembering what we found, in Chapter 7, about the direction of causation, how it was associated with the contrast between fixity and non-fixity and with the way in which events become fixed, we can see another important difference between basic laws of working and collocations. Since laws of working cover the ways in which (some) things become fixed, there is, while not an absolute requirement, yet something of a presumption that there should be such laws. The universe needs to know where to go next. Of course we must concede Hume's point that it is in a way conceivable that there should be complete chaos, that every occurrence should be random—though we must also concede Strawson's point that we cannot say or even imagine in detail what chaos would be like. But this would be a very strange state of affairs, at variance with expectations which are presumably instinctive and which are certainly involved in and satisfied by our whole method of interpreting our experience, whereas chaotic *collocations* would be harmless and in no way out of the ordinary. Mill overstated the case in claiming that the 'law of causation' is a general axiom which somehow guarantees that there must be uniformities of succession, whereas there is no such axiom requiring uniformities of coexistence,[30] but at least there is a presumption in favour of the former though not in favour of the latter. To this extent, then, what I called the seventh job for necessity, the notion that it is somehow necessary that every event should have a cause, contributes in a weakened form to the distinctive necessity of basic laws of working—and, of course, facilitates their inductive establishment, which in turn explains their so-called counterfactual force.

The dictum that 'the universe needs to know where to go next' may require some explanation and defence. I am suggesting that there is some truth in the notion that what happens next *flows from* what is there already. The immediate future is, so to speak, *extruded* by the present and the immediate past. Of course all that is observed and all that ever could be observed

---

[30] Quoted above, p. 205.

about this process amounts to a vast and intricate collection of persistences, continuities, and complex regularities. But there is perhaps also something more elusive, which my talk about fixity and fixing is an attempt to capture. Ayer, endorsing what I called in Chapter 1 Hume's third exclusion, suggests that 'everything that happens in the world can be represented in terms of variations of scenery in a four-dimensional spatio-temporal continuum'.[31] Represented, yes; but is the representation adequate? Does everything that happens in the world simply consist of varied four-dimensional scenery? I want to deny this, but it is very difficult to say just what the denial means. The notion of flowing from, of extrusion, would mean that there had to be *some* relations of the general sorts mentioned above—persistence, continuity, regularity—that what happens fits into such categories as the continued existence of objects, motion, change (which involves also some persistence), growth, development, decay, composition, disintegration, but not—or at least not in most cases—annihilation or coming to be from nothing. I am not, of course, suggesting that the laws or regularities in accordance with which things come about must themselves be intelligible, but only that if we are right to see the future as flowing from the present we are justified in expecting that there will be some *ways* in which it flows.

The implausibility of the 'four-dimensional scenery' account can be brought out by considering how strange a world—or bit of the world—we should have if the time dimension changed places with one spatial dimension. Each persisting object or continuant would turn into a very long but very short-lived worm. The sudden changes that we encounter as we move along some spatial straight line would become successive events in the same place. The direction of explanation (for example, from a common cause to joint effects) would run from, say, south to north (but not from north to south) between simultaneous existents. It is obvious how serious a loss of intelligibility such an interchange of axes would carry with it. It is worth noting that this is a kind of transformation which the Special

---

[31] *Probability and Evidence*, pp. 10–11 (quoted more fully above, pp. 23–4).At this point he presents this just as an equivalent of Hume's thesis, but he says that it is 'scientifically most respectable' and 'at least very plausible', and he goes on to defend it.

Theory of Relativity neither imposes nor even allows. No change of co-ordinate system within that theory will turn what had been a line of simultaneity into a line of temporal succession in one place; no line representing the possible history of any persisting thing or causal process, however rapidly moving, can become in some other co-ordinate system the locus of a set of simultaneous events; possible light-paths constitute a rigid barrier between possible causal succession and what can, from any point of view, be seen as coexistence.

To say this is not merely to say, what is obviously true, that time does not present itself in our experience as just another dimension like the spatial ones. It is to say that if what is now experienced as temporal were experienced as spatial, and part of what is now experienced as spatial were experienced as temporal, the result would be very strange. For example, an ultimate uniformity of coexistence, say that a thing of one sort should always shade off, in a northerly direction, into a thing of a certain other sort, would strike us as a very odd coincidence if there were no causal sequences, no laws of working through time, of which it was a resultant. To bring out the strangeness, to us, of an exchange of roles between a spatial and a temporal dimension is to display, by a contrast, something that is at least firmly built into our ordinary conceptual scheme. But the facts also fit in with this scheme. Even if we started, as we may well have, with an innate prejudice in favour of something like it, we should not have been able to work with it unless the data of observation had been amenable. If we take the world just as Ayer's four-dimensional stage-setting, it is remarkable that nearly all the long worms it contains are temporal ones, occupying possibly causal lines, and hardly any are spatial ones, occupying what could be lines of simultaneity—even telephone wires, railway lines, oil pipelines, and the like have a considerable temporal persistence as well as spatial extension, and so come out not as worms but as thin but two-dimensionally extended spatio-temporal sheets. Now if there were nothing in the notion of what happens next flowing from what is there already, it would be a surprising coincidence that worms should be distributed through the four-dimensional scene in the selective way that they apparently are, whereas if there were something in this notion, the actual distribution is just what we should expect. To this extent we can defend a presumption that does something like what I called the seventh job for necessity.

We can sum up this discussion by referring to the other six jobs for necessity. In Chapter 1, after distinguishing necessity$_2$ from necessity$_1$, I suggested that it might have a variety which I called necessity$_{2.2}$, something that would support a probabilistic *a priori* inference, as contrasted with a necessity$_{2.1}$ which would support a deductively valid *a priori* inference. We have found nothing that could play the part of necessity$_{2.1}$, but qualitative or structural continuity of process, along with the persistence of objects, might count as necessity$_{2.2}$. Such continuities and persistences up to a point—for example, over the stretch *A–B–C* in our diagram—seem to constitute some presumption in favour of their own continuance. But this is only a hint, which would need to be developed as part of a wider discussion of induction. There might be something that contributed a little to the second job, therefore, and hence also to the first. The third job, that of necessity$_3$, is done by the regularity aspect of causal laws. But for the fourth job, that of necessity$_1$, we need not only regularity but also the natural necessity that does the fifth job, the marking off of causal from non-causal regularities. This has been our main topic in this chapter, and we have located it first in the distinction of basic laws of working from collocations and mixed laws which involve collocations, and secondly in the qualitative and structural continuity which processes that obey those basic laws seem to exhibit, in the fact that they are forms of partial persistence, once we move from the events at the perceptual level to the 'transcendent hypotheses' with which those events are, on a scientific realist view, identified, and by which they are explained. This account has been built upon foundations provided by Kneale's theory, but we have rejected his suggestions that this natural necessity can be assimilated either to logical necessity or to the incompatibility of colours; our continuity, as I said, is an empirical counterpart of the rationalists' logical or near-logical necessity. And of course these continuities and partial persistences, while joining with the notion of basic laws of working to do the fifth job, do the sixth job on their own: it is they that would really constitute the long-searched-for link between individual cause and effect which a pure regularity theory fails, or refuses, to find.

We can now, at last, reply to the sceptical suggestion made near the end of Chapter 2, that since singular causal statements involve in their analysis counterfactual conditionals which cannot be true, they cannot be true either, and that necessity$_1$, the distinguishing feature of causal sequences, cannot be observed. These comments hold, indeed, for statements of singular causal sequence as we ordinarily mean them, for what is contained in our concept of necessity$_1$. But we can now offer a revised account of what causation is in the objects. If our speculations are correct, a singular causal sequence instantiates some pure law of working which is itself a form of partial persistence; the individual sequence therefore is, perhaps unobviously, identical with some process that has some qualitative or structural continuity, and that also incorporates the fixity relations which constitute the direction of causation. Here, then, we have what was foreshadowed at the end of Chapter 5: a general characteristic of causal processes, sometimes observable, sometimes not, which constitutes a link between cause-events and effect-events similar to but more selective than the relation defined by Ducasse, since it relates specifically relevant causal features to those features which constitute the result. This is an answer to the question, 'What is the producing that Hume did not see?' And it is easy to apply to this an explanation already suggested in Chapter 1: Hume failed to see it not, as Kneale suggests, because he confined himself to 'impressions', but because he was looking for something else, for an *a priori* justification of inference, and gratuitously assumed that 'productive quality' could be only another name for such a necessity.

These aspects of causation as it is in the objects—the holding of pure laws of working which are forms of partial persistence, and hence the qualitative or structural continuity in each individual process that instantiates them—are related in various ways to the important counterfactual conditionals. The inductive evidence that supports or corroborates the laws justifies the use of the counterfactuals which they seem to sustain, and the continuities, when observed or inferred, give at least further psychological encouragement and perhaps further justification for their use. Thus the counterfactual conditionals which emerge from the analysis of causal statements, though not themselves true, are surrogates for clusters of statements which can be true.

Of these objective aspects of causation some are sometimes observed, for example in the experiences which, according to Michotte, provide our basic 'perception of causality', and in many of the experiences in which we learn to use common transitive, causal, verbs, as Anscombe and Holland insist. Where they are not observed, such features may be postulated in transcendent hypotheses which are confirmed in the usual scientific way. Other aspects of causation in the objects, in particular the pure laws of working, are never the subject of observation, but are reached by the framing and testing of hypotheses, by the gradual sorting out of these laws from what depends upon collocations or initial conditions. But that does not make them any less objective.

9
Statistical Laws

IT has become clear in several of the preceding chapters that a study of causation need not presuppose causal determinism, or even use it as a regulative idea. Chapter 2 showed that we do not always require a cause to be a necessitating cause, sufficient in the strong counterfactual sense, Chapter 3 that even in those methods of discovering and establishing causal relations that rely upon assumptions of uniformity, the form of assumption required is not that of a 'law of universal causation'. Chapter 4 revealed fatal flaws in Kant's attempts to establish the general validity of the categories within our experience and to show that, in the phenomenal realm of common sense and science, every alteration must take place in accordance with some law. In Chapter 5 we criticized Ducasse's attempt to prove that '*every* event of necessity must have a cause from which it follows in a uniform manner'; in Chapter 7 we found that universal determinism would undermine the contrast between fixity and unfixity used in our preferred analysis of the direction of causation; and nothing that Chapter 8 could uncover about natural necessity amounted to any strong presumption that all events have sufficient causes. Of course, none of these points amounts to a disproof of determinism; but they suggest that we can get along without it.

But if determinism goes, what takes its place? The orthodox answers are, freedom of the will in the realm of human choice and action, and statistical laws in the realm of physics. I shall not, in this book, be discussing freedom of the will, but I want now to take up the question, Just what is a statistical law? Or, so as not to prejudge the question whether there are any, Just what would a statistical law be?

Here, as elsewhere, I mean by the term 'law' an objective law, not a law statement; 'laws' without further qualification means what Bunge calls laws₁, and defines as 'the *immanent patterns of being and becoming*', as opposed to laws₂, 'the *conceptual reconstructions thereof*'.[1]

At first sight, the answer to my question may seem obvious: take any universal law—perhaps of the complex regularity form—substitute '*x* per cent of' for 'all', and you have a statistical law. A universal law states what always happens, a statistical law what happens in some definite proportion of cases: universal laws, if there are any, can be regarded as a limiting case of statistical laws with $x = 100$.

Before criticizing this simple analogy, let us examine a corollary of it. According to the Humean tradition, the only sense in which an individual effect is necessary is that it is necessitated, logically, by the conjunction of a contingent law and a cause. (More accurately, the conjunction of the law statement with some description of the cause-event logically necessitates the statement that an effect of this sort occurs.) Analogously, this tradition would suggest that an individual outcome, such as the disintegration of a particular atom within some period of time *t*, is probable only in the sense that it is probabilified, logically, by the conjunction of a statistical law with an antecedent situation. If the law is to the effect that of atoms of a certain sort in a certain condition *x* per cent disintegrate within time *t*, then this statement, in conjunction with the statement that this is an atom of that sort in those conditions, probabilifies to degree *x* per cent the statement that this atom will disintegrate within time *t*. We may wish to impose the restriction that no fuller true description of the antecedent conditions, conjoined with any other genuine law, should probabilify this outcome to any different degree or entail either that it will or that it will not occur. But the important point is that this tradition would reduce the probability of individual events to logical probabilification by statistical laws plus antecedent conditions just as it reduces the necessity of caused individual events to logical necessitation by laws of sufficient causation plus antecedent conditions.

It is true that we have found reason to supplement the

<hr/>

[1] M. Bunge, *Causality*, p. 249.

Humean account of sufficient causation—as well as to insist that our ordinary concept does not require a cause to be a sufficient cause. What we have added is the direction of causation, the sorting out of pure laws of working, and the suggestion that these are forms of at least partial persistence, that they typically involve some qualitative or structural continuity. We may well add these features also to our Humean picture of a statistical law. Indeed it is particularly easy to add the direction of causation to a statistical law, where the antecedent conditions will be fixed before the outcome occurs, while that outcome will presumably not be fixed until it actually occurs. And at least in the central case of quantum mechanics, the mathematical description in terms of ψ-functions yields a kind of structural continuity, though it is controversial whether these functions can be interpreted realistically. But even when these features are added, the *probability* of individual outcome events is still being reduced to the logical probabilification of the corresponding statements by statistical law statements plus descriptions of antecedent conditions.

There are, of course, other concepts of probability, other senses of 'probable' and its associates. For example, 'It is probable that P (to a certain degree)' may mean 'There are inconclusive reasons (of such and such strength) for believing that P'. There is the 'range' or 'measure' concept of which the classical definition in terms of a ratio of possibilities is a primitive version. There are frequency concepts. And there is a notion of objective chance or propensity.[2] But the first three of these would make no substantial difference here. If there are reasons of some strength, but inconclusive, for belief about an individual outcome that falls under a statistical law, this will be just because the law and the antecedent conditions together probabilify it; the measure concept comes in only as a way of explaining and systematizing such probabilifications; the relevant frequencies will be those within the class of events referred to by the antecedent of the statistical law. Only objective chance or propensity would give the individual outcome event an intrinsic probability as distinct from the frequency in a class of events and the consequential logical probabilifications. But,

[2] I have examined these concepts and their interrelations in Chapter 5 of *Truth, Probability, and Paradox.*

as I have argued,[3] Hume's reasons for denying logical connections between distinct occurrences would tell equally against
a corresponding intrinsic probability, an objective chance or
propensity. A Humean, then, would say that if antecedent
conditions ever probabilify, rather than necessitate, a certain
outcome, this relation will consist simply in this individual
situation's being an instance which falls under a statistical law,
just as any necessitating would have consisted simply in its
being an instance that fell under a universal law, a law of
sufficient causation.

But let us then go back to the question, Just what is a
statistical law? There is no difficulty or obscurity in the notion
of a statistical *fact*, for example that 30 per cent of dwellings
occupied in the United Kingdom at a certain date have no
bathrooms. But what constitutes a statistical *law*? Is it a
statistical fact about the universe, differing from such a
statistical fact as that just mentioned only in being free from
spatio-temporal restriction ('in the United Kingdom at a certain date')? Would it be a statistical law, if it were true, that
nine-tenths of all the human beings (defined, like Popper's
moas, by some biological structure) that ever have lived, are
now alive, or ever will live anywhere in the universe had, have,
or will have brown eyes? This would be only a semi-uniformity
of coexistence. If, with Mill, we have recognized laws of coexistence we might recognize statistical laws of the same sort,
which might arise in several ways.

First, it could be that events of type *A*, when conjoined with
ones of type *B*, regularly led to ones of type *C*, and that those of
type *A*, when conjoined with ones of type *D*, regularly led to
ones of type *E*, but it was a mere fact of collocation that in
x per cent of cases when an *A* was conjoined with a *B*, it was
conjoined also with a *D*. This, if *C*s came about in no other
way, would have the consequence that *x* per cent of *C*s had *E*s
associated with them. Thus a semi-uniformity of coexistence
could be derived from a mere statistical fact of collocation:
but Mill refused the title of law to those uniformities of coexistence that had an analogous source.[4]

---

[3] *Truth, Probability, and Paradox,* especially pp. 179–87 and 232–3; also in my review
of D. H. Mellor's *The Matter of Chance,* in *Philosophical Quarterly,* xxiii (1973), 85–7.
[4] *System of Logic,* Book III, Ch. 5, Sect. 9; cf. Chapter 8 above, pp. 204–5, n. 12.

Secondly, it could be that some assemblage of conditions A led uniformly, by a law of sufficient causation, to Cs, but only by a statistical law to Es, producing Es only in x per cent of cases; then again if Cs were produced in no other way, x per cent of Cs would have Es associated with them. *This* semi-uniformity of coexistence would be analogous to those uniformities of coexistence which Mill *was* ready to call laws: but it would be only a derived law, and what is of greater interest is the supposed law by which As produced Es in x per cent of cases.

Thirdly, just as Mill was willing to recognize ultimate uniformities of coexistence,[5] so we must recognize the possibility of ultimate semi-uniformities of coexistence of a statistical sort, not derived in either of the two ways just mentioned.

However, the statistical laws that we need most to elucidate are not any such semi-uniformities of coexistence, but laws of working such as we used in the second case above, a law of the form that As produce Es in x per cent of cases. It seems that it would be a statistical law, if it were true, that 50 per cent of all radium atoms, if left alone, not subjected to nuclear bombardment and so on, disintegrate within a period of 1590 years from the time at which they become radium atoms. But there is still a difficulty. It might be that, in the whole history of the universe, only 2^n million radium atoms ever have come or will come into existence, that the first half of these, the first 2^{n-1} million, all disintegrate within 1590 years of their becoming radium atoms, while none of the other half ever have disintegrated or ever will. But if there were a statistical fact of this sort about the universe, although this is a fact about changes rather than coexistences, and although it is free from spatio-temporal restriction, it seems that it would not constitute what we mean by a statistical *law*. To be a law, it must in some way apply to radium atoms severally, distributively, not merely collectively. The proportionality of the outcome must be exhibited repeatedly, it must in some way crop up wherever the antecedent conditions occur. How can we reconcile this distributiveness, this severalty, with a merely statistical character?

It looks as if a statistical law should have the form of a universal quantification of some statistical fact, it should assert that in all such and such, a certain statistical relation (about changes, comings about) holds. But, if so, the simple analogy between universal and statistical laws has broken down; the latter will have some more complex form than '*x* per cent of *A*s are (become, produce, lead to, and so on) *B*s'.

'Where there are three doctors, there are two atheists.' In whatever sense this might be true, it could not be that for every set of three doctors, exactly two members of that set are atheists. If there are four or more doctors in the world, then however atheism is distributed among them it is mathematically inevitable that there should be at least one set of three which contains either more or fewer than two atheists. Similarly, it cannot be true that for every collection of radium atoms existing at time t_1, exactly half the atoms in the collection will have decayed by $t_1 + 1590$ years. It will be possible to find collections all of whose members decay within this period, other collections none of whose members decay, and others again with decay ratios all the way up and down the scale between 0 per cent and 100 per cent. No doubt one would be most unlikely to be able to specify in advance one of these atypical collections, but that is not to the point. We are trying to find a form for an objective law of working, and any law-statement of the form suggested above is necessarily false.

We seem able to do better with a Mendelian example. With a plant species *S*, which displays contrasting genetically determined characteristics *A* and *a*, of which *A* is dominant, we might try this formulation: 'In *S*, whenever a plant from a pure strain displaying *A* is crossed with a plant from a pure strain displaying *a* and one plant from the first filial generation (F_1) thus produced is self-pollinated, exactly three-quarters of the plants in the second filial generation (F_2) thus produced will display *A*.' Unlike the last, this suggested law-statement is not necessarily false. But it is contingently false: most collections of F_2 plants thus produced will not show this exact proportion of *A*s.

Nor will it do to substitute 'approximately' for 'exactly'. This is too indeterminate for a statement of how nature actually works in this field, and yet if any definite limits are set, for example, if it is said that the proportion of *A*s in F_2 plants thus produced will always lie between 70 per cent and 80 per cent, the proposed law-statement will still be contingently false.

It is worth noting why these proposed Mendelian laws are only contingently false and not necessarily so. We are now applying the universal quantification not to sets or collections in general of the individuals of the kind in question, but to groups of these individuals which are marked out independently of our choices. The proposed law is about groups each of which consists of all the individual F_2 plants produced by the self-pollination of one F_1 plant. So while a statistical law could not be of the form 'For every collection of As, x per cent of the As in the collection will be B', it could be of the form 'For every collection of As produced in such and such a way . . .'; it could be a universal quantification over *basic groups* of a certain kind—where each basic group might be, say, all the radium atoms in a continuous lump of radium at time t_1.

All the 'laws' of this form so far suggested are contingently false. On the other hand, there could be genuine statistical laws of this form. Let us construct an example, using only slight distortions of some biological facts. Let us suppose that the female golden eagle always lays exactly two eggs at a time and that it always happens either that both chicks hatch out or that both fail to do so. The two chicks in each brood then compete for the food brought by the parents, and whichever of the two has some slight initial advantage competes more successfully and in consequence grows bigger and stronger than its sibling. Eventually the chicks grow too big for the nest to hold both of them, and the weaker of the two is pushed out and dies. Assuming that eagle chicks are safe from every other hazard, it will follow that of every pair of chicks just one reaches maturity. Consequently a 50 per cent survival rate holds for basic groups of golden eagle chicks, where the basic group is the single brood.

An essentially similar example would be a law that has been suggested for political triumvirates, namely that every triumvirate is unstable, because it will always be to the advantage of two of its members to combine against the third and exclude him from power. If so, there will be a $33\frac{1}{3}$ per cent casualty rate among triumvirs, where the basic group is each particular triumvirate.

In both these examples, a statistical truth results from a certain pattern of competition within basic groups. But what is essential is interaction, not necessarily competition. There might be South Sea Island economies in which all the necessities of life, and even all the known luxuries, were provided easily by the activity of half the community, and in which there was, in consequence, an amicable division of communities into workers and idlers in equal numbers. But statistical laws of this sort hold, if and when they do hold, because some particular pattern of interaction is displayed within each basic group of the kind in question. These laws are always derived laws; they result from interaction which goes on in accordance with other, more basic, laws, which may well be universal, deterministic ones. If there are any statistical laws of this sort, let us call them interaction resultant laws, or IRLs. We could put under this heading the fact that a heterozygous parent produces, by meiosis, equal numbers of gametes carrying the two genes that form a pair of allelomorphs: the 'interaction' here is just the separation of the two halves of the cell. This equal proportion of the sub-classes within this basic group (gametes produced by a single individual) is a statistical outcome of a process (cell division) which in this respect at least is deterministic.*

But the most important examples of statistical laws of working are not of this sort: their statistical outcomes are not the product of proportions thus causally maintained within any basic groups. Even in the genetic process, only some parts are thus covered by IRLs. What happens at fertilization is covered by laws of chance of a different sort: interaction in basic groups is no longer relevant, and even the basic groups themselves seem to lose their importance. A statistical discussion of, say, haemophilia and its carriers will deal with frequencies in large populations rather than the proportions in individual families which, since the families are fairly small, will often differ widely from the theoretical probabilities. Again, physicists do not tell us that the decay rate of radium depends upon interaction (in even the loosest sense) between adjacent atoms: no basic group is relevant here. But if basic groups go, over what can a statistical law be universally quantified? How are we to reconcile its statistical character with the need for repetition, for distributiveness, to distinguish a law of working from a mere statistical fact about the universe?

The obvious answer which I have been withholding so long is that a statistical law assigns the corresponding *probability* or *chance* to each individual that falls under it, that it has the form 'Every *A* has an *x* per cent chance of becoming *B* (or of producing a *B*)'. It is this assignment of a measured chance of the change in question to each individual instance of the relevant assemblage of conditions that allows a law to be at once universally distributive, as a law of working, it seems, should be, and yet merely statistical in its outcome. Bernoulli's Law of Large Numbers ensures that if each instance of *A* has an *x* per cent chance of becoming *B*, there is a high probability that the frequency, in any large collection of *A*s, of becoming *B* will be near to *x* per cent.[6]

But this answer, though obvious, is paradoxical in the light of what has been said earlier. If we are to reduce the probability of individual outcome events to the probabilification of the corresponding statements by the conjunction of descriptions of antecedent conditions with statements of statistical laws, we cannot without circularity take those laws to assign a probability of such an outcome to individual antecedent situations. The probability interpretation of a statistical law requires that the probability thus assigned should be some genuinely intrinsic feature of each individual occurrence of the antecedent conditions; in other words, an objective chance or propensity. But I have argued elsewhere against the recognition of any such entities,[7] and it would clearly be inconsistent to introduce them while keeping even as close as I have kept to the Humean reduction of necessity to universality. On the other hand, the rejection of intrinsic, not logically relational, objective single case probabilities leaves us nothing to use as the predicate in the proposed formulation of a statistical law. Of course, this proposed formulation will do as a rough indication (it is not as rough as the alternative '*x* per cent of *A*s are *B*'), and in conjunction with Bernoulli's Law and Bayes's Theorems it indicates how such law-statements are to be applied and tested; but it will not do as a formulation of a law by which the world actually works, as a literal description of what goes on. If there

[6] I have examined the interpretation and application of this law in *Truth, Probability, and Paradox*, pp. 204–13.

[7] Ibid., pp. 133–45, 179–87, and 232–5.

are no such probabilities, a law statement that assigns them to all situations of a certain sort cannot be literally true. So we still have on our hands the problem of saying just what a statistical law of working could be.

The only way out of this difficulty is that indicated by the theory of limiting frequency. We know what it is for, say, tosses of a coin to approach a certain limiting frequency for heads: in short runs the frequency may diverge widely from this limit, but most longer runs approach it more closely, and greatly divergent longer runs are rare. If there is a statistical law of working about, say, the decay of radium atoms, the state of affairs must be similar to this. If radium atoms are considered in one or other possible series, for example a series determined by increasing distance at a time t_1 from some arbitrarily chosen point, their decaying or not decaying within some period of time may exhibit the sort of pattern that makes a series look as if it were a random collective approaching a certain limiting frequency. Its doing this, I suggest, would constitute the holding of a statistical law of working. This statement may well seem crude. But this is deliberate. It is all too easy in this area to sacrifice reality to precision. We are tempted to say that in a series that has a limiting frequency for some feature there is a low *probability* for long runs that diverge widely from that limiting frequency. But in the formulation of a law which is intended to provide a reductive analysis of objective probability this 'probability for long runs' cannot remain unanalysed, it in turn will have to be analysed in terms of limiting frequency; and then we shall not be able to avoid a vicious infinite regress if such a probability turns up in the account of what a series with a limiting frequency is. Again, it is plausible to interpret probability statements about individual objects, such as 'This penny, tossed in the normal way, has an x per cent chance of falling heads', as assertions of limiting frequency in a merely *hypothetical* series, as being about what *would* happen if this penny as it now is were tossed indefinitely.[8] But no such hypothetical statement can be an adequate formulation of a fully objective law of working. Of course, we can and must frame hypotheses to the effect that such and such a law holds. There is no objection to laws, statistical or otherwise, being hypo-

[8] Cf. *Truth, Probability, and Paradox*, pp. 177–8, 231–2.

STATISTICAL LAWS 241

thetical in this sense. All laws of nature will be the objects of such hypotheses and will be known only in so far as such hypotheses are confirmed or corroborated. But it would be quite another matter, and quite inadmissible, to include a statement about what *would* happen *if* . . . within the formulation of a (potentially) objective law.

A statistical law, then, must consist in some outcome's having some limiting frequency in certain actual series or sequences of instances of the assemblage of antecedent conditions. Its distributive character must lie not in any universal assignment of a *probability* of that outcome to each such instance, nor even in any universal assignment of *probabilities of various frequencies* of that outcome to runs of such instances of various finite lengths, but merely in the fact that long runs of such instances in various spatio-temporally determined series usually exhibit frequencies close to the limiting one.

There is, indeed, another way in which we can interpret such terms as 'tendency' or 'propensity' and which allows for a universal assignment of a certain propensity to each antecedent instance. A loaded die has, at every throw, the same physical asymmetry which somehow accounts for its landing 6-up more than one-sixth of the time. We could identify its propensity to favour 6-up not with the disposition whose manifestation is the limiting frequency but with the occurrent ground of that disposition, the physical asymmetry. In this sense, every throw of the die contains this propensity. And by contrast an unbiased die is physically symmetrical; if its propensity to fall equal numbers of times with each of the six faces up is identified with this symmetry, we can assign this equality-favouring propensity to every throw. Similarly, all radium atoms share a nuclear composition which somehow accounts for their being unstable and for radium having the half-life that it has, a nuclear composition which is different from that of a stable element like lead or of a radioactive element with a different half-life like radon. If we again equate their propensity to decay not with the disposition but with this occurrent ground of the disposition, we can assign this propensity universally, to every radium atom at all times up to that at which it actually decays. But it is very obvious that these universal assignments are not in themselves statements of any laws of working. They would become so only if the propensity were interpreted as a disposition rather than as the ground of a disposition. But if we analyse dispositions, as we must, in terms of laws, we cannot without circularity include the assignment of dispositions in a strict formulation of those laws. This approach would give us a law of working as a universally quantified propensity-assignment only by way of an equivocation about 'propensity'.

This exclusion of chance or probability from the formulation of statistical laws not only makes that formulation cruder and clumsier than we might desire but also deprives us of what looks like an explanatory concept. We feel that if each instance of the antecedent conditions had the appropriate *chance* of producing such and such an outcome, this would explain why, in most long runs of such instances, this outcome occurs with a frequency fairly close to that chance. But since the supposed chance can be introduced only as an unknown somewhat which, by obeying the standard probability calculus, issues in a much higher chance for corresponding frequencies in long runs, and hence in a high chance that most long runs of instances of the antecedent conditions will exhibit the corresponding frequency of the outcome, where this last 'chance' is taken to justify a corresponding degree of belief, the supposed explanation is spurious. The explanatory item is a mere 'that which would account for' what it is supposed to explain. There is, indeed, no objection to talk about 'powers' or (more old-fashioned) 'virtues' if these terms are taken as place-holders for genuinely explanatory items still to be discovered;[9] but a 'chance' or 'propensity' assigned to each individual instance of the antecedent conditions cannot serve as such a place-holder: nothing could ever fulfil the promise it offers. Such items as the nuclear composition of atoms or the physical symmetry or asymmetry of a die will not fill this bill; they will not explain, in the way promised by the term 'chance', the appearance of an approach to a limiting frequency which is the observed fact in question.

This last claim may be disputed. In the case of the die we can at least sketch an explanation. There is a considerable range of variation between possible ways of placing the die in the dice-box and throwing it onto the table. Any one such way leads deterministically, by strict laws of sufficient causation, to

[9] Cf. *Truth, Probability, and Paradox*, p. 143.

a certain result, a certain face's being uppermost when the die comes to rest. If the die is symmetrical, equal portions of this range of possible variation will thus lead to the results 1-up, 2-up, and so on. But if the die is asymmetrical, say if it is loaded to favour 6-up, a larger portion of this range of possible variation will lead, deterministically, to 6-up than to any other result. Add to all this the vital further fact that in a certain long run of throws of the die the actual ways of placing the die in the dice-box and throwing it were scattered fairly evenly over the whole range of possible ways, and we have an explanation why in this run the six faces came up about an equal number of times each (if the die was symmetrical) or unequally, with 6-up the most frequent (if it was loaded).

But this explanation depends on the conjunction of physical symmetry or asymmetry with deterministic laws of working and with a brute fact of collocation, the actual scatter of throwing methods used in this run.

A similar explanation could be given, or at least sketched, of the frequencies that result from the genetic lottery. For example, a heterozygous parent plant produces male and female gametes carrying the allelomorphs A and a in equal numbers. In a particular process of self-pollination, these gametes are shuffled around in such a way that about half the A females are fertilized by A males and about half by a males, and the a females likewise. In this individual process, the frequencies among the offspring of close to one quarter AA, one half Aa, and one quarter aa result from the equal numbers of A and a gametes (itself the product of an IRL) conjoined with deterministic laws of working and a fact of collocation, the actual shuffling that occurred.

If we now go on from a particular process of self-pollination in one plant to what regularly happens in the self-pollination of plants that are heterozygous with respect to this pair of allelomorphs, the main problem is what to say about these shufflings. It is a mathematical fact that if there are m male and n female gametes $(m > n)$, and half of each are A and half a, then of the possible unions resulting from all possible shufflings exactly one quarter will be AA, and so on. But what sort of fact is it that actual self-pollination processes incorporate shufflings which are pretty fairly representative of the range of mathematically possible shufflings? Comparison with other examples of shuffling, say of large numbers of grains of sand of different colours placed in a tray that is then mechanically agitated, shows that the characteristic apparently random results of shuffling need not, and presumably in general do not, depend upon any indeterminism in the pure laws of working, but simply on the conjunction of facts of collocation—the exact shape of the tray, the exact initial arrangement and shapes of the variously coloured grains, and so on—with deterministic laws. That actual shufflings are pretty fairly representative of the range of mathematically possible shufflings is then, in terms of the distinctions drawn in Chapter 8, a mixed law. Various applications of this and analogous principles have the consequence that certain kinds of set-up regularly produce outcomes which are apparently random in order and arrangement but which seem to approach definite limiting frequencies for the different possible kinds of outcome. Some such set-ups—dice-throwing, card-shuffling, the stirring up of marbles in a lottery-barrel, and so on—are typically used as gambling devices. These in general involve fairly close approximations to equality between certain aspects of the set-up—a die is meant to be physically symmetrical with respect to all six faces, the cards in a pack are equal in size and surface texture, and so on—and consequently also in the resulting limiting frequencies for alternative outcomes. But exactly analogous explanations underlie the *unequal* limiting frequencies generated by asymmetrical dice and unequal set-ups in general. We may, then, give the name of gambling device laws, or GDLs, to all those laws each of which consists in a certain kind of set-up regularly generating outcomes in apparently random order with limiting frequencies for alternative outcomes, where this can in principle be explained in the sort of way indicated by our examples. GDLs, then, are mixed laws; they are derivative from deterministic pure laws of working in conjunction with certain relevant and fairly permanent features of the set-up—the symmetry or the exact asymmetry of the die, the equality or inequality of the numbers of A and a gametes, and so on—and with other more obscure facts of collocation, almost impossible to describe in detail, which by the complexity and scattering of their relevant aspects help to introduce the appearance of randomness into the results. Consequently, even if we

state a GDL in a hypothetical form, putting into the antecedent explicit descriptions of all the fairly permanent relevant
features of the set-up, we cannot thereby 'purify' it, and turn
the mixed law into a pure law of working, as we could (in
principle) with the mixed laws discussed in Chapter 8. What
I have called the more obscure facts of collocation keep it
impure. If their obscurity could be overcome and we could, for
any particular process or run of trials, include in the antecedent of a hypothetically formulated law a description of all
the relevant detail, then we should have a derivative pure law
of working, but a deterministic one, which this particular process or run would exactly instantiate. But if we put into the
antecedent only a rough general description of these obscure
contributory facts of collocation, our law will still be a statistical,
not a deterministic, one, assigning only limiting frequencies to
series of the antecedent conditions, but also it will remain a
mixed law, dependent on the unstated and obscure facts of
collocation, not a pure law of working.

GDLs are different from IRLs, although, as we have seen,
laws of both kinds may play a part in the same complex phenomenon, covering, for example, different phases of a genetic
process. IRLs rest upon patterns of interaction of some kind
within basic groups and may issue in exact proportions within
each basic group (and therefore, automatically, in any collection of such basic groups); GDLs rest rather on an input of
complex, scattered, detail in relevant collocations, and issue
only in limiting frequencies. But both are only mixed laws, and
in both cases the pure laws of working from which they are
partly derived may be, and in all the ordinary cases presumably
are, deterministic laws, laws of sufficient causation.

Consequently, we can reaffirm our thesis that such items as
the symmetry or asymmetry of a die will not explain in the
way required the appearance of an approach to a limiting frequency of this or that outcome. We can concede that it helps
to explain this, but only in conjunction with some obscure facts
of collocation. What is even more serious is that such explanations dispense with statistical laws of working, resolving what
appear to be such into mixed laws derived from the conjunction
of collocations with deterministic laws of working. Any such
explanation, then, is very far indeed from fulfilling the promise

offered by the assignment of an objective chance or propensity to each instance of the antecedent conditions. We can then, in the light of this discussion, reaffirm the thesis that whereas talk about 'powers' or 'virtues' can be interpreted, harmlessly, as merely foreshadowing the discovery of genuinely explanatory items, the analogous talk about 'chances' or 'propensities' cannot; at any rate not without departing from the claim that what these terms explain, or foreshadow an explanation of, are statistical *laws of working*.

What our discussion brings out, then, is the need to distinguish such statistical laws of working (if there are any), which we may call SLWs, from both IRLs and GDLs. Whether there are any SLWs is a question that we cannot answer with confidence. The orthodox view of quantum mechanics asserts that there are, and indeed that what look like macroscopic deterministic laws are derivative from SLWs at the micro level, and are therefore (in general) themselves only SLWs that approach determinism as a limit. But a heretical view of quantum mechanics in effect suggests that the quantum laws themselves are what I have called GDLs rather than SLWs. I cannot adjudicate this controversy; I have been concerned merely to bring out what SLWs, if there are any, would involve. The concept of an SLW can be developed coherently and without conflict with our empiricist, semi-Humean, treatment of natural necessity. And yet when it is clarified and distinguished, something rather mysterious is left. There is, I have argued, an unavoidable crudity of formulation: an SLW must find its distributiveness simply in the fact that certain actual series appear to approach limiting frequencies and that most long runs in such series do not diverge far from the limiting frequencies: we cannot make this formulation neater by introducing universal assignments of chances or probabilities without abandoning the claim that such a law-statement is an objective description of how things work. Also, there is an inevitable lack of explanation: we cannot go behind the brute fact of actual approaches to limiting frequency with random distribution without sliding from SLWs to GDLs and hence to deterministic laws of working.

There may, indeed, seem to be a gap in our argument here. I have said only that the laws of working from which GDLs are partly derived *may be* and in ordinary cases *presumably are* deterministic, not that they *must* be so. There is nothing in theory to preclude the derivation of a GDL from the conjunction of collocations (both the relatively permanent features and the obscure, scattered, details) with pure laws of working some of which are SLWs. True, but that only shifts the problem. If what we initially took to be an SLW is explained as being, after all, a GDL which itself is dependent partly on an SLW, then it is this new SLW that both calls for and resists explanation.

We cannot, however, make very much of this, since our empirical counterpart to Kneale's necessity gave even deterministic laws only a partial intelligibility even in principle: even a deterministic interaction requires, inescapably, a law of working which does not consist just in the regular persistence of anything. That any interaction should go one way rather than another, however regularly it does so and however many items or quantities are conserved through the transaction, remains in part a purely contingent fact which no penetration into underlying features, no transcendent hypotheses, could ever render completely intelligible. Yet it remains true that a statistical law of working resists intelligibility still more. On the other hand, it is worth repeating that statistical laws of working make it particularly easy to feed in our criterion for the direction of causation, and that those suggested for the central quantum mechanical case clearly provide for a recognizable kind of structural continuity.

Extensionality—Two Kinds
of Cause

Of what kind are the entities that stand in causal relations?
Between what sorts of item does causing go on? In Chapter 2
this question was brushed aside with the interim suggestions
that although causes and effects would be spoken of as events,
'event' would be used just as a general term to stand in for such ·
items as 'the hammer's striking the chestnut', and that in constructing conditional analyses of singular causal statements we
could go back from such nominalizations to the corresponding
clauses or their negations: 'The chestnut would not have become flatter if the hammer had not struck it.' Similarly in
Chapter 3 regularities were formulated in terms of types of
event or situation. But these ways of speaking slurred over a
cluster of issues which deserve attention.[1]

At least two questions have been raised. Are causes events or
facts? And are causal statements extensional? Both are controversial. Philosophers have long been inclined to speak of one
event causing another. The double assassination at Sarajevo was
surely an event, and it was at least the triggering cause of the
First World War. Standing conditions and states of affairs are
admitted to be also causally relevant, to be perhaps predisposing
causes, but they can be accommodated, under a tolerant interpretation of the term, as static events, as Ducasse's *unchanges*.[2]

---

[1] They are discussed, for example, by Donald Davidson, 'Causal Relations',
Journal of Philosophy, lxiv (1967), 691–703; Zeno Vendler, 'Causal Relations', ibid.,
pp. 704–13, also in Vendler's earlier 'Effects, Results, and Consequences' in *Analytical
Philosophy*, ed. R. J. Butler; G. E. M. Anscombe, 'Causality and Extensionality',
Journal of Philosophy, lxvi (1969), 152–9; and Adam Morton, 'Extensional and
Non-truth-functional Contexts', ibid., pp. 159–64.

[2] Though Ducasse seems to distinguish a standing condition from an unchange:
cf. Chapter 5.

Yet it is also tempting to say '*The fact that* there was a short circuit *caused it to be the case that* there was a fire' or that Caesar's having crossed the Rubicon caused the Civil War; these go together because the phrase 'Caesar's having crossed the Rubicon' is an *imperfect nominal,* and the word 'fact' goes with the imperfect nominals whereas the word 'event' goes with the perfect nominals.[3] Again, the extensionality of at least some causal statements seems intuitively obvious. We can surely substitute co-referring expressions in singular causal statements: if the assassination at Sarajevo in 1914 caused the First World War, so did the assassination in the capital of Bosnia in 1914, and so did Gabriel Prinzip's best-known action; if Caesar's crossing of the Rubicon caused the Roman civil war, so did Caius Julius's crossing of the boundary of Italy; and so on. On the other hand, even if we agree that there was an international crisis because President de Gaulle made a speech we may hesitate to say that there was a crisis because the man with the biggest nose in France made a speech;[4] moreover, there is a logical argument which is believed to show that any context which is extensional must also be truth-functional, which causal contexts certainly are not.[5] In favour of another aspect of extensionality it might be argued that statements of causal regularity relate types of event or situation, and must necessarily retain their truth-value when coextensive predicate terms are substituted for one another. An excessively simple regularity will serve to illustrate this point: if every event of type A is also of type B and vice versa, then 'Every event of type A is followed contiguously by an event of type C' will retain its truth-value when 'B' is substituted for 'A'. But against this it might be argued that of the coextensive features A and B one might be causally relevant to C and the other not; for example, someone who held a double aspect theory of mind and brain might say that the neurophysiological aspect has effects which cannot properly be ascribed to the mental aspect of the same events; he could not deny the corresponding regularities, but he might reply that this shows only that there is more to causing than regular sequence.

[3] Vendler, 'Causal Relations'; this is discussed below.
[4] Anscombe, op. cit.
[5] Davidson, op. cit.; Anscombe, op. cit.

Since the logical argument mentioned above has tended to dominate recent discussions, we may consider first whether it is sound and what, if anything, it shows. It purports to show that if a context is extensional it is truth-functional, so that it can be applied to prove that since causal contexts are not truth-functional they cannot be extensional either. However, 'extensional' is ambiguous. It may mean that the substitution of co-referring singular terms does not affect truth-value, or that the substitution of coextensive predicates does not affect truth-value. Let us use Quine's term 'referentially transparent' (or, briefly, just 'transparent') for the former meaning, and reserve 'extensional' for the latter. The argument we are to consider is then concerned with transparency, not extensionality: it purports to show that if a context is transparent it is truth-functional. It runs as follows.

Let 'p' represent any sentence, and '$F(p)$' any sentence containing the sentence represented by 'p'. That is, '$F(...)$' is a sentence-forming operator on sentences, or briefly a context. Suppose that '$F(...)$' is such that logical equivalents are interchangeable within it *salva veritate*. Suppose further that '$F(...)$' is referentially transparent, so that co-referring expressions are interchangeable in '$F(p)$' *salva veritate* provided that they are so in 'p' itself. Then consider $\hat{x}(x = x \,\&\, p)$, that is, the class of xs such that both (x is identical with x) and p. If p is true, this will be the class of xs such that $x = x$, but if p is false it will be the empty class. Consequently '$\hat{x}(x = x \,\&\, p) = \hat{x}(x = x)$'—the statement that {the class of xs such that both (x is identical with x) and p} is identical with {the class of xs such that (x is identical with x)}—will be logically equivalent to 'p', since, whatever 'p' may be, it is necessarily true when 'p' is true and false when 'p' is false. Moreover, if 'q' has the same truth-value as 'p', $\hat{x}(x = x \,\&\, p)$ will be the same class as $\hat{x}(x = x \,\&\, q)$, since each will be $\hat{x}(x = x)$ if 'p' and 'q' are both true, and each will be the empty class if 'p' and 'q' are both false. We then have the following steps:

1	(1)	$p \leftrightarrow q$	—assumption
2	(2)	$F(p)$	—assumption
2	(3)	$F(\hat{x}(x = x \,\&\, p) = \hat{x}(x = x))$	—from (2), by substitution of logical equivalents in '$F(...)$'
1, 2	(4)	$F(\hat{x}(x = x \,\&\, q) = \hat{x}(x = x))$	—from (3), by substi-

tution of co-referring expressions in '$F(...)$', in the light of (1) and the above remarks.

1, 2   (5) $F(q)$—from (4), by substitution of logical equivalents in '$F(...)$'

1   (6) $F(p) \rightarrow F(q)$—from (2), (5), by conditional proof.

1   (7) $F(q) \rightarrow F(p)$—by a similar series of steps to (2)–(6).

1   (8) $F(p) \leftrightarrow F(q)$—from (6) and (7).

     (9) $(p \leftrightarrow q) \rightarrow (F(p) \leftrightarrow F(q))$—from (1), (8), by conditional proof.

Now (9) says that the context '$F(...)$' is truth-functional, and this has been proved from the suppositions that '$F(...)$' is such as to allow substitution within it of logical equivalents and of co-referring expressions. That is, if '$F(...)$' is both transparent and allows substitution of logical equivalents, it is truth-functional.[6]

This argument has been widely accepted and respected, but is it sound? As Professor Anscombe says, someone might complain about its artificiality, but that is beside the point. The most suspect move is that from (2) to (3), resting on the alleged logical equivalence of 'p' and '$\hat{x}(x = x \,\&\, p) = \hat{x}(x = x)$'—with of course, the reverse move from (4) to (5). The point of this move is that it replaces the proposition 'p', which may be about any subject whatever, with one which asserts the identity of two classes, and therefore allows the substitution at (4) of another expression '$\hat{x}(x = x \,\&\, q)$' which refers to the same *class* as does '$\hat{x}(x = x \,\&\, p)$'. Cummins and Gottlieb say roundly that this step is fallacious. If the set abstraction operator is defined contextually, so that

$$\hat{x}(Fx) = \hat{x}(Gx) =\ _{df}(x)(Fx \leftrightarrow Gx)$$

we can no longer move validly from (3) to (4), since the apparent class-identity of (3) has been reduced by this definition to a statement that two predicates are coextensive, and our initial assumption was only that '$F(...)$' was transparent, not that

[6] The argument is credited originally to Frege and variants have been used by Gödel ('Russell's Mathematical Logic' in *The Philosophy of Bertrand Russell*, ed. P. A. Schilpp, p. 129, n. 5) and Quine ('Three Grades of Modal Involvement' (1953), reprinted in *The Ways of Paradox*, pp. 156–74) as well as by Davidson and Anscombe in the papers referred to above, p. 248, n. 1. It is discussed by Morton in the paper referred to above and by Robert Cummins and Dale Gottlieb in 'On an Argument for Truth-functionality', *American Philosophical Quarterly*, ix (1972), 265–9.

it was extensional in the sense of allowing interchange of coextensive predicates. If, alternatively, the set abstraction operator makes definite descriptions out of predicates—that is, if we take sets seriously as individual objects to which reference can be made—then 'p' and '$\hat{x}(x = x \,\&\, p) = \hat{x}(x = x)$' are not logically equivalent, for the latter implies the existence of the class of xs such that $x = x$, whereas the former does not. It might be objected, however, that the class of xs such that $x = x$—the universal set—is guaranteed by logic alone to exist and to be non-empty, and therefore that the explicit commitment to it in '$\hat{x}(x = x \,\&\, p) = \hat{x}(x = x)$' does not destroy the latter's logical equivalence to 'p'. As Anscombe says, what we need is the description of a class $\hat{x}(Gx \,\&\, p)$ where 'G' is a respectable class-forming predicate such that $\hat{x}(Gx)$ logically cannot be empty. There is room for dispute here.[7] The argument could, then, be blocked by a narrow interpretation of the term 'logical equivalents' in the assumption that '$F(...)$' is such that logical equivalents are interchangeable within it *salva veritate*, or vindicated by a broader interpretation of this term. It is hard to see how anything of importance could turn upon this choice.

Still, the conclusion of this argument is paradoxical. It seems intuitively obvious that *some* causal statements are transparent without being truth-functional, even if *others* are referentially opaque, and we must be suspicious of an argument that purports to exclude the former possibility. In 'The fact that Smith fainted caused it to be the case that Jones ran for help' truth-value will be preserved by any substitution of co-referring expressions for 'Smith' or for 'Jones' and by any substitution of

---

[7] Cummins and Gottlieb discuss Quine's version of the argument, which introduces as equivalent to 'p' the formula '$\hat{x} \, (x = \phi \,\&\, p) = \hat{x} \, (x = \phi)$' where '$\phi$' is a name for the empty set. They rebut an objection that the existence of $\hat{x} \, (x = \phi)$ is guaranteed by first-order theory with identity because $(\exists x)(x = c)$ is a theorem, and also point out that the proof fails if the schematic letter 'c' is used throughout instead of 'ϕ', but they do not consider the more serious objection that the existence of the empty class ϕ itself, and hence of the class of which this is the only member, is specifically guaranteed by logic. This would be the analogue of the claim mentioned above, that the existence and non-emptiness of the class $\hat{x} \, (x = x)$ are logically guaranteed. Anscombe points out that the argument could be constructed in terms of numbers rather than classes: the number of numbers n such that (n is an even prime, and p) will be 1 if 'p' is true and 0 if 'p' is false, so that 'the number of numbers n such that (n is an even prime and p) is 1' will be logically equivalent to 'p'. But this would still be open to the objection that the former statement implies the existence of the number 1 whereas 'p' does not.

predicate-expressions with the same sense for 'fainted' or 'ran for help', and equally by any substitution of logical equivalents for the sentences 'Smith fainted' and 'Jones ran for help', since these will naturally preserve the reference and the sense of each sentence as a whole—for example, 'Smith either fainted or both walked and didn't walk' and 'Jones didn't not run for help'.[8] What is peculiar about the argument we are examining is that the sense of 'p' is lost at step (4).

This has come about not by any substitution of co-referring expressions *in* 'p' *itself*, nor by any substitution of logical equivalents *for* 'p' *itself*, but by the substitution of what may be considered as a logical equivalent of 'p' followed by the substitution of a co-referring expression *within that equivalent*. In constructing the argument, one construes the assumptions about '$F(...)$' as meaning not merely that each kind of substitution is allowed on its own, but that substitutions of one kind are allowed within the products of substitutions of the other kind.

If the assumptions apply to the *context* '$F(...)$' as such, and hence to *any* statement of the form '$F(p)$', then we must so construe them. But there might be a *particular* sentence 'p'— or a whole special class of such sentences—such that when it was inserted into the context '$F(...)$' each kind of substitution was allowed separately but successive substitutions of the two kinds were not allowed. A modification of the story of Puss in Boots may illustrate this. The giant might well have said to the cat, 'Certainly you may eat any mice you find in this castle, and, to amuse and impress you I shall be happy to change myself temporarily into an animal of any sort you care to name', but if he had had his wits about him he would have added, 'But this does not mean that after I have changed myself into a mouse to oblige you, you may *then* eat any mice you find in this castle'. And we should show a like caution when we realize that successive substitutions of the two kinds can produce a loss or change of sense which no substitution of either kind could produce on its own in such a sentence as ordinarily enters, as a clause, into causal statements of the sort we are discussing. We can concede that if the *context* '$F(...)$' is such that substitutions of both kinds in the contained sentence *always* preserve the truth-value of the whole statement, then it must be

[8] Cummins and Gottlieb, op. cit., p. 269.

truth-functional—allowing, that is, the broad interpretation of logical equivalence which escapes the criticism of Cummins and Gottlieb—and yet defend the intuitive claim that a *particular sentence* '$F(p)$' may be such that replacements either of 'p' itself by logical equivalents or of singular terms in 'p' by co-referring expressions do not alter the truth-value of '$F(p)$', but that replacement of 'p' by a sentence of the same truth-value may alter the truth-value of '$F(p)$'. The point is that when 'p' is replaced by its logical equivalent at step (3), a singular term '$\hat{x}(x = x \;\&\; p)$' is introduced in a position different from that occupied by, say, 'Smith' in our last example (which is typical of the position occupied by names in ordinary causal sentences, the ones which intuitively look transparent); and it may well be that when this new sentence is embedded in the context '$F(...)$', a singular term in this new position is not replaceable *salva veritate* by a co-referring one.

These considerations draw the claws of the argument, to which excessive deference has been shown. We can therefore consider the substantive questions directly, free from the threat that any transparent context for sentences will have to be merely truth-functional.

Those who have deferred to the argument have moved in different directions. Anscombe 'finds it harmless to say that causal statements are intensional', and to say that this applies not only to those of the form 'p because q', but also to those of the form 'A brought it about that p'—whether 'A' designates an event or a substance—and indeed to all in which a proposition 'p' is embedded in a context to yield a statement '$F(p)$'. But her reason for welcoming this conclusion is merely that there is *a* way of construing a clause containing a definite description which makes it important which of a number of co-referring definite descriptions is used. If we read 'There was a crisis because the man with the biggest nose in France made a speech' in such a way as to assert that there was a crisis because his was the biggest nose, it is false, whereas 'There was a crisis because the French president made a speech', read in the same way, is true. But there is also a way of reading both sentences, giving, Anscombe suggests, the definite description a different scope, which gives the two sentences the same truth-value so long as the two descriptions refer to the same man. But this reading, which makes the occurrence of the definite descriptions transparent, escapes the conclusion of the logical argument by taking these descriptions out of the embedded sentence and prefixing them to '$F(...)$' as a whole, presumably allowing the embedded sentence to be intensional: 'Concerning the man with the biggest nose: there was a crisis because he. . . .'[9]

We can link this suggestion with what was said above. What I referred to as the position occupied by 'Smith' in our example—and normally by names in ordinary causal sentences—is one such that a definite description there would naturally be read as having large scope, as being prefixed to '$F(p)$' as a whole, whereas the position occupied by '$\hat{x}(x = x \, \& \, p)$' in (3) is such that a definite description there has small scope.

Quine's versions of the argument have been criticized on these grounds by Richard Sharvy (following Arthur Smullyan): 'definite descriptions given large scope will behave properly with respect to substitutivity of identity' but 'there is no justification for performing such substitutions for or of definite descriptions which are given smaller scope'.[10] Thus '$F(...)$'—which may be, as in our examples, a causal context, or a modal one, or a belief one, and so on—may well be transparent with respect to definite descriptions with large scope but not with respect to definite descriptions with smaller scope (and names can be treated correspondingly). The moves from (2) to (3) and from (4) to (5) will be valid only if the descriptions of the classes $\hat{x}(x = x \, \& \, p)$ and $\hat{x}(x = x \, \& \, q)$ are taken as having small scope, as being strictly inside the context '$F(...)$' and as governed by 'F'; but the move from (3) to (4) would be valid only if these descriptions of classes had large scope. We can concede that if '$F(...)$' were such as to allow substitutivity of identity for *all* names and definite descriptions it would have to be truth-functional, as the argument shows: but it could be, and some causal contexts clearly are, such as to allow substitutions of co-referring terms which function as definite descriptions with large scope only, without being truth-functional.

----

[9] Cf. Anscombe, op. cit., p. 156.

[10] 'Truth-Functionality and Referential Opacity', *Philosophical Studies*, xxi (1970), 5–9, referring to Arthur Smullyan, 'Modality and Description', *Journal of Symbolic Logic*, xiii (1948), 31–7. Similar points are made and applied to other, but related, Quinean arguments in an unpublished article by C. J. F. Williams, who brought Sharvy's treatment to my attention.

Davidson, on the other hand, thinks that the argument's conclusion is to be evaded by denying that the logical form of a statement like 'The short circuit caused the fire' is given by 'The fact that there was a short circuit caused it to be the case that there was a fire', and by saying that its true logical form is that of a two-place relation whose terms are events, where an event is something complex and concrete with features beyond those that we use to describe it. The event which is Flora's drying of herself is also Flora's drying of herself with a coarse towel on the beach at noon: 'we must distinguish firmly between causes and the features we hit on for describing them'.[11] It is a consequence of this treatment that we can be said to have specified the whole cause of an event even when we have not wholly specified it. The event which is a certain man's eating of a particular dish, which, as Mill remarked, we should be apt to call the cause of his death, is, from this point of view, the whole cause, since as a concrete occurrence it is an eating of food containing just whatever poison it did contain by a man with just such a bodily constitution in just such a state of health, and so on. The event *qua* concrete occurrence includes everything that was relevant to the production of the effect and much more besides. Yet Davidson stops short of including all the circumstances in the event: since Caesar's death was the death of a man with more wounds than Brutus inflicted, Brutus's stab, even if it was sufficient for Caesar's dying, was not the whole cause of Caesar's death. Although Brutus's stabbing of Caesar was a stabbing of him shortly after the other conspirators had stabbed him, Davidson does not take the concrete event, Brutus's stabbing of Caesar, to include these other stabbings as parts of itself, but says that it 'was literally (spatio-temporally) only part of the cause'.[12] And this is just as well: if we included the circumstances in the event we should have to conclude, in a far more damaging sense than Hume intended, that anything may cause anything. The unfortunate Cinna the poet might have been rightly blamed for Caesar's death, since his writing of some bad verses was, no doubt, a writing-of-bad-verses-at-a-time-when-not-far-away-the-conspirators-were-stabbing-Caesar.

[11] Davidson, op. cit., p. 697.
[12] Ibid., p. 699.

We can identify events, in this concrete occurrence sense, simply by their spatio-temporal regions, well enough to allow one event but not another roughly contemporaneous event to be the cause of a certain effect. We then have a view of causing very similar to that of Dúcasse;[13] a cause leads on to or produces an effect by being followed contiguously by it, and by being the only change (or unchange) upon which the effect so follows. I think we can and sometimes do think and speak of such concrete occurrences as causes. We can plausibly say, of such a cause-event, that if in the circumstances it had not occurred the effect-event would not have occurred either: a possible world constructed from the actual world by excising the whole concrete occurrence and then letting things run on in accordance with the actual laws of working will not contain the effect. (Presumably we should have to insert some fairly harmless, neutral occurrence in the place of the one excised: if we cut out Flora's drying of herself, we may put in her simply lying on the beach for that period of time.) Such a counterfactual conditional will be particularly plausible if we know some law or set of laws of working by which it would be sustained; but even where we do not know such a law, we may believe *that there is* some such law.[14]

We can, then, and sometimes do, take causes (and effects) as concrete occurrences and causing as a two-place relation between such events. But it is far from clear that this is the best treatment, and it is certainly not the only possible one. Even if we deferred, unnecessarily, to the logical argument discussed above, we could keep 'The fact that . . . caused it to be the case that . . .' as an operator on propositions or sentences in Anscombe's way, by taking these contexts as intensional and by interpreting the transparent occurrences of definite descriptions within them as having large scope, that is, as being prefixed to the whole sentence rather than being governed by this

---

[13] Cf. Chapter 5.

[14] Davidson (op. cit., p. 702) says that 'Ducasse is right that singular causal statements entail no law; Hume is right that they entail there is a law'. I have argued against the latter claim in Chapter 3, and the arguments of Chapter 2 would show that even if a law were so entailed it would not need to be one of Hume's form, making the cause an event of some type that is *sufficient* for events of the same type as the effect. We may, but need not, believe that there is a law which makes the cause *necessary* in the circumstances for the effect: the other half of the regularity is still more dispensable.

causal operator. It seems a disadvantage of concrete occurrence causes that they will nearly always include irrelevant components. In Mill's example, this man's eating of this dish was also, perhaps, an eating of something with a silver fork by a man with a red moustache, and neither of these features may have had any bearing at all on his subsequent death. And we saw, in Chapter 5, how Ducasse was forced to include the air waves from the song of a canary in the cause of a particular breaking of a particular window pane. We are, sometimes at least, interested in a more selective, more discriminating relation than can hold between concrete occurrences. I spoke in Chapter 3 of the progressive localization of a cause. This is an important kind of advance in knowledge, but it would be severely restricted if only concrete occurrences were recognized as causes. Davidson himself gives examples of sentences in which particular features of events, or facts rather than events, are mentioned as causes: 'The slowness with which controls were applied caused the rapidity with which the inflation developed'; 'The collapse was caused, not by the fact that the bolt gave way, but by the fact that it gave way so suddenly and unexpectedly.' Davidson suggests that these are 'rudimentary causal explanations', that 'Explanations typically relate statements, not events', and that the 'caused' of these sentences is different from that of 'straightforward singular causal statements' and 'is best expressed by the words "causally explains" '.[15]

We need not dispute about which sort of statement is the more straightforward: what matters is that there is room, and need, for statements of both kinds. And if the logical argument had any force, it would clearly raise a difficulty for the context 'The fact that . . . causally explains the fact that . . .', since it is a context for sentences, it is obviously not truth-functional, and yet singular terms (for example, 'the bolt' in Davidson's sentence above) can occur transparently in such an explanation sentence.

Zeno Vendler argues from linguistic evidence that it is facts, rather than events, that count as causes. His thesis is that if noun phrases denoting events are represented by 'e' (with subscripts if necessary) and those denoting facts by 'f', our sentences have the three distinct forms:

[15] Op. cit., pp. 702–3.

e_1 is the effect of e_2.

f_1 is the result of f_2.

f is the cause of e.

In other words, effects and what they are effects of are events (that is, what I have been calling concrete occurrences), results and what they are the results of are facts, but a fact is said to be the cause of an event.

Vendler's linguistic argument centres upon the distinction between perfect nominals and imperfect nominals: 'the noun phrases typically associated with the "fact"-group turn out to be imperfectly nominalized sentences, whereas those appropriate to the "event"-group are exclusively perfectly nominalized sentences'. The difference is that 'In the imperfect nominal the verb keeps some of its verb-like features: it retains the verb-object intact; tenses, modals and adverbs may be present; and the whole structure is subject to negation', whereas 'The verb in the perfect nominal sheds these verb-like features and behaves like a noun: it may take relative clauses, adjectives, articles, and prepositions'.[16] Thus 'that he sang the song' and 'his having sung the song' are imperfect nominals, 'his singing of the song' and 'the beautiful singing of the song we heard' are perfect nominals.

To me, one part of Vendler's thesis, namely that imperfect nominals can stand very naturally as subjects of 'caused' and as occupants of the second gap in 'The cause of . . . was . . .' is entirely convincing. But I cannot accept the other part, that perfect nominals *cannot* play these roles. We can accept 'Caesar's having crossed the Rubicon caused the war' and 'The cause of the Roman civil war was Caesar's having crossed the Rubicon'; but can we not accept also 'Caesar's crossing of the Rubicon caused the war' and 'The cause of the war was Caesar's crossing of the Rubicon'? However, this is a purely linguistic issue, with which I am not much concerned. Even if Vendler were right, we could say 'Caesar's crossing of the Rubicon had-as-one-of-its-effects the Roman civil war' or we could coin a term, perhaps borrowing Mill's 'producing cause', for an event of which some other event is the effect, and say 'The producing cause of the war was Caesar's crossing of the Rubicon'. However the point is to be linguistically accommodated, we want both events and facts as antecedents in (different) causal relations.

[16] Vendler, op. cit., p. 707.

But there is a further issue. According to Vendler, facts are referentially transparent. Oedipus's having married Jocasta is the same fact as his having married his mother, and if the latter caused the tragedy, so did the former. Yet the latter description helps to explain the tragedy in a way that the former does not. What is referentially transparent may be, for that very reason, explanatorily opaque. But, as Davidson suggests, it is particularly when we are concerned with explanation that we take facts rather than events as causes. Vendler's transparent facts may be what the linguistic evidence picks out as the most favoured category for causes, and may none the less be only half way to a thoroughly explanatory sort of cause.

Let us work with the notion of a *causally relevant feature*. That Brutus's dagger had a sharp point was, presumably, causally relevant to Caesar's death, that it had an ornamented hilt presumably was not. That the bolt in Davidson's example gave way suddenly was causally relevant to the collapse of the bridge, that it gave way noisily was not. We can then form the concept of a *minimally complete causal account*, one which mentions all the features that were actually causally relevant to some event. This is, of course, an ideal: we do not in general expect to be able to give such an account. If determinism is not presupposed, we should not assume that the complete set of relevant features was in the strong, counterfactual, sense sufficient for the event, but if the account is causal rather than probabilistic we can assume that each relevant feature was necessary in the circumstances for that event. Now these relevant features will all be *general*: what is vital is not *this* bolt's giving way but the giving way of *a* bolt at this place; what mattered about the assassination at Sarajevo was not that it was committed by Prinzip but that it was committed by *a* Bosnian who had received arms and instruction in Serbia.

The same drive towards explanation, however, will lead us to take also what is caused not as an event but as a fact, as what Vendler calls a result: war's breaking out in August 1914 rather than the outbreak of war, or Caesar's dying rather than Caesar's death. For it will be such facts only that can be explained rather than a concrete occurrence in all its infinite detail. But again we cannot stop at a referentially transparent fact. Oedipus's having certain obvious and conscious motives causally explains his marrying the one woman who had a certain combination of physical and social attractions; to explain his marrying his mother we must either add the fact that his mother was the unique possessor of these attractions in the relevant spatio-temporal region, or substitute, in Freud's manner, some unconscious motives for the conscious ones.

But in a minimally complete causal account, not everything dissolves into generality. It is *Caesar's* being stabbed in such and such a way, conjoined with *his* having just such a physical make-up, that caused, or causally explains, *Caesar's* dying. It is such and such features of one or more things of such and such kinds being together *at this place and time* that causally explains the fact that an event of such and such a sort occurred *near this place at a time slightly later than this*. It is still a singular causal account that is being given, and at least one singular term will be included in the description alike of the cause and of the result—the same term in both—holding together what are otherwise general, existentially quantified statements. With respect to this term, then, the whole account will be referentially transparent, but this term can be considered either as a pure proper name or as a definite description with large scope, prefixed to the account as a whole: 'Concerning Caesar,'—or 'Concerning the bald Roman dictator,'—'his being stabbed....' Everything causally relevant will have been mentioned elsewhere. This singular term, which as it were stands outside the clauses which state the cause and the result and enters into them (in the shape of pronouns that refer to it) only to connect them with one another, is a much purified version of the causal field introduced in Chapter 2.

The typical form of a minimally complete causal account will then be:

> 'a's being B and there being an x such that x is C and x has relation R to a and . . . caused there to be a z such that z is D and z has relation S to a.'

What is here said to cause something may be called an *explanatory cause*. An explanatory cause is a fact, but of an unusually pure sort. Everything causally relevant about it is expressed by general terms and existential quantifications; the individual that this fact is about, the only item with respect to whose description the expression that states this fact is referentially transparent, is causally irrelevant, everything that is causally relevant about this individual having been covered by explicit monadic, dyadic, or polyadic predicates. And the result of which this is the cause is a fact of an equally pure sort.

A minimally complete causal account is explanatory in at least two ways. The conjunction of features in the cause will be related to that in the result by some regularity which makes the former necessary and perhaps also sufficient for the latter. Also, since the first conjunction includes all the features that are causally relevant to the latter, this regularity will be what we called in Chapter 8 a pure law of working, and as such will be at least in part a pattern of persistence, that is, there will be some qualitative or structural continuity uniting the former set of features to the latter.

Pushed to this extreme, facts as causes seem to have every advantage over events. Why, then, do we bother to recognize producing causes as well as explanatory causes? The reason lies, as so often, in the extent of our ignorance. A minimally complete account is an ideal which we can hardly ever reach. But we can use this concept to elucidate some of the peculiarities of the kinds of causal statements we actually make.

Let us start with the following approximation to a minimally complete account: 'There being an explosion here just after midnight was caused by' or, rather, according to Vendler, 'was a result of'—'someone's pressing at midnight a button which was connected to a pair of contacts which were connected by electrical conductors to a charged battery and a detonator which was in contact with a quantity of TNT which was here'. Apart from 'here' and 'at midnight' all the components of the explanatory cause are relevant general features. If we change 'a button' to 'the button', yielding a definite description, it makes little difference, though no doubt the uniqueness of the button satisfying the general description was not causally relevant. But other changes are more serious.

Suppose we replace 'someone' by 'Tom' and 'a button' by 'the button on the red box'. We have now added, let us suppose, true but irrelevant bits of description, and if we still read it as purporting to be a minimally complete account, and hence as asserting that it was causally relevant that *Tom* pressed the button and that it was (the only one) on the red box, the statement must be counted false. But we can read these items as giving some gratuitous but true and harmless further information, that is, in Anscombe's way as 'Concerning Tom and concerning the red box, there being an explosion . . . was a result of his pressing . . . a button on it which . . .'; and this will still be true. Again we may leave out part of the explanatory cause: 'There being an explosion here just after midnight was a result of someone's pressing a button.' This is still true if it claims that some button's being pressed was causally relevant, though not if it claims that this was the whole explanatory cause, that the pressing of a button *as such* brought about the explosion.

Alternatively, we may replace part of the explanatory cause by what we previously introduced as an irrelevant definite description: 'There being an explosion here just after midnight was a result of someone's pressing at midnight the button on the red box.' Now the explosion was not a result of the button's being on the red box, but it was a result of features which the button on the red box uniquely possessed; the phrase 'the (one) on the red box' is a kind of substitute for the unstated relevant features. Taken in this way, the statement remains true, and although it is hardly more relevantly informative than the last variant it is more helpful in indicating where further relevant information is to be sought. We should still construe it as starting 'Concerning the button on the red box, there being an explosion here just after midnight was a result of someone's pressing it at midnight' but as going on 'and of its (uniquely) possessing certain other qualities and relations'. Moreover, someone might use this statement not perversely, suppressing parts of a known minimally complete account, but because it expressed all he knew. Observing the red box, the button on it, someone's pressing it and, immediately afterwards, the explosion, and employing the method of difference either explicitly or implicitly, he might well arrive at just that mixture of knowledge and ignorance which this statement as we have construed it would express. Since this is how the phrase 'the button on the red box' is functioning, its occurrence is referentially transparent: any other unique description of this object would do the same job equally well, and we can explain this logically by saying that this description is prefixed to the whole statement, not governed by the intensional operator 'was a result of'. We might then be tempted to argue that in the original minimally complete account with 'a button' changed to 'the button', the whole phrase 'the button which was connected . . . which was here' also occurs transparently, since *it* can be replaced *salva veritate* by any other correctly identifying phrase, such as 'the button on the red box'. But this would be wrong. Truth is preserved through this replacement only by a thorough reconstrual of the sentence, by moving the description from the place where it is governed by 'was a result of' to a place where it is not. The sentences which, as Vendler says, present referentially transparent facts as causes, or as what have results, are typically of the form illustrated by 'There being an explosion here just after midnight was a result of someone's pressing at midnight the button on the red box'; but an in principle superior, but often unattainable, account has the minimally complete form which is intensional throughout.

Finally, we may say 'The explosion here was caused by Tom's midnight movement'. Tom's midnight movement is an event, not a fact, and what we now have is a producing, not an explanatory, cause. All the causally relevant features are now concealed under a blanket phrase. But again it is easy to tell a story in which someone's actual knowledge of the incident would be accurately expressed by this sentence: the observer sees Tom enter a darkened room, hears him moving about and immediately afterwards hears, and sees, the explosion. Of course, an event description may include features that were causally relevant to the effect, but a statement which says that one *event* was the effect of another, or was caused by another, makes no claim that the features used to identify the cause-event were causally relevant. There is nothing false or even misleading about 'The international crisis was an effect of the speech made by the man with the biggest nose in France'.

Ignorance is the main reason for taking referentially transparent facts as causes rather than giving minimally complete accounts with only existentially quantified expressions to introduce causes, but of course the advantages of brevity or of saying just as much as is needed for the purpose in hand often

justifies our saying less than we know. Similar reasons will
often explain our taking concrete events as causes rather than
facts. We may know that a certain event caused another without knowing what features of the former event were relevant,
and therefore without being able to specify any facts as causes.
And since less knowledge is needed to pick out an event as a
cause, the knowledge that is needed is more easily acquired.
One event's causing another is observable whereas the identification of a fact as a cause requires some theory, some assumptions, or some comparison of cases with one another. As we
saw in Chapter 5, Ducasse identifies causing with a relation
between concrete events with spatio-temporal boundaries, and
thereby makes causing observable. It is one concrete event that
in the most obvious sense leads on to or produces another.
But it is general features that enter into regularities and continuities.

We need then, to recognize both kinds of cause, producing
causes and explanatory causes, events and facts, and at the
same time to distinguish them, in order to understand what we
think and say about causal relations. Two problems touched
upon earlier may be further clarified with the help of this distinction. One is that of quantitative over-determination: the
hammer-blow that flattened the chestnut was harder than it
needed to be to produce this result, and this seemed to make
questionable the judgement that this blow was necessary in the
circumstances for the flattening.[17] We can now say that the
concrete event, this hammer-blow, was the producing cause
of the chestnut's change of shape, it was what actually led on to
this change; but the explanatory cause was the fact that there
was here a blow of at least such-and-such a momentum. Each
can be said, in a slightly different sense, to have been necessary
and sufficient in the circumstances for the result; our earlier
difficulty arose from the fact that the concrete event was not
necessary in the sense in which the fact was; the event could
have been a bit different without altering the result, whereas
the fact as stated could not. But this is only a further refinement
of the contrasts drawn earlier between plugging in or leaving

[17] Cf. Chapters 2 and 6. The corresponding distinction, between facts and events
as results or effects, has already been used in Chapter 2 (pp. 46–7) to clear up a
similar problem about alternative over-determination.

out, from a possible world, the hammer-blow as a whole and altering its momentum, and between neolithic and functional concepts of causation.

.   The other problem is the legal difficulty in the case of the uncertificated officer, Sinon.[18] Sinon's navigation of his ship on the date in question was part of the cause of the collision; that is, this bit of navigating as a concrete event (or perhaps performance) was a partial producing cause of the collision. Among the features of this concrete event were that it was navigation by an uncertificated officer, that it was none the less navigation by an experienced and in general competent officer, and that it was, however, negligent. The very reasonable finding which the judge had some difficulty in formulating can be put in our terms as follows: the fact that the navigation was negligent was part of the explanatory cause of the collision, but the fact that it was by an uncertificated officer was not; whereas if the officer who navigated negligently had been incompetent as well as uncertificated, then the fact that he was uncertificated would have been (indirectly, by way of the fact that he was incompetent) a part of the explanatory cause. Speaking in terms of Vendler's referentially transparent facts, we can say that the collision was a result of Sinon's navigating negligently, and also, therefore, of an uncertificated officer's navigating negligently, but we must remember that the phrase 'an uncertificated officer' occurs here transparently, that is, it is really prefixed to the whole account and not governed by the intensional operator 'was a result of'.

The distinction between these two kinds of cause is, then, clear and useful. But there are still very close relations between them. That Sinon navigated negligently is a fact; for that very reason negligence in navigation was a feature of the concrete event or performance, Sinon's navigation on that date; someone's navigating negligently is a type of event, and Sinon's performance was an instance of that type just because the fact mentioned is a fact. These close systematic connections between events, their features, event-types, and facts make it legitimate to move freely and without excessive caution between them in the way that I have done in earlier discussions, in particular in Chapter 3. For some purposes we need to attend to these

---

[18] Chapter 5, quoted from Hart and Honoré, *Causation in the Law*, pp. 112–13.

distinctions, but for most of our investigation of causal regularities and our ways of discovering them we do not. The
presence on some occasion of one of the 'factors' or 'conditions'
discussed in Chapter 3 would be a fact: but it would also be a
concrete event's having a certain feature and being an instance
of a certain type of event.

In the light of this distinction, we may also take up again
the question raised in Chapter 3 whether causal statements are
implicitly general. If a singular causal statement about events
were implicitly general, its analysis would include the claim
that the producing cause and the effect could be described in
such a way that the existence of one was related to that of the
other by some causal law.[19] But such a *statement* does not entail
this, but only that the one event led on to the other and that
if the one had not occurred, in the circumstances, the other
would not, and while this counterfactual might be backed by
laws, we saw in Chapters 2 and 3 that it does not need to be
backed even by the claim that there is a law that would back
it. But what about a singular explanatory cause statement? It
is explicitly general in the sense that it makes essential reference
to certain general features, but does it implicitly claim that
there are laws connecting the general features mentioned on
the cause side with those on the result side? Does 'The fact that
Sinon navigated negligently caused his ship to collide with
another' entail that there is some law in which '*x* navigates
negligently' and '*x*'s ship collides with another ship' are con-
stituent elements? I have little doubt that there *is* such a law:
there are circumstances the conjunction of which with negligent
navigation will always lead to a collision, but the conjunction
of which with careful and skilful navigation would lead to no

---

[19] Cf. Davidson, op. cit., p. 699. I have omitted his suggestion that the law would
make cause and effect both necessary and sufficient for one another, which could
not be defended for concrete events even if we accepted thoroughly deterministic
laws. Though a cause-event may be necessary for its effect, it is so only in the sense
that a possible world from which it was excised would not contain the effect-
event; all that a law could demonstrate as being necessary for the effect is that *an*
event of a certain sort should have occurred, not that *this* one in all its concrete
detail should have done so. And the same applies to sufficiency: this concrete
cause-event may be shown by laws to be sufficient for the existence of *an* effect
with such and such features, but, even if strict determinism holds no isolable
event, but only the previous condition of the whole neighbourhood, would be
sufficient for the effect in all its concrete detail.

collision: that is, there is a law which makes negligent navigation an inus condition of collisions. Such a law, if known,
could be used to back up the explanatory cause statement. But
I do not think that that statement *entails* that there is such a
law. All it *entails* is that the causal feature mentioned was
necessary in the circumstances for the result feature mentioned,
and this claim is to be analysed into the appropriate counterfactual conditional along with an assertion of causal priority.

Finally, we may return to the question raised earlier whether
causal statements are extensional in the sense of allowing the
substitution of coextensive predicates. Statements about producing causes will be extensional, since in them predicates are
used only to identify concrete occurrences, and if one of a pair
of coextensive predicates helps to do this, the other will serve
equally well. But this is not true of explanatory cause statements. On a pure regularity theory it would be true: coextensive
predicates are interchangeable *salva veritate* in statements of
regularity. But the sorts of structural and qualitative continuity
suggested in Chapter 8 could link one, but not the other, of
a pair of coextensive features with some result. Even if the
features A and B were coextensive, A's being regularly followed
by C might be a pure law of working, but B's being followed by
C a mixed law—if B's being coextensive with A were a fact of
collocation or partly derivative from collocations. And even if
the coextensiveness of A and B were the result of pure laws of
working, each being produced by some common cause D in
accordance with such laws, we could have A's being followed
by C as a pure law, and while B's being followed by C would
then be a derivative pure law, the direction of causation
(between B and D), as the diagram shows, would be such as
to prevent B's *causing* C in virtue of the relationships shown

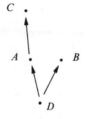

Diagram (vii)

(though of course there could *also* be an additional relationship that would need an arrow from B to C to represent it).

The considerations we have dealt with under the headings of causal priority and the necessity of causes, when added to a regularity theory, may prevent coextensive features from being interchangeable in causal laws. I have just argued that explanatory cause statements do not entail regularities or that there are regularities; still less do they reduce to them. Our use of such statements involves some employment of the notions of causal priority and the necessity of causes which I have tried to clarify in Chapters 7 and 8. Explanatory cause statements, therefore, are not extensional in the way that pure regularity statements would be.

I I

Teleology

ARE there final causes as well as efficient causes? Or can teleology be somehow reduced to efficient (or 'physical' or 'mechanical' or 'Humean') causation? When this question is discussed, it is commonly assumed that the efficient causation with which teleology may be contrasted or to which it may be reduced is essentially a matter of laws or regularities, and that these laws make causes sufficient for their effects, that these causes are necessitating causes. Little account, if any, is taken of what I have called the direction of causation or of what I have discussed in Chapter 8 under the heading of the necessity of causes. If I have been right in earlier chapters in rejecting or qualifying this cluster of assumptions, it is very likely that an inadequate concept of efficient causation will have produced false contrasts and incorrect solutions of the problem of relating final to efficient causes I have already argued in Chapter 5 that Hart and Honoré concede too much to Mill with regard to physical causation, and as a result take as distinctively characteristic of interpersonal causation features which are in fact common to it and physical causation. Much the same may have happened in the discussion of final causes.

Let me then sum up the main points that I have suggested and have tried, with varying degrees of conclusiveness, to establish about efficient causation. First, the conceptual and epistemological priority of singular causal statements to generalizations (Chapters 1, 2). Secondly, an initial analysis of the meaning of those singular statements in terms of conditionals, especially those which claim that a cause (whether event or fact) is necessary in the circumstances for its effect or result, with a further analysis of those conditional statements which shows that they may, or may not, be backed by belief in

regularities (Chapter 2). Thirdly, an account of the form of
causal regularities, typically highly complex and very incompletely known, with a demonstration that this form is closely
related to the standard basic methods of observation and
reasoning through which we discover and can up to a point
establish such regularities, these observations in turn being
similar to those which give rise to even the most elementary
and least sophisticated counterfactual conditional thinking
involved in causal judgements (Chapter 3). Fourthly, a demonstration that laws of functional dependence introduce a causal
concept which is in some ways new, but which has such close
connections with and formal similarities to the 'neolithic' concept that the former is best regarded as a development and
refinement of the latter rather than a rival or complete replacement for it; and with this a plea for two other extensions of the
causal concept to cover successive phases of persisting things
and self-maintaining processes (Chapter 6). Fifthly, I argued
that we have a concept of the direction of causation as something intrinsic to causal processes, which, though discovered
initially in our active and apparently free interventions, is not
incurably anthropocentric, nor is it simply derived from the
asymmetry of time; I attempted to define this causal priority
in terms of a contrast between fixity and unfixity, and to relate
it both to the dispersal of order and to the direction of explanation (Chapter 7). Sixthly, in considering the necessity of causes,
I accepted Hume's argument that there can be no logically
necessary connection between causes and effects either as they
are known or as they are in the objects, and that there is no
necessity$_{2.1}$ which would support a deductively valid *a priori*
inference from cause to effect or vice versa; I argued that the
apparent power of causal laws to sustain counterfactual conditionals was to be explained without assuming that such laws
differ in form or content from accidental generalizations; but
I tried to show that an important distinction can be drawn
between pure laws of working, collocations, and mixtures of the
two, and speculated that processes in accordance with pure laws
of working would display certain kinds of continuity or persistence (Chapter 8). Seventhly, although I rejected Kantian
and transcendental arguments not only for the principle that
all alterations take place in accordance with rules but also for

the more modest claim that there must be some regularity and some persistence, I noted that instantiations of the latter presumption are required for our ordinary basic methods of detecting causal relationships, and that they could be defended as an avoidance of arbitrarily selective scepticism and perhaps also more directly (Chapters 4 and 8). Eighthly, I showed how statistical laws of working might fit into this general theory (Chapter 9). And ninthly I argued that this theory left room for the explanation of common-sense and legal restrictions on the use of causal terms, and that puzzles about both extensionality and the observability of causation could be cleared up by recognizing that both events and facts can be causes, in slightly different but closely related senses (Chapters 5, 8, and 10).

It is against the background of such a richer concept of efficient causation that questions about the distinctness and irreducibility of final causation should be considered. A rough general definition of teleology or final causation—I shall take these two terms to be synonymous—is that an account or explanation is teleological if it makes some essential use of the notion that something—perhaps an event, or a state, or a fact— is an end or goal to which something else is, or is seen as, a means. But exactly what it would be for something to be an end or a goal, or again a means, remains to be clarified, and different teleological concepts result when these terms are given various more exact meanings.

One elementary case is where we see something (a type or an individual) as necessary for something else. The repeated contractions of the heart are necessary for the continued circulation of the blood in this animal body or in some large class of animal bodies; the defeat of the Persians at Salamis was (perhaps) necessary for the flowering of Athenian culture in the age of Pericles. But this relationship, where one thing is necessary (in the circumstances) for another is, as we have seen, the very one which is central in our ordinary concept of efficient causation: once we have seen that efficient causes need not be sufficient (even in the circumstances) for their effects or results we must admit that we have *as yet* no distinction at all between final and efficient causes. But there is a difference if we see the result as good, from our own point of view or from some point of view which we for the moment endorse or play along with.

If we regard the art and literature of fifth-century Athens as a good thing, then we may see the Greek victory at Salamis, because it was necessary for this good thing, as fitting satisfactorily into a certain pattern, and in a much-extended sense of that elastic word 'explain', we may feel that its place in that pattern explains that victory. But of course this does not in itself (without, say, the postulation of some divine or immanent historical purpose) explain the *occurrence* of that victory, it does not explain why the Greeks got the better of the Persians. Similarly, once we see the circulation of the blood as good for the individual animal, we see the fact that repeated contractions of the heart are necessary in the circumstances for that circulation as giving a certain point to those contractions: we in a sense explain them just by showing that they have this 'function'; but in this case it is possible to add two further sorts of explanation: if (in a certain large class of animals) the circulation of the blood is in turn necessary for continued life, the fact that heart-contractions are necessary for circulation helps to explain why all living animals (of that class) have repeatedly contracting hearts; and it may also (in a way that I shall examine later) figure in an evolutionary explanation of how it comes about that all such animals have hearts which contract regularly. More simply, we may just (as von Wright puts it)[1] take the occurrence of the result for granted, and in relation to this we shall see something's being necessary for that result as explaining that something. But this relation itself, the antecedent's being necessary in the circumstances for the result (whether in an individual case or generally) is, for all we have so far found, just that of efficient causation: all that makes it distinctively teleological is either a subjective or a relative point of view—we take the result for granted, or see it as good, or note that it is good for the animal in question—or the incorporation of this relation into some wider account—purposive or evolutionary or referring simply to conditions for individual survival—which explains either why the antecedent came about or came into existence or simply why it does exist in all members

---

[1] *Explanation and Understanding*, p. 58. von Wright calls such examples as that of the heart *quasi-teleological*, but examples like our Salamis one *quasi-causal*, because he thinks that there are distinctively teleological steps in the chain that connects, say, Salamis with the Parthenon.

of a certain class. It is in such further accounts, then, that distinctively teleological features must be sought, not in the mere relation of something's being necessary for a certain result.

On the other hand, we must reject the view of, for example, Moritz Schlick that there is, necessarily and trivially, no real difference between final and efficient causes, that 'it makes no difference whether we say "the past determines the future" or "the future determines the past" '.[2] In Schlick's thought, this is simply a consequence of a pure functional dependence view of causation, that is, a refined pure regularity view, and more generally of an extreme positivism. Given his assumptions, there is no room for the sort of causal priority I have tried to elucidate in Chapter 7, or indeed for anything except one or other sort of regularity or functional dependence and inferences and calculations based on these, which of course may move in either direction. But if I am right there is a distinctive order in which events come to be fixed, and an explanation by way of efficient causes retraces this path of fixing, and (as we saw) this is why we can explain the co-occurrence of collateral effects by reference to their common cause, but not the co-occurrence of joint or over-determining causes by reference to their common effect. In ordinary simple cases it would be simply wrong, not a trivially equivalent alternative, to explain the *occurrence* of a cause-event (or cause-fact) by reference to its effect or result. But of course if there were backward causation, then indeed the later event would explain the earlier one(s), and (as we saw with Scriven's precognition experiment) would explain the co-occurrence of a set of earlier events. It would be through such a later event that the earlier ones became fixed. Now if there were such a case, we could call the later event an end or goal, simply in virtue of its relative temporal position, rather than (as we have been doing) a time-reversed cause. And then this would be in a very clear sense a case of teleology or final causation: the 'end' would indeed be responsible for the coming about of the 'means', and any adequate explanation of these earlier-occurring items would have to refer to this end. Of course, it would be a trivial, merely verbal, choice whether we called this final causation or time-reversed efficient causation;

---

[2] 'Causality in Everyday Life and in Recent Science', in Feigl and Sellars, *Readings in Philosophical Analysis*, pp. 515–33, especially p. 527.

but it would be radically and intrinsically different from ordinary, forward, efficient causation, and it might well be described as the purest and simplest kind of teleology. The only trouble is that such cases seem never to occur. This possibility has, nevertheless, some importance in that opponents of teleology are inclined to assume that this would be the only sort of teleology that was really worthy of the name, and to conclude that objections to it are fatal to teleology in general. Thus Charles Taylor quotes Hull as saying that 'In its extreme form teleology is the name of the belief that the *terminal* stage of certain environmental-organismic cycles somehow is at the same time one of the antecedent determining conditions which bring the behaviour cycle about.'[3] Defenders of teleology, however, do not adopt this 'extreme form'. It would be characteristic of this extreme form that the end or goal must actually occur or be realized; it must, in our terminology, be fixed first in order to be able both to fix and to explain the earlier items: only an already concrete remoter future could drag the immediate future into existence. But it is not in this way that ends or goals figure in plausible teleological accounts: in them a goal can play its part even if it fails to be realized at all in the individual case, and *a fortiori* even if, though it is realized, its occurrence is not fixed in advance.

There are several distinguishable kinds of example to be considered. First, there is conscious purposive human action; it is obviously from this that we first acquire the notions of end or goal, of a means to an end, and so on. Secondly, there is the goal-seeking action or behaviour of the higher but non-verbal animals, which are unable to report to us any conscious purposes that they may have, but whose behaviour itself invites purposive description; a stock example is a carnivore stalking and catching its prey. Thirdly, there is the apparent teleology of goal-seeking and feedback mechanisms, homing rockets, thermostats, and the like. Fourthly, there is the functional appropriateness of organs and their working seen in the light of actual or possible evolutionary explanations. I shall discuss all of these, but in what may seem to be a less natural order, taking first the purposive behaviour of non-verbal animals.

[3] Taylor, *The Explanation of Behaviour*, p. 16, quoting C. L. Hull, *Principles of Behaviour*, p. 26.

The mere fact that such animals are unable to tell us that they have purposes does not, indeed, show that they do not have them, and it is possible that their thinking and acting are closely analogous to those of human beings: if so, they will be covered by the analysis of conscious purposive human behaviour which is still to be given. But for the present I shall ignore this possibility, and consider only what we can say on the basis of rather unimaginative observation of animal behaviour.

The stock example[4] is of a carnivorous animal in a certain state—hungry, with eyes, sense of smell, muscles, and so on in good working order—all of which I sum up as 'this A'; an environment E which includes an appropriate victim; a sequence of behaviour B—looking, smelling, stalking, leaping, and so on—and a goal G—the predator's catching and eating its prey. This A's performing B in E can be said in some sense to lead to G; we need not specify whether it is necessary for G or sufficient for G or both or whether it merely favours G, considerably increases the likelihood of G. The description and explanation that we naturally give is that this A does B in E because B (in E) leads to G; and this is a teleological account, it refers essentially to the goal G. Now that B (in whatever precise sense) leads to G is a fact of efficient causation: this kind of teleology at any rate presupposes and involves efficient causation. But the controversial question is whether the teleological account is somehow equivalent or reducible to an efficient causal one. If we construe the 'because' as a reference to a law, we are led to formulate a teleological law, 'Whenever an animal of sort A is in a situation such that B would lead to G, it does B, but when it is in a situation such that B would not lead to G, it does not do B'. It can then be argued[5] that all (and only) situations which satisfy the teleological description of being such that B would lead to G must also satisfy some intrinsic description, say 'I', and hence that the teleological law can be replaced by the law 'Whenever an animal of sort A is in a situation of kind I it does B, but when it is in a situation of a kind other than I it does not do B'. This clearly has (if we add, as we can, the right direction of causation) the form of

[4] Cf. Taylor, op. cit., pp. 9–17.
[5] Cf. D. Noble, 'Charles Taylor on Teleological Explanation', *Analysis*, xxvii (1966–7), 96–103.

a law of efficient causation, and it could be used to back up an ordinary causal explanation about an individual case, 'This A did B in E because E was of kind I'. It must be conceded that there will always be some intrinsic description 'I' which is coextensive with the teleological description 'such that B would lead to G'.[6] But I have argued (at the end of Chapter 10) that coextensive predicates need not be interchangeable in explanatory cause statements as they are in pure regularity statements. It would therefore in principle be possible that this A should have done B in E because B (in E) would lead to G but not because E was of kind I, although it was, and although all and only situations in which B would lead to G are, of kind I. But how can this formal possibility be realized? We have deliberately excluded any appeal to the notion that the animal sees E as being such that B would lead to G: this would be relevant to an account in terms of conscious purpose, which we are for the moment leaving aside. Again, there might be an evolutionary story to be told, that this A has an instinctive tendency to do B in situations of kind I because those members of some ancestral species which happened to have a stronger tendency than others to do B in I-situations achieved G more often than those others, survived when those others did not, and passed on this tendency to their descendants including this A. In this story mention of B's leading to G cannot be eliminated in favour of the coextensive predicate-term 'I'. But this is a further explanation, it involves another species of teleology to which we have still to turn: is there anything irreducibly teleological in the behaviour of *this A*? Well, there might have been some process of 'reinforcement' in the individual history of this A; it might have acquired a stronger tendency to do B in I-situations as a result of often getting food when it did so but remaining hungry when it did not. This explanation too refers essentially to B's having led to G: it is this feature of I-situations, not their being I as such, which has produced the reinforcement. But this too is a further explanation and we can still ask: Is there anything irreducibly teleological in the behaviour of this A *as it is now*? If we exclude conscious purpose, further explanations in terms of evolution and reinforcement, and backward causation, there seems to be no way in which the fact that E is such

[6] Cf. Taylor, 'Teleological Explanation—a Reply to Denis Noble', ibid., pp. 141–3.

that B would lead to G, rather than the fact that E is of kind I, could be causally relevant. This A (as it is now, including its instincts and its acquired or developed characteristics) must surely be reacting to some occurrent intrinsic features of E, it must be instantiating some law (perhaps only an approximate regularity) that As do B in situations of kind I, where their being I is the causally relevant feature. But, as Taylor shows,[7] the teleologist has one further resource. This A displays appropriately different behaviour in different situations. Where E is such that B_1 would lead to G, it does B_1; where E is such that B_2 would lead to G, it does B_2, and so on. And though each performance on its own could be explained by a law that As do B_1 in situations of kind I_1, or that As do B_2 in situations of kind I_2, and so on, we find no common feature of all the I_n–B_n correlations ($n = 1, 2, \ldots$) until we note that B_n is what in I_n leads to G. Doing in various Es whatever in each E would lead to G is the common feature of this A's diverse performances. (Of course, this will hold only over some range of variation in E; there will be limits to our predator's versatility.) This teleological law is superior to the mere conjunction of a set of efficient causal laws (As in I_1 do B_1 and As in I_2 do B_2 and so on) both because it explains them all by subsuming them under a more general theory and because it enables us to predict, as the finite set (As in I_n do B_n for $n = 1, 2, \ldots r$) does not, that if in a situation of some *further* kind I_{r+1} some performance B_{r+1} would lead to G, then in an I_{r+1}-situation an A will do B_{r+1}.

It is clear that our knowledge and understanding of a particular thing—say this A—or things of a certain kind—say As—can be such that the most unitary general account that we can give, and the one with the greatest predictive value, is a teleological one. But it is misleading to say that this teleological account is therefore more basic than its efficient causation rivals. The fundamental laws of working, the ways in which the B_n events actually come about, are here still laws of efficient causation and involve no reference to G—that is, as long as we attend only to what happens now, and do not go back to further explanatory accounts concerning reinforcement or evolution. We have so far, then, found a place for indispensably

7 In the *Analysis* article referred to in footnote 6, p. 277.

teleological accounts within our knowledge and understanding of, and predictions about, certain kinds of behaviour; but we have not yet found processes which are objectively, in themselves, irreducibly teleological.

This sort of example does, however, refute a move sometimes made by anti-teleologists who suggest that any causal law whatever can be recast, by mere verbal juggling, in a teleological form, and therefore that this form reveals no important distinction: 'do not basic causal laws in effect say that in any situation, things of a certain kind . . . will do whatever is required in order that they remain in certain relations one to another, or in order that they continue to move in a certain direction of change?'[8] A Newtonian solar system does indeed do whatever is required to keep constant the total sum of potential and kinetic energy, to keep each body's acceleration directly proportional to the resultant force acting on it and inversely proportional to its mass, the force being a certain function of all the masses and distances in the system; but such *keeping constant* and *keeping proportional* are not results causally brought about by what the system initially does as G is causally brought out by B_n. What the solar system persistently 'achieves' is a certain mathematical form which is realized in different concrete arrangements of the positions and velocities of the various bodies; but this is quite different from the convergence of the different sorts of behaviour, B_1 in I_1, B_2 in I_2, and so on, towards a single type of goal-event G. The different actions that As initially perform in these different kinds of situation do not, as we have seen, lend themselves to any intrinsic common description: we can reach a common description of B_1 in I_1, B_2 in I_2, and so on only by saying that each is what there leads to the remoter result G; but the various moves that the solar system initially makes from various prior positions are open to an intrinsic common description (though of an essentially mathematical sort) and do not call for any common remoter result to unify them.

The very fact that what unifies an A's different patterns of behaviour is teleological, whereas its fundamental laws of working are non-teleological, creates a problem: why does it do, in

[8] T. L. S. Sprigge, 'Final Causes', *Aristotelian Society Supplementary Volume* xlv (1971), 149–70, esp. p. 161.

each kind of situation, whatever would lead to G? It must have one inbuilt pattern of response to I_1, another inbuilt pattern of response to I_2, and so on: but how does it come about that it has this odd collection of inbuilt features? That each response when triggered by the appropriate situation should lead to the same goal G is, on the face of it, an extraordinary coincidence which demands some further explanation in a way that the regular conformity of a solar system to Newtonian laws does not. This is the element of truth in the theological Argument from Design: there are kinds of things, notably the behaviour of various organisms, which exhibit 'marks of design', co-existences of features which taken in themselves would be remarkable coincidences, and which call for *some* further explanation. But, in principle, several different kinds of explanation are possible. Our 'coincidence' could be resolved by reference to the conscious purposes of a very skilful and powerful designer and maker, or (up to a point) by reference to reinforcement, or by reference to an evolutionary process; or an initial explanation of the 'coincidence' might be given in terms of the animal's own conscious purpose to achieve G. But *something* is called for to resolve the tension between the teleological common description and the mere conjunction of efficient causal laws.

Although it is not true that *any* causal law whatever can be trivially recast in a teleological form, *some* special kinds of mechanism do invite teleological description of a sort analogous to that which we have been examining. The governor on a steam engine sometimes opens and sometimes closes a valve in such ways as to bring the engine speed near to a certain value, and a homing rocket changes its direction in such ways as to bring it eventually into contact with an elusive target, though either of these is far less versatile than a hungry wolf. *These* teleological descriptions are literally true of such devices: they are in no way metaphorical or animistic or anthropomorphic. They are, of course, quite compatible with detailed mechanical descriptions in terms of purely efficient causation, and are indeed deducible from some such descriptions. On the other hand, it is quite possible that the teleological description should be the best one that we know, providing more general explanations and more powerful predictions than any *available* causal account. We may find out by a few experiments *that* the governor does something that keeps the engine speed fairly constant without knowing *how* it does this; and after rockets of·this kind have had one or two spectacular successes in reaching targets that have done a fair amount of zigzagging about we may predict that no movements of the target, however erratic, will elude them, and yet not know at all how this comes about. Once again our knowledge and understanding of something may be distinctively and irreducibly teleological, a teleological account may be the best one available to us, and yet the basic laws of working will be efficient causal laws. And here again the teleological aspect calls for some further explanation, and the more versatile the device, the more clearly it calls for this, because the greater would the coincidence be if there were no unitary explanation for its achieving the same result by diverse means in diverse conditions. But with these devices the required explanation is at hand in the conscious purpose, ingenuity, and skill of their makers.

In fact, we know in outline how such devices work: by feedback. Some (perhaps random or externally caused) change brings the device in some sense nearer to its goal. The control mechanism reacts to this increased 'nearness' by producing a further change in the same direction. But if some change takes the device further from its goal, the control mechanism reacts to this decreased 'nearness' by producing a change in the opposite direction. The evolutionary explanation of teleological behaviour in organisms has a rough formal analogy to this. Some differential genetic characteristic X_1 tends to produce behaviour B_1 in situations of type I_1; if B_1 in I_1 tends to lead to G, where G is in turn something that increases the organism's chance of having descendants, the organisms that have X_1 will have more descendants than otherwise similar ones that do not, and if X_1 tends to be inherited in some way there will, as time goes on, be proportionately more members of the species that do B_1 in I_1; but, conversely, if X_z tends to produce behaviour B_z in situations of type I_z, and B_z in I_z tends to prevent G, there will in time be fewer members of the species that have X_z and so do B_z in I_z: natural selection constitutes a kind of feedback. Taking the species as a whole as the system, various moves that actually bring an earlier phase of the system 'nearer' to G are fostered, while any move that actually takes it further from G is attenuated; that is why later phases of the system tend to display in various situations whatever behaviour favours G. In this story, as I mentioned earlier, the reference to G is uneliminable: actual attainings of G by doing B_1 in I_1 and actual failures to attain G as a result of doing B_z in I_z are part of the causal process by which X_1 has been multiplied and X_z made rare. It is the fact that situations of kind I_1 are such that an A's doing B_1 in them leads to G, not the fact that they are I_1 (though these features are, by hypothesis, coextensive), conjoined with the fact that As possessing X_1 tend to do B_1 in I_1, that has fostered X_1, and conversely it is the fact that I_z situations are such that an A's doing B_z in them tends to prevent G, not the fact that they are I_z, that has made X_z rare. But although the (type-event) G that is the goal in the teleological description of the behaviour of *this* A, the product of the evolutionary development, thus plays an uneliminable part in the evolutionary explanation of this developed behaviour, it is not *as a goal*, not as something for the sake of which something else is done, that it figures in that story, but simply as a result that has come about from certain causes on some occasions and that has been prevented from coming about by other factors on other occasions, and that, when it occurs, has certain further effects. We thus have the slightly paradoxical but not, I hope, really obscure consequence that although the evolutionary explanation of what, taken on its own, invites a teleological description makes essential reference to the G which is the goal in that description, that evolutionary story is not itself a teleological one. The steps it narrates both are and are described as processes of efficient causation only.

I have here discussed an evolutionary explanation of the goal-seeking behaviour of an animal. A closely analogous account could be given of the functional appropriateness of organs in organisms of all sorts. The presence and the operation of each organ will correspond to our B_1, B_2, and so on. The co-operation and mutual support of the various organs and their operations (in a healthy organism) correspond to the convergence of B_1 in I_1, B_2 in I_2, and so on to the single type-event G; it is these that make a teleological description appropriate and (since the detailed workings themselves involve only efficient causation) call for some further explanation. And again it is an evolutionary story that provides this explanation, making essential mention of some goal G—the harmony of organic functions which promotes the survival and reproduction of organisms—and yet itself involving only processes of efficient causation.

It would be labouring the obvious to show that the same applies to a psychological story about reinforcement—though such a story gives only an incomplete explanation, since it needs a further evolutionary story to explain why the organisms in question are capable of having tendencies reinforced.

It is worth stressing that when we say of this A that it does B_1 in I_1 because B_1 in I_1 leads to G, and B_2 in I_2 because B_2 in I_2 leads to G, and in general B_n in I_n because B_n in I_n leads to G—in other words, that in each situation it does whatever leads to G because it leads to G—we are speaking correctly about the extended evolutionary process, whereas if we were speaking only about the short-term response of this A as it now is to its environment, we should say that it does B_1 in I_1 because this environment is intrinsically of kind I_1, B_2 in I_2 because it is intrinsically of kind I_2, and so on. (In each case we are speaking of fact-causes, explanatory causes, as these were distinguished in Chapter 10, and we could hardly make the present point without the help of this or some equivalent distinction.) The distinctively teleological description of this A's behaviour, that in each situation it does whatever leads to G, can therefore be appropriately used in two very different states of knowledge. As we saw, it can be used as the most general and most predictively powerful account available to us after a fairly superficial observation of this A's behaviour in several different situations, and while we as yet know nothing of the detailed causal processes by which this A now responds to its environment, let alone any evolutionary process by which it has come into existence with these tendencies and capacities. In this use it is not an explanatory cause statement, nor a producing cause statement either: it is what we may call a surface teleological account. But this same description can be used in the knowledge of and with reference to at least the sketch of an evolutionary story: it is then serving as a condensation of an explanatory cause statement, that this A does (for all n) B_n in I_n and so tends to achieve G because some ancestral proto-As did B_n in I_n and so achieved G and so survived and reproduced their kind better than other proto-As which did something else in I_n and so failed to achieve G. It is only because the same type-event G is mentioned twice in this explanatory cause statement, as the general result of this A's present (versatile) behaviour and as what some proto-As achieved while others did not, and also because the same set of type-events B_1, B_2, and in general B_n, in situations of types I_1, I_2, and in general I_n, are also mentioned twice, as what this A now does and as what some proto-As did, that the condensation of this explanatory cause statement takes the teleological form: this A does in each situation whatever leads to G because it leads to G. There is, in these respects, an essential logical connection between the description of the evolutionary explanatory cause and the description of the behaviour which it explains. Yet no one can doubt that this is a statement of efficient causation of a thoroughly standard kind, relating logically distinct *occurrences* and discovered only empirically—facts which should warn us against concluding hastily in other cases that *any* logical connection between antecedents and consequents is an obstacle to ordinary efficient causal relations.

In all the kinds of case mentioned so far an initially teleological description has been underpinned and replaced by a story about efficient causation. But, it might be said, it is logically possible that there should be something which called for an *ultimately* teleological description. There might be an animal—or, for that matter, an inanimate system—which was found to do in a wide range of Es whatever in each E would lead to G, so that it was inductively reasonable to predict that it would do so even in further, unobserved, kinds of E, and yet these diverse performances (B_1 in I_1, B_2 in I_2, etc.) might not lend themselves to any intrinsic common description, the only distinctive common feature of these performances might be their leading to G, and there might be no further explanation to be found either in terms of the animal's—or the system's—having been skilfully designed and manufactured by a maker whose purpose was that it should achieve G, or in terms of evolution or reinforcement or anything of that sort. Even a backward causation explanation might be excluded by the occasional failure of G to be actually realized, even where the animal had done the right B for the E as it then was. That is, the animal's—or the system's—behaviour might invite teleological description for the reasons indicated by Taylor, and yet this might be left as ultimate by the non-realization of any efficiently caused underpinning.

It must be conceded that this is a logical possibility; but there is no evidence that anything of this sort actually occurs. If it did occur, it would be very natural to suppose that this animal—or system—had a conscious purpose of achieving G, and knew or rightly believed that each B_n in I_n would lead to G, and that this explained its diverse G-ward performances. That is, this case would then be assimilated to that of conscious purposive action which we have still to consider. But if this explanation also were excluded we should be faced with a very puzzling situation indeed. The sheer unexplainable coincidence of such ultimate non-conscious teleology, of the animal's—or the system's—doing in each E whatever would lead to G but for no reason whatever in which the type-event G figured *anywhere*, would be far more surprising than, say, mere indeterminism (as in the random differences in the outcome of relevantly identical situations covered by quantum mechanics). So it is just as well that it seems not to occur.

So far, then, we have found several uses for distinctively teleological accounts and explanations, but no objective processes which are in themselves teleological in a way that either excludes their being instances of efficient causation or makes their teleological aspect objectively more basic than their efficient aspect. It remains to be considered whether this holds good when we come to what must be the hard core of final causation—as well as being the original source of our teleological concepts—our own experience of conscious purposive human action.

The central and crucial case may be represented by the same letters as before: A—now a human agent—does B in situation E in order to bring about G. But since we are now concerned with conscious action, not with automatic responses to the environment, it matters less of what kind the situation E is than of what kind A sees it as being; so let us say that A sees E as being a situation of kind I. Then if A does B in order to bring about *G*, he must believe that his doing *B* in this *I*-situation will lead to *G*. As before, 'lead to' is deliberately imprecise: *A* may believe that his doing *B* is necessary in the circumstances for *G*, or sufficient in the circumstances, or both, or merely that it will increase the likelihood of *G*'s coming about: there will be examples of all these sorts, but the differences between them do not affect the main issues. Equally it does not matter whether *A*'s belief is dispositional or occurrent, confident or uncertain, true or false, or even whether it is knowledge rather than belief. But what *A* believes is that there is some relation of efficient causation between his doing *B* in *E* and the occurrence of *G*. He need not, of course, be making any explanatory causal judgement, he need not claim to know what it is about *E*, or *B*, that will make the doing of *B* in *E* lead to *G*; rather he must see his doing of *B* in *E* as some sort of producing cause of *G*. Purposive action, then, involves in this respect not efficient causation itself but a belief about efficient causation. But, of course, more than this belief is required: *A* also desires or wants or intends to bring about *G*.

Now the natural and traditional[9] view is that *A*'s believing this and his wanting (or desiring or intending) that are joint efficient causes of his doing *B*; that is, they are factors which together constitute the cause or at least a partial cause of his doing *B*. Moreover, on this view they would be, in our terminology, explanatory causes. It is causally relevant that *A*'s conative state should be wanting to bring about *G*, and that his cognitive state should be believing that *B* would lead to *G*, with the same description of the goal *G* in both. And it is causally relevant that what he believes to be some sort of efficient cause of *G* is the same *B* that, when he finally acts, he sees himself as doing. If *A* turned on the burner in order to boil the kettle, what is causally relevant about his wanting is that it was his wanting this kettle to boil, what is causally relevant about his believing is that it was his believing that his turning on of this burner would lead to this kettle's boiling, and it is causally relevant that the subject of this belief is his turning on of this burner, while the performance of which all this is the explanatory cause is seen by *A* as his turning on of this burner. If, for example,

---

[9] Cf. D. Davidson, 'Actions, Reasons, and Causes', *Journal of Philosophy*, lx (1963), 685–700.

A saw his ultimate action simply as his rotating that white knob ninety degrees anticlockwise, this action could not be caused in the proposed way by his wanting to boil the kettle and his believing that turning on this burner would make the kettle boil. And equally, even if he saw his action as his turning on of the burner, it could not be caused in the proposed way if what he wanted was that the kettle should boil while what he believed was that his turning on of the burner would lead to the production of a quantity of water vapour. We need the descriptive links between his action as he sees it, the content of his belief, and the (intentional) object of his desire.

But these descriptive links which seem to be required for such an explanatory cause statement have been seen as fatal to the traditional view, as showing that there is no efficient causal relation here at all. Efficient (or 'Humean') causation requires logically independent causes and effects, whereas the supposed 'cause' and 'effect' in any voluntary action are logically connected. Thus Melden, arguing indeed against a rather simpler theory of 'acts of volition', says: 'Let the interior event which we call "the act of volition" be mental or physical (*which* it is will make no difference at all), it must be logically distinct from the alleged effect—this surely is one lesson we can derive from a reading of Hume's discussion of causation. Yet nothing can be an act of volition that is not logically connected with that which is willed—the act of willing is intelligible only as the act of willing whatever it is that is willed.'[10] This *logical connection argument* has been widely accepted; and yet, as it stands, it is little more than a bad pun on the phrases 'logically distinct' and 'logically connected'. What we can learn from Hume's discussion is that cause and effect must be logically distinct occurrences (or 'existences'), that it must be logically possible that either should occur while the other does not. But the supposed act of volition would need to be connected with its alleged effect (in a successful voluntary performance) only by the appearance of some true description of that effect in the content of the act of volition. Acts of volition would be identified (at least partly) by their content; if *A* voluntarily does *B* the act of volition theory is committed to saying that what happens is truly describable as *A*'s doing *B*, and that this

[10] A. I. Melden, *Free Action*, p. 53.

same description, A's doing B, is the content of A's act of volition, it is *as* his doing of B that he 'wills' it. But of course this 'logical connection' would not prevent the act of volition from being a logically distinct occurrence from the doing of B, it would not make it logically impossible that either should occur without the other. There is no more logical connection here than there is between someone's hoping that Leeds will win the Cup Final and Leeds's winning the Cup Final, and though these two may not be causally connected, it is no lack of logical distinctness that prevents this.

But this is liable to be confused with a different and trickier point. On the act of volition theory, A's voluntary raising of his arm consists of his willing that his arm should rise and its rising as a result: the voluntary action as a whole consists of an act of will, a bodily movement, and an efficient causal connection between them. But it is tempting to say rather that what A wills is that he should raise his arm, and that the effect of his willing is that he raises his arm. If we say this, we are taking the *whole* voluntary action as the 'effect'—and also a description of it as the content of the act of will. That is, on the act of volition theory, we have now incorporated the act of volition in the 'effect', and that 'effect' is indeed no longer a distinct occurrence from the act of volition, not because a description of the 'effect' occurs as the content of that volition, but because the volition has been included in the 'effect'. But we can, and should, present the theory coherently by keeping them apart. Analogously, the movement of a cricketer's bat cannot cause a drive, for the supposed effect, the drive, includes that movement. None the less, part of the movement of the bat (leaving out the follow through) is a partial cause of the movement of the ball, and the whole process of bat-movement temporally overlapping with ball-movement and causally related to it is what is called a drive.

Such arguments as Melden's have been criticized on such grounds as these,[11] and the force of these criticisms is recognized by, for example, von Wright: 'The logical dependence of the specific *character* of the will on the nature of its object is fully

[11] e.g. by Davidson in the article mentioned in footnote 9, p. 286 and by F. M. Stoutland in 'The Logical Connection Argument', *American Philosophical Quarterly Monograph* iv (1970), 117–30.

compatible with the logical independence of the *occurrence* of an act of will of this character from the realization of the object.'[12] It is worth stressing that in order to bring out the latter logical independence it is not necessary to say—though it may be true—that the agent's willing or intending or desiring is open to some other description which is independent of the nature of its object. And, as I have insisted, it is the description which is 'logically dependent on the nature of its object' which presents the causally relevant feature of this willing, the one which must be mentioned in an explanatory causal statement.

But though von Wright accepts these criticisms, he still endorses a version of the logical connection argument. His thesis is that if it is asked 'how . . . one ascertains (verifies) whether an agent has a certain intention, "wills" a certain thing—and also how one finds out whether his behavior is of a kind which his intention or will is supposed to cause' it will turn out that one *cannot* answer the one question without also answering the other, and hence that 'the intention or will cannot be a (humean) cause of his behavior', because 'The facts which one tries to establish [are] not logically independent of one another'.[13] There is, he holds, a schema of practical inference (or practical syllogism) which is that of a teleological explanation turned upside down. If the teleological explanation is '*A* does *B* in order to bring about *G*' the practical inference is (roughly):

A intends to bring about *G*.
A considers that he cannot bring about *G* unless he does *B*.
Therefore *A* sets himself to do *B*.[14]

And, von Wright argues, the practical inference, *when properly formulated*, is logically binding. Several precautions are needed. *A* will not set himself to do *B* if he thinks (or knows) that he cannot do *B*. So von Wright takes it that the first premiss 'contains, in a concealed form, that the agent thinks he knows how to bring about' *G*.[15] Also, what *A* intends and considers at one time cannot, in the required sense, be logically connected

[12] *Explanation and Understanding*, p. 94.
[13] Ibid., pp. 94–5 and 115–16.
[14] Ibid., p. 96. I have altered the letters to agree with those used above.
[15] Ibid., p. 103.

with his setting himself to do something at a later time: the logical connection argument cannot apply to *previous* intentions but only, if at all, to *concurrent* intentions. So the practical inference schema, in its final—and, von Wright argues, logically binding—form, becomes:

From now on *A* intends to bring about *G* at time *t*.

From now on *A* considers that, unless he does *B* no later than at time *t*, he cannot bring about *G* at *t*.

Therefore, no later than when he thinks time *t* has arrived, *A* sets himself to do *B*, unless he forgets about the time or is prevented.[16]

Now von Wright argues that in order to verify that *A* sets himself to do *B*, it is not enough to observe that he did *B* in the sense that the result came about through *A*'s movements: even if this happens, we must ascertain that *A*'s behaviour 'is intentional *under the description* "doing *B*" '. Also, we may need to verify that *A* set himself to do *B* but failed to do *B*. So (in either case) to verify the conclusion we have to verify either the premisses of this practical inference or those of some other similar inference which would show the behaviour to be intentional under the description 'doing *B*'. He also argues, in a Wittgensteinian vein, that one can verify the premiss that *A* has such and such an intention (even if *A* is oneself!) only by recognizing intentionality in *A*'s behaviour, and 'Behavior gets its intentional character from being *seen* by the agent himself or by an outside observer in a wider perspective, from being *set* in a context of aims and cognitions', as happens 'when we construe a practical inference to match it'.[17]

Non-Wittgensteinians might suspect that if we accepted both von Wright's arguments we should be caught in a vicious circle which made it impossible to 'verify', or to have any good reason for believing, either the premisses or the conclusion of any practical inference whatever. But let that pass. There are several more important comments to be made.

---

[16] *Explanation and Understanding*, p. 107. I am here concerned only with von Wright's use of this 'practical syllogism'; but there is another and I think more interesting sort of practical syllogism which is not, like this, merely descriptive of an agent but systematizes an agent's own rational deliberation, by which he may arrive at a decision to act. I have examined this briefly in a discussion on 'Practical versus Theoretical Reason' in *Practical Reason*, ed. S. Körner.

[17] *Explanation and Understanding*, pp. 114–15.

First, the possibility of verifying the conclusion by verifying the premisses of some *other* practical inference is a red herring. Except in special cases where an action is intentionally over-determined—where the agent is killing two birds with one stone—there will be just one teleological explanation of an action and so, when it is turned upside down, just one relevant practical inference. In such a case von Wright's first argument seems to show that the conclusion of this practical inference can be verified only by verifying the premisses of *this* practical inference.

But, secondly, would this show that what the conclusion describes is not *as an occurrence* logically distinct from what the premisses describe? Surely not. What the conclusion describes, A's setting himself to do B, has been taken to include A's intending to do B. But even if A's only reason for intending to do B is that he intends to bring about G and sees doing B as necessary for G, his having this reason and his intending to do B can still be distinct occurrences. Further, if his setting himself to do B only includes, and is not exhausted by, his (now) intending to do B (right away), it would for that reason be partly a distinct occurrence from his having the reason specified by the premisses, even if his intending to do B were not so distinct. The obstacles to independent verification mentioned in this first argument have no tendency to show that the occurrence described by the conclusion is included in those described by the premisses.

A third and still more important point is this. The tendency of von Wright's second argument is indeed to suggest that these occurrences are not distinct, because the 'occurrence' described by the premisses is just that described by the conclusion seen in a certain way. Of course this view is supported by well-known difficulties about inner mental states or events, difficulties which, I believe, can be met, though I cannot discuss them here. But whatever we make of these difficulties, we cannot consistently take von Wright's view about concurrent intentions if we admit that there are also literally preformed intentions, intentions which exist before any behaviour manifests them. For these intendings must be, as occurrences, logically distinct from any related actions: it cannot then be impossible that exactly similar items should continue to exist and so be concurrent with, but logically distinct from, the actions that fulfil them. No problems about independent verification can undermine this possibility of independent existence. We could evade this argument only by interpreting the talk about previous or preformed intentions as fictitious in a high degree.

I have discussed von Wright's account because it seems to me to make the best case that can be made for even a partial acceptance of the logical connection argument; but it seems to me that it fails completely.

But suppose that we were to waive all these objections, and concede von Wright's conclusion, what would follow? The proposed practical inference, as a logically valid schema, would hold within and for a certain systematic way of interpreting the actions in question. The descriptions '*A* intends to bring about *G*', '*A* considers that he cannot bring about *G* unless he does *B*', and '*A* sets himself to do *B*'—or rather their more exact counterparts in the final version—are now being so read that the first two entail the third: anything that counts as falsifying the third automatically falsifies at least one of the others. We have a network of interlocking descriptions which must be applied or withheld as a whole. Then since the teleological explanation is, as von Wright says, just this schema turned upside down, it too is only a network of interlocking descriptions: we have to read '*A* does *B* in order to bring about *G*' as short for '(*A* does *B*) and (*A* believes that he cannot bring about *G* without doing *B*) and (*A* intends to bring about *G*)' with such senses that the first of these conjuncts is entailed by the two others together, with a hint that this entailment holds. And this is a conceptualist view of teleology with a vengeance: we have nothing but a set of interlocking concepts, with no shadow of an account or explanation of how *A came to* do *B*. Once we have a genuine logical connection between the action on the one hand and the belief and intention on the other, as opposed to the spurious logical connection that Melden offered—the mere 'dependence of the specific *character* of the will on the nature of its object'— we do indeed exclude efficient or Humean causation, but we also abandon all claim to be explaining how things come about. We cannot now speak of processes of final causation. Nor are there, in this sense, any teleological laws of working that would

be alternatives or rivals to those of efficient causation. A teleological account, thus construed, simply leaves the question of
how things come about off to one side, and so leaves it wide
open.

Although this is a possible and consistent view, it is an
extremely unnatural one—so unnatural that it is almost impossible to adhere to it for long. Our natural way of speaking
of conscious purposive human action treats intendings, desir-
ings, believings, and so on as elements in accounts of how
actions come about. It seems that von Wright himself so treats
them when, in the next chapter, he discusses the course of
historical events. But if we revert to this natural treatment, we
cannot consistently read into it the logical connection barrier
to efficient causation. If intendings, and so on, are so construed
as to be permissible elements in any genetic account, they can
figure there, as I suggested earlier, as factors that help to make
up (explanatory) efficient causes of people's doing what they
consciously do. Only an indefensible confusion of two separately defensible interpretations of teleological descriptions of
human action produces the appearance of a special kind of
causation by which actions come about but which includes
features that prevent it from being a species of efficient causation.

We can, if we like, accept von Wright's conceptual teleology:
I do not think that either the ordinary meaning of the terminology of intentions or any epistemological difficulties about
mental events force us to do so. Alternatively we can interpret
teleological descriptions of human action (and perhaps some
animal action also) as explanatory causal accounts. But then
if A does B because he intends (or wants or desires) to bring
about G and believes that his doing B would lead to G, there
is not only A's belief about efficient causation between his
doing B and the occurrence of G, there is also an objective
relation of efficient causation between A's intending (or wanting
or desiring) this, his believing that, and his doing of B.

A view which is almost equivalent to von Wright's (and to
which von Wright refers with approval) is taken by Stoutland.[18]
After arguing, correctly, that the weak type of logical connection mentioned by, for example, Melden does not exclude a

[18] In the article referred to in footnote 11, p. 288.

contingent connection such as causation is now commonly taken to be, Stoutland says that there is also a strong type of logical connection between an intention and its fulfilment which does exclude a contingent connection. Intending that p makes it '*a priori* necessary that p occur if normal conditions obtain', and in general 'To attribute a goal to a system, in the sense involved in a teleological theory, is to say that it is *a priori* necessary that the system realize the goal *if normal conditions obtain*, that is, if nothing interferes'.[19]

Now this last remark is far too weak distinctively to characterize a teleological account. If I call something a reflector I am saying that it is *a priori* necessary that it reflects light if normal conditions obtain, and similar comments apply to the calling of something a conductor, a cure for chilblains, or indeed a cause of such-and-such in the inus-condition sense, and while such a way of speaking describes an antecedent in terms of a consequent and (given some positive valuing of the consequent) develops easily into at least a functional description, it is obviously quite compatible with saying that the antecedent causally brings about that consequent.

There are some hints[20] that Stoutland regards a system as having a goal if it tends by some *internal* process to achieve some result, external conditions needing only not to interfere, but not if external conditions play some more positive role in bringing about the result. But even if any distinction of this sort could be drawn firmly, it would be no more than a distinction between 'transeunt' and 'immanent' causation, that is between what is ordinarily called causation and the sort of self-maintaining process for whose inclusion, in an extended notion of causation, I have argued in Chapter 6. There is nothing intrinsically non-contingent about such an 'immanent' relation.

Stoutland must then fall back on a conceptual relation between intention and fulfilment. 'It is not simply contingent that my intention to visit my friend should result in my visiting him; my visiting him, given normal conditions, is a criterion of my intending to visit him. That is part of our concept of intention.'[21] But this, with a sense of 'criterion' strong enough to exclude a

[19] *Explanation and Understanding*, pp. 126, 128.   [20] Ibid., p. 127.
[21] Ibid., p. 128.

contingent (causal) relation, *is* equivalent to von Wright's conceptual teleology: the intending, as intending, is not now a distinct occurrence from the visiting, and does not explain how the visiting came about, any more than the infant Edward Heath's being a future Prime Minister explains his eventually becoming Prime Minister. If it were claimed (though, I think, neither Stoutland nor von Wright does claim this) that an intention to do *p* is a previous existent which in itself, and not just in being described as an intention to do *p*, logically requires that if circumstances are normal *p* will be done, we should have to reply that there can be no such animal. Hume's arguments exclude this from reality, not merely from our concept of efficient causation.

We can, then, repeat part of our interim conclusion: though we have found several uses for distinctively teleological accounts and explanations, we have found no objective processes which are in themselves teleological in a way that precludes their being instances of efficient causation. On the other hand, conscious purposive action which calls for the kind of explanatory causal account suggested does seem to involve a distinct *species* of efficient causation. This might be challenged by someone who adopted a physicalist or epiphenomenalist view. While I am sceptical about such theories, it seems to me to be more important to insist that even if some such theory were adopted, an adequate explanatory causal account in its terms would have somehow to reproduce the characteristic teleological form, keeping intact the descriptive links between the repeated occurrences of our terms '*B*' and '*G*'. Some physicalist counterpart would have to be found for the agent's *seeing his action as* of a certain kind, for his intending a certain event *under a certain description*, and for his believing that a certain *kind* of action would lead to a certain *kind* of outcome. And if this were done, even the physicalist account would be teleological in that some representation of a *B–G* causal sequence would figure essentially in the explanatory cause of what we now describe as *A*'s doing *B*. It *might* be that this teleological sort of account could be reduced to a more basic causal account which eliminated what I am here calling the teleological form; but there is no obvious reason why this should be possible. Even if it were possible, an adequate explanatory account would involve some repetitions of descriptive terms, just because the pure laws of working would, as I have argued, involve some element of continuity and persistence. In any case, teleology as a species presents no challenge to efficient causation, of the richer sort for which I have argued, as the genus that covers all actual laws of working and perhaps all processes by which things come about.

It is, then, causation, in the sense of what satisfies the wider and richer concept for which I have argued, that holds the universe together, that makes it more than just a collection of four-dimensional scenery. Moritz Schlick, like others in the Humean tradition, was very critical of the notion of a causal tie: 'After the scientist has successfully filled up all the gaps in his causal chains by continually interpolating new events, the philosopher wants to go on with this pleasant game after all the gaps are filled. So he invents a kind of glue and assures us that in reality it is only his glue that holds the events together at all. But we can never find the glue; there is no room for it, as the world is already completely filled by events which leave no chinks between them.'[22] But this criticism does not touch the view for which I have argued. Causation is not something *between* events in a spatio-temporal sense, but is rather the way in which they follow one another. It involves regularities, universal or statistical, in particular what I have distinguished as pure laws of working, but it is not exhausted by them; it includes also the spatio-temporal continuity stressed by Ducasse, the qualitative or structural continuity, or partial persistence, which I have sorted out from Kneale's more rationalist concepts, and the features which constitute the direction of causation. When Hume said that the principles of association are *to us* the cement of the universe,[23] he meant that they are the links that connect the ideas of unobserved things with impressions, that give rise to the non-rational inferences which we naturally make. Inference is not as central in causation as Hume thought, but the causal inferences which we undoubtedly make have sometimes more authority than he allowed. When we get things right, our causal inferences retrace or anticipate the sequences by which the universe creates itself.

[22] 'Causality in Everyday Life and Recent Science', in *Readings in Philosophical Analysis*, ed. H. Feigl and W. Sellars, pp. 515–33, at p. 522.
[23] *Abstract*, p. 32.

APPENDIX

Eliminative Methods of Induction

(Mill's Methods of Induction)

1. *Introduction*

JOHN STUART MILL, in his *System of Logic*[1] set forth and discussed five methods of experimental inquiry, calling them the method of agreement, the method of difference, the joint method of agreement and difference, the method of residues, and the method of con- comitant variation. He maintained that these are the methods by which we both discover and demonstrate causal relationships, and that they are of fundamental importance in scientific investigation. In calling them eliminative methods Mill drew a rather forced analogy with the elimination of terms in an algebraic equation. But we can use this name in a different sense: all these methods work by eliminating rival candidates for the role of cause.

The inductive character of these methods may well be questioned. W. E. Johnson called them demonstrative methods of induction,[2] and they can be set out as valid forms of deductive argument: they involve no characteristically inductive steps, and no principles of confirmation or corroboration are relevant to them. But in each case the conclusion is a generalization wider than the observation which helps to establish it; these are examples of *ampliative* induction.

The general nature of these methods may be illustrated by examples of the two simplest, those of agreement and of difference.

Mill's canon for the method of agreement runs: 'If two or more instances of the phenomenon under investigation have only one circumstance in common, the circumstance in which alone all the instances agree is the cause (or effect) of the given phenomenon.' For example, if a number of people who are suffering from a certain disease have all gone for a considerable time without fresh fruit or vegetables, but have in other respects had quite different diets, have lived in different conditions, have different hereditary backgrounds, and so on, so that the lack of fresh fruit and vegetables is the only

---

[1] Book III, Chs. 8–10.   [2] *Logic*, Part II, Ch. 10.

feature common to all of them, then we can conclude that the lack of fresh fruit and vegetables is the cause of this particular disease.

Mill's canon for the method of difference runs: 'If an instance in which the phenomenon under investigation occurs, and an instance in which it does not occur, have every circumstance in common save one, that one occurring in the former; the circumstance in which alone the two instances differ, is the effect, or the cause, or an indispensable part of the cause, of the phenomenon.' For example, if two exactly similar pieces of iron are heated in a charcoal-burning furnace and hammered into shape in exactly similar ways, except that the first is dipped into water after the final heating while the second is not, and the first is found to be harder than the second, then the dipping into water while it is hot is the cause of such extra hardness—or at least an essential part of the cause, for the hammering, the charcoal fire, and so on may also be needed. For all this experiment shows, merely dipping iron while hot into water might not increase its hardness.

The method of agreement, then, picks out as the cause the one common feature in a number of otherwise different cases where the effect occurs; the method of difference picks out as the cause the one respect in which a case where the effect occurs differs from an otherwise exactly similar case where the effect does not occur. But in both the conclusion is intended to say more than that this was the cause of that effect in this instance (or this group of instances). The conclusion in our first example is that this particular disease is always produced by a lack of fresh fruit and vegetables, and in our second example that dipping iron which has been heated and hammered in a particular way into water while it is hot always hardens it.

There are many weaknesses in Mill's description of these methods, but there is no need to criticize his account in detail. The interesting questions are whether there are any valid demonstrative methods of this sort, and if so whether any of them, or any approximations to any of them, have a place in either scientific or commonsense inquiry. Several reconstructions of the methods have been offered; the most thorough treatment I know of is that of von Wright, but I find it somewhat unclear.[3] I shall, therefore, attempt another reconstruction.

In giving a formal account of the reasoning involved in these methods, I shall use an old-fashioned sort of logic, traditional (roughly Aristotelian) logic but with complex (conjunctive and

[3] G. H. von Wright, *A Treatise on Induction and Probability*. Earlier accounts are those of Johnson (referred to above, p. 297) and C. D. Broad, 'The Principles of Demonstrative Induction', *Mind*, xxxix (1930), 302–17 and 426–39.

disjunctive) terms. The letters 'A', 'B', and so on stand for kinds of event or situation, or, what comes to the same thing, for features the possession of which makes an event or situation one of this or that kind. These *conditions* (Mill's 'circumstances') can therefore be present or absent on particular occasions (in particular *instances*). To say that all A are B would be to say that whenever feature A is present, so is feature B. To say that A is necessary for B is to say that whenever B is present, A is present, and to say that A is sufficient for B is to say that whenever A is present, B is present also. A conjunctive feature AB is present whenever and only when both A and B are present. A disjunctive feature (A or B) is present whenever at least one of A and B is present. A negative feature not-A (written $\bar{A}$) is present whenever and only when A is absent. The following argument forms are obviously valid:

(i) All A are C
Therefore, All AB are C

(ii) All A are BC
Therefore, All A are B (and All A are C)

(iii) All (A or B) are C
Therefore, All A are C (and All B are C)

(iv) All A are B
Therefore, All A are (B or C)

(v) All A are C
and All B are C
Therefore, All (A or B) are C.

In expounding the reasoning implicit in these methods, I shall also use the letters 'X', 'Y', 'Z' as variables whose instances are the features or kinds of occurrence represented by 'A', 'B', and so on, and I shall take the liberty of quantifying with respect to them; for example, to say that for some X, X is necessary for B will be to say that some feature occurs whenever B occurs; this statement would be true if, say, all B are C. There is nothing unsound in these procedures, and I hope nothing obscure. The slight unfamiliarity of these techniques is, I believe, more than compensated for by the fact that for this particular task they are more economical than the obvious alternatives.[4]

To avoid unnecessary complications, let us assume that the

---

[4] The classic exposition of this extension of traditional logic to allow for complex terms is in J. N. Keynes's *Formal Logic* (4th edition, 1906), Appendix C, pp. 468–538. It was much discussed by John Anderson in lectures at Sydney University. For our present purposes we can take the universal propositions as not having existential import, and thus avoid the need for restrictions on the valid argument forms.

conclusion reached by any application of one of these methods (other than that of concomitant variation which we shall leave aside for the present) is to have the form 'Such-and-such is a cause of such-and-such a kind of event or phenomenon', where a 'cause' will, in general, be both necessary and sufficient for the phenomenon, though in some variants of the methods it will be taken as necessary only, or as sufficient only. Let us assume also that we can distinguish in some way causes from effects, and think of the methods only as identifying causes. (Mill, as the canons quoted show, mixes this task up with that of identifying effects, and so far as their logical form is concerned the methods could be applied to any problem about conditions that are necessary for something, or sufficient, or both, but their most interesting applications, and the ones for which the required assumptions are most plausible, are to the identification of causes.)   However, the cause will be such, and will be necessary or sufficient or both, in relation to some field, that is, some set of background conditions: our question is, say, 'What causes this disease in human beings living in ordinary conditions, breathing air, and so on?' or, 'What causes the greater-than-ordinary hardness in iron in ordinary circumstances and at ordinary temperatures?' To say that A is necessary for B in the field F will be to say that whenever B occurs in (or in relation to) something that satisfies the conditions summed up as F, A occurs there also—which will be expressed accurately enough by 'All FB are A'—and so on. I shall use 'P' to represent the 'phenomenon' whose 'cause' is being sought, and I shall call an occasion on which P is present a *positive instance*, and one on which it is absent a *negative instance*. The observation that supports the conclusion will be an observation of the presence or absence of various conditions, each of which *might* be causally relevant, in one or more (positive or negative) instances.

But since, as I said, the conclusion regularly goes beyond the observation, and yet each method is supposed to be demonstrative, that is, deductively valid, the conclusion must be drawn not from the observation alone, but from it in conjunction with an assumption. This pattern, *assumption* and *observation* together entailing a *conclusion*, is characteristic of all these methods. And there are obvious proportional relations between the three items. The less rigorous the assumption, the stronger the observation needs to be if we are to get the same, or perhaps even any, conclusion. With the same observation, a less rigorous assumption will yield a weaker conclusion, if any. And so on.

But what sort of assumption is required, and what is it for it to be more or less rigorous? Since we are to arrive at the conclusion that

ELIMINATIVE INDUCTION301

a certain condition is, in the sense indicated above, a cause of the phenomenon, and to do so by eliminating rivals, we must assume at the start that there is *some* condition which, in relation to the field, is necessary and sufficient (or which is necessary, or which is sufficient) for this phenomenon, and that it is to be found somewhere within a range of conditions that is restricted in some way.

For a formal exposition, it is easiest to take the assumption as indicating some set (not necessarily finite) of possibly relevant causal features (Mill's 'circumstances' or 'antecedents'). Initially I shall speak in terms of a list of such *possible causes* (p-cs), but, as I shall show, we can in the end dispense with any such *list*. A p-c, since it is possibly causally relevant in relation to the field in question, must—like the phenomenon itself—be something that is sometimes present and sometimes absent within that field: it must not be one of the conditions that together constitute the field.

But are we to assume that a p-c acts singly, if it acts at all? If the p-cs are A, B, C, etc., are we to assume that the cause of P in F will be either A by itself or B by itself, and so on? Or are we to allow that it might be a conjunction, say AC, so that P occurs in F when and only when both A and C are present? Are we to allow that the actual (necessary and sufficient) cause might be a disjunction, say (B or D), so that P occurs in F whenever B occurs, and whenever D occurs, but only when at least one of these occurs? Are we to allow that our p-cs may include counteracting causes, so that the actual cause of P in F may be, say, the absence of C (that is, not-C, or $\overline{C}$), or perhaps $B\overline{C}$, so that P occurs in F when and only when B is present and C is absent at the same time?

There are in fact valid methods with assumptions of different kinds, from the most rigorous, which requires that the actual cause should be just one of the p-cs by itself, through those which progressively admit negations, conjunctions, and disjunctions of p-cs and combinations of these, to the least rigorous, which says merely that the actual cause is built up out of some of the p-cs in some way. There are in fact eight possible kinds of assumption, namely that the actual cause is:

1. one of the p-cs.
2. either one of the p-cs or a negation of one.
3. either a p-c or a conjunction of p-cs.
4. either a p-c or a disjunction of p-cs.
5. a p-c, or the negation of a p-c, or a conjunction each of whose members is a p-c or the negation of a p-c.
6. a p-c, or the negation of a p-c, or a disjunction each of whose members is a p-c or the negation of a p-c.

7. a p-c, or a conjunction of p-cs, or a disjunction each of whose members is a p-c or a conjunction of p-cs.

8. a p-c; or the negation of a p-c; or a conjunction each of whose members is a p-c or the negation of one; or a disjunction each of whose members is a p-c, or the negation of one, or a conjunction each of whose members is a p-c or the negation of one.

Analogy with the use of disjunctive normal form in the propositional calculus makes it easy to show that any condition made up in any way by negation, conjunction, and disjunction from a set of p-cs will be equivalent to some condition allowed by this eighth kind of assumption, which is therefore the least rigorous kind of assumption possible. The form of the observation determines whether a method is a variant of the method of agreement, or difference, and so on. But since each form of observation may be combined with various kinds of assumption, there will be not just one method of agreement, but a series of variants using assumptions of different kinds, and similarly a series of variants of the method of difference, and so on. To classify all these variants we may use a decimal numbering, letting the figure before the decimal point (from 1 to 8) indicate the kind of assumption, and the first figure after the decimal point the form of observation, thus:

1. a variant of the method of agreement.
2. a variant of the method of difference.
3. a variant of the joint method (interpreted as an 'indirect method of difference').
4. a new but related method.

Further figures in the second place after the decimal point will be used for further subdivisions.

A complete survey would take up too much space, but some of the main possibilities will be mentioned.

2. Agreement and Difference—Simple Variants

Positive method of agreement

Let us begin with an assumption of the first kind, that there is some necessary and sufficient condition Z for P in F—that is, for some Z all FP are Z and all FZ are P—and Z is identical with one of the p-cs A, B, C, D, E. We obtain a variant of the method of agreement (1.12) by combining this assumption with the following observation: a set of one or more positive instances such that one p-c, say A, is present in each, but for every other p-c there is an instance from which that p-c is absent. This yields the conclusion that A is necessary and sufficient for P in F.

For example, the observation might be:

	A	B	C	D	E
I_1	p	a	p	.	a
I_2	p	p	a	a	.

where 'p' indicates that the p-c is present, 'a' that it is absent, and a dot that it may be either present or absent without affecting the argument. I_1 and I_2 are positive instances: I_1 shows that neither B nor E is necessary for P in F, and hence that neither can be the Z that satisfies the assumption, similarly I_2 shows that neither C nor D can be this Z; only A can be, and therefore must be, this Z; that is, A is both necessary and sufficient for P in F.

Since this reasoning eliminates candidates solely on the ground that the observation shows them not to be necessary, there is another variant (1.11) which assumes only that there is some necessary condition Z for P in F and (with the same observation) concludes only that A is necessary for P in F.

Negative method of agreement

Besides this positive method of agreement in which candidates are eliminated as not being necessary because they are absent from positive instances, there are corresponding variants of a negative method of agreement in which they are eliminated as not sufficient because they are present in negative instances. The required observation consists of one or more negative instances such that one p-c, say A, is absent from each instance, but for every other p-c there is an instance in which it is present. For example:

	A	B	C	D	E
N_1	a	p	.	.	.
N_2	a	.	p	p	.
N_3	a	.	.	.	p

If the assumption was that one of the p-cs is sufficient for P in F, this observation would show (1.13) that A is sufficient, while if the assumption was that one of the p-cs is both necessary and sufficient, the same observation yields the conclusion (1.14) that A is both necessary and sufficient.

Method of difference

The simplest variant of this method (1.2) combines the assumption that one of the p-cs is both necessary and sufficient for P in F with this observation: a positive instance I_1 and a negative instance

N_1 such that of the p-cs present in I_1 one, say A, is absent from N_1, but the rest are present in N_1. For example:

	A	B	C	D	E
I_1	p	p	p	a	.
N_1	a	p	p	.	p

Here D is eliminated because it is absent from I_1 and hence not necessary, and B, C, and E because they are present in N_1 and hence not sufficient. Only A therefore can be, and so must be, the Z that is both necessary and sufficient for P in F. Note that with an assumption of this first kind it would not matter if, say, E were absent from I_1 and/or D were present in N_1: the presence of the actual cause A in I_1 but not in N_1 need not be the only relevant difference between the instances. But this would matter if we went on to an assumption of the second kind. We may also remark that the method of difference, unlike some variants of the method of agreement, requires the assumption that there is some condition that is both necessary and sufficient for P in F. As we shall see with variants 4.2 and 8.2, the conclusion may not fully specify the resulting necessary and sufficient condition, and the factor picked out as (in another sense) the cause is guaranteed only to be an inus condition or better; but the assumption needed is that *something* is both necessary and sufficient.

Joint method of agreement and difference

Mill's exposition of this method mixes up what we may call a *double method of agreement*, that is, the use of the positive and negative methods of agreement together, with what Mill himself calls an *indirect method of difference*, in which the jobs done by the single positive instance and the single negative instance in the method of difference are shared between a set of positive and/or a set of negative instances. The latter is the more interesting and distinctive. Its simplest variant (1.3) combines the assumption that one of the p-cs is both necessary and sufficient for P in F with this observation: a set S_i of positive instances and a set S_n of negative instances such that one of the p-cs, say A, is present throughout S_i and absent throughout S_n, but each of the other p-cs is either absent from at least one positive instance or present in at least one negative instance. For example:

		A	B	C	D	E
S_i	I_1	p	p	p	p	a
	I_2	p	p	p	a	p
S_n	N_1	a	p	a	a	a
	N_2	a	a	p	a	a

This assumption and this observation together entail that A is necessary and sufficient for P in F. As the example shows, none of the other p-cs, B, C, D, E, could be so, given such an observation: yet S_i by itself does not yield this conclusion by the positive method of agreement, nor S_n by the negative method, nor does any pair of positive and negative instances from those shown yield this conclusion by the method of difference.

3. *Agreement and Difference—Complex Variants*

When we go on to an assumption of the second kind, allowing that the actual cause may be the negation of a p-c, we need slightly stronger observations. Thus for variants of the positive method of agreement (2.11 and 2.12) we need this: two or more positive instances such that one p-c (or a negation of a p-c) say A, is present in each instance, but for every other p-c there is an instance in which it is present and an instance from which it is absent. The observation described for 1.11 and 1.12 above would be too weak: for example, if D were absent from both I_1 and I_2 as we there allowed, $\overline{D}$ would not be eliminated, and we could not conclude that A was the actual cause.

For the corresponding variant of the method of difference (2.2) we need this: a positive instance I_1 and a negative instance N_1 such that one p-c (or a negation of a p-c), say A, is present in I_1 and absent from N_1, but each other p-c is either present in both I_1 and N_1 or absent from both. For example:

	A	B	C	D	E
I_1	p	p	a	a	p
N_1	a	p	a	a	p

Since B is present in N_1, B is not sufficient for P in F, but since B is present in I_1, $\overline{B}$ is not necessary for P in F. Since C is absent from I_1, C is not necessary for P in F, but since C is absent from N_1, $\overline{C}$ is not sufficient for P in F. Thus neither B nor C, nor either of their negations, can be both necessary and sufficient for P in F; D and E are ruled out similarly, so, given the assumption that some p-c or negation of a p-c is both necessary and sufficient, A must be so. This is the classic difference observation described by Mill, in which the only possibly relevant difference between the instances is the presence in I_1 of the factor identified as the actual cause; but we need this, rather than the weaker observation of 1.2, only when we allow that the actual cause may be the negation of a p-c.

The joint method needs, along with this weaker assumption, a similarly strengthened observation: each of the p-cs other than A

must be either present in both a positive instance and a negative instance or absent from both a positive instance and a negative instance; this variant (2.3) then still yields the conclusion that A is both necessary and sufficient for P in F.

We consider next an assumption of the third kind, that the actual cause is either a p-c or a conjunction of p-cs. This latter possibility seems to be at least part of the complication Mill described as an *intermixture of effects*. This possibility does not affect the positive method of agreement, since if a conjunction is necessary, each of its conjuncts is necessary, and candidates can therefore be eliminated as before. But since the conjuncts in a sufficient (or necessary and sufficient) condition may not be severally sufficient, the negative method of agreement is seriously affected. The observation described and exemplified above for 1.13 and 1.14 would now leave it open that, say, BC rather than A was the required sufficient (or necessary and sufficient) condition, for if C were absent from N_1, B from N_2, and either from N_3, then BC as a whole might still be sufficient. We can, indeed, still use this method with a much stronger observation (3.14), namely a single negative instance N_1 from which one p-c, say A, is absent, but every other p-c is present. This will show (with our present assumption) that no p-c other than A, and no conjunction of p-cs that does not contain A, is sufficient for P in F. But even this does not show that the actual cause is A itself, but merely that it is either A or a conjunction in which A is a conjunct. (We may symbolize this by saying that the cause is $(A.\,.\,.)$, where the dots indicate that other conjuncts may form part of the cause, and the dots are underlined, while A is not, to indicate that A must appear in the formula for the actual cause, but that other conjuncts may or may not appear.)

The corresponding variant of the method of difference (3.2) needs only the same observation as 1.2; but it, too, yields only the weaker conclusion that $(A.\,.\,.)$ is necessary and sufficient for P in F (but therefore that A itself is necessary, but perhaps not sufficient). For while in the example given for 1.2 above B, C, D, and E singly are still eliminated as they were in 1.2, and any conjunctions such as BC which, being present in I_1, *might* be necessary, are eliminated because they are also present in N_1 and hence are not sufficient, a conjunction such as AB, which contains A, is both present in I_1 and absent from N_1, and therefore might be both necessary and sufficient. Thus this assumption and this observation show only that A is, as Mill put it, 'the cause, or an indispensable part of the cause'. The full cause is represented by the formula '$(A.\,.\,.)$', provided that only p-cs which are present in I_1 can replace the dots.

The corresponding variant of the joint method (3.3) needs a *single* negative instance instead of the set S_n, for the same reason as in 3.14, and the cause is identified only as $(A. \underline{\ \ .}.)$.

With an assumption of the fourth kind, that the actual cause is either a p-c or a disjunction of p-cs, the negative method of agreement (4.13 and 4.14) works as in 1.13 and 1.14, since if a disjunction is sufficient, each of its disjuncts is so. It is now the positive method of agreement that suffers. For with the observation given for 1.12 above, the necessary and sufficient condition might be, say, $(B$ or $C)$; for this disjunction is present in both I_1 and I_2, though neither of its disjuncts is present in both. Thus the observation of 1.12 would leave the result quite undecided. We need (for 4.12) a much stronger observation, namely a single positive instance in which one p-c, say A, is present but from which every other p-c is absent, but even this shows only that the cause is—with the same interpretation of the symbols as above—$(A$ or $. . .)$. This assumption (that the cause may be a disjunction of p-cs) allows the possibility of what Mill called a *plurality of causes*, each disjunct being a 'cause' in the sense of being a sufficient condition. What we have just noted is the well-known point that this possibility undermines the method of agreement.

The method of difference, on the other hand, still survives and still needs only the observation of 1.2; this eliminates all p-cs other than A, and all disjunctions that do not contain A, either as being not sufficient because they are present in N_1 or as not necessary because they are absent from I_1. The only disjunctions not eliminated are those that are present in I_1 but absent from N_1, and these must contain A. Thus this observation, with the present assumption, still shows that $(A$ or $. . .)$ is necessary and sufficient for P in F; that is, the actual cause is either A itself or a disjunction one of whose disjuncts is A and the others are p-cs absent from N_1. Hence A itself, the differential feature, is sufficient for P in F but may not be necessary.

The joint method with this assumption (4.3) needs a *single* positive instance instead of the set S_i, but can still use a set of negative instances, and it too identifies the cause as $(A$ or $. . .)$.

As the assumptions are relaxed further, the method of agreement needs stronger and stronger observations. For example in 6.12, a variant of the positive method with the assumption that there is a necessary and sufficient condition which may be a p-c, or a negation of one, or a disjunction of p-cs and/or negations of p-cs, the observation needed is this: a set S_i of positive instances such that one p-c, say A, is present in each, but that for every other possible combination of the other p-cs and their negations there is an instance in which this combination is present (that is, if there are n other p-cs, we need 2^n *different* instances). This observation will eliminate every disjunction that does not contain A (showing it not to be necessary) and will thus show that $(A \text{ or } \ldots)$ is necessary and sufficient, and hence that A itself is sufficient, for P in F. A corresponding variant of the negative method of agreement (5.14) shows that $(A. \ldots)$ is necessary and sufficient, and hence A itself necessary, for P in F—a curious reversal of roles, since in the simplest variants the positive method of agreement identified a necessary condition and the negative one a sufficient condition.

The method of difference, however, continues to need only the observation prescribed for 1.2, if negations are not admitted, or, if negations are admitted, that prescribed for 2.2. But the conclusions become progressively weaker, that is, the cause is less and less completely specified. By far the most important variant of this method—indeed it is the most important of all those that deal in agreement or disagreement or any combination of them—is 8.2. This has an assumption of the eighth kind, in effect that for some Z, Z is necessary and sufficient for P in F, and Z is a condition represented by some formula in disjunctive normal form all of whose constituents are taken from the p-cs. With the observation of 2.2, this yields the conclusion that $(A. \ldots \text{ or } \ldots)$ is necessary and sufficient for P in F. For every condition built up in any way from p-cs other than A will either be present in both I_1 and N_1, and so not sufficient (because it is present in N_1), or absent from both I_1 and N_1, and so not necessary (because it is absent from I_1); also any condition in normal form in which A occurs only negated will similarly be absent from I_1 if it is absent from N_1, so it will either be absent from both, and hence ruled out as not necessary, or it will be present in N_1, and hence ruled out as not sufficient. Consequently Z must be identical with some condition in disjunctive normal form in which A occurs unnegated, that is, with something covered by the expression '$(A. \ldots \text{ or } \ldots)$'. Since each disjunct in such a necessary and sufficient condition is itself sufficient, this observation, in which the presence of A in I_1 is the only possibly relevant difference between I_1 and N_1, shows even with the least rigorous kind of assumption that A is at least a necessary part of a sufficient condition for P in F (this sufficient condition being $(A. \ldots)$), that is, that A is an inus condition of P in F, or better. (It is this method 8.2 that has been discussed in Chapter 3; as was said there, the conclusion can also be expressed thus: For some X and for some Y (which may, however, be null), all F $(AX \text{ or } Y)$ are P, and all FP are $(AX \text{ or } Y)$.)

The joint method, as an indirect method of difference, ceases to work once we allow both conjunctions and disjunctions of p-cs as candidates for the role of actual cause. But what we called the double method of agreement, which in the simplest variants involved redundancy, the positive and negative halves merely, as Mill says, corroborating one another, comes into its own with our eighth, least rigorous, kind of assumption. In 8.12, as in 6.12, if there are n p-cs other than A, the set of 2^n positive instances with A present in each but with the other p-cs present and absent in all possible combinations will show that $(A \text{ or } . . .)$ is necessary and sufficient and hence that A is sufficient. Similarly in 8.14, as in 5.14, the corresponding set of 2^n negative instances with A absent from each will show that $(A. . .)$ is necessary and sufficient and hence that A is necessary. Putting the two observations together, we could conclude that A is both necessary and sufficient for P in F.

A new method, similar in principle, can be stated as follows (8.4): if there are n p-cs in all, and we observe 2^n instances (positive or negative) which cover all possible combinations of p-cs and their negations, then (assuming that some condition somehow built up out of these p-cs is both necessary and sufficient) the disjunction of all the conjunctions found in *positive* instances is both necessary and sufficient for P in F. For example, if there are only three p-cs, A, B, and C, and we have the observation set out in the following table:

P	A	B	C
a	p	p	p
p	p	p	a
p	p	a	p
a	p	a	a
a	a	p	p
p	a	p	a
a	a	a	p
a	a	a	a

then $(AB\overline{C}$ or $A\overline{B}C$ or $\overline{A}\overline{B}\overline{C})$ is necessary and sufficient for P in F. For if these are the only possibly relevant factors, each combination of p-cs and their negations along with which P occurs at least once must be sufficient for P, and each such combination in whose presence P is absent must be non-sufficient for P; but the disjunction of all the sufficient conditions must be both necessary and sufficient, on the assumption that *some* condition is so.

We find thus that while we must recognize very different variants of these methods according to the different kinds of assumptions used, and while the reasoning which validates the simplest variants fails when it is allowed that the actual cause may be constituted by negations, conjunctions and disjunctions of p-cs combined in various ways, nevertheless there are valid demonstrative methods which use even the least rigorous kind of assumption, that is, which assume only that there is *some* necessary and sufficient condition for P in F, made up in *some* way from a certain restricted set of p-cs. But with an assumption of this kind we must be content either to extract (by 8.2) a very incomplete conclusion from the classic difference observation or to get more complete conclusions (by 8.12, 8.14, the combination of these two, or 8.4) only from a large number of diverse instances in which the p-cs are present or absent in systematically varied ways.

There are two very important extensions of these methods, which consist in the relaxing of restrictions which have been imposed for the sake of clarity in exposition. First, since in every case the demonstration proceeds by eliminating certain candidates, it makes no difference if what survives, what is not eliminated, is not a single p-c but a cluster of p-cs which in the observed instances are always present or absent together: the conclusion in each case will be as stated above but with a symbol for the cluster replacing 'A'. For example, if in 2.2 we have, say, both A and B present in I_1 and both A and B absent from N_1, but each other p-c either present in both or absent from both, it follows that the cluster (A, B) is the cause in the sense that the actual cause lies somewhere within this cluster. *Given that this cluster will either be present as a whole or absent as a whole*, its presence is necessary and sufficient for P in F. A similar observation in 8.2 would show that, subject to the same proviso, this cluster is an inus condition of P in F, or better, and hence that either A or B is an inus condition, but perhaps each is an inus condition and perhaps their conjunction (AB) is so. Secondly, in order to eliminate candidates it is not really necessary to list them first. The observation required for 2.2 or 8.2, for instance, is only that a certain p-c (or, as we have just seen, a certain cluster of p-cs) should be present in I_1 but absent from N_1 while in every other respect that might be causally relevant these two instances are alike. Or for 8.12 we need only observe that A is present throughout a set of diverse positive instances while all the other factors that might be causally relevant occur, and fail to occur, in all possible combinations in these instances. To be sure, we could check this conclusively only if we had somehow counted and listed the possibly relevant factors, but without this we could have a mass of evidence that at least seemed to approximate to the required observation.

4. *The Method of Residues*

We have, in the wide range of variants so far indicated, covered only three of Mill's five methods. His method of residues needs only brief treatment: it can be interpreted as a variant of the method of difference in which the negative instance is not observed but constructed on the basis of already known causal laws.

Suppose, for example, that a positive instance I_1 has been observed as follows:

	A	B	C	D	E
I_1	p	p	a	p	a

Then if we had, to combine with this, a negative instance in which B and D were present and from which A, C, and E were absent, we could infer (according to the kind of assumption made) either by 2.2 that A was necessary and sufficient for P in F, or by 8.2 that $(A \ldots \text{or} \ldots)$ was so, and so on. But if previous inductive inquiries (of whatever sort) can be taken to have established laws from which it follows that given $\bar{A}B\bar{C}D\bar{E}$ in the field F, P would not result, there is no need to *observe* N_1; we already know all that an observation of N_1 could tell us, and so one of the above-mentioned conclusions follows from I_1 alone along with the appropriate assumption.

Again, if the effect or phenomenon in which we are interested can be *measured*, we can reason as follows. Suppose that we observe a positive instance I_1, with the factors present and absent as above, in which there occurs a quantity x_1 of the effect in question, and suppose that our previously-established laws enable us to calculate that given $\bar{A}B\bar{C}D\bar{E}$ in F there would be a quantity x_2 of this effect; then we can regard the difference $(x_1 - x_2)$ as the phenomenon P which is present in I_1 but absent from (the calculated) N_1. With an assumption of the first, second, fourth, or sixth kind—that is, any assumption which does not allow conjunctive terms in the cause—we could conclude that the cause of P in this instance I_1 was A alone, and hence that A is sufficient for the differential quantity $(x_1 - x_2)$ in F.

To make an assumption of any of these four kinds is to assume that effects of whatever factors are actually relevant are merely additive, and that is why we can conclude that the extra factor in I_1, namely A, itself produces the extra effect $(x_1 - x_2)$. But with an assumption of the third, fifth, seventh, or eighth kind, which allows conjunctive causes and hence Mill's *intermixture of effects*, we could conclude only that a (sufficient) cause of $(x_1 - x_2)$ was $(A \ldots)$. Given the other factors that were present in both I_1 and N_1, A was sufficient for this differential effect; but it does not follow that A is sufficient for this in relation to F as a whole.

Though Mill does not say so, it is obvious that such a use of constructed, calculated, instances is in principle possible with all the methods, not only with the method of difference in the way outlined here.

5. *Methods of Concomitant Variation*

Whereas Mill called this just one method, there is in fact a system of concomitant variation methods mirroring the various presence-and-absence methods we have been studying. These too will be forms of ampliative induction: we shall argue from a covariation observed in some cases or over some limited period to a general rule of covariation that covers unobserved instances as well. These methods, then, work with a concept of cause which makes the (full) cause of some quantitative phenomenon that on which the magnitude of this phenomenon functionally depends: causation is now the converse of dependent covariation. As I have argued in Chapter 6, this functional dependence concept is best regarded as a development and refinement of 'neolithic' concepts of causation defined in terms of necessity and (perhaps) sufficiency, that is, in terms of conditional presences and absences of features. To let it count as causation, functional dependence requires, of course, the addition of the relation of causal priority. This indeed plays some part in the formal methods that we are studying in so far as it is used in deciding what are possibly relevant causal factors (that is, what can count as p-cs) and in interpreting a covariation as a directed causal relation, but we can take these points for granted and leave them aside in most of the analysis.

The typical form of a functional causal regularity will then be that the magnitude of P in the field F is always such-and-such a function of the magnitude of the factors, say, A, B, C, and D, which we can write:

$$P_F = f(A, B, C, D).$$

Where such a regularity holds, we may call the whole right hand side of this equation, that is, the set of actually relevant factors together with the function f which determines how they are relevant, the *full cause* of P in F, while we may call each of the actually relevant factors a *partial cause*. The full cause is that on which the magnitude of P in F wholly depends; a partial cause is something on whose magnitude the magnitude of P in F partly depends.

A thorough investigation of such a functional dependence would involve two tasks, the identifying of the various partial causes and the determination of the function f. Only the first of these two tasks can be performed by concomitant variation methods analogous to those already surveyed.

There are concomitant variation analogues of both the method of agreement and the method of difference; that is, there are ways of arguing to a dependence of P on, say, A both from the observation of cases where P and A remain constant while other possibly relevant factors vary and from the observation of cases where P and A vary while other possibly relevant factors remain constant.

As before, we need an assumption as well as an observation, but we have a choice between different kinds of assumption. The more rigorous kind (corresponding to the second kind of assumption above) would be that in F the magnitude of P wholly depends in some way on the magnitude of X, where X is identical with just one of the p-cs. The less rigorous and in general more plausible kind (corresponding to the eighth kind of assumption above) would be that in F the magnitude of P wholly depends in some way on the magnitudes of one or more factors X, X', X'', etc., where each of these is identical with one of the p-cs.

The simpler covariance analogue of the method of difference combines the more rigorous assumption with this observation: over some period or over some range of instances in F, P has varied while A has varied but all the other p-cs have remained constant. None of the other p-cs, then, can be identical with the X in the assumption, so A must be so. That is, the conclusion is that the magnitude of P in F depends wholly *in some way not yet determined* on that of A.

The more complex covariance difference analogue combines this same observation with the less rigorous kind of assumption above. The observation does not now show that some p-c other than A, say B, is *not* a partial cause. But it does show that the magnitude of P in F cannot depend wholly, in any way, on any set of factors that does not include A, for every function of every such set has remained constant while P has varied. This ensures, therefore, that A is a partial cause, but leaves it open whether the full cause is simply of the form $f(A)$ or whether there are other partial causes as well. This observation and this assumption, therefore, show that a full cause of P in F is $f(A, \cdots)$. Repeated applications of this method, with other factors being varied one at a time, could fill in further partial causes, but could not close the list.

The simple covariance analogue of the method of agreement combines our more rigorous kind of assumption above with this observation: over some period or range of instances in F, P has remained constant while A has remained constant while every other p-c has varied. We want to argue here that since B, say, has varied while P has not, B cannot be identical with the assumed X on whose magnitude that of P depends. But this does *not* follow. It might be that P's magnitude varied with and in sole dependence upon the magnitude of B, and yet that P was not responsive to *every* change in the magnitude of B: there might be flat stretches, plateaux, in the curve for $P_F = f(B)$, with values for B plotted on the x-axis and values for P_F on the y-axis. So to eliminate B we must either strengthen the assumption by adding that P is *responsive* to every change in the magnitude of X, or strengthen the observation to include every possible degree of variation of every p-c other than A, or strengthen both assumption and observation together, so that we can say that every p-c has varied to a degree to which, if this p-c were our X, P would be responsive. Only in some such way could we validly reach the conclusion that the magnitude of P in F depends *in some way* on that of A alone.

A complex covariance analogue of the method of agreement encounters much the same problem as complex variants of the original method. Even if P has remained constant while all the p-cs other than A have varied, this does not, with our less rigorous assumption, exclude the possibility that $P_F = f(B, C)$, say. For it might be that the actual variations of B and C and the actual function f were such that the effects of these variations cancelled out: f might be such as to allow the actual changes in B and C to compensate for one another. It will not help now to strengthen the assumption to include the claim that P is responsive to all variations in the Xs. But will it do if we greatly strengthen the observation, to claim that all the p-cs other than A have varied independently (and hence in all possible combinations) over the whole possible range or magnitude of each? Even this claim—which is in any case so extreme that we could not hope to do more than approximate to its fulfilment— would yield only the conclusion that the magnitude of P in F does not depend *wholly* on p-cs other than A, that is, that A is at least *a* partial cause. It does not, as we might be tempted to suppose, show that all p-cs other than A are irrelevant, and that P depends only upon A. For it might be that at *some* values of A changes in the values of all the other p-cs were ineffectual, and yet that at *other* values of A some variations in some of the other p-cs made a difference. Consequently, if with an assumption of our less rigorous kind we are to be able to *close* the list of partial causes, nothing less than an analogue of 8.4 will do. That is, we must be able to say that A, as well as all the other p-cs, has joined in this mutually independent variation over the whole possible range of each. And then if the value for P has remained constant for *each* constant value of A, we can conclude that P's magnitude depends on that of A alone.

As I have said, these concomitant variation methods only identify partial causes of the functional dependence sort, and may in an extreme case tend to close the list of partial causes: they do not in themselves help with the task of determining the function f. But there is another device, still within the range of eliminative induction methods, which at least makes a start on this task. As we saw when discussing the method of residues, we can regard a quantitative difference in some magnitude, something of the form $(x_1 - x_2)$, as the effect or phenomenon whose cause is identified by some application of the method of difference. Various observations interpreted in this way will ascribe such-and-such a change in the quantity of P to such-and-such a change in the magnitude of, say, A at certain (temporarily fixed) values of the other p-cs, and will so at least impose constraints on the function f. That is, even when we are dealing with functional dependences there is an important place for applications of the neolithic presence-and-absence method of difference.

6. *Uses and Applications of these Methods*

I have so far been concerned to show only that there are many demonstratively valid methods of these sorts. But in reaching a more exact formulation of them for this purpose I have incidentally removed some of the more obvious objections to the view that such methods can be and are applied in practice. Thus the introduction of the notion of a field gives these methods the more modest task of finding the cause of a phenomenon only in relation to some field, rather than that of finding a condition which is absolutely necessary and sufficient. By contrasting the p-cs with the field we have freed the user of the method of agreement from having to make the implausible claim that his instances have only one 'circumstance' in common. He has merely to claim that they have only one of the p-cs in common, while conceding that whatever features constitute the field or are constant throughout the field will belong to all the instances, and that there may be other common features too, but ones that the user has initially judged not to be possibly relevant to this phenomenon.

Similarly, the user of the method of difference has only to claim that no *possibly relevant* feature other than the one he is picking out as (part of) the cause is present in I_1 but not in N_1. Also, we have taken explicit account of the ways in which the possibilities of counteracting causes, a plurality of causes, an intermixture of effects, and so on, need to be allowed for, and we have seen how valid conclusions can still be drawn in the face of these complications, provided that we note explicitly the incompleteness of the conclusions we can now draw or the much greater strength of the observations required for complete conclusions (for example in 8.4).

By making explicit the need for assumptions we have abandoned any pretence that these methods in themselves solve or remove the problem of induction. If the requisite observations can be made, the ultimate justification for any conclusion reached by one of these methods will depend on the justification for the assumption used, and since this proposition is general in form, any reliance that we place on it or on its consequences will have to be backed by some other kind of inductive reasoning or confirmation or corroboration. The eliminative methods cannot be the whole of the logic of scientific discovery. But it does not follow that they cannot be any part of this. It is, I think, instructive to see just how far 'deduction from the phenomena' (in Newton's phrase) can go, in the light of some not implausible assumptions.

It is worth stressing the precise form of assumption that our analysis has shown to be required. It is not a general uniformity of nature, a universal determinism, but merely that this particular phenomenon, in this particular field, should have some cause. But we have also found that whereas our ordinary concept of cause *requires* a cause only to be necessary in the circumstances, the assumption needed for almost all our methods is that *something* (though this will usually not be the factor that is eventually picked out as, in a popular sense, the cause) should be both necessary and sufficient for this phenomenon in this field. We do have to assume what might be called *particular determinism*. We must reject the view of Mill that there is some one 'law of causality' to which every application of these methods appeals. But at the other extreme we should stop short of the view of Wittgenstein in the *Tractatus* that this 'law' dissolves into the mere logical form of laws in general. Specific deterministic assumptions play a part that makes them in at least one way prior to the laws discovered with their help.

What may seem more of a problem is that we have to assume a somehow restricted range of possibly relevant factors, p-cs. But, as we shall see, some inquiries are conducted against a background of general knowledge that supplies such a restriction; in others we simply assume that the only items that are possible causes for some result, some change, are other perceptible changes in the spatial neighbourhood and not long before. And what counts as near enough in space and time, and as being perceptible, can itself be a matter of working hypotheses. If a conclusion demonstrated with the help of some particular limitation of p-cs is subsequently falsified, that limitation can and must be relaxed: we must look further afield or try other ways of detecting changes that we did not at first perceive. It must be emphasized that though the eliminative methods are themselves demonstrative, there is no hostility whatever between the use of them and the use of hypotheses whether as working assumptions or otherwise. The demonstrative methods need not be associated with any theory that the method of inquiry as a whole is watertight, or simply aggregative, or mechanical.

The eliminative methods are in fact constantly in use in the sense that innumerable procedures of search, discovery, and checking have implicit within them the forms of reasoning that I have tried to formulate and make precise. I have argued in Chapter 3 that all our basic causal knowledge is founded on what are in effect applications of the method of difference, and that this knowledge has, in consequence, just the form (of elliptical double regularities) that one would therefore expect it to have. It is by before-and-after contrast observations that we know that fire burns, that it cooks meat, that rattlesnakes are poisonous; Becquerel discovered that the radium he carried in a bottle in his pocket caused a burn by noticing that the presence of the radium was the only possibly relevant difference between the time when the inflammation developed and the earlier time when it did not, or between the part of his skin where the inflammation appeared and other parts.

But the causal relations revealed in this way need not be so general as to be of scientific interest. Fault-finding procedures aim only at discovering why this particular machine does something wrong, and hence how it can be put right; but they, too, depend on trying one change after another and seeing what *results*.

Suppose that a new drug is being tested. It is administered to some subject, and some change (good or bad) is noticed in the subject soon afterwards. There is a prima facie case for supposing that the administration of this drug can cause—that is, is an inus condition of—that change. But why, if the method of difference is a demonstrative method, is it only a prima facie case? Simply because the experimenter cannot be sure that the requirements for that method's observation have been met: some other relevant change may have occurred at about the same time. But if the experiment is repeated and we keep on getting the same result, it becomes less and less likely that on each occasion when the drug was administered, some one other, unnoticed but relevant, change also occurred. But (as I said in Chapter 3) such repetition should not be taken as a resort to the method of agreement, it is not the repetition of the A–P sequence as such that we are relying on: we are using the repetition merely to check whether on each occasion the requirements for the method of difference were met. If we keep getting the same result, we can say that it is probable that they were met, that no other relevant change occurred, and therefore (given the assumption) that the conclusion demonstrated by the method of difference holds. But repetition can have another function as well. Even if we are reasonably sure that a particular experiment (or set of experiments) has shown that A is an inus condition of P in F (or better), we may repeat it under varying conditions in the hope—which *may* be fulfilled—of showing that various factors which were present in our original I_1 and N_1, and so *might* be essential conjuncts with A in the full cause $(A . . . \text{or} . . .)$, are not in fact essential: we are reducing the indeterminacy represented by the first row of dots in this formula. Such repetition under varying conditions *is* an application of the method of agreement, and turns the whole procedure into something that can be called (in yet another sense) a joint method: it is in fact an approximation to 8.4.

As I have said in Chapter 3, the controlled experiment, in which a control case is deliberately set up alongside the experimental case and made to match it as closely as possible except with regard to the item under test, is another well-known application of the method of difference.

It is often supposed, and the examples I have given might encourage the belief, that these methods operate only at superficial levels of science, that they establish causal connections only between directly perceivable features. But they are subject to no such restriction. A physicist may take himself to be firing deuterons at bismuth atoms when all that a superficial observer could perceive was his twiddling knobs and switches on a large and impressive piece of apparatus; but if the physicist subsequently finds evidence that some of the former bismuth atoms are now behaving like polonium atoms, it will be method of difference reasoning that enables him to say that deuteron bombardment of bismuth can *produce* polonium. Of course in such applications the conclusion reached by a method which is in itself demonstrative is established only subject to the proviso that the interpretation of the antecedent conditions and of the result is correct. But once we have detached the use of these methods from the claim that they achieve certainty, this is quite in order. It is also very obvious that the eliminative methods can be used, not only as part of a mere response to experiences that force themselves upon us, but also in procedures for testing hypotheses, for finding answers to questions that we ask.

Mill thought that these were methods both of discovery and of proof; and so they can be, but not very easily at once. Rather an observation which appears to conform to the requirements for one of the methods may suggest that a certain causal relationship holds, and a causal hypothesis—whether suggested in this way or in some other—may be tested and perhaps confirmed by a more thorough survey or by a carefully constructed experiment, the results of each being interpreted by another application of the appropriate method.

The method of agreement is frequently used in medical contexts—locating a source of infection, identifying the substance to which someone has an allergic reaction, deciding what bacillus is responsible for a certain disease, and so on. It is particularly in such contexts that a previously developed background of theory supplies the fairly rigorous kind of assumption needed for the simpler variants of this method. In a country in which typhoid is rare, we may hope that if a dozen cases occur within a few days in one town they all result from a single source of infection. A person may be allergic to just one substance, and his response to it may not depend much on other circumstances. But in these applications too the eliminative method of reasoning may well be combined with asking questions, framing and testing hypotheses, rather than the passive reception of information.

The methods of concomitant variation, particularly those that are counterparts of the method of difference, along with statistical procedures that can be regarded as elaborations of these methods, are constantly used when one or more factors are varied while other possibly relevant factors are held constant, and calculations are based on the observed results. In practice the two tasks which I distinguished, the identifying of actual partial causes of a phenomenon and the determination of the function f, tend to be mixed up together; but the separation of these tasks in our analysis may help to distinguish different degrees of conclusiveness with which different parts of an hypothesis have been confirmed.

7. Criticisms of these Methods

We have already met most of the stock objections to these methods. One still outstanding is that they take for granted the most important aspect of inquiry, the detection, isolation, and analysis of the possibly relevant factors. Mill, of course, does not ignore this: he devotes a whole book to 'operations subsidiary to induction'. But what most needs to be stressed is that there is no need for a finally satisfactory analysis of factors before the eliminative methods can be applied: as I argued in Chapter 3, we can start using the methods with a very rough distinction of factors and obtain some correct results, which can be later refined by what I called the progressive localization of a cause. Also, though classification may be subsidiary to induction, it is not purely preliminary to it. Things are classified mainly by their causal properties; it will be by using, in effect, the method of difference that we find that *this* material regularly does such-and-such to that other material, and so recognize it, and other samples that act similarly, as all specimens of some one kind of stuff. A mass of elementary eliminative inductions helps to provide the setting for more sophisticated ones.

Another stock criticism is that causal relations are not the whole, or even the most important, concern of science. (We have already rejected, in Chapter 6, the argument that science is not concerned with causation at all.) We can concede that science has other concerns as well, but this criticism is otherwise to be rebutted by insisting on a wide concept of causation and by seeing that these methods assist the discovery of causes in this wide sense. Especially since entities on all levels are identified largely by dispositional properties, that is, by their causal powers, the detection of causation by particular objects as well as the discovery of causal regularities runs through all processes of discovery.

Thirdly, it is often thought that the use of and reliance on these methods is somehow a discredited and discreditable alternative to the hypothetico-deductive method. In fact there is no incompatibility, hostility, or even any necessary difference of spirit between the use of these two procedures. Though the eliminative methods are in themselves demonstrative, they are naturally and unavoidably used in contexts which make their conclusions only tentative. Their assumptions require to be confirmed in ways in which these methods cannot themselves confirm them. And the Popperian principle that hypotheses are corroborated by being subjected to severe tests— that is, ones which, if an hypothesis is false, are likely to show it to be false—is admirably illustrated by the methods of agreement and difference. The hypothesis that A is necessary for P in F is severely tested by looking for instances of P which fall within the field F but otherwise differ widely in all conceivably relevant ways, and seeing whether A is present in them all; if the hypothesis stands up to this test, it is by the method of agreement that we draw the (in practice still tentative) conclusion. The hypothesis that A is an indispensable part of a sufficient condition for P in F that was present in I_1 is severely tested by finding or constructing an instance that is as like I_1 as possible in all conceivably relevant ways, except that it lacks A, and seeing whether P occurs there or not. And if it does not, this counts as the N_1 from which, along with I_1, we draw our conclusion in accordance with the method of difference.

Additional Notes

(These notes are indicated in the text by an asterisk)

p. 80.   I offer a solution in 'A Defence of Induction', in *Epistemology in Perspective: Essays in Honour of A. J. Ayer*, edited by G. Macdonald (Macmillan, forthcoming).

p. 143.   But Hume was anticipated by Hobbes and (in a slightly different kind of compatibilism) by various theologians. See 'Compatibilism, Free Will and God' by A. G. N. Flew in *Philosophy*, xlviii (1973).

p. 190.   The analysis suggested in this paragraph needs revision. See the Preface to the Paperback Edition, pages viii–xvi.

p. 214.   This book has been republished as *Laws, Modalities, and Counterfactuals*, with a foreword by Wesley C. Salmon (University of California Press, 1976).

p. 238.   An interesting and important class of IRLs is found by ethologists investigating 'evolutionarily stable strategies' when there is a mixture of strategies in equilibrium with one another or a single corresponding mixed strategy. See, e.g., R. Dawkins, *The Selfish Gene* (Oxford, 1976), esp. Ch. 5.

Bibliography

Including only works mentioned in the text, and showing the editions referred to or quoted

ANDERSON, J. *Studies in Empirical Philosophy*. Sydney, 1962.

ANSCOMBE, G. E. M. *Causality and Determination*. Cambridge, 1971.

—— 'Causality and Extensionality.' In *Journal of Philosophy*, lxvi (1969), 152–9.

ANSCOMBE, G. E. M., and GEACH, P. T. *Three Philosophers*. Oxford, 1961.

AYER, A. J. *The Problem of Knowledge*. Harmondsworth, 1956.

—— *Probability and Evidence*. London, 1972.

BENNETT, J. F. *Kant's Analytic*. Cambridge, 1966.

BERKELEY, G. *The Principles of Human Knowledge*. In *The Works of George Berkeley*, ed. A. C. Fraser, Oxford, 1901.

BLACK, M. 'Why Cannot an Effect Precede its Cause?' In *Analysis*, xvi (1955–6), 49–58.

—— *Models and Metaphors*. Ithaca (N.Y.), 1966.

BROAD, C. D. *The Mind and its Place in Nature*. London, 1925.

—— 'The Principles of Demonstrative Induction.' In *Mind*, xxxix (1930), 302–17 and 426–39.

BUNGE, M. *Causality*. Harvard, 1959.

CHISHOLM, R. M. 'Freedom and Action.' In *Freedom and Determinism*, ed. K. Lehrer, New York, 1966.

CHISHOLM, R. M., and TAYLOR, R. 'Making Things to have Happened.' In *Analysis*, xx (1959–60), 73–8.

CUMMINS, R., and GOTTLIEB, D. 'On an Argument for Truth-functionality.' In *American Philosophical Quarterly*, ix (1972), 265–9.

D'ALEMBERT, J. *Traité de dynamique*. Paris, 1921.

DAVENEY, T. F. 'Intentions and Causes.' In *Analysis*, xxvii (1966–7), 23.

DAVIDSON, D. 'Actions, Reasons, and Causes.' In *Journal of Philosophy*, lx (1963), 685–700.

—— 'Causal Relations.' In *Journal of Philosophy*, lxiv (1967), 691–703.

DESCARTES, R. *Principles of Philosophy*. In *Descartes: Philosophical Writings*, tr. G. E. M. Anscombe and P. T. Geach, London, 1969.

—— *Rules for the Guidance of our Mental Powers*. In *Descartes' Philosophical Writings*, tr. N. K. Smith, London, 1952.

DRAY, W. 'Taylor and Chisholm on Making Things to have Happened.' In *Analysis*, xx (1959–60), 79–82.

DUCASSE, C. J. *Nature, Mind, and Death*. La Salle, 1951.

—— *Truth, Knowledge, and Causation*. London, 1968.

DUMMETT, M. 'Can an Effect Precede its Cause?' In *Proceedings of the Aristotelian Society*, supplementary volume xxviii (1954), 27–44.

—— 'Bringing about the Past.' In *Philosophical Review*, lxxiii (1964), 338–59.

EWING, A. C. *Idealism*. London, 1934.

FITZGERALD, E. *Rubáiyát of Omar Khayyám*. Ed. G. F. Maine, London, 1953.

FLEW, A. 'Can an Effect Precede its Cause?' In *Proceedings of the Aristotelian Society*, supplementary volume xxviii (1954), 45–62.

—— 'Effects before their Causes?—Addenda and Corrigenda.' In *Analysis*, xvi (1955–6), 104–10.

—— 'Causal Disorder Again.' In *Analysis*, xvii (1956–7), 81–6.

GALE, R. M. 'Why a Cause Cannot be Later than its Effect.' In *Review of Metaphysics*, xix (1965), 209–34.

—— 'Professor Ducasse on Determinism.' In *Philosophy and Phenomenological Research*, xxii (1961), 92–6.

GARDINER, P. *The Nature of Historical Explanation*. Oxford, 1952.

GÖDEL, K. 'Russell's Mathematical Logic.' In *The Philosophy of Bertrand Russell*, ed. P. A. Schilpp, Evanston (Ill.), 1944.

GOROVITZ, S. 'Leaving the Past Alone.' In *Philosophical Review*, lxxiii (1964), 360–71.

GRÜNBAUM, A. *Philosophical Problems of Space and Time*. New York, 1963.

—— 'Temporally-asymmetric Principles, etc.' In *Philosophy of Science*, xxix (1962), 146–70.

HARRÉ, H. R. *The Principles of Scientific Thinking*. London, 1970.

—— *The Philosophies of Science*. Oxford, 1972.

HART, H. L. A., and HONORÉ, A. M. *Causation in the Law*. Oxford, 1959.

HUME, D. *A Treatise of Human Nature*. Ed. L. A. Selby-Bigge, Oxford, 1888.

—— *Enquiries*. Ed. L. A. Selby-Bigge, 2nd edn., Oxford, 1902.

—— *An Abstract of a Treatise of Human Nature*. Ed. J. M. Keynes and P. Sraffa, Cambridge, 1938.

JOHNSON, W. E. *Logic*. Cambridge, 1921.

KANT, I. *Critique of Pure Reason*. Tr. N. K. Smith, London, 1929.

—— *Prolegomena to Any Future Metaphysic*. Tr. P. G. Lucas, Manchester, 1953.

KEYNES, J. N. *Formal Logic*. 4th edn., London, 1906.

KIM, J. 'Causes and Events: Mackie on Causation.' In *Journal of Philosophy*, lxviii (1971), 426–41.

KNEALE, W. C. *Probability and Induction*. Oxford, 1949.

—— 'Natural Laws and Contrary to Fact Conditionals.' In *Philosophy and Analysis*, ed. M. Macdonald, Oxford, 1954.

LOCKE, J. *An Essay Concerning Human Understanding*. Ed. A. C. Fraser, Oxford, 1894.

LYON, A. 'Causality.' In *British Journal for the Philosophy of Science*, xviii (1967), 1–20.

MACKIE, J. L. 'Responsibility and Language.' In *Australasian Journal of Philosophy*, xxxiii (1955), 143–59.

—— 'Counterfactuals and Causal Laws.' In *Analytical Philosophy*, 1st ser., ed. R. J. Butler, Oxford, 1962.

—— 'Causes and Conditions.' In *American Philosophical Quarterly*, ii (1965), 245–64.

—— 'The Direction of Causation.' In *Philosophical Review*, lxxv (1966), 441–66.

—— 'Mill's Methods of Induction.' In *Encyclopedia of Philosophy*, ed. P. Edwards, New York, 1967.

—— *Truth, Probability, and Paradox*. Oxford, 1973.

—— Review of *The Matter of Chance* by D. H. Mellor. In *Philosophical Quarterly*, xxiii (1973), 85–7.

—— 'Practical versus Theoretical Reason.' In *Practical Reason*, ed. S. Körner, Oxford, 1974.

McLAUGHLIN, J. A. 'Proximate Cause.' In *Harvard Law Review*, xxxix (1925–6), 149 ff.

MARC-WOGAU, K. 'On Historical Explanation.' In *Theoria*, xxviii (1962), 213–33.

MARTIN, R. 'The Sufficiency Thesis.' In *Philosophical Studies*, xxiii (1972), 205–11.

MELDEN, A. I. *Free Action*. London, 1961.

MICHOTTE, A. *La perception de la causalité*. 2e éd, Louvain, 1954.

MILL, J. S. *A System of Logic*. 8th edn. (reprinted), London, 1941.

MORTON, A. 'Extensional and Non-truth-functional Contexts.' In *Journal of Philosophy*, lxvi (1969), 159–64.

NAGEL, E. *The Structure of Science*. London, 1961.

NERLICH, G. C., and SUCHTING, W. A. 'Popper on Law and Natural Necessity.' In *British Journal for the Philosophy of Science*, xviii (1967), 233–5.

NEWTON, I. *Philosophiae Naturalis Principia Mathematica*. London, 1686.

NOBLE, D. 'Charles Taylor on Teleological Explanation.' *Analysis*, xxvii (1966–7), 96–103.

PEARS, D. F. 'The Priority of Causes.' In *Analysis*, xvii (1956–7), 54–63.

POPPER, K. R. 'The Arrow of Time.' In *Nature*, clxxvii (1956), 538, also in *Nature*, clxxviii (1957), 382, and *Nature*, clxxix (1958), 1297.

—— *The Logic of Scientific Discovery*. 6th impression, London, 1972.

—— *Objective Knowledge*. Oxford, 1972.

QUINE, W. V. *The Ways of Paradox*, New York, 1966.

REICHENBACH, H. *Nomological Statements and Admissible Operations*. Amsterdam, 1954.

—— *The Direction of Time*. Berkeley, 1956.

ROBINSON, J. A. 'Hume's Two Definitions of "Cause".' In *Hume*, ed. V. C. Chappell, London, 1968.

RUSSELL, B. A. W. *Mysticism and Logic*. New York, 1918.

—— *The Analysis of Mind*. London, 1921.

—— *An Inquiry into Meaning and Truth*. London, 1940.

—— 'Reply to Criticisms.' In *The Philosophy of Bertrand Russell*, ed. P. A. Schilpp. Evanston (Ill.), 1944.

SCHLICK, M. 'Causality in Everyday Life and Recent Science.' In *Readings in Philosophical Analysis*, ed. H. Feigl and W. Sellars, New York, 1949.

SCRIVEN, M. 'Randomness and the Causal Order.' In *Analysis*, xvii (1956–7), 5–9.

—— Review of *The Structure of Science* by E. Nagel. In *Review of Metaphysics*, xviii (1964), 403–24.

—— 'The Logic of Cause.' In *Theory and Decision*, ii (1971), 49–66.

SHARVY, R. 'Truth-Functionality and Referential Opacity.' In *Philosophical Studies*, xxi (1970), 5–9.

SMULLYAN, A. 'Modality and Description.' *Journal of Symbolic Logic*, xiii (1948), 31–7.

SPRIGGE, T. L. S. 'Final Causes.' In *Proceedings of the Aristotelian Society*, supplementary volume xlv (1971), 149–70.

STOUTLAND, F. M. 'The Logical Connection Argument.' In *American Philosophical Quarterly Monograph*, iv (1970), 117–30.

STOVE, D. C. 'Hume, Probability, and Induction.' In *Hume*, ed. V. C. Chappell, London, 1968.

—— *Probability and Hume's Inductive Scepticism*. Oxford, 1973.

STRAWSON, P. F. *The Bounds of Sense*. London, 1966.

SUCHTING, W. A. 'Popper's Revised Definition of Natural Necessity.' In *British Journal for the Philosophy of Science*, xx (1969), 349–52.

SUPPES, P. *A Probabilistic Theory of Causality*. Amsterdam, 1970.

TAYLOR, C. *The Explanation of Behaviour*. London, 1964.

—— 'Teleological Explanation—a Reply to Denis Noble.' In *Analysis*, xxvii (1966–7), 141–3.

VENDLER, Z. 'Effects, Results, and Consequences.' In *Analytical Philosophy*, 1st ser., ed. R. J. Butler, Oxford, 1962.

—— 'Causal Relations.' In *Journal of Philosophy*, lxiv (1967), 704–13.

VON WRIGHT, G. H. *A Treatise on Induction and Probability*. London, 1951.

—— *Explanation and Understanding*. London, 1971.

Additional Bibliography

DAWKINS, R. *The Selfish Gene*. Oxford, 1976.

MACKIE, J. L. 'A Defence of Induction.' In *Epistemology in Perspective: Essays in Honour of A. J. Ayer*, ed. G. Macdonald, London, forthcoming.

—— *Ethics: Inventing Right and Wrong*. Harmondsworth, 1977.

—— 'Mind, Brain, and Causation.' In *Midwest Studies in Philosophy*, iv (1979), 19–29.

—— *Problems from Locke*. Oxford, 1976.

—— 'Self-Refutation: A Formal Analysis.' In *Philosophical Quarterly*, xiv (1964), 193–203.

—— 'The Transitivity of Counterfactuals and Causation.' In *Analysis*, forthcoming.

Index